JEWISH BOOK ANNUAL

VOLUME 52
1994-1995
5755

Edited by
JACOB KABAKOFF

JEWISH BOOK COUNCIL
15 East 26 Street, New York, N.Y. 10010

Library of Congress Catalogue Card Number: 44-6602
ISBN 1-885-838-02-6

Designed by Kalman Shiloni

Produced by Shofar Magazine

Printed in the United States of America
by Thomson-Shore, Inc.

Contents

BIBLIOGRAPHIES OF NEW BOOKS

JACOB KABAKOFF

Introduction

WE DEVOTE OUR WORDS of introduction this year to the anniversaries of three literary figures and bookmen whose 100th birthdays occur during 1995. The anniversaries of Menachem Ribalow, Eliezer Raphael Malachi and Isaac Rivkind afford us a welcome opportunity to recall the contributions of these unique personalities who played vital roles in our cultural life.

Menachem Ribalow is the individual most closely identified with the development of the American Hebrew press and literature from the early 20s down to his passing in 1953. He arrived from Russia in 1921 at the age of 27 and from the start was imbued with the idea that the evolving American Jewish community must take the place of the declining Jewish cultural centers in Europe.

The early 20s were a period of letdown for Hebrew cultural activity in America. After the weekly *Hatoren* and *Haivri* and the monthly *Miklat* ceased publication the Hebraists pinned their hopes on the daily *Hadoar*, which was edited by Mordecai Lipson. Ribalow became a staff writer for *Hadoar* and in his very first article made a plea for establishing the cultural independence of American Hebrew letters from Europe. When it became apparent that *Hadoar* could not continue as a daily it was turned into a weekly and Ribalow eventually assumed the editorship.

Ribalow believed firmly in the future of Hebrew and the development of a Hebrew cultural center in America. He maintained that unless American Jews would suport a vital Hebrew press and literature they could not fully share in the Hebrew rebirth with the new literary center that was being established in Palestine.

In addition to editing *Hadoar*, Ribalow was the driving force behind the activities of the Histadruth Ivrith and its Ogen publishing agency which brought out the works of American Hebrew authors. During the 30s and 40s he edited the

1

impressive literary miscellanies *Sefer Hashanah li-Yhudei Amerikah* (American Hebrew Yearbook). In 1938 he edited an anthology of American Hebrew poetry in which he traced the development and growth of Hebrew verse writing in America from its early maskilic days.

During his lifetime Ribalow published four volumes of literary criticism and a fifth volume was issued posthumously. He devoted his critical efforts to an exposition of the themes and ideas of such established figures as Bialik, Tchernichowsky, Schneour and Shimoni. In some of his later essays, such as those devoted to Shin Shalom and to Shofmann, we find examples of his finest critical writing.

Undoubtedly Ribalow's greatest contribution to literary criticism is to be seen in his evaluations of American Hebrew writers. His first volume of essays, published in 1928, consisted in the main of writings from his European period, but it also contained an essay on Halkin as well as one on Dolitzky. With each additional volume, Ribalow placed greater emphasis on American Hebrew writers and covered the main representatives of poetic and prose expression.

In a lengthy survey of American Hebrew writing which Ribalow published in 1943 in *Ahisefer*, a volume he co-edited with S. Niger on the literature and languages of the Jews, he offered an optimistic summary of American Hebrew creativity in the period between the two World Wars. He enumerated the contributions of some 120 authors in various fields of literary endeavor, including belles-lettres, essays and criticism and scholarship. He was led to conclude that due to their efforts, "Hebrew literature in this country had become a basic and indispensable part of the cultural life of the Jewish community." He was sanguine also regarding the future of Hebrew writing in America, for he could not conceive of a creative Jewish community in which the Hebrew language and literature would be allowed to languish. Terming the years between the two World Wars a "period of transition," Ribalow hoped that "What had been done until now will serve as the basis for continuation, a seed planted for the future." In 1953 he launched a new literary quarterly, *Mabua*, in order to give greater scope to American Hebrew writing. Unfortunately, he did not live to see the completion of the first year of publication. *Hadoar*, the Hebrew magazine which he nourished and cultivated for close to three decades, still appears and continues to serve as a forum for Hebrew writers. It also remains as his most enduring monument.

We recall also Ribalow's participation in the early work of the Jewish Book Council. He served as associate chairman of the Council in 1943-44 and as editor of the Hebrew section of the first two volumes of the Jewish Book Annual in 1942-43. To his five books of Hebrew literary criticism must be added a book of Yiddish critical essays and a volume of literary evaluation in English entitled *Modern Hebrew Literature,* which was published posthumously in 1959 under the editorship of Judah Neidich.

II

Eliezer Raphael Malachi, who died in 1980, had a long and distinguished career as a historian, bibliographer and journalist. Born in Jerusalem, he made his debut at the age of 15 as the author of a historical survey of the Palestine press which was published in A.M. Luncz's *Luah Eretz-Yisrael* (Palestine Miscellany). For some 70 years he continued to publish the fruits of his research primarily in Hebrew but also in Yiddish.

Malachi arrived in America in 1912 and remained here through the World War I years. He returned to Palestine in 1919 but three years later took up permanent residence in New York. Already in 1913 he became a contributor to the newly established *Hatoren*. His expertise as a bibliographer and historian was revealed in his pioneering historical survey of the American Hebrew press and in his well annotated bibliography of the works of Mendele Mokher Sefarim which he prepared on the occasion of the author's death.

Malachi soon earned prominence as an authority in various specialized fields. He became known as an expert on the history of the Palestinian Yishuv and on the worldwide Hebrew press. Endowed with a phenomenal memory, he was able to utilize his talents to compile the bibliographies of a whole roster of authors and scholars, including Bialik, Tchernichowsky, Sokolow and Dubnow, among many others.

He turned his attention also to the writings of his fellow
American Hebrew authors and among his bibliographies in
this area were the separate publications devoted to Chaim
Tchernowitz and Hillel Bavli.

In his studies dealing with modern Hebrew literature
Malachi was especially attracted to authors and journalists
who adopted a militant literary stand. Among these were
Judah Leib Kantor, editor of *Hayom*, and David Frishman,
who excelled as a creative writer, translator and editor. Seventeen of Malachi's essays on Hebrew authors were gathered in
his volume *Massot u'Reshimot* (Essays and Jottings, 1937).
Here one can be enlightened on such subjects as Judah Leib
Gordon as a critic, Shalom Aleichem as a Hebrew writer and
Bialik as a feuillitonist. Among Malachi's other contributions
are a critical edition of the letters of Frishman and a collection
of miscellaneous letters of other writers.

Only a small part of Malachi's writings have appeared in
book form and a good deal that is worthy of collecting remains
scattered in periodicals and collective volumes. In 1940 there
was published his book of historical sketches *Tsilelei Dorot*
(Shadowy Generations), which drew upon various martyrological chapters in Jewish history. Previously he had brought
together his series of articles published in the Yiddish press
and issued it as a volume entitled *Mekubolim in Erets Yisroel*
(Kabbalists in Palestine, 1929), which dealt with the leading
figures who were active in the mystical movement.

The Institute For Zionist Research of the Tel-Aviv University recognized Malachi's central role in Palestine research
when it re-published twenty-three of his studies in the volume
Perakim be-Toledot ha-Yishuv ha-Yashan (Studies in the History of the Old Yishuv, 1971). These studies encompass the period beginning with the aliyah in 1810 of Rabbi Elijah Gaon's
disciples to the stirrings of the new settlement movement. The
volume depicts the struggle of the representatives of the old
system with the Hovevei Tziyon who advocated a new
approach. The personalities of such leading figures like Luncz,
Frumkin, Ben-Yehuda and Pines are effectively portrayed.

Malachi compiled not only the individual bibliographies of
numerous literary figures but published detailed thematic
bibliographical surveys of the literature dealing with

various subjects. In 1955 there appeared his *Otzar ha-Leksikographiah ha-Ivrit* (Treasury of Hebrew Lexicography) as an appendix to the American edition of Mandelkern's biblical concordance. Here he offered detailed descriptions of all the biblical concordances and dictionaries that had been published in Hebrew and other languages. Other examples of his thematic approach are his Hebrew monograph on "The Kishinev Pogroms in the Mirror of Hebrew and Yiddish Poetry," published in vol. 3 of *Al Admat Bessarabia* (On Bessarabian Soil, ed. G. Kressel, 1964), and his bibliography of "Hebrew Educational Literature in America," published in *Sefer ha-Yovel shel Agudat ha-Morim ha-Ivrim* (Jubilee Volume of the Hebrew Teachers Ass'n, ed. Zvi Scharfstein, 1944).

Malachi's archives, containing his collection of documents and letters, have been transferred to the Ben-Zvi Institute in Jerusalem, where they will be of aid to scholarly research. Readers of the Jewish Book Annual are indebted to him for the articles and bibliographical materials he contributed to its pages over the years.

III

Isaac Rivkind, who died in 1968, had a varied career as librarian, bibliographer and cultural historian. He was born in Lodz, Poland, and studied in leading yeshivot. He immigrated to America in 1920 and beginning with 1923 served as Hebraica librarian of the Jewish Theological Seminary of America Library.

An indication of the esteem in which Rivkind was held as a librarian-scholar can be had from the volume *Minha le-Yitshak* (An Offering to Isaac, 1949), which was published by the then Jewish Librarians' Association in honor of the completion of 25 years of his services in the Library of the Jewish Theological Seminary. The volume consists of Rivkind's bibliography compiled by Mordecai Kosover and Abraham G. Duker, together with appreciations of his work. We find here not only a detailed enumeration of Rivkind's writings arranged by category but also a listing of over 80 scholarly works in which the authors expressed their appreciation to Rivkind for his assistance.

Because of his lifelong association with the Hebrew book
Rivkind was able to make significant contributions to the
history of Hebrew printing. Among the subjects of his research
were some of the rare Passover Haggadah editions. His ability
to combine wide bibliographical knowledge with scholarly
research into Jewish cultural history was seen in his Hebrew
volume *Le-Ot u'le-Zikkaron* (For a Sign and a Reminder,
1942), which was devoted to the history of the Bar Mitzvah.
The first part consists of seven chapters which are devoted to
various aspects of the custom. Rivkind traces its origin to as
far back as Geonic times and surveys the manner of its
observance in various communities. The synagogue ceremony,
the Bar Mitzvah speech and the festive meal are among the
subjects that are authoritatively treated. The second part of
the volume presents a comprehensive annotated bibliography
of 468 items which cover halakhic literature and responsa,
speech collections, poetry and piyyut, as well as other types of
literature.

Among Rivkind's major interests were old Yiddish texts
and philology, which were seen by him as keys to an understanding of the folklore of Eastern European Jewry. A fascinating and little explored area of Jewish life was illuminated
by him in his Yiddish work *Der Kamf Kegn Azartshpilen bay
Yidn* (The Fight Against Gambling Among Jews, 1946). Rivkind indicated that this work was "A Study of Five Centuries
of Yiddish Poetry and Cultural History." He uncovered many
poems and ditties that had to do with games of chance and
revealed that the life of our ancestors had also a lighter side.
He drew attention as well to the strong words of condemnation
regarding the widespread custom of card playing which are to
be found in the works of mussar and ethical admonition.

Rivkind's most important work was perhaps his unique
lexicological Yiddish work *Yidish Gelt in Lebenshteyger,
Kultur Geshikhte un Folklor* (Jewish Money in Folkways, Cultural History and Folklore, 1959). Offered here are numerous
insights into the ways that money was used to enhance Jewish
life and which by inference give the lie to charge that Jews are
"money mad." In his introductory chapters Rivkind described
how money was used to carry out various religious and
cultural functions. Hundreds of detailed alphabetical entries
are listed and explicated in order to indicate how special terms

were created for these functions which embraced the life cycle and the daily regimen of the Jew. The entire gamut of Jewish literature and folklore is explored in order to determine the origin and the popular usage of these terms. Typical entries include: *shatkhones gelt* (matchmaker's fee); *rebbe gelt* (tuition); *dire gelt* (rent); *Khanike gelt* (Hanukkah money gift); and *oysleyzgelt* (ransom). Rivkind has skillfully shown how material concerns were transformed into spiritual concepts and has erected a lexicological memorial to the Jewish way of life as practiced particularly in Eastern Europe.

Rivkind was also the author of many articles and studies on such varied subjects as the history of Eretz Yisrael, Zionism, the holidays, personalities, the Volozhyn Yeshiva and early American Hebrew documents. But his overriding concern was ever the Jewish book. In a moving essay entitled "Sefarim Bokhim" (Weeping Tomes) he related that on his way to the synagogue one Sabbath morning he was shocked to find that a pile of sefarim had been placed at the curb for removal. Apparently the family had no use for these volumes which had belonged to their deceased father. Despite the fact that this sacrilege had occurred on the Sabbath, Rivkind took the necessary steps to see that the books were saved. Throughout his life he remained the guardian of the book.

IV

Our profound thanks go to our contributors for enriching our volume with their articles and studies and to our bibliographers for providing us with their listings of the literary output in America, Europe and Israel. These listings cover broadly the period between April 15, 1993 and April 15, 1994. Because the National Jewish Book Awards for 1994 will be presented in November instead of June, our regular feature devoted to the Awards will appear in our next volume.

We again express our appreciation to the Lucius N. Littauer Foundation for its valued support. We are pleased also to acknowledge the contributions of the Jacob and Hilda Blaustein Foundation, the Morris and Betty Kaplun Foundation, the I. Edward Kiev Foundation, the Joseph Meyerhoff Fund and the Irving and Bertha Neuman Foundation.

MICHAEL CHERNICK

The English Language
Rabbinics Revolution

THE BABYLONIAN TALMUD has never been an "easy read." Maimonides, speaking for his own time and community, noted, "The commentaries, legal monographs, and responsa that the gaonim authored and viewed as clear have become difficult [for those] in our day. Hardly anyone understands their contents properly, save for a very few, and this is even truer for the Talmud itself...." (Introduction to *Mishneh Torah*). Perhaps this is also the thrust of R. Jeremiah's midrash of Lamentations 3:6, " 'He [God] has placed me in the dark like the eternal dead....' —this refers to the Talmud of Babylonia." Nevertheless, the Talmud's ability to capture perenially the imagination of the Jewish people has, repeatedly, turned it into a best seller, or at least enough of a "seller" for profitable publishing houses to print it.

To the amazement of some observers of the Jewish scene, the arcane treasury of debates and discussions about Jewish law, life, philosophy, theology, folkways and folk tales which is the Talmud has re-appeared on the scene in several English language editions. Random House has begun publishing Rabbi Adin Steinsaltz's English translation of the Talmud accompanied by his line-by-line, step-by-step commentary, a veritable reader's map through the intricate dialectics of the Talmudic argument. The Talmud text itself was preceded by an introductory volume that included traditional notions about the Talmud's history and detailed information about personalities, rhetorical forms, specialized terms, and legal rubrics found therein. Though Steinsaltz chose to start with *Baba Mezi'a*, a fairly difficult tractate dealing with torts, his work attempts quite successfully to be "user friendly." His translation is far superior to the Soncino Talmud's, and his prowess as an elucidator of the Talmudic argument is universally acknowledged.

On the heels of the Steinsaltz Talmud, the prolifiç Art Scroll/Mesorah Press began to produce the Schottenstein Talmud. Like the Steinsaltz edition, this publication, the Schottenstein family's memorial to Jerome Schottenstein, contains the traditional Hebrew and Aramaic text of the Talmud. That text is effectively translated, and a commentary that runs beneath it guides the reader through the tractate's issues and arguments. The Schottenstein Talmud has come out quite quickly and now covers 18 Talmudic tractates. Its commentary is quite lucid and a credit to the various contributors and collaborators who participated in its creation.

Were these Talmud editions the only works of their kind to appear in the last few years, I believe that alone would be a very interesting phenomenon. But the last five years have witnessed the appearance of a host of English language academic studies of the Talmud and related rabbinic literatures that is quite amazing. Today it is possible for an English reader to enter a world of Talmud studies that was, until recently, the preserve of a small circle of scholars and their students. That world speaks more about the Talmud as a whole than about its parts and their specific contents. It is interested in how the Talmud came to be; why it developed; what purpose it served in its own era; and why it expresses itself as it does. It wants to know whether the Talmud came into being as a literary whole, or if not, what the nature of its editorial and redactional history is. Given the vast Talmudic collection of what appear to be records, academicians are interested in their accuracy and original meaning. Further, how accurate is the tradition that the Talmud was formally canonized? Is the work unique, or is it a typical artifact of its time and place?

RESEARCH GOALS

Answers to these questions, and others like them, impact quite substantially on a number of weighty modern Jewish intellectual and practical concerns. For example, if the Talmud's purpose in recording certain events is primarily a matter of religious and moral teaching, the Talmud may not be a credible source for the history of its times. In another direction, a conclusion that the Talmud was never formally canonized impacts on the historical credibility of the approaches and attitudes of Orthodox and Conservative Judaism to Jewish law, its application, and potential for development and change. Similarly, the discovery that attributed Talmudic dicta were the fictional creations of the Talmud's sixth, seventh, or early eighth century authors would mean that we have no intellectual history for early Judaism nor truly ancient rabbinic tradition. The academic study of the Talmud has not reached hard and fast conclusions about any of these matters, but research is certainly closing in on some of them. Who are the researchers and academicians who are presenting their studies, methods, and findings to the English-reading public, and what are they telling us?

Had this been a mere decade ago, the answer to the question would have been: Jacob Neusner and his circle of students. These include David Goodblatt, William Scott Green, Gary Porton, Robert Goldenberg, and the lamented Baruch Bokser, of blessed memory, to name a few. His work and that of his "students circle" comprises most of the Judaica titles published by Brill (Leiden), the Brown Judaica Series, and Scholars' Press (Missoula). These works have generated both light and heat, but no matter what may be said of him or his students' methodologies or views, credit must go to him for opening up the "closed book" of the entire spectrum of formative rabbinic literature to the English-reading academic community. Once that was achieved, it was only a matter of time before others joined the enterprise.

What is it that Neusner introduced? First, Mishnaic, Midrashic and Talmudic texts in modern translations with extensive commentaries. The commentaries generally provided sufficient information to make the texts or citations involved understandable to the academic community interested in the history of religion, the Hellenistic and Roman worlds, antique Judaism, or intertestamental and New Testament scholarship. Because the audience was as often non-Jewish as Jewish, the writers assumed that every specifically rabbinic issue or idea needed to be fully and clearly explained in a way that connected the sages' world and reality with ours. Thus, at the most elementary level, that of plain and simple comprehension of a "foreign" literature, Neusner and his students opened a whole world to Jews separated from their literary tradition and to non-Jews seeking entree to it.

Secondly, Neusner connected the sages' intellectual and spiritual world to ours by claiming that their manifestly legal works were expressed in their own idiom: religious, ethical, philosophical, and social concerns similar enough to ours, or to the classical Western tradition's, to be comprehensible. This approach made the "mysterious" universe of the Mishnah and related rabbinic works somewhat more accessible to contemporary Western readers and whetted the appetite of some for more.

Finally, Neusner, unlike his predecessors in rabbinic research, consistently applied form criticism to his analysis of Mishnah and other formative rabbinic documents. This methodology, long part of the arsenal of methods used in historical-critical Biblical research, now served as a bridge to the study of rabbinic documents. People familiar with the assumptions, terminology, and applications of form criticism could now feel a bit more at home in rabbinic literature because how it was being handled was familiar.

CHARACTER OF MISHNAH

Neusner, however, had something considerably more important than making his audience comfortable in mind when he applied form criticism to Mishnah. He sought to determine whether that rabbinic classic preserved original rabbinic traditions or only synthetic, edited ones. On the basis of his findings, he claimed that the Mishnah preserved edited views and that the final redaction provided a basically uniform style and world-view for the whole work.

Furthermore, form critical method also uncovered various literary strata and techniques for conveying rabbinic views and debates. According to Neusner and his students some of the techniques represented the characteristic usage of a particular generation of contributors to the Mishnah. This helped to identify a tradition's temporal origin and often the intellectual milieu from which it issued as well. Thus they

claimed a tradition cast in the form of a lemma, that is, a
primary proposition with a connected, subsidiary one,
literarily favors the view stated in the primary proposition
and proclaims that view "winner." If the Ushan scholars (c.
135-165) favored the lemma-form, it could reasonably be
argued that they were interested in codifying the law by
determining whose view "won." Implicitly, a form which
communicated a more balanced "feel" or valence would
indicate a formulator's or group's interest in simply preserving
traditions without judging which tradition "won." These
attitudes, communicated by particular formulary choices,
provide a key to the intellectual concerns and history of the
early rabbinic movement. Form criticism obviously had
something to contribute to understanding early rabbinism's
documents and developments alongside the tested philological
and source critical methods employed in earlier studies.

Critical reaction to Neusner's work was sharply divided.
The doyens of academic rabbinics, most of whom wrote their
major works in Hebrew, were severely critical of his
translations, methodology, and conclusions about rabbinic
culture. Many chose to ignore him all together, at least
initially. On the other hand, academics whose language
capabilities did not include rabbinic Hebrew or Aramaic were
grateful to him for revealing the significance of rabbinic
Judaism to their areas of interest and reviewed his works
positively. Whether one praised, criticized or ignored Neusner,
it eventually became clear that his was the dominant
American voice in the academic study of rabbinic literature. If
one wished to argue the merits of other methods of approach
to rabbinic texts than Neusner's or to make different claims
than his about the nature and meaning of early rabbinic
culture, one had to produce studies accessible to the English-
reading public interested in these issues. Thus began the
English language rabbinics revolution.

Among the most prominent participants in what I have
termed a revolution is David Weiss-Halivni. Like Neusner,
Halivni has encouraged his students, notably Judith
Hauptman, Richard Kalmin, and David Kraemer, to publish
their research in English. He himself has contributed works
like *Midrash, Mishnah, and Gemara: the Jewish Predilection*

for *Justified Law* (1986) and *Peshat and Derash: Plain and Applied Meaning in Rabbinic Exegesis* (1991).

Halivni has built his scholarly reputation primarily on his Hebrew source critical Talmudic commentary, *Mekorot u'Mesorot* (1968-1982) and the introductory essays to its volumes. Source criticism, which Halivni has used more consistently than any of his predecessors, assumes that most of the Talmud's forced interpretations result from the replacement of an original source with a closely related, but ultimately different version or formulation of that source or with a different source altogether. In fact, Halivni frequently replaced sources in particularly strained Talmudic discussions with alternative sources and thereby obviated the need for the Talmud's forced interpretation, thus validating his methodological approach.

REDACTION THEORY

While source criticism's application to Talmudic texts is Halivni's most original and profound contribution to the Talmud's academic study and modern exegesis, he has played a major role in circulating the idea that the Talmud is the product of two stages of redaction. According to this theory, the first redactional process preserved the terse, attributed dicta of the early Talmudic sages, the amoraim. This redactional effort was essentially contemporary with the teachings themselves. During the second redactional stage rich discussions were added to the amoraic records creating the Talmudic discourse, or *sugya*, as we know it.

Halivni is not the first to recognize the phenomenon of two diverse elements in the Talmudic text. Earlier Talmudic critics like Julius Kaplan, Abraham Weiss, and Hyman Klein had already described it and attempted to account for the origins of the Talmud's terse and discursive elements. Interestingly, Kaplan's book, *The Redaction of the Babylonian Talmud* (1933) and most of Hyman Klein's articles on the Talmud's redaction [*Jewish Quarterly Review* 35:4 (1947), 38:1 (1953) and 50:2 (1959) and the *Journal of Semitic Studies* 3:4 (1958)] were written in English, yet they never achieved notice beyond

academic circles. Partly this was due to sociological factors.
American Jewish readers interested in the Talmud were often
not fluent English-readers during the first decades of this
century. Their children, striving for Americanization and
frequently uncomfortable with their inherited Jewish tradition
and traditional education, were English-readers with little
knowledge of or interest in the Talmud. Therefore Kaplan and
Klein "fell between the cracks." On the other hand, their
extensive, untranslated citation of original Talmudic material
was itself enough to make their works incomprehensible to
those uninitiated in Talmud study. Weiss wrote only in
Hebrew, as did those other great lights of rabbinic research,
Jacob Nahum Epstein and Saul Lieberman.

Halivni has avoided the pitfalls that undermined Kaplan
and Klein's efforts to put their findings before the English-
reading public. He knows his audience and recognizes that
they are trying to reclaim an intelligent understanding of
their Jewish heritage. He knows that they may not be
Talmudists, but he also knows that they are willing to put in
the effort to feel as intellectually adequate in the Jewish realm
as they are in other endeavors. He, therefore, meets them at
least halfway. His scholarly findings and academic conclusions
are stated in a concise manner unburdened by more technical
terminology than is necessary. Perhaps Halivni's presentation
sacrifices something in a less detailed presentation than one
would find in his *Mekorot u'Mesorot,* but clarity is certainly
well served. Further, the texts he cites in support of his views
are short, clearly translated, and frequently introduced in a
way that eases the reader's way into them. In short, his
English works have been constructed in a manner which
makes Halivni's scholarship available to non-specialists. This
means that his views have better circulation and more
acceptance than others, and he has acquired a readership who
feel empowered and informed by him.

'JUSTIFIED LAW'

Essentially, Halivni has introduced his readers to what the
scholarly world calls redaction criticism. In his *Midrash,*

Mishnah, and Gemara Halivni explains the two redactional stages he and others have recognized as part of a larger picture of what he calls "the Jewish predilection for justified law." By this Halivni means there was within early rabbinic Jewish circles a resistance to accepting unrationalized legal dicta. Halivni therefore regards the entire mishnaic enterprise as a deviation, though a fairly short-lived one. This "deviation" from the "justified" legal dicta of the more discursive halakhic midrashim was accepted in order to preserve the rabbinic tradition when it was still deemed unacceptable to write it down. The mishnaic style influenced the amoraic period, the Babylonian Talmud's earliest stratum. Though, according to Halivni, the amoraim renewed legal justification for the mishnaic era's laws, they, too, tended to preserve only the legal results of their discussions rather than the justificatory discussions themselves.

At a later date, however, the penchant for justified law resurfaced, and a group of redactors, whom Halivni calls the *stammaim*, tried to collect what they could of the amoraim's rationales and legal discussions. When that was impossible, they reconstructed what they believed to have been the generative argument for the amoraic dicta. Often they wove the amoraic dicta, truncated sources or "stranded," uncontexted material into their reconstructions. The result was the discursive Talmudic unit called the *sugya*. As Halivni notes, these reconstructions were not always in accordance with the traditional material's "natural inclination."

Here we would do well to compare Halivni and Neusner's views. Neusner regards Mishnah as the most basic statement of early rabbinic Judaism. It is a unified work whose legal dicta are organized to make major statements about human beings' decisive role in determining the nature of things, to protect Israel's psyche in the wake of the Temple's destruction, and to move Jewry away from messianic and apocalyptic fantasizing toward the safer realms of study and intellection. It is a "sectarian" work because, according to Neusner, rabbinic Judaism is just one of a number of competing Judaisms.

For Halivni, Mishnah is an atypical deviation from formative rabbinic literature's major penchant, justified law. Mishnah is certainly an edited text, but its editor edited texts in order to provide the Jewish people, not a sect, with an authoritative code (*Midrash, Mishnah and Gemara*, pp. 46 and 67). The code's function was to make a great statement primarily about law with occasional sallies into non-legal fields like ethics and theology. To the extent Mishnah dealt with practical laws, it viewed those laws as applicable to Jewish observance and life. Its tractates dealing with Temple law and ritual purity, no longer practiced in the post-Destruction period, were part of the mishnaic effort to preserve all aspects of the Jewish legal tradition.

DIFFERING APPROACHES

Obviously, Neusner and Halivni's views on Mishnah and its purposes are quite distinct and distant from one another. This holds true for their approach to the Babylonian Talmud as well. Neusner has often stated that the last level of redaction determines a work's "meaning." This obviates the need for expending more than minimal effort on redaction criticism. Furthermore, Neusner is generally distrustful of our ability to regain earlier levels of the tradition with any high degree of certainty. Thus, for example, he takes up the question of attributed sayings in *In Search of Talmudic Biography* (1984) and, for the most part, concludes that fluidity of attributions and lack of coherence between various statements attributed to a single teacher preclude knowing what early sages really said. This, however, does not preclude understanding what a total work communicates.

Here Halivni would argue that the Talmuds of Palestine and Babylonia, like Mishnah, have no "great meaning" to communicate. They are what they appear to be: well preserved collections of law and other rabbinic thought. Their meaning lies in the meaning of each preserved dictum (*memra*) and unit of discussion (*sugya*). If a redactor imbedded a dictum into a discussion, or claimed that a certain discussion generated a particular view, the original meaning of that view may have been changed. How else but through redaction criticism can we proceed to recapture original meaning? How, other than through reconstruction of a passage's redaction history, can we understand why obviously forced and circuitous arguments appear in the Babylonian Talmud's generally wise and intelligent contents? For Halivni the most important academic task is properly understanding the Talmud. For Neusner the task is understanding the Talmud's statement about the Judaism that created it.

By the mid-1980's there were sufficient major statements by Neusner and his students and Halivni to recognize their distinct views and approaches. It took the work of David Kraemer in *The Mind of the Talmud* (1990) to synthesize their approaches. His work, another English language contribution to Talmudic studies, began as a doctoral thesis guided by Halivni. In that thesis, summarized and, to some extent re-presented in *The Mind of the Talmud*, Kraemer traced the development of interpretive statements and argumentation as major forms of amoraic expression from the first to the sixth amoraic generation. In the first two generations there were few interpretive dicta and little preservation of discussion and argument. In the next two there was a gradual increase in interpretive statements and preservation of argument, with the most striking shift in emphasis occurring in the fourth generation. As we enter the last two amoraic generations, preservation of interpretation and re-interpretation of earlier sources and argument are fairly standard. What is novel are these last two generations' challenges to earlier authorities based on personal reasoning rather than sources. These developments set the stage for the explosion of argumentation, questions and answers that characterize what Halivni calls the "stammaitic period" and others like Zecharias Frankel, Abraham Weiss and Hyman Klein called the "saboraic period."

Thus far Kraemer's work is a contribution to redaction studies. He, however, raises a central question that is typical of Neusner's approach. Given that we can trace a stylistic development which moves in three stages from simple statements of legal opinion to re-interpretation, "give and take", and challenges from reason, what do these developments mean? In short, what is the relationship between the form of expression that Babylonian Talmud comes to prefer and the ideology it wishes to communicate?

ESTABLISHING TRUTH

Kraemer's answer is that the Babylonian Talmud's form expresses its belief in the indeterminacy of truth. God's Torah, for it, contains the truth. That truth, however, is mediated through human reason and interpretation which is fallible and, therefore, perceives and transmits only a portion of the whole truth. The Babylonian Talmud's style expresses that one can never underestimate the worth of even a portion of truth. The Talmud's creators also knew that prophecy was no longer available, and the interpretive route was the only one open for applying God's Torah to the realities that the Jewish community faced. Therefore, interpretation and human reason were precious and worthy of preservation and presentation. All views potentially contained some truth; therefore, all views warranted inspection, critique, and discussion. The more entrenched this world-view became, the more reason was valued, and simple appeals to authority eschewed. Thus, the Babylonian Talmud is, finally, a great statement about the necessary interplay between Divine revelation and human reason and the partnership of God and humanity in organizing the world.

If Kraemer is correct, and there is much in his documentation to recommend his view, the Babylonian Talmud was unique, if not avant-garde. Generally, the classical philosophical and religious traditions, as Kraemer notes, have claimed that it was possible to know the truth either through autonomous human reason or revelation. The Babylonian Talmud claimed truth to be unknowable. Scripture simultaneously revealed and concealed; human reason was fallible; where was one to find "the truth?"

According to Kraemer's view, the Babylonian Talmud seems to bring us to where some contemporary thinkers believe "post-modernity" begins: to indeterminate truth and authority with only human reason and choice to help us muddle through. Here Kraemer's presentation identifies the Talmud's unique religious position. God's word still guides and informs human reason. Therefore, proclaims the Babylonian Talmud, humanity is not alone without any secure moorings, but neither is it fettered by "the Word." The process of living in light of both revelation and human reason is sacred and sustaining.

NEW RESEARCH

This review has only touched the surface of the English language rabbinics revolution. Other authors besides those reviewed here have written fine works on Mishnah and Talmud. Among these are Louis Jacobs, the eminent British rabbinic scholar, Judith Hauptman and Richard Kalmin, students of David Weiss Halivni, and Baruch Bokser. Jacobs has concentrated on the Talmudic argument's structure and rhetorical forms in two works, *The Talmudic Argument* (1984) and *Structure and Form in the Babylonian Talmud* (1991). Hauptman and Kalmin have contributed important details to our picture of how the Babylonian Talmud was redacted. Hauptman in her *Development of the Talmudic Sugya* (1988) has suggested that the earliest level of the Talmud began with commentaries on the Mishnah produced within the mishnaic era. Kalmin's *The Redaction of the Babylonian Talmud* (1984) strongly suggests that the Talmud's final redaction took place later than Halivni proposes, namely, during the saboraic period, that is, the seventh century. This view supports the theories of Halivni's predecessors. Finally, Baruch Bokser's *Post-Mishnaic Judaism in Transition* (1980) proves that Samuel, an early third century Babylonian sage, created a Mishnah commentary a single generation after the Mishnah was created. This documents the powerful impression the Mishnah made on Diaspora rabbinic circles and how it served as a rallying force for those circles. His study also traces the transition from Mishnah to *Gemara* and how Mishnah commentary evolved into independent traditions.

As a teacher of Talmud I am gratified by the publication in such a short time of so many books in my field of interest. I am also surprised. Why has this occurred now? Why not earlier?

I believe two forces are promoting the English language rabbinics revolution: the widespread development of university level Judaic studies programs and a search for Jewish "roots" in part of the Jewish community. Judaic studies programs now exist in practically every major university in the United States. They have refined the Jewish tastes, thinking and study habits of those who have majored in Jewish studies and those who have only dabbled. The

programs' students have come to understand that it is
virtually impossible to understand contemporary Judaism or
Jewish life without knowing Jewish history and the
literatures that informed it. Hence, they want and need books
that will help them access those sources. Fortunately, there
are well-trained Judaic scholars familiar with them and their
Jewish and secular backgrounds ready to provide for them.

The second factor engendering the English language
rabbinics revolution, especially the popular Steinsaltz Talmud,
is the search for Jewish "roots." While prophecies of Jewish
doom in America abound, there has also been a renascence of
Jewish consciousness. Orthodox Judaism's "coming of age" in
America has been partly responsible for this, and America's
shift toward multiculturalism and "ethnicity" has added its
force to the movement. Intelligent Jews wondering what has
impelled Jewish survival are now searching the Jewish past
for answers. Authors who help contemporary Jews in that
search, or search along with them, are welcomed fellow-
travellers. I believe those authors, who are contributing so
richly to a deeper understanding of the Jewish tradition and
its sources, know the depth of these readers' interest and
commitment to Jewish continuity. After all, they have
dedicated their life's work to interpreting the classic sources of
the Jewish past for the sake of the Jewish present and future.

JOSEPH LOWIN

The Call of the Midrashic Muse

A Defining Trend in Contemporary American Jewish Fiction

DURING THE PAST thirty years, the Jewish literary community in America—novelists, poets, pundits, and mavens—has been telling us that we are on the verge of becoming the locus for the next Golden Age of the Jews. In the lead article of the New York Times Book Review of May 30, 1965, for example, we are told the following: "It is, in this country, as happy a time for the cultural-intellectual life of Jews as any since 12th-century Spain under the Moors."[1] How could it fail to be, the author fairly boasts, with the likes of Bellow, Malamud, Mailer, Salinger, Roth, Howe, Trilling, Kazin, and others, taking hold of the center of America's literary universe?

The problem with such an approach is that the writer is speaking not of Jewish culture but of American culture. Many writers in the American canon of twenty-five years ago were possessed of that thing called "Jewishness." What these writers lacked, however, was not so much Judaism, that is, the Jewish religion, but what we might call "Judeity," an immersion in the totality of Jewish culture, especially its textual tradition. In the final analysis, if we are going to have a Jewish civilization in America at all comparable to the one in Golden Age Spain, we are going to need a few Ibn Ezras, a couple of Ibn Gabirols, and one or two Yehuda ha-Levis.

And while we do not have these yet, we are, nevertheless, *within* a great American Jewish cultural revolution, one in

---

1. Stanley Kauffmann. "Some of Our Best Writers." *The New York Times Book Review*. (May 30, 1965):1

21

which American Jewish writers are creating works from inside the Jewish textual tradition and are thereby inserting themselves into that tradition. The Jewish textual tradition is being transformed into a new, American, version of that thing we call Jewish Civilization.

Nessa Rapoport is a novelist in the vanguard of this trend. She has also given much thought to and articulated clearly the details of what it is that constitutes this tendency. "We are bound together," she states, "not only by our history as a people but by a history of passion for one book, a book that has sustained us, as well as much of what is called 'culture.' From that book, over thousands of years, and inextricably part of the way we read it, have come commentaries, arguments, parables, laws, legends, mystical meditations, poems and songs. These writings constitute an astonishing literary civilization."[2]

Jewish fiction in America does not need to be, as Irving Howe has claimed, about the immigrant experience. It can, as Rapoport asserts, "equally be a dialogue with earlier Jewish books." This is the "midrashic mode." And to write in it, a writer must be, as Rapoport asserts, both "Jewishly educated" and "culturally confident."

HEEDING THE CALL

What I propose to present in this essay are four Jewishly educated and culturally confident Jewish writers, writers who have come under the spell of the midrashic muse. These are: Nessa Rapoport, Rebecca Goldstein, Melvin Jules Bukiet, and Allen Hoffman.[3] Not yet household names, each of these is

---

2. Nessa Rapoport. "Summoned to the Feast." In Ted Solotaroff and Nessa Rapoport, eds., *Writing Our Way Home: Contemporary Stories by American Jewish Writers*. New York: Schocken, 1993, p. xxviii.

3. By focussing on these four writers, I do not mean to imply that they are the only practitioners of the "midrashic mode." In our day, to cite only the best known, Herman Wouk, Joseph Heller, and Cynthia Ozick in the United States; Elie Wiesel and Primo Levi in Europe; Amos Oz and Aharon Appelfeld in Israel have all had recourse to this most Jewish of Jewish modes of literary expression.

nevertheless a serious literary artist. And each of these artists strives to marry cutting-edge formal innovation to traditional Jewish content. It is inevitable that such a marriage will, in many ways, be subversive of traditional Jewish content. That, I will hold, is the essence of the "Midrashic Mode."

What exactly is midrash? Midrash is first of all the quintessentially Jewish way of telling a story. It is a writing style, a strategy adopted by the Rabbis to teach their value system to the Jews by deriving that system from Torah itself. Midrash is created by the Rabbis when they find something in a biblical text which intrigues them, whether it be a missing word, a word they are puzzled by, or an incomplete narrative. We get our values from the Torah, they insist, even if it means we have to re-interpret Torah to do so. Constantly rewriting Torah, engaging Torah in an ongoing synchronic conversation, whether it is with the Written Torah of Moses or the Oral Torah of the Rabbis, that is the "midrashic mode."

And that is also the activity of those of our contemporary Jewish writers in America who feel impelled to write in response to the call of the midrashic muse.

Let us return now to the case of Nessa Rapoport, who is not only a theoretician of the "midrashic mode" but one of its foremost practitioners. Born in Canada in 1953, Rapoport has been a book editor and a teacher of writing at universities. She has published one novel, *Preparing for Sabbath* (1981), has co-edited a volume of American Jewish short stories, *Writing Our Way Home* (1992), written a televised screenplay, *Saying Kaddish* (ABC, 1991), has a meditative book recently published by Morrow, *A Woman's Book of Grieving*, and has just completed her most midrashic work, *The Perfection of the World*.

The Perfection of the World—the title is itself an English translation of the kabbalistic concept of *tikkun olam*—is a novel that, in the author's own words, "asks to be read Jewishly: that is, as a book in which story and commentary are indivisible." It is a novel in which each of five parts is a rewriting of a different book of the *Tanakh*, the Hebrew Bible, the books of Esther, Ecclesiastes, Lamentations, Ruth, and the Song of Songs. Says Rapoport, "I wrote this book to be read as a Jewish text: the same words can be read for the story they tell; for the texts they hint at; for the commentary they render on the greatest of Jewish books; and for their mystical sympathy with the original texts."

Preparing for Sabbath can be read similarly. On the surface, it is a novel about a young girl growing up in a warm Jewish family, in a Jewish neighborhood, going to a Jewish day school, attending Jewish summer camp, making the Jewish teenager's pilgrimage to Israel. It is also the story of an adolescent coming to terms with both her intellectual and sexual selves. The narrative relates the story of the heroine's struggles with her family's and her religious community's moral code of behavior. It recounts how she tests her newly-acquired ideas on her passionately–loved girlfriends and how she comes to grips with her passion for a boy who, as happens in many instances of this sort, does not deserve her.

METAPHYSICAL QUEST

Beneath the surface, however, *Preparing for Sabbath* is much more than sociology or psychology. It is metaphysics. It is about asking ultimate questions and about the search, from inside Judaism, for the secret meanings of the universe.

Asserting the organicity and the necessity of its Jewish core, the novel uses Hebrew throughout as an organizing language. It is certainly not by accident that the author chooses *not* to italicize the dozens of Hebrew words and phrases with which she seasons her text. "Illui," "birkat hamazon," "v'choshekh al pnei tehom," and "ir pituach" are not foreign words and concepts but the very sinews and muscles of Rapoport's discourse, from which it derives its vitality.

In a further, highly formal assertion of its essential Judeity, the novel is not only divided into chapters one through seven; it also has chapters alef through vav, mirroring the six days of the week one spends preparing for the Sabbath. And the Sabbath here is not only the physical Sabbath, that one day of the week when we rest and refresh our bodily selves; it is also the spiritual Sabbath, a Palace in Time, in which we are redeemed.

It is in chapter Gimel that Rapoport demonstrates what it means to write in the "midrashic mode." What Rapoport does here is to take the tale of a young girl's initiation into the world of Eros and turn it into a daring rewriting of the Song of Songs. She does this, first of all, by incorporating into her text reworked verses from the biblical text in such a way that they sound like poetic prose: "She was looking for him but she could not find him"; Who is it that waits at the door?'; "A young prince over water"; "I have entered his house"; "His left hand was under her head and his right arm held her"; "Who was like her beloved, chosen over all others?"; "She would seal him into a tower"; "She was little and had not breasts." All of these phrases resonate with scriptural power. What Rapoport does with them is to weave them into her narrative and create not only a new "Shir ha-Shirim," a Song of Songs, but a new book of prayer. What she does is to take her own text—a work of literature after all—and transform it into a piece of highly personal, and highly sensuous, liturgy. That is the way to read the otherwise incomprehensible final phrase of this chapter: "Now all her body was praise and her being exulting, holy, holy, holy, who enabled her to reach this day."

As the novel progresses, and as we immerse ourselves into the magic of its language, we come to realize more fully that, even on the cosmic level, it is still a religious humanist's reworking of "Ma'aseh Bereshit," the biblical telling of the six days of Creation. Is there no chapter Zayin, to correspond to Chapter Seven, because on the seventh day God rested and so, therefore, should Jewish novelists? Or is there no chapter Zayin because, in the final analysis, even the liturgy which we create for ourselves, whether out of our primary source texts or out of our Rabbis' commentaries on them, must be brought down from the Sabbatical realm of holiness into the domain of dailiness? The conclusion of the novel hints strongly that dailiness is where both we and Judeity belong.

RICH BACKGROUND

If the future of the Jewish novel in America resides, for the most part, in the realms of metaphysics and ethics, then it should come as no surprise that one of its most deft practitioners should herself be a student of philosophy. A 1976

Ph.D. in the philosophy of science from Princeton University, Rebecca Goldstein spent ten years teaching the subject at Barnard College when, not many years after publishing her first novel, she decided to abandon academia to become a full-time writer. Born in 1950, Goldstein grew up in an Orthodox Jewish home, the youngest daughter of the *hazzan* of the Hebrew Institute of White Plains. By her own admission a rebellious and somewhat refractory student, she did eventually graduate from an Orthodox Jewish high school. She maintains, however, that she received the better part of her Jewish education from study with her father[4] and, later, from study with her daughters, who themselves attend Orthodox Jewish day schools in New Jersey.

What is interesting about all this background is that Goldstein is a very unorthodox Jewish novelist. In fact, for many years she did not consider herself a Jewish novelist at all. "I was at first," she wrote in a letter to me, "both intellectually and emotionally opposed to taking the 'Jewish' in Jewish writer too seriously." Like Spinoza—"that pious apikoros," she calls him—she did not want the accident of birth to determine her identity. And then, she also had an "awful lot of anger toward a scholarly tradition that I felt had excluded me, by virtue of my being female."

Although Spinoza's metaphysics of the human spirit "came through to me like an old Ladino prayer melody sounding softly beneath the great formal system of his metaphysics," it was, she asserts, her art that brought her to the point where she could say that she was becoming a Jewish writer. "I find myself now," she writes, "with characters who are immersed in Jewish tradition—not just the ritual but the literature: Chumash, Navi, Gemara, Cabala—but have been displaced and are now in a world at odds with that tradition. But," she emphasizes, "they themselves are not at odds with that tradition. Or even when they are, that tradition is still exerting a powerful influence."

---

4. Father-daughter Jewish study is, of course, a theme of I.B. Singer's "Yentl." It is even more poignantly described—and with greater depth—in Goldstein's essay "Looking Back at Lot's Wife," *Commentary* 94.3 (September 1992): 37-44. The essay itself is written in the "midrashic mode."

Goldstein's four books to date include: *The Mind-Body Problem* (1983), *The Late Summer Passion of a Woman of Mind* (1989), *The Dark Sister* (1991), and *Strange Attractors* (1993). From the beginning of her literary career, Goldstein staked out a territory in the Jewish literary landscape that was uniquely her own, combining "kishkaesque" Jewish knowledge with an academic background in philosophy and a deep appreciation for the beauty and elegance of mathematics.

Her most recent book, *Strange Attractors*, a collection of short stories, contains two stories that bear directly on the Jewish condition in America, "Mindel Gittel," and "Rabbinical Eyes," and one story, "The Legacy of Raizel Kaidish," that presents a new perspective on the problematics of Holocaust survival. All three stories are distinguished by the freshness of their point of view and the opportunity and context they provide for rethinking some of the problems of identity faced by Jews in America.

SEEKING HARMONY

The title story, "Strange Attractors," presents a fresh take on a millennial Jewish dilemma, the confrontation between Western Civilization and Judaism, and the ongoing desire by some to harmonize them. Phoebe Saunders, the heroine of the tale, is one of Goldstein's most successful and delectable creations, a female schlemiel to rival Peretz's "Bontshe Schveig." Phoebe's duality comes from her genes. She is the granddaughter of a Yiddish actress and the daughter of a professor of classics. An unworldy mathematician, she has gone on an academic visit to a mathematical institute on the outskirts of the world's center of worldliness, Paris. At the institute, which is barely distinguishable from the madhouse across the way, Phoebe encounters her ideal, the mathematical god for whom the secrets of the universe have no mystery. She also encounters an even bigger schlemiel than herself, an Israeli mathematician who steers her from the gods to God. An appreciation for the beauty of God's universe seems to be at the center of both the mathematical and the Jewish-fictional enterprises. As the story ends, all the mathematicians rush

out into the street to stare in awe at a double rainbow. One of
these rainbows can easily be explained by the physics of light.
Could not the other be an allusion to the biblical covenant
with man, a covenant which placed man at the center of God's
universe and concerns?

This speculation is justified by a midrashic reading of
Goldstein's first novel, *The Mind-Body Problem*. On the
surface, this volume constitutes the by-now commonplace
American literary sub-genre, the academic novel. The title
itself and the epigraphs preceding each of its chapters lead us
directly to that sort of reading. And yet, there are hints strewn
throughout the book that lead us elsewhere, into the realm of
the midrashic. What else to make of the dozens of terms and
phrases taken directly from the vocabulary of observant
Jewish life—kashrut and shuckling, glatt and trayf, flayshig
and milchik, mikvah ladies and yeshivah bochurs, Bais
Yaakovs and kollels, the Shulchan Aruch and the Eshet
Hayyil? What else are we to make of the definition of adultery
taken directly from the Talmud? How else are we to
understand the insertion directly into the text, not once but
twice, of the awe-inspiring litany found in the *Netaneh Tokef*
prayer of the Days of Awe?

The Mind-Body Problem is a tale of three cities, Princeton,
New Jersey, Lakewood, New Jersey, and White Plains, New
York. Renee Feuer is in the process of dropping out of the
graduate program in philosophy at Princeton, replacing
cogitation with copulation, when she meets, seduces, and then
marries Noam Himmel, a mathematical genius. Life in
Princeton is characterized by a dialectic—in the classroom, in
the lunchroom, and in the bedroom—on the mind-body
problem. Do we gain our identity from the mind or the body?
Renee's attachment to the body's side of the mind-body
problem is related to her rebellion against her strictly
Orthodox Jewish education.

Himmel has nothing to rebel against. He thinks that all
Jews are products of the Enlightenment and that Jewish
religious orthodoxy went out with the Middle Ages. Noam and
all the Jewish *goyim* on campus, as Renee calls them, have no
inkling that in Lakewood, New Jersey, where Renee's brother
"sits and learns" in the Jewish institute for advanced study

known as a kollel, there exists what Goldstein calls a "Princeton of *yiddishkeit*."

Noam may not enjoy being called a pagan by his pious brother-in-law, and yet, in Vienna to deliver a paper, Noam, who usually can't even find his way to the refrigerator, has the uncanny ability to navigate Vienna's streets expertly, as though he had lived in Vienna's *Judengasse* in some previous existence. Noam draws two conclusions from this experience: that there is such a thing as the transmigration of souls, in Jewish mysticism, *gilgul ha-nefesh*; and, perhaps even more surprisingly, that his Jewishness is essential to his identity, and not at all accidental.

BACK TO THE SOURCE

For all her refractoriness to her background, Renee recognizes that her "interior is unmistakably Jewish." In Budapest, she stumbles on a group of Jews observing Shabbat, and suddenly feels herself back in her father's world, "inside Shabbos." Between Princeton and Lakewood, there is White Plains, as between the mind and the body there is the soul. "Here," says Renee, meaning Princeton, "intelligence is the issue that draws the boundaries, provides the distinctions that make the difference: who are the somebodies and who the nobodies; who the cherished and who the despised; who the heroes and who the misfits." And Renee adds that these words recall the "Who shall live, Who shall die" liturgy that her father used to chant on the high holidays. So crucial is this liturgy that it is repeated verbatim at the novel's conclusion. Making the liturgy hers, Renee concludes: "Long after I ceased believing in these words, the sound of them has caused my spine to tingle and eyes to tear, as there is often a lag between one's rationality and emotive responses. *I'm not even confident that today the words would entirely fail in their effect were I to put them to the test.*" (Emphasis mine.)

A metaphor that runs through this narrative has to do with a "mattering map" which Renee had elaborated as a way to judge herself and the world. Renee's namesake, the seventeenth-century philosopher René Descartes, had affirmed his existence by stating "I think, therefore I am." Feuer wants

above all to feel that she exists, that she matters, that she has
a place on the mattering map. Although she acknowledges that
"most of us manage to situate ourselves in that region of the
mattering map where one's own self comes out mattering," she
herself had chosen to matter by marrying someone who did.
When, inevitably, the great mathematician loses his powers,
Renee has to get beyond her husband's genius to his suffering.

In Rebecca Goldstein's metaphysics this is both an ethical
and an esthetic move. As Noam had taught her earlier, "the interesting thing about art is you're being presented with another's point of view, looking out into the world from his perspective." When she learns that artistic technique, Renee Feuer
learns—and teaches the reader—the Jewish lesson taught by
Jewish history, that "people and their suffering matter."

FAMILY BURDENS

Born in 1953 in New York City, Melvin Jules Bukiet
received a 1974 B.A. from Sarah Lawrence College, where he
currently teaches, and an M.F.A. in writing from Columbia in
1976. He grew up in a family steeped in Jewish history, his
mother having lived on a Baron de Hirsch farm settlement in
Southern New Jersey and his father having survived
Auschwitz, Buchenwald and Theresienstadt, and, as he puts it,
the culinary delights of poison ivy eaten during a forced
march.

Like Elie Wiesel, and other writers for whom life itself is de-
fined by the concentration camp experience—either their own
or their parents'—Bukiet is unashamedly willing, as he puts it
in a letter to me, "to call the Jewish deity to account for his
sins." He refuses to engage in any literary justification of God's
ways to man; rather, he seeks, as he wrote, "through fiction, a
retribution upon divinity for the unfair punishment meted out
on Israel."

In an understandable act of hubris that places man not only
at the center of the universe but on top of it, his aim is "to establish a human divinity more exemplary than our maker."
And yet, Bukiet, for all his professed lack of faith, maintains a
Jewish faith in the power of the book. "As I see Judaism," he
writes, "it's the commentary that keeps us going rather than

the thing commented upon, and this," he is happy to conclude, "makes for especially fortuitous fiction today. . . . I think it's the utopian streak that echoes most potently in the fictional dialogue, whether it looks backward to a state of primordial perfection or forward to the Messiah."

In *Stories of an Imaginary Childhood* (1992), Bukiet rewrites the story of the Garden of Eden and provides his own American portrayal of the literary redemption of the Jews. The childhood in the title of this refreshingly original—and insidiously thoughtful—work of fiction is doubly imaginary. First of all there is the Eastern European shtetl of Proszowice, so "lovingly" imagined by the author. There, one encounters the twelve-year old narrator, his parents, and their herring-selling dry goods-hardware-grocery store. There, one observes how the narrator escapes successfully from violin lessons and how he fails miserably in his effort to hook up with the town harlot.

The crowning glories of this work are the chapters entitled "New Words for Old" and "Torquemada." In the latter story, the narrator, having been hit on the head and knocked unconscious by a local Polish bully, imagines himself as all the anti-Semites of history and thereby raises the problems of both Jewish self-hatred and suffering. The former tells of the arrival in town of a great Jewish poet who is asked to give a public reading of his works. Desirous of preserving his vocal chords, he agrees to the public performance on condition that a reciter can be found. The choice falls on our narrator and the venerable bard whispers the words of his opus into the ears of the young poet. What comes out of his mouth, however, is not what has been transmitted, but a whole new Torah, a work of youth and rebelliousness, in which the story of the Garden of Eden is totally recast.

OPTIMISTIC OUTLOOK

Allen Hoffman, born in 1942, grew up in the Jewish community of St. Louis. His mid-western upbringing is very possibly accountable for the breath-of-fresh-air optimism and the humanistic view of Judaism that pervades his writing. A 1965 B.A. in American history from Harvard University,

Hoffman spent several years learning in Yeshivot in both Jerusalem and Brooklyn. After a teaching stint in the New York
City public school system, he moved with his wife, Stefani
Hoffman—a specialist in Russian Studies and the main translator of Natan Sharansky's biography—and their children to
the Old City of Jerusalem, where he continues to write.

Since 1981, when *Kagan's Superfecta and Other Stories* was
published, Hoffman has been receiving a great deal of word-of-
mouth attention from a special brand of literary cognoscenti,
those who are also knowledgeable about Jewish texts and
tradition. Although the book has been out of print for some
time, the title story, "Kagan's Superfecta," has been making
the rounds, Samizdat-style, in third- and fourth-generation
photocopies. Hoffman's readers have also been eagerly
awaiting the appearance of a major novel, rumors of which
have been circulating for several years.

That novel, which promises to be Hoffman's *magnum
opus*—1,250 pages in typescript—has been completed and is
awaiting publication. Titled *Small Worlds*, the novel appears
to fulfill all of Hoffman's fans' expectations of him as an
important innovator in Jewish fiction. What distinguishes
Small Worlds is its unmistakable grounding in the Jewish
textual tradition. As the novel's epigraph points out, the title
comes from the Talmud where we are told that every man's
eye is a small world that contains within itself the reflection of
the Holy Temple and therefore the seeds of redemption.

Hoffman's real talent lies in his ability to create small
worlds out of macrocosmic events. He does this by using the
Joycean technique of focusing our attention on one Jewishly
significant day in the life of each of his main characters. Thus,
the pogrom suffered in the Polish shtetl of Krimsk takes place
on Tisha B'Av, the day on which the destruction of the Temple
is commemorated; the Jewish major league baseball player
caught in a web of corruption remembers the ethical lessons of
the Krimsker Rebbe, and turns a Saturday afternoon into
Shabbat; the Jewish KGB investigator, who is trained to elicit
guilt from the most innocent of Moscow's citizens, has a
Dostoyevskyan confrontation with his own guilt on Rosh
Hashanah when all Jews are judged; on a secular Israeli
kibbutz, a member teaches his refractory comrades to light the

Hanukkah lights, with the blessing; two teenage boys in St. Louis watch the Krimsker Rebbe climb a table and re-enact for them the ascent of Moses to Mount Sinai to receive the Torah, on the holiday of Shavuot, which commemorates the Giving of the Law.

COMIC TALE

Yom Kippur, the most solemn day of the Jewish year, is the focus of Hoffman's boisterous, raucous novella, a Rabelaisian comedy in a Jewish register, "Kagan's Superfecta." The main character of this story, Maurice Kagan, and several of his Upper West Side Manhattan cronies seem to come straight out of Damon Runyon. Moe Kagan is a remedial English teacher— for a while he also had a routine as a stand-up comic—living in a modest New York City apartment with his wife Fran, who hails from Connecticut—for Kagan, the essence of bucolic Middle America. On the one hand, Kagan can only be described as a low-life. He plays mind games with his wife, he is constantly trying to borrow—or rather mooch—money from his friends, and, compulsive in his search for betting action, he could be a poster boy for Gamblers Anonymous.

Kagan, however, is ripe for repentance, rehabilitation and redemption. The gambler's credo—"Winning is better than losing. But losing is action. And action is better than no action"— can also be read as a metaphor for life. Kagan does care sincerely for his students, whom he would like to bring up to "grade level" not only in reading but in life. He is able to see the good in people whom society relegates to the margins: Katzi, the bookmaker who takes bets almost after the race has been run and the game has been played, because betting is in his blood; Big Abe, the information addict whose ear is constantly glued to his transistor radio; Pakooz, a cut-rate shrink open all night, who also sells to his patients, from suitcases under his couch, everything from ties to trays of canapes. It is clear that Kagan relishes the margins, not only of New York life, but of Jewish life as well. It is from the margins that Kagan enters into Jewish society. It is from the margins—from the limits of reality—that Kagan exits Jewish society to enter—by way of the fantastic—into the world of Jewish metaphysics.

The seriousness with which we are to take the comic effects of this story owes a great deal to the sixteenth-century French religious humanist François Rabelais. Rabelais had admonished his readers to go beneath the surface of his often crude humor, reminding them that, in the reading room as at the groaning board, to get at the marrow, it is necessary to crack the bone. The marrow in question is an educational philosophy appropriate for the renascence of a European culture that will be at once religious and humanist. The marrow of Hoffman's bone is an outlook on Jewish life appropriate to the 21st century.

Hoffman is good at making distinctions: Tradition is at odds with modernity; what's clever is not necessarily funny; understanding is not the same thing as acceptance; and, most of all, information is not knowledge. The novella teaches that despite man's vulnerability and subsequent failures, God's intention is that man take his fate into his own hands and continue with the business of living. As Kagan puts it, borrowing his language from the stage, "the show must go on."

It is erev Yom Kippur 1973[5] and Kagan is making last-minute preparations for the holiday, which he will spend at the local shtibl (which Kagan takes pains to distinguish from the local temple). Everywhere he goes, however, the four digits 5734 loom before him. It is the number tattooed on the

---

5. Astonishingly, the story makes no mention at all of the 1973 Yom Kippur War, news of which buzzed through virtually every congregation in America as Jews prayed that day. Obviously, Hoffman's silence on the subject is pregnant with meaning. In a telephone conversation, Hoffman revealed that he was "very much aware" of the coincidence. Aside from the fact that "I wanted Shabbat to coincide with Yom Kippur" for the conclusion, Hoffman asserts that, especially from God's point of view, from the perspective of kedushah, holiness, "all Yom Kippurs are the same." Hoffman agreed that his silence on the subject was a pointed silence, a metaphysical silence. As my analysis attempts to show, one of the points that Hoffman makes is that information, "news," is on not the same level with knowledge, and certainly not with understanding.

arm of the mikvah-man, a refugee from Europe's Holocaust, who will turn out to be Elijah the Prophet. It is the number of a police car with which Kagan becomes entangled. It is the number of the Jewish year. Kagan believes that it is also the number for that evening's superfecta, the order of finish of the first four horses. The problem is that Kagan does not, as a matter of principle, bet on a sporting event that takes place on the Sabbath or a Jewish holiday, despite the fact that there is no legal prohibition against doing so.

How does Kagan, not a Torah scholar, know about Jewish law? True, Kagan had begun to study with a Rabbi. But it seems that Kagan owes much of his Jewish learning to supernatural means. He has an angel, Ozzie, who not only confirms that if he bets on the number he will win, but also gives him religious sanction to do so.

USE OF FANTASY

It is at the point where the story enters into the realm of the fantastic that it also enters into the world of the "midrashic mode." Here, in the realm of the midrashic, is where ultimate Jewish questions are asked. Why is Kagan a compulsive gambler? Why does Kagan's angel want to place ethical stumbling blocks before Kagan? Is there a theological meaning to Jewish survival? What, finally, is the deep meaning of Yom Kippur, and what is it supposed to teach the Jewish people? After all, it is on Yom Kippur that the ultimate Jewish issue of life and death is raised.

It seems that Kagan and Katzi, the bookmaker, gamble because "it's in the blood." A bit of Jewish folklore crucial to an understanding of this story is that certain family names indicate that one is likely to be a descendant of the biblical priests. Among these names, are Cohen, Katz, and Kagan. The Torah, in Leviticus 16, and the Babylonain Talmud, in Yoma 4, recount how the High Priest would draw lots—gamble—on Yom Kippur in order to determine the order of the day's atonement.

It seems that Kagan's angel, whom Kagan knows only as Ozzie, is in reality Azazel, an angel involved since biblical times in the atonement process. Ozzie tries to corrupt Kagan, to get him to bet, because, according to the midrash, the angels are mankind's antagonists since the Creation. The angels had even tried to convince God not to create man and give him dominion over the earth, because, they argued, man would sin. God rebukes the angels by telling them, first, that, placed on earth, the angels would do worse than mankind, and that, in the second place, humans will take advantage of the opportunity to repent.

"Kagan's Superfecta" is a midrash on this midrash. The theological lesson it teaches is that it is possible to move from information to knowledge, and from thence to an understanding of God's ways. It is God who places humanity, and not the angels, at the center of Creation. Human beings have within themselves the capacity to be like Elijah the Prophet and bring the Messiah, that is, the Redemption. It is by acquiring this wisdom that the Jewish people will decide for themselves on Yom Kippur that the Jewish people shall live and not die.

As Kagan recites the Priestly Blessing that concludes the Ne'ilah Service of a Yom Kippur that coincides with a Shabbat, he raises his hands in the appropriate gesture. As he intones the primordial chant, he realizes that his fate, and that of the company he keeps, is literally in his hands.

Allen Hoffman, like Nessa Rapoport, and not unlike Melvin Jules Bukiet and Rebecca Goldstein, has artfully wrought a work of art that determines to teach the Jewish people at the dawn of a new, admittedly non-Jewish, millennium that, however marginal their texts may appear, however subversive of the Jewish tradition their texts may aim to be, they are in reality at the center of a Jewish tradition that seeks to build on itself and to create itself eternally in such a way that tradition and modernity will be perceived as one and the same thing.

Works Analyzed

BUKIET, MELVIN JULES. *Stories of an Imaginary Childhood*. Evanston, IL: Northwestern University Press, 1992.

GOLDSTEIN, REBECCA. *The Mind-Body Problem*. New York: Random House, 1983.

_____. *Strange Attractors*. New York: Viking, 1993.

Hoffman, Allen. *Kagan's Superfecta*. New York: Abbeville Press, 1989.

RAPOPORT, NESSA. *Preparing for Sabbath* (1981). Sunnyside, NY: Biblio Press, 1988.

LEWIS GLINERT

Modern Hebrew Lexicography: The Last 100 Years

IN THE REPUBLIC OF LETTERS, power is with the lexicographer — a shadowy species of technocrat, an anonymous engineer with his fingers on the linguistic switches that supply a whole nation. The power that such men and women pack has only recently come under the scrutiny of sociologists of language, themselves a relatively new breed.[1] Studies of language planning[2] and language engineering pay frequent attention to the doings of language academies, educational authorities and similar official or quasi-official agencies in the lexicographic field; less light has been thrown upon the activities of the private lexicographer, although their fallout can be as pervasive and persistent as any.[3]

In the evolution of Hebrew in the past 100 years from literary language to multipurpose written medium, native vernacular, and all-functional national tongue, the dictionary has constantly occupied centre stage. On the diaspora sidelines, too, wherever the study of Modern Hebrew has mattered, the dictionary has mattered a great deal.

It thus comes as a matter of particular dismay that Modern Hebrew lexicography has lagged far behind that of other modern Western cultures, quantitatively and qualitatively, in

---

1. On the sociology of language, see for example the writings of Uriel Weinreich, Einar Haugen, John Gumperz, Joshua Fishman, John Edwards, and David Laitin. On the sociology of Hebrew in general, see Fishman 1981, 1985 and Glinert 1993b.
2. Overviews of the field are Eastman 1983 and Cooper 1990. On the planning of Modern Hebrew, see Fellman 1974, 1977, Nahir 1979, Rabin 1976, 1983, and Glinert 1991, 1993a.
3. Noteworthy studies of lexicography are Householder and Saporta 1967, Hartmann 1983 and 1986, Ilson 1985, 1986 and 1987, and Landau 1984.

terms of scope and format and sheer self-awareness. We shall presently set this in the context of Modern Hebrew language studies and language attitudes in general.

THE HISTORICAL BACKDROP

An acute sense of lexical inadequacy has in fact long haunted Hebrew writers, expressing itself in Saadia's fascination with biblical hapaxlegomena, in the linguistic bravado of the rabbi in Yehudah Halevi's *Kuzari* ("Is it conceivable that their rulers such as Moses, Joshua, David, and Solomon lacked the words to express what they wished, as is the case with us today, because it is lost to us?"), in the decision of a whole Sephardic Medieval culture to use Arabic in all things but poetry,[4] and, paradoxically, even in the faintly hysterical lexical coinages of the *paytanim*. Even while Jews beyond the realm of Arabic contrived to produce a rich Hebrew literature in the sciences and humanities, involving lexical retrieval and coinage on a massive scale,[5] no attempt was made to record, let alone codify, this lexical wealth, mathematical, medical, philosophical. The purpose of dictionaries, it was felt, was to serve as aids to biblical and talmudic study or as guides to biblical good style,[6] but not as witnesses to the scientific achievements of Hebrew, let alone as guides or standards for the aspiring Hebrew academic.

The first glimmer of evidence that Hebrew lexicographers were becoming conscious of the present came with the German Haskalah.[7] Yehuda Ben-Zeev's Hebrew-German-Hebrew *Otzar Ha-Shorashim* (1807-8) was the most used and

---

4. See Blau 1962, Halkin 1963 and Roth 1983, 1985.
5. See, for example, Sarfatti 1969.
6. See Hirschfeld 1926, Malachi 1956, and Tene 1971, pp. 1364-7; Talmudic and Rabbinic lexis featured in the lexicons of Elia Bahur (Tishbi) and Johannes Buxtorf.
7. In the words of Shavit (1993), "the achievement of the Berlin Haskalah was not only to prove that Hebrew could act as a modern cultural medium. With this proof went a carefully argued ideology that saw Hebrew as a secular national tongue..." See also Yitzhaki 1970.

influential Hebrew dictionary of the nineteenth century. The German-Hebrew side in the first edition is replete with words for things like post, kitchen, potato, spectacles, elastic.[8] Even the Hebrew-German side, though constructed around biblical roots, throws out the occasional tantalizing modernism. But the nineteenth century, while quite prepared to create vernacular-to-Hebrew equivalence lists — one small set of equivalences out of many — to service its modernistic Hebrew activity, made no attempt at databases of Diaspora Hebrew, whether monolingual or Hebrew-to-vernacular. To the individual lexicographer, it all appeared too diffuse and disorganized.

Once the Zionist movement was committed to creating a Hebrew society, a comprehensive lexicon of the Hebrew language assumed critical importance, in both symbolic and practical terms.

The keynote statement to this effect came in 1908 with Bialik's essay *Hevlei Lashon* ("language pangs"), in which he set out an agenda for Hebrew lexicographers. His dominant theme was that Hebrew should develop organically, from within, by virtue of sheer use, above all by speakers and by creative writers with a feel for the language. He proposed the retrieval *(kinnus)* of the vast "authentic" Hebrew riches of the past, with particular attention to phraseology; and with all modernisms being kept apart and listed in a separate volume, by no means unwanted but strictly for use in referring to the unheard of or the new-fangled. Could Bialik be said to have been calling for a historical dictionary? No, if by this one means a dictionary that both collates and demarcates the various historical layers of a language, leaving no illusions as to what is obsolete. What Bialik was calling for might be termed an ahistorical dictionary. And this was to be the consensual goal of Hebrew lexicography until recent years. The monolingual dictionary was its lynchpin, but not a "native-speaker's" dictionary (as is the norm in Western

---

8. From its very beginnings in efforts like the periodical *Kohelet Musar* (1750) and Satanov's *Mikhtav Shema Shelomo* (1788), the Haskalah had generally preached a rapid expansion of the Hebrew lexicon, both by scouring the postbiblical sources and by coinage.

cultures), rather a "learner's dictionary" of a peculiar kind: the whole society was "learning" its mother tongue (be they immigrants or third generation native Hebrew speakers!) and it had to be learned from historical basics. The bilingual dictionary would meanwhile be left to simmer.

PIONEERING EFFORT

Eliezer Ben-Yehuda launched the first serious, and massive, assault on this target. The first edition of his thesaurus appeared in 1900-1905 (Berlin: Langenscheidt), and the second edition entitled *Millon ha-Lashon ha-Ivrit ha-Yeshanah ve-Ha-Hadashah* between 1908-1959 (Berlin, then Jerusalem) in sixteen volumes, the last nine written after his death by M.H. Segal and N.H. Tur-Sinai, accompanied by a massive introduction representing the only serious lexicographic study by a Hebrew lexicographer until Goshen-Gottstein's prolegomenon (1969). Mirkin (1973, 1975, 1981) has traced the twists and turns in Ben-Yehuda's purposes. Ironically, the original idea was a thoroughly modern dictionary "for anyone wishing to write and speak Hebrew" (as Ben- Yehuda put it in *Ha-Zvi* in 1887), rather than an aid to Bible study — arranged both alphabetically and thematically, and with many of his own coinages. And indeed, Ben-Yehuda did just this with his little-known pocket Hebrew-Russian dictionary (1901). His Hebrew-Hebrew dictionary project, however, quickly developed into a vast historical-cum-contemporary canvas, with rich examples and etymologies and with hosts of Haskalah coinages — citations coming from as late as 1902. The one thing lacking, by deliberate decision, was the wealth of Persian, Greek and Latin words that are morphologically and culturally part and parcel of Hebrew. While the first edition did include foreignisms susceptible of Hebrew inflection where "needed for the enrichment of our language," the second edition relegated a large amount of non-Semitic material to a projected separate volume — words like אטליז, גמטריא, הדיוט, מלפפון. This was an extreme degree of purism that no other Hebrew dictionary has followed, save the tellingly entitled Ben-Yehuda

Pocket Dictionary edited by David Weinstein and Ben-Yehuda's son in 1961. One user-friendly feature, however, that all have taken up is the listing of all nouns and adjectives under their own form rather than by root.

While the thesaurus begun by Ben-Yehuda slowly took shape, another of the educator-heroes of the Revival, Yehuda Gur, devoted seven years to producing an altogether more realistic monolingual pocket dictionary — with some 25,000 headwords, based on primary sources. Done in collaboration with David Yellin (a traditionalist where Ben-Yehuda was a radical Semitist, see Ben-Asher 1977), *Ha-Millon ha-Ivri* (Tel-Aviv: Dvir, 1927) made no attempt to exclude Aramaisms and foreignisms in the name of Hebraic purism — though, as Avineri (1964) has noted, later Diaspora reinterpretations of ancient expressions such as אין מזל לישראל are sometimes ignored. Gur's preface portrays his dictionary as serving the needs of the Revival above all but wherever possible drawing on the past, all the while avoiding explicit challenge to biblical norms:

> This new dictionary is a lexicon of Hebrew language and literature in its many and varied periods, from earliest biblical times down to our own days, the days of our national and linguistic rebirth. Biblical Hebrew is here in its entirety [...] while from the talmudic and midrashic language, as well as other branches of ancient literature, this book gathers only those words that may be adjudged Hebrew in form and are unattested in the Bible by mere chance or those words of which the Revival has need [...] From the coinages of the Geonim, Poskim, Paytanim, Parshanim, and translators, and those of our own times, we have chosen only what has become more or less accepted, in particular words desperately needed in living usage, easy to grasp, and of clear Hebrew derivation... [my translation]

To these he adds the Aramaisms that "have become naturalized in our language," and a very few foreignisms. Here, as with Hebrew-based coinages, Gur explicitly reserves the liberty to exclude words "with which this author is dissatisfied."

Gur's compendious *Millon ha-Safah ha-Ivrit,* with citations galore, followed in 1936 (Tel Aviv: Dvir), a concise version without citations in 1937, and a revamped unabridged *Millon*

Ivri in 1946. A further edition was planned but never completed.[9]

Gur's agenda set new benchmarks for Hebrew lexicography. It differed strikingly from Bialik's. Public acceptability and the realities of the Yishuv rather than documentary idealism was being portrayed as setting some of the parameters, within the post-Classical database at any rate (though the sheer logistics of the task may have counted for even more — Bialik had the luxury of being able to theorize without ever writing a dictionary.) In its format, too, Gur trumpeted, this was a "popular" dictionary, not "research-oriented and scientiflc" (in current parlance, a desk dictionary). True, but as we have seen, popular Hebrew dictionaries were nothing new.

In practice, however, this was still something of an *embarras de richesses*. As Rabin (1985) has noted, Gur's dictionary, and that of Kaufman/Even-Shemuel, functioned "like a sort of display window offering a choice of words for one's use." Avineri thundered at the many unattested neologisms that came and went in the various editions of Gur's dictionaries — words like אפן, עיין, אבחמץ for "ear doctor, eye doctor, oxygen" respectively. By contrast, monolingual dictionaries post-'48 (Even-Shoshan and Knaani) aimed, in Rabin's words, "at presenting words that readers are liable to find in the books they read or to hear in a speech or lecture." Note that Gur, as good as his word, enters every biblical word and virtually all that the Mishnah has to offer. A statement about the realities of Yishuv education, or about his ideals? Note too the words "lexicon of Hebrew... literature": Citations from good sources serve not just as illustrations but as models.

AMERICAN CONTRIBUTION

1929 saw the appearance in Tel Aviv of Kaufman's dictionary. A unidirectional *English-Hebrew Dictionary*, published by Dvir, it was the work of three American Hebraists, the poet-philosopher Israel Efros, Benjamin Silk (Silkiner),

---

9. I am indebted to Reuven Mirkin for this information. The 1946 edition was no larger in content but much changed.

and editor-in-chief Judah Kaufman (Even-Shemuel); an addendum followed in 1948. In a Hebrew preface, the Russian Zionist leader Shemaryahu Levin relates that while in the USA during World War One he resolved that an English-Hebrew dictionary would "give millions of English-speaking Jews a means of approaching Hebrew" and thus "show all who consider Hebrew an impoverished tongue how wrong they are." He proceeded to commission the aforesaid gentlemen to do the work. The authors' own Hebrew preface sees the dictionary as acting in reverse, serving Hebrew-literate Jews studying English. They also hail the Balfour Declaration as opening new contacts between "our national culture" and English; however, despite appearing in Tel Aviv, the dictionary's inspiration was clearly American rather than British and the target readership English-speaking Jews, or Hebrew-literate Jews seeking to write American English. Thus, the English is based on Webster's (adding some Anglo-Jewish expressions), and no guidance is given as to British pronunciation.

The Hebrew data still reveal no clear sense of a definitive current usage; they add their own "two cents" to the Revival by wholesale suggestion of calque phrases like זכוכית החול for "sandglass" (Yishuv language planners, by contrast, were firmly committed to a policy of single words rather than phrases, see Sivan 1985:87ff.).

Another strategy for dealing with the lack of intertranslatability was to pile the entries high with competing translations, e.g. for "rose" both ורד and שושנה, for "orange" תפוח סיני, פלסין, תפוח זהב, סינית, and for "elevator" no less than seven alternatives! Avineri (1964) found this fault in several dictionaries of the time, an extreme case of the lexicographer-as-corpus-planner sending signals to other like-minded lexicographers while quite ignoring the needs of the user. Even where the Hebrew translations could be differentiated in meaning, there was no attempt to do so — just mystifying strings of Hebrew words, creating the impression that Hebrew vocabulary itself is prone to be "woolly," a feeling that had long dogged Hebraists and had given rise to a veritable literature on "synonym discrimination" in the Haskalah years. And down to the present, most bilingual Hebrew dictionaries have blindly continued to neglect sense discriminations.

The riches of the past, biblical, talmudic, and, rabbinic, were served up, as usual, and with generous citations— Hebrew, after all, was not to be thought of as impoverished. But Kaufman struck a particularly modern, anti-classical note (maybe an American one, for his readership?) by including Yiddishized and generally folkloristic matter: אפסן "good-for-nothing," סך הכל "total," ידעות "conscience." No other dictionary has ever picked up on this initiative.

Nine years later, in 1938, Dvir of Tel Aviv published a battery of dictionaries with an altogether British rather than American slant: (a) *The Compendious Hebrew-English Dictionary*, a revision by the Hebrew University Semitist M.H.Segal of an earlier work by the American-born writer Reuben Avinoam (Grossman) and H. Sachs, "designed to assist the English-speaking reader in his studies of the Hebrew language and literature of all periods, and especially of the Hebrew Bible and the literature of contemporary Hebrew"; (b) *A Concise Hebrew-English Dictionary*, a slimmed-down version of the same by M.H.Segal, "designed chiefly to assist the English-speaking reader in his study of Modern Hebrew"; and (c) a sister *Concise English-Hebrew Dictionary* by Anglo-Christian Hebraist Herbert Danby and M.H.Segal.

These dictionaries use British, *Concise Oxford Dictionary* spelling and British pronunciation, and make much fuss of the latter. The British were firmly ensconced in Palestine; American dictionaries were presumably not to their taste.

The Grossman-Segal effort, like Gur (whose work they acknowledge), can be seen as a pragmatic reflection of current *literary* norms, of what the educated and very educated were reading and what the educated were writing. The concise version reflects essentially the same principle, but on a narrower scale: "In addition to the whole of Biblical Hebrew, our book gives also of the vocabulary of Mishnaic Hebrew and of Medieval Hebrew as much as has been preserved in the speech and general literature of Modern Hebrew"— a reflection of the dominant role of the Tanakh in Yishuv education of the times, Talmud and other traditional texts, by contrast, having largely faded into the general background. All three dictionaries furnish "a large number of technical terms" but

without any of the Hebrew colloquialisms and slang whose
English counterparts might find a place in Webster's or in the
English side of an English-Hebrew dictionary for that matter.
This can be accounted for within a model of literary norms: It
was only with the 1940's native-born "Palmach Generation" of
writers that colloquialisms began slowly to find their way into
Hebrew literature; indeed, they would not capture the "low
ground" of literature in translation until the seventies.[10] This
same model can probably account for the less than friendly
representation of verb forms, still organized by root with
grudging cross-referencing of the most opaque of verb stems —
while הוסיף, הביט are cross-referenced to the roots נבט, וסף, there
is no cross-referencing of הבין to בין let alone of straightforward
Hiphil verbs to their roots. If this is "designed to assist the
English-speaking reader in his studies of the Hebrew language
and literature," it is a somewhat elitist construal of the notion.

LEXICOGRAPHY POST-'48

If Ben-Yehuda and Gur produced (in Avineri's words)
מקוה מים (a pond), Avraham Even-Shoshan's dictionary was
באר מים חיים (a well of living waters). Even-Shoshan's *Millon
Hadash* (Jerusalem: Kiryat Sefer, 1948-52), revised in 1966 as
Ha-Millon he-Hadash (an addendum appeared in 1986), was
the first monolingual Hebrew dictionary to put descriptivism
on a par with revivalism. A Hebrew-speaking state was now in
being, with institutions guaranteeing the primacy of the
language. Current Hebrew usage could now be assessed and
safely underwritten; and Diaspora folk usage and talmudic
idiom need not be eschewed for its own sake — Even-Shoshan,
in Avineri's words, "gathered Aramaic idioms as a loving
mother gathers up her children."

Even-Shoshan's introduction contains none of the reserva-
tions expressed by Gur about un-Hebrew-looking new words; it
claims in fact to embrace not only colloquialisms but even
"slang" (Hebrew for "non-normative"). Also in the name of
descriptivism, it claims to provide the biblical and talmudic

---

10. See Ben-Shahar 1989.

inventory — though here there is more than a hint of revivalism once again: "There is hardly a word, however rare, that the Hebrew reader might not come across in study or conversation. Better then to err on the side of completeness." And even Qumran and archaeological vocabulary are also to be included. Another sign that conventional Western lexicographical concerns were not foremost in his mind was the lack of indication of how much technical vocabulary was being included.

How Even-Shoshan proceeded in practice, and why, was the subject of a study by Glinert 1987. It emerged that large numbers of non-normative words or semantically non-normative uses of words were included (e.g. אחרת (=אם לא), בלגן, זיפתי, בטח טנדר, טוסטר,), but large numbers were omitted, with no apparent rhyme or reason. By contrast, substandard words and uses were excluded (e.g. מלאן, טוסיק, למה ש–). Clearly, Even-Shoshan's descriptivism was still constrained by revivalism. Even more remarkable was the complete omission of any phonologically or grammatically non-normative forms (e.g. ישן, זאתי אופנוע,). Grammatical and phonological deviance from the classics topped Hebrew normativists' agendas then, as it still does today. Even-Shoshan, true to his claims, included virtually all (but not all), biblical lexis and a large dose of talmudic vocabulary; but, unworthy of true descriptivism, he almost nowhere indicates where a word (e.g. אבל (=אכן), איכה, אימתי, עשתי-עשר) is archaic – and labels such as "poetic" and "literary" are entirely lacking.

Descriptivism run wild is a fitting label for Yaakov Knaani's *Otzar ha-Lashon ha-Ivrit* (Jerusalem: Masada, 1960-1). Designed to be an utterly comprehensive historical monolingual dictionary, shunning purism and including "not only all Hebrew words, however rare, but the Aramaic, Greek and Latin and all the other foreign academic words, ancient and modern, that have come into the language," Knaani's majestic tomes are a gross act of lexicographic technology with nothing of the lexicographer's art and craft: Lacking, as Sarfatti (1961) has noted, are any criteria for when a foreign word becomes a loan word, for when an unbound phrase becomes a lexical item, any guidance on style and register or on case prepositions. The only compensation is a veritable mass of authentic citations, and a creditable selection of collo-quialisms (e.g. מצוברת, חתיך, אוטו, טרמפיסט, טרמפ) to the extent that these crop up in Yizhar or in Knaani's newspaper files.

The sixties brought rapid advances and bizarre regressions in bilingual Hebrew lexicography. Ben-Ami Scharfstein and Raphael Sappan's *English-Hebrew Dictionary* (Tel Aviv, Dvir/Shilo, 1961) appears to have been the first English-Modern Hebrew dictionary to approach contemporary Western standards of descriptivism for a bilingual dictionary. Even-Shoshan's influence was probably significant, but so too was the fact that Raphael Sappan was one of the first students of Israeli slang; his *Darkhei ha-Sleng* (1963) marked a significant stage in the painful emergence of Israeli linguistic realism. The introduction pulled no punches: "...an approach to language that is realistic rather than moral... Hebrew educators are particularly reluctant to accept as a natural part of the language much of what is in fact said by ordinary people. We think this reluctance is excessive." They were not minded to screen for internationalisms, nor to give false standing to official coinages that never caught on ("We have cited the official word wherever it has been or may still be adopted").

This was the first — and, save for Wittenberg 1975, the only — Hebrew learner's dictionary: Rather than draw its English entry list from monolingual native speaker dictionaries, it is based on *The Teacher's Word Book of 30,000 Words* (chiefly American usage, but with some British and Jewish additions). The entries themselves are splendidly organized, using sense discriminations (e.g. wild *of animals*, wind: air in motion... breeze...) and distinguishing polysemes by semicolon.

The same year, however, saw the appearance of quite the oddest Hebrew-English-Hebrew dictionary to appear since 1948. The cover blurb and the very title of *Ben-Yehuda's Pocket English-Hebrew Hebrew-English Dictionary*, by Ehud Ben-Yehuda and David Weinstein (New York, 1961) — Ehud was a son of Eliezer Ben-Yehuda — proclaim that it "derives from the eight-volume Dictionary and Thesaurus of the Hebrew Language by Eliezer Ben-Yehuda, the father of modern Hebrew." A confusing message: on the one hand, Ben-Yehuda's dictionary was a historical dictionary, on the other, the brand name value of the man himself is his association with *modern* Hebrew. The product itself is confusion incarnate: In strict line with Ben-Yehuda *père's* Semitic purism (which was adjudged extreme even in its own day, see above), internationalisms are out: no טלוויזיה, אינפלציה, אנרגיה, ביולוגיה etc.[11] In their place come a swarm of Hebraic substitutes, words like סכיון for television, נפח for inflation, and — a source of undying embarassment to learners unaware of its current use as "striptease" – חשפנות for archaeology, most of these being Ben-Yehudisms which never found general acceptance.[12] Both authors were based in the USA, and the dictionary is unusual among Hebrew dictionaries in containing substantial American material. By contrast, the Israeli colloquial is entirely lacking. Yet this is otherwise very much a modern Hebrew dictionary, and one with some practical features lacking in many other, newer dictionaries: verbs are entered by stem, including all hiph'il and hitpa'el verbs; and plurals of nouns are supplied.

COMPREHENSIVE WORK

An altogether more significant endeavor, though not without its own fetishes, was Reuven Alcalay's *Complete English-Hebrew Hebrew-English Dictionary*, Tel Aviv 1959-61 (English-Hebrew) and 1963-5 (Hebrew-English). It appeals to a broad, literary cum technological model of native Hebrew competence — embracing the major Classical sources along with the flood of technical coinages by official Israeli agencies since statehood. However, as the author himself states, this is a dictionary for "the advanced student, the technician and the professional no less than the general reader" — and indeed, items like "anthrophobia" and "stipiform" and the whole of Israel's flora and fauna ("running into thousands") place this

---

11. For some reason, an exception is made for טלפון.
12. A large majority of Ben-Yehuda's coinages suffered this fate, see Sivan 1985. Some of the un-Israeli words in Ben-Yehuda–Weinstein actually represent American usage, e.g. סכיון, used by Daniel Persky in *Hadoar*; some of them may even have become common in summer camp parlance as a result of appearing in this pocket dictionary.

in the category of technical lexicon, but a technical lexicon of a very special sort: With Alcalay, 150 years of Hebrew lexicography as advocacy of Hebrew's modern capabilities reached a climax; if Even-Shoshan embodied the new Jewish territorial-linguistic state to itself, Alcalay represented it to the outside world, arguing on every page that Hebrew had now achieved truly modern and westernized status: standardization, intertranslatability, and hence parity with languages of wider international communication — except that in the interests of Hebrew's standing (and possibly his own, as ex-Hebrew Translator-in-chief for the Mandatory Press Bureau), Alcalay took the gross liberty of entering many as yet unaccepted words of his own making.

As if to bring a Jewish-traditional counterweight to bear on this cosmopolitan-modernist leaning, this dictionary gives unprecedented space to Jewish cultural realia and to hawking "phrases, idioms, proverbs, adages and familiar Bible quotations exemplifying the use of words." Cultivating the idiom and the proverb, in fact, had always been a major value of Hebrew revivalism .

Peculiarly, however, Alcalay's image of a normalized Hebrew did not extend to legitimating the colloquial. His Hebrew-English preface self-consciously states: "The purist may take exception but I think that current, even vulgar, usages ought not to be primly disregarded." Sadly, his actions failed to match his words. The result is a dictionary in which the two "edges" — the modern-technological and the classic-literary — are heavily present, while the "center" of any general dictionary, the everyday, is seriously lacking.

Just as regrettable, the "new enlarged" edition of 1990 fails to include words like עיצומים, מדרחוב, דרגנוע, קלטת which have meanwhile become so familiar.

Formatting is moderately friendly. Large numbers of synonyms are listed "for enrichment sake" — in both directions, suggesting that we have here a case of didactism rather than just Hebrew revivalism; sense discriminations are provided, but perversely in the target rather than source language; full vocalization is the rule. The preface claims that this is as much a Hebrew-speaker's as an English-speaker's dictionary, which is to a large extent true.

MEGIDDO DICTIONARY

Edward A. Levenston's and Reuven Sivan's *Megiddo
Modern Dictionary* (Tel Aviv: Megiddo, 1965, reprinted in
1993 as the Galil Dictionary) was, like Scharfstein and
Sappan, a fairly realistic endeavor, in two large volumes:
Hebrew-English as well as English-Hebrew. However, as the
introduction acknowledged, it was of more use to the Israeli
than to the English-speaker, i.e. aimed at Hebrew recognition
rather than production; indeed, no major Hebrew dictionary
since Scharfstein and Sappan has catered for the English-
speaker — far more Israelis need to know English than
English-speakers Hebrew, and publishers know it.

The Megiddo Dictionary was neither historical nor highly
technical; it reflected general usage, including "new or revived
words from science and technology" as well as the "substandard," but omitting "words no longer in use in literature or colloquial speech" — a departure from the neologizing tendencies
of Hebrew lexicography. An example of this new descriptivism
was the use of *huf'al* verb forms rather than *hof'al* and
sporadic colloquialisms such as טרמפ and פיספס. At the same
time, archaic biblicisms like סות still take up valuable space.
The trail-blazing comprehensive plene spelling, hints of which
could already be sensed in Alcalay, reflected growing official
and popular trends; so too the decision (anticipated by the
Ben-Yehuda Pocket Dictionary) to list verbs by stem rather
than by root — neither Israeli users nor students of Hebrew
can be expected to identify roots. However, plene spelling by
itself is inadequate: non-plene spelling of sorts is still so
widespread, particularly in the vocalized texts that learners of
Hebrew regularly use, that some type of cross-referencing
system, or at least running explanatory footers, are essential.
Sense discriminations were provided, though still in the target
rather than the source language. Stylistic labels appeared,
such as "poetic, literary, colloquial." Commas and semicolons
set polysemes aside from distinct lexemes.

A concise, pocket version of the Megiddo dictionary
appeared in 1975, the Bantam-Megiddo, claiming to be "up-to-
date" and "comprehensive", with 46,000 entries — but a mystifying sense of priorities: no space for sense discriminations but

space for hundreds of obscure English headwords that should have no place in a pocket dictionary: just on one page alone, "buzz-saw, buttonwood, butt weld, bushing, burgess" (meanwhile, I looked in vain for "disco, nuts, stodge"). The Hebrew word list was anything but an "up-to-date" listing of Israeli usage which the English-speaker might encounter: the same old hang-ups about the colloquial and the contemporary foreignism — no טירטר, טרמפ, מבסוט, פיספס, פלונטר, פשלה, צ'ופר, חבר"ה, no acknowledgement that די means "rather" and המון means "lots of," and no mention of standard anglicisms and slavisms such as חלטורה, בלגן, סטיישן, טוסט — and an indefensible absence of realia such as גרבונים, סוודר, בקלה, בורקה. It may not be coincidental that the Hebrew editor, Reuven Sivan, is a noted normative stylist with several studies of the Hebrew Revival to his name.

Another confused endeavor of the seventies was M. Wittenberg's Hebrew-English *Millon Ivri-Angli* (Jerusalem: Yeda, 1975, 2 volumes), claiming to represent "Modern Hebrew as spoken in day-to-day life, [...] as printed in our copious literature, in newspapers and periodicals for all professions and sciences." Here was a dictionary aimed at least as much at English-speakers as at Israelis, and in many respects it was a cut above the others: Abundant sense discriminations, collocations and idioms, colloquialisms, and examples. Thus the entry המון furnishes the various syntactic subcategorizations of the word הוא סבל המון (3 המון ילדים (2 המון בעיות (1. Here and there, too, are comments appropriate to a Hebrew learner's dictionary — e.g. on TO LOSE אבד: "actually this verb means: to get lost to. Instead of saying I lost my pencil, you say: my pencil was lost to me." Learner's dictionaries using this approach are standard for major European languages; it is an indictment of the Hebrew teaching establishment that to this day only two dictionaries can remotely be described as Hebrew learner's dictionaries.

As if to compensate for this usefulness, Wittenberg used non-plene spelling in his headwords; listed verbs by root and not by stem; and included archaisms such as אבה (התאבה סיגריה "Would you care for a cigarette?").

Dov Ben Abba's *Signet Hebrew-English English-Hebrew Dictionary* (New York: Signet/Masada, 1977) is a pocket

dictionary that claims to be both "modern and comprehensive,"
to embrace the slangy and the technical, the "Biblical,
Talmudic, and Medieval." Not surprisingly, it manages just
sporadic coverage of all of these. Sense discriminations too are
sporadic and verbs are listed by stem — but one looks in vain
for case prepositions or inflectional information or (particularly perverse in the late seventies) plene spelling. In short, a
dictionary for Hebrew-speakers but not for Hebrew-learners.

Haim Shachter's *New Universal English-Hebrew Hebrew-
English Dictionary* (Tel Aviv: Yavneh, 1960 (H-E) and 1983
(E-H)) caters for both English and Hebrew speakers. The
Hebrew-English side, a product of the fifties, betrays this in
its coverage of "all periods of Hebrew — Biblical, Mishnaic,
Talmudic, Midrashim, Medieval and recent developments of
our modern, living language" — even glossing אבל in its biblical sense of 'indeed.' Similarly, spelling is "short" with little
plene cross-referencing, and verbs are listed by root. Moreover,
while claiming to offer a "big selection of so-called 'slang' ", it
provides a very sporadic selection. However, unlike most
Hebrew dictionaries, this one recognizes the importance of
sense discriminations — in the English-Hebrew side at any
rate: the various Hebrew equivalents are given numbers (e.g.
STOP: ... 11. עצר 14. שהה, התעכב) keyed to discriminative
examples (e.g. 11. The policeman stopped the car, 14. Do you
intend to stop here?), a unique and valuable resource. It also
gives case prepositions.

THE LAST DECADE

Menachem Dagut's *Dictionary of Contemporary Israeli
Hebrew* (Jerusalem: Kiryat Sefer, E-H 1979, H-E 1986), a
thorough revision of M. Segal's 1938 dictionary, but still with
a British bias, claims — as one might expect from a
professional British semanticist of Dagut's stature — to offer a
Hebrew-English list that is strictly contemporary and non-
technical, with "full representation of colloquialisms and slang
expressions." And indeed, here at last is a fairly good coverage
of standard (as against substandard) Hebrew colloquialisms:
טייפ, מבסוט, פלונטר, פשלה, טרמפ, טרטר, חבר"ה (cassette recorder),

though not צ'ופר or פלאגים (spark-plugs). Concomitantly, biblicisms are omitted, unless they are a living part of contemporary literature: no עשתי–עשר, סלה, אימתי. Revealingly, however, lexico-grammatical colloquialisms such as די as 'rather' and זאתי for זאת are missing, evidence that grammar is the last frontier of Hebrew normativism (see Glinert 1987).

Hebrew headwords are spelled in short followed by plene, and additionally entered as a plene cross-reference. Verbs come with case prepositions and inflectional peculiarities, and are given by stem, including *pu'al* and *huf'al* and nonpassive *nif'al* verbs, a practice that has unfortunately become widespread in the last few years — it is surely not for dictionaries to list grammatically near-automatic inflections like *pu'al* and *huf'al*. Welcome use is made of style labels (lit., coll., sl.), though not nearly enough; likewise, sense discriminations are only sporadic and only in the target language. Especially disappointing, this is yet again a unidirectional effort: The E-H side caters for Israelis, not for English-speakers seeking the Hebrew *mot juste*.

If ever an English-Hebrew dictionary were likely to suit Hebrew learners, it would, ironically, be the English-Hebrew *Oxford Student's Dictionary for Hebrew Speakers* (Tel Aviv: Kernerman/Kahn, 1985), edited by Bar-Ilan linguist Joseph Reif from A.S. Hornby's *Oxford Student's Dictionary of Current English*. The very organization of homographs and polysemes as distinct subentries ensures that STOP = 'put an end to' is translated as לעצור, STOP = 'prevent' as למנוע and so on. Spelling is plene *plus* pointing (perfect for a Hebrew production dictionary), verbs are given with case prepositions. Adjectives, however, are not; indeed, I know of no Hebrew dictionary that specifies דומה ל, שונה מ, גאה ב, עד ל — one more indication that Hebrew lexicography is less than professional. Reif's descriptivism is also patchy: while sweater is rendered סוודר and hitch-hiker טרמפיסט, sandwich is given as כריך and arm as זרוע rather than יד. Nonetheless, this has already become one of the best-selling English-Hebrew dictionaries of all times.

Shimshon Inbal's *Hebrew-American English-Hebrew User-Friendly Dictionary* (Jerusalem: Zack, 1988) appeared as a desk dictionary and then (slightly abridged) in pocket format.

It makes the by-now ritual boasts of descriptivism, of Arabisms and Yiddishisms, of sparing us the old lists of near-synonyms and specialized terms, while zealously listing the "correct" Hebraic alternatives to foreignisms like פרופיל. But here, as in Dagut-Segal, is indeed a fairly good picture of Hebrew as she is spoke: you will find פשלה, טרמפ, טרמפ, טרטר, חבר"ה, פלונטר, צ'ופר, though no פלאגים (spark plugs) or טייפ (cassette recorder) — the desire to Hebraize the realia of life appears still to be a potent force among "liberated" Israeli lexicographers, as indeed it is to some extent among the populace as a whole, witness the success of certain recent hebraizations such as תקליטור, קלטת (see Glinert 1991) Similarly, an ambivalence still persists toward grammatical "errors," thus "quite" is rendered די but די is not rendered "quite." Inexplicably, the English-Hebrew side still provides follies such as "sweater: סורגה, סוודר, פרקס, מיזע, אפודה" (this cannot reasonably be aimed at Israelis, but could it seriously be aimed at Americans?) However, this does seem once more to be a dictionary for Israelis: sense discriminations are sporadic; spellings are plene, without "defective" cross-references and without any guide on how to find the plene form; neither case prepositions nor inflectional hazards are indicated.

Avraham Zilkha's *Modern Hebrew-English Dictionary* (New Haven: Yale University Press, 1989) describes itself explicitly as a dictionary for special purposes, namely for comprehension of Israeli texts, particularly the media; and it indeed assembles an impressive vocabulary of current affairs and lifestyles. In many ways, this dictionary complements Hornby-Reif. But the media being what they are, one might have expected more colloquialisms and less literarisms. Hebrew lexicographers committed to modernity have yet to comprehend that there is no shortage of places for looking up רמה, אבה or אימתי — nor that listing automatic *pu'al* and *huf'al* verbs while ignoring verbal irregularities is to blur the distinction between lexicon and grammar book. Most recently, the pocket Shimon Zilberman's *Up-to-date English-Hebrew Hebrew-English Dictionary* (Jerusalem: Zilberman, 1992) seems to have been specifically designed to be of no use to Hebrew-learners: the Hebrew in the English-Hebrew side has no *nikkud*, probably the first ever Hebrew dictionary with this dubious feature. Further enigmas: a full listing of *pu'al* but no *huf'al,* plene spelling of *u* but defective spelling of *i*. In the version for a smaller pocket (a third less entries), 1993, the *nikkud* has been restored. Generally, however, this dictionary maintains the great Hebraic lexicographic tradition of patchy descriptivism and paltry sense discrimination, while contriving to do without case prepositions and inflectional warnings altogether.

LINGUISTIC AND SOCIAL CONTEXT

The past 100 years of Modern Hebrew lexicography have seen a slow progression from an historical, or more strictly speaking, an ahistorical focus to a contemporary one — as the creation of an all-purpose, self-regulating modern tongue has run its course. Even-Shoshan's monolingual dictionary, coinciding with the creation of the State of Israel in 1948, was something of a watershed in this process; however, the lack of any major successor or major revision to Even-Shoshan's popular opus in the past 25 years points to a serious weakness in the Hebrew lexicographic profession, and indeed in the expectations of the Israeli public.

Furthermore, few of the many Hebrew-English-Hebrew dictionaries to have appeared have done justice to everyday standard Hebrew. This might appear particularly perverse in view of the popularity of the Ulpan teaching method, with its emphasis on speech rather than grammar or the written word. However, as I have suggested elsewhere (Glinert 1979), Hebrew language teaching is still acting out the drama of the Spoken Revival, in which Classical purism and fear of translationese play major roles. A further striking feature, to anyone familiar with general Western lexicographic practice, is the poverty of resources and method at every level: confusion of functions that are sometimes best served by separate dictionaries (production vs. comprehension, specialized vs. general, literary vs. mundane, classic vs. modern), a dearth of dedicated Hebrew learner's dictionaries and children's dictionaries, a failure to develop standards of sense discrimination, semantic arrangement, stylistic labelling, grammatical arrays, spelling retrievability and so on.

Modern Hebrew lexicography in the 1990's still exhibits something of the idealism and *halutzic* amateurism that flourished in the period of linguistic revival. In this, it runs broadly parallel to Modern Hebrew linguistics in Israel, a field of study that appeared, a generation ago, to be on the verge of a great leap forward (Rabin 1970) but which has been in steady retreat and today has little to show in terms of academic positions or productions. Both disciplines would seem to be out of synch with the general evolution of political and cultural values from the ideologically charged atmosphere of the forties and fifties to the disillusion and laissez faire of the nineties. A crucial factor may be the sheer decline in the Hebraic humanities in Israel; radical elements may gravitate elsewhere, leaving conservative forces to fill the vacuum.

If real progress is to be made in Modern Hebrew-English lexicography, it may have to come from the Diaspora.

References

Avineri, Yitzhak. Yad ha-Lashon, Tel Aviv: Davar, 1964.

Ben-Asher, Mordechai. "Innovators versus conservatives during the language revival," Balshanut Shimushit 1, pp. 5-19, 1977.

Ben-Shahar, Rina. "Normot Leshoniyot-Signoniyot be-Targum Mahazot Angliyim ve-Tzarfatiyim le-Ivrit bi-Shenot ha-Hamishim ve-ha-Shishim. *Dappim le-Mehkar be-Sifrut* 5-6, 1989.

Blau, Yehoshua. "Al maamadan shel ha-ivrit ve-ha-aravit," *Leshonenu* 26, pp. 281-284, 1962.

Cooper, Robert. *Language Planning and Social Change*. Cambridge University Press, 1990.

Eastman, Carol M. *Language Planning: An Introduction*. San Francisco: Chandler and Sharp, 1983.

Fellman, Jack. "The Academy of the Hebrew Language: Its History, Structure and Function," *International Journal of the Sociology of Language* 1, pp. 95-104, 1974.

____. Hebrew Language Planning and the Public. In Joan Rubin et al. (eds.) *Language Planning Processes*. Berlin: Mouton de Gruyter, pp. 151-156, 1977.

Fishman, Joshua A. *Language and Nationalism*. Rowley, Mass.: Newbury House, 1972.

____. (ed.), *The Sociology of Jewish Languages* = *International Journal of the Sociology of Language* 30, 1981.

____. (ed.), *Readings in the Sociology of Jewish Languages*. Leiden: Brill, 1985

Glinert. Lewis H. "Linguistics and Language Teaching: The Implications for Modern Hebrew," *Hebrew Annual Review* 3, pp. 105-127, 1979.

___. "Le-shitot ha-millonaut be-millon Even-Shoshan — Normativiut vedeskriptiviut," *Mehkarim be-Lashon* 2-3, pp. 399-409, 1987.

___. "The back-to-the-future syndrome in Language Planning: The case of Modern Hebrew," in David F. Marshall (ed.), *Focus on Language Planning*. Amsterdam: John Benjamins, pp. 215-243, 1991.

____. "The first conference for Modern Hebrew, or when is a congress not a congress?," in Joshua A. Fishman (ed.), *The Earliest stage of language planning: The "first congress"phenomenon*. Berlin: Mouton De Gruyter, pp. 85-115, 1993a.

____. (ed.), *Hebrew in Ashkenaz: A Language in Exile*. New York: Oxford University Press, 1993b.

Goshen-Gottstein, Moshe. *Mavo la-Millona'ut shel ha-Ivrit ha-Hadasha*. Tel Aviv: Schocken, 1969.

Halkin, A.S. "The Medieval Jewish Attitude Toward Hebrew, in Alexander Altmann (ed.), *Biblical and Other Studies*. Cambridge: Harvard University Press, pp. 233-248, 1963.

Hartmann, R.R.K. (ed.), *Lexicography: Principles and Practice*. London: Academic Press, 1983.

____. *The History of Lexicography = Studies in the History of the Language Sciences*. 40. Amsterdam: John Benjamins, 1986.

Hirschfeld, Hartwig. *Literary History of Hebrew Grammarians and Lexicographers Accompanied by Unpublished Texts*. London: Oxford University Press, 1926

Householder, Fred and Sol Saporta (eds.), *Problems in Lexicography*. The Hague: Mouton, 1967.

Ilson, Robert. *Dictionaries. Lexicography and Language Learning*. Oxford: Pergamon, 1985.

____. *Lexicography: An Emerging International Profession*. Manchester: Manchester University Press, 1986.

____. (ed.), *A Spectrum of Lexicography*. Amsterdam: John Benjamins, 1987.

Landau, Sidney. *Dictionaries: The Art and Craft of Lexicography*. New York: Scribner's Sons, 1984.

Maimon, N.Z. Review of Ben-Ami Scharfstein and Raphael Sappan *English-Hebrew Dictionary, Bitzaron* 47:3,1963, pp. 186-188.

Malachi E.R. *Otzar ha-Leksikografia ha-Ivrit* (Addendum to Mandelkern's Hebrew Concordance). New York: Shulsinger, 1956.

Mirkin, Reuven. "Perakim be-Toledot ha-Millonut ha-Ivrit ha-Hadashah, *Leshonenu* 37, pp. 165-186, 1973, 39, pp. 73-98, 1975, 54, pp. 311-323,1991.

_____. "Ha-Millonut ha-Ivrit ba-Me'ah ha-Tesha-Esrei," In Moshe Bar-Asher (ed.), *Kovetz li-Shenat ha-Lashon*, Jerusalem: Academy of the Hebrew Language, pp. 178-185, 1990.

Nahir, Moshe. "Lexical Modernization in Modern Hebrew and the Extra-Academy Contribution," *Word* 30, pp. 105-116, 1979.

Rabin, Chaim. "Hebrew." In T.A. Sebeok (ed.), *Current Trends in Linguistics*, vol. VI, The Hague: Mouton, pp. 304-346, 1970.

"Language Treatment in Israel," *Language Planning Newsletter* 2.4, 1976.

_____. "The Sociology of Normativism in Israeli Hebrew," *International Journal of the Sociology of Language* 41, pp. 41-56, 1983.

_____. "Millona'ut ha-mikra," *Peraqim* 5, pp. 33-53, 1985.

Rosén, Haiim. *Contemporary Hebrew*. The Hague: Mouton, 1977.

Roth, Norman. "Jewish Reactions to the Arabiyya and the Renaissance of Hebrew in Spain," *Journal of Semitic Studies*, 28.1, pp. 63-84, 1983.

_____. "Maimonides on Hebrew Language and Poetry," *Hebrew Studies* 26.1, pp. 93-101, 1985.

Sarfatti, Gad B. Review of Knaani, *Otzar ha-Lashon ha-Ivrit*, *Leshonenu* 25, pp. 206-214, 1961.

_____. *Munahei ha-matematika ba-sifrut ha-mada'it ha-ivrit shel yemei ha- beinayim*. Jerusalem: Magnes, 1969.

Shavit, Yaacov. "A Duty too Heavy to bear: Hebrew in the Berlin Haskalah, 1783-1819: Between Classic, Modern, and Romantic." In Lewis Glinert (ed.), *Hebrew in Ashkenaz: A Language in Exile*. New York: Oxford University Press, pp. 111-128, 1993.

Sivan, Reuven. *Tehiyyat Leshonenu*. Jerusalem: Rubinstein, 1985.

Tene, David. "Linguistic Literature, Hebrew," *Encyclopedia Judaica*, vol. 16, pp. 1352-1390, 1971.

Yitzhaki, Yosef. "Deoteyhem shel sofrei ha-haskalah al ha-lashon ha-ivrit," *Leshonenu* 34, pp. 287-305, 35, pp. 39-59,140-155, 1970.

REUVEN KIMELMAN

Liturgical Studies in the 90's

IF THIS DECADE LIVES UP to the promise of its first several years, it will be a banner decade for liturgical studies. The year 1993 alone has witnessed the publication of a massive bibliography on Jewish liturgy, an encyclopedia of Jewish prayer, an English rendition of Ismar Elbogen's classic on the history of Jewish prayer, *Der jüdische Gottesdienst in seiner geschichtlichen Entwicklung,* two comprehensive treatments of the liturgy and prayer, even a *Festschrift*, not to mention more popular works and a host of articles.

When the promise of the decade is realized major credit will go to the *sine qua non* of research–bibliography. A yeoman's service has been rendered by Joseph Tabory in his Hebrew work, *Jewish Prayer and the Yearly Cycle: A List of Articles,* a Supplement to volume 64 of *Kiryat Sefer*, the bibliographical quarterly of the Jewish National and University Library in Jerusalem. This 1993 volume consists of close to three hundred pages of bibliography on a wide range of liturgical issues through 1991. There are fifteen chapters under the rubric "The world of prayer;" nine chapters under the rubric "The history of the liturgy according to its periods and its communities," (with an appendix on the Falashas); five chapters under the rubric "Daily liturgies and their histories;" and fifteen chapters under the rubric "Jewish holidays." The book opens with a bibliographic essay on liturgical research and concludes with a list of authors in Hebrew and in English.

Another boon for students of the liturgy is Macy Nulman's, *The Encyclopedia of Jewish Prayer: Ashkenazic and Sephardic Rites*, published by Jason Aronson. This book is a *vade mecum* of matters liturgical. If there ever was a book for "everything you wanted to know about the liturgy but were afraid to ask," this is it. In more than four hundred pages, some twelve hundred entries on the prayerbook are extensively documented. At the end, there is a helpful list of prayers, a list of Hebrew first lines, an index to biblical verses, and an index of names. In addition, the book is introduced by a glossary and a "How to use this book." Every Hebrew entry is given in transliteration followed by the Hebrew.

The book is informative, accessible, and comprehensive. Peculiarly, it lacks an entry for *'Amidah* (though there are entries for the individual blessings) or *Birkat Ha-Minim.* There is also a problem with the completeness of the documentation. While the bibliographical information covers the range from traditional to modern studies, there is a dearth of references to the academic periodical literature as well as to recent scholarly books. Especially helpful would have been references to two recent works on the development of custom that deal significantly with the history of liturgical practice. The first are the two Hebrew volumes of Daniel Sperber on *Jewish Customs: Sources and History,* published by Mossad Harav Kook in 1989 and 1991; the second is the 1992 Hebrew book of Israel M. Ta-Shma, *Early Franco-German Ritual and Custom,* published by Magnes Press, which includes nineteen studies, ten on the Sabbath most of which deal with liturgical matters, four on Passover, and five on blessings and prayer. The extensive indices and the listing of sources, both ancient and medieval, make both of these works especially accessible.

Two other path breaking works that would have been helpful deal with Hekhalot and Genizah material. The first is that of Meir Bar-Ilan,*The Mysteries of Jewish Prayer and Hekhalot,* published by Bar-Ilan University Press in 1987, which documents the type of parallels between the liturgy and *Hekhalot* literature that can contribute to a history of liturgical formulation. The second is that of Ezra Fleischer, *Eretz-Israel Prayer and Prayer Rituals as Portrayed in the Genizah Documents,* published by Magnes Press in 1988, which documents the significance of the Genizah material for our understanding of the origins of the liturgical rites of Eretz-Israel and thus the formation of the classical liturgy. These two Hebrew volumes contain extended bibliographies as well as excellent indices of the discussed prayers and *piyyutim,* making them especially useful for scholarly referencing. Had this literature been incorporated, *The*

Encyclopedia of Jewish Prayer would have realized more fully the promise of its title and enhanced its use for scholar and layman alike.

ELBOGEN REVISITED

If these deficiencies mar the above work they scar the next one. The aforementioned work by Elbogen has merited a splendid edition and translation by Raymond P. Scheindlin entitled *Jewish Liturgy: A Comprehensive History*, published by The Jewish Publication Society. Although it is a boon to the English reader to have this German classic, especially with the additions of the Hebrew edition, available in the vernacular, it is unclear what the purpose of such a corrected translation is in 1993.[1] At least when the work appeared in Hebrew, for a second time in 1972, the editors updated it. If the work was considerably dated in 1972, it is all the more so in 1993. Not to have updated it is not only a disservice to the reader, but undermines its scholarly usefulness. A publisher more attuned to scholarly needs would have been more demanding especially in the light of the effort expended in making the book aesthetically pleasing and accessible to the reader.

A case that could have been a model is the new English version of Emil Schürer's *The History of the Jewish People in the Age of Jesus Christ*. It had as its agenda a revision that includes "the removal of out-of-date-items of bibliography, ...the revision of bibliographies, ...the correction and modernization of all references (to), ... [and] the addition of relevant new archaeological, epigraphic, papyrological and numismatic material" (I. vi). Through this revision and reshaping, the editors expressed the hope that "they will have secured its

---

1. Although Scheindlin has done a commendable job in correcting miscitations, some still got through. For instance, on p. 23, the citation of *Mishnah Ber.* 1:2 should be 2:2 and *Antiquities* 218 should be 212. Nonetheless, even the corrected source does not support Elbogen's contention that Josephus knew of all three passages of the *Shema'*.

useful survival into the twenty-first [century]" (III. 1. vi). Had
this been the agenda of Elbogen's reissue such an expectation
would also have been in order.

It is precisely because Scheindlin is such a sensitive scholar
that he feels obliged to excuse these deficiencies. In the
Forward, he says, "Though Elbogen's reconstruction of liturgical history and the book's intellectual matrix are somewhat
outdated, his work remains the most exhaustive compendium
of factual information about the Jewish liturgy, and it is likely
to remain so for some time" (p. xi).

A reason for this slavish adherence to Elbogen's legacy is
noted in Scheindlin's next paragraph. He says, "Elbogen's book
can be read in two ways: as a scientific history and description
of the Jewish liturgy; or as a monument to the outlook of a
religious Jewish intellectual in nineteenth- and early twentieth-century Germany." Both parts of this statement deserve
comment. When humanistic endeavors such as history are
dubbed "scientific," it is unclear whether the intention is
descriptive or evaluative. If "scientific" means verifiability,
then no history is verifiable in the sense of subject to
repetition especially not under controlled conditions. If by
"scientific" is meant the use of the best methods and
information available, then if a work was "scientific" seventy
years ago, it, by definition, can no longer be so in the 1990's.
There would be much wisdom in replacing the term "scientific"
by "academic," and meaning that the work conforms to the
current standards of the historians' guild. Anything more is
special pleading.

Since the concern for "science" in the first part of the
statement does not explain the slavishness of the English
rendition to the original with the revisions of the Hebrew
edition, the second part may. Scheindlin explains the inclusion
of Elbogen's idiosyncrasies even "to the point of crankiness"
(p. xi) because "In our age of fundamentalist revival, Elbogen
needs to be heard again, for he reminds us that the path of
uncompromising traditionalism leads nowhere" (p. xii).
Scheindlin also believes that Elbogen's opposition to mysticism "provides us with a badly needed corrective. For in our
desperate late twentieth-century quest for spirituality we tend
to forgive mysticism its ties to intellectual reaction and

superstition...Thus Elbogen's peculiarly objective yet engaged work has wisdom for our own time" (p. xii). The result is a monument to a cranky *fin de siécle* religious Jewish intellectual who, reflecting the prejudices of the translator, merits a full hearing under the guise of a "scientific" history of the liturgy. Clearly "scientific" denotes here more an endorsement than a description.

This would have been bearable had more of the book withstood the ravages of subsequent research and if the analysis had significantly enhanced the understanding of liturgy as liturgy. There is little hope for that, however, since, as Scheindlin says in his conclusion, he hopes that a successor will rise and "update his work and go beyond it to deal with the religious meaning of the liturgy, a meaning Elbogen felt keenly but had not the tools to describe" (p. xvi). Indeed, the bibliography is bereft of any reference to works on the problems of textual analysis for historical reconstruction, the meaning of prayer in the history of religion, or literary analysis. It thus reflects well the classical approach of 'holy insularity.'

WRONG EMPHASIS

It must seem strange to modern students of religion how so many classical *Wissenschaft* scholars of Judaica could invest so much effort in description and so little in meaning. Examples of this is Elbogen's discussion of *Mah Tovu* and *Adon Olam*. With regard to *Mah Tovu*, he says, "The passage is composed of biblical verses, especially verses beginning with the word ואני 'and I' " (p. 76). Elbogen was clearly right in stressing this emphasis on "I" verses.[2] Indeed, the drive for such verses was so strong that Psalm 95:6, which reads "Come, let us worship and bow down; let us bend the knee before the Lord our Maker," was transformed into the "I" statement, "I will worship and bow down; I will bend the knee

---

2. See the survey of the various versions by A. Hilvitz, "The Saying of the Verses of 'Mah Tovu' before the Liturgy," *Sinai* 78 (5736) 263-278 [Hebrew].

before the Lord my Maker."[3] Yet, no effort at accounting for this focus on the self as particularly suited for a morning entrance liturgy is forthcoming. There is thus no discussion of how the liturgy deals with the ego in its effort to create a divine focus in the opening moment of prayer.

The failure to deal with meaning is even more noticeable in the treatment of *Adon Olam*. It is described, "As a prayer of purest poetry and universal religious content" (p. 77) without a single observation on its poetics or on its religious content. This is lamentable since of all medieval poetry *Adon Olam* achieved the greatest liturgical prominence. Some observation on its poetics would have been in order such as how the ten lines (of the Ashkenaic version) of the hymn comprise a chain of five couplets with a uniform rhyme scheme carried by the second line of each couplet. Or a comment on how the ten lines break down into two blocks: the first six making the case for God's transcendence as reflected through the notions of God's eternity, sovereignty, and uniqueness; the last four making the case for divine immanence as reflected through the notions of care, protection and trustworthiness. By interlocking both divine greatness and compassion a mental matrix for prayer is formed through which *Adon Olam* emerges as the theological introduction to the service, thereby accounting for one of its strategic locations in the prayerbook.

Similarly, *Ashre* is referred to some seven times without any comment on its significance as an introductory psalm to the afternoon service or the morning psalms that introduce the Shema' and its blessings besides noting the talmudic citation that "Whoever recites 'A Psalm of David' *three times a* [should be: every] *day* is assured of belonging to the world to come" (p. 71).[4] It is also annoying when Elbogen relies on

---

3. It is rarely adequate to note an allusion without noting how the liturgy reformulated the original; see Menachem Schmelzer, "Some Examples of Poetic Reformulations of Biblical and Midrashic Passages in Liturgy and Piyyut," *Porat Yosef: Studies Presented to Rabbi Dr. Joseph Safran*, Ktav: 1992, 217-224, with the literature cited there in note 1.

4. For its meaning and liturgical significance, see Reuven Kimelman, "Psalm 145: Theme, Structure, and Impact," *Journal of Biblical Literature* 113 (1994).

secondary literature when appearing to cite primary literature. For instance, after noting that the *Lekhah Dodee* that was adopted was that of R. Solomon Alkabez, he states that "The kabbalistic rite of welcoming the Sabbath [was] first described in *Seder hayom* by R. Moses b. Makhir (1599)" (p. 92), without mentioning that the *Lekhah Dodee* cited in *Seder Hayom* is different from the one attributed to Alkabez. From the literature cited in endnote 4, it appears that Elbogen was misled by the secondary literature.

On the other hand, Elbogen is to be commended when avoiding the scholarly tendency of his day of ascribing so much of the liturgy to either periods of persecution (see p. 79) or political events (see p. 26). He, however, does not resist entirely the pull of either the persecution theory (see p. 56) or the political theory (see p. 28) to explain the presence of the *Shema'* in the *Mussaf Kedushah* or the national petitions in the daily *'Amidah*. Subsequent research has shown the flimsiness of such theories. One of the legacies of the "scientific" study of the liturgy is a Hegelianism that considers political theories of liturgical formulation as "scientific" while explanations due to internal developments or the religious situation as something less. Thankfully, contemporary understanding of "real" explanations far exceed the realm of the political.

Elbogen dedicates considerable attention to both the recitation of the *Shema'* and the *'Amidah*. Much of his treatment of the *Shema'* and its Blessings has become standard. Noteworthy is his understanding of the tannaitic recitation of the *Shema'*. According to him, "The recitation was antiphonal, with the congregation and the precentor alternating... [with the] precentor, reciting the beginning of the verse - for example, "Hear O Israel." The Congregation would repeat his words and finish the verse: "Hear O Israel, the Lord our God, the Lord is One" (p. 24). The most recent treatment of the tannaitic recitation of the *Shema'* has nuanced this a bit, but accepts the basic thesis with regard to the antiphonal recitation of the *Shema'* verse.[5]

---

5. See Reuven Kimelman, "The Shema' and Its Rhetoric: the Case for the Shema' Being More than Creation, Revelation, and Redemption," *Journal Of Jewish Thought and Philosophy* 2 (1992): 111-156, esp. 154.

Elbogen's understanding of the 'Amidah has not fared as well. He accepts the idea that "The Amidah is divided into three sections: The first three benedictions form a hymnic introduction; the final three are a conclusion with thanksgiving; and the thirteen middle ones contain petitions" (p. 25). According to his footnote, this description is talmudic. In actuality, it is not the Talmud that makes this distinction between the nature of the opening and closing three benedictions but Maimonides, who may be based on Saadyah Gaon.[6] More to the point is the fact that the designation of the first three benedictions as a "hymnic introduction" is unhelpful. It not only does not note what is being introduced, it says nothing of its content. Also the designation of the final three as "a conclusion with thanksgiving" says nothing about what is being concluded and overgeneralizes the content, for as Elbogen himself notes, "Benediction 17 and Benediction 19 contain petitions" (p. 27)[7] and thus cannot be subsumed under the rubric of thanksgiving. Elbogen is left to conclude that "the order and organization can be understood only on the assumption that the parts of the prayer come from different periods" (p. 27).

The assumption that a composite document reflects different periods is a standard technique of the "scientific" (read: historical) school for dealing with literature that does not conform to preconceived notions of coherence. It is not clear how much this assumption is helpful in detecting the prior history of the 'Amidah. Although benedictions of the 'Amidah did not come into being at one time, there is no evidence for the existence of an extra-Temple daily communal liturgy other than that of the 'Amidah whose existence in Temple times cannot be documented. While there were prayers in Second Temple times whose themes overlapped one or another of the benedictions of the 'Amidah, there was no proto-'Amidah in the sense of a daily prayer said by the

---

6. See Reuven Kimelman, "The Daily 'Amidah and the Rhetoric of Redemption," *Jewish Quarterly Review* 79 (1988/89) 167, n. 5.

7. This observation had long ago been attributed to R. Hai Gaon; see *Otsar Ha-Geonim: Berakhot, Perushim,* 47.

people.[8] After all, if every theme that overlaps that of the 'Amidah were to be taken as evidence of a proto-'Amidah, then the statements in Deuteronomy 10:17 and Nehemiah 9:32 that "God is great might and awesome" would also be candidates.[9] On the other hand, the order of the 'Amidah, according to the Talmud, is that of Yavneh.[10] Since there is no evidence of an alternative order and since recent research has underscored the overall thrust of the theme of redemption as the generative idea behind its structure,[11] there is reason to attribute the order of the benedictions to a single period.

Two other discussions by Elbogen require significant revision and updating. The first is his identification of the Nazarenes in the Genizah version of Birkat Ha-Minim with Christians (p. 31). Recent research points to their identification with Jewish-Christians not Gentile ones.[12] The issue was one of internal schism, not one of Jewish Christian relations. The second is the Kedushah. Despite Heinemann's significant updating of Elbogen (pp. 59-61), the number of entries under Kedushah in Tabory's aforementioned bibliographical work that were published in the last twenty years attests to the need for further updating.

---

8. See Ezra Fleischer, "On the Beginnings of Obligatory Jewish Prayer," Tarbiz 59 (1990) 397-441 [Hebrew] with English summary iii-v.

9. See the assumptions with regard to them in B. Yoma 69b and Y. Berakhot 7:4, llc.

10. B. Berakhot 28b; B. Megillah 17b; see J. Berakhot 2:4, 4d.

11. Kimelman, "The Daily 'Amidah," 165-198.

12. See Reuven Kimelman, "Birkat Ha-Minim and the Lack of Evidence for an Anti-Christian Jewish Prayer in Late Antiquity," Jewish and Christian Self-Definition: Judaism from the Maccabees to the Mid-Third Century CE, Fortress Press: 1981, 2:226-244, 391-403; and idem "Birkat Ha-Minim: the Status of the Question," forthcoming in the Lou H. Silberman Festschrift, ed. by W. Dever and J. Edward Wright.

COMPREHENSIVE STUDY

Some of the deficiencies in this work are made up for by the new book by Stefan C. Reif entitled *Judaism and Hebrew Prayer: New Perspectives on Jewish Liturgical History.* This 1993 book by Cambridge University Press is *au courant* with current liturgical research. It not only covers the development of the classical liturgy including a chapter on its "biblical inspiration" but also chapters on the evolution of the prayer-book, the various medieval rites and texts, and even recent liturgical developments. The bibliography contains entries up to 1992. Among the indices, which include sources, names, and subjects, is an especially helpful one on prayers and rituals. It is a pity that the indices only refer to the text and not to the eighty pages or so of valuable notes.

Reif's opening chapter, "On Jewish liturgical research," surveys the history of scholarship from Zunz and Elbogen through contemporary approaches. His critique of Elbogen complements many of the above animadversions. From the perspective of understanding liturgy as liturgy, Reif pays considerable attention to integrating the history of liturgical development into the history of understandings of prayer. This type of linkage is frequently speculative, but quite necessary for placing the history of the liturgy within the framework of the history of Judaism. Nonetheless, it must be noted how often the same evidence can be read in opposite ways. For example, Reif argues that, "the traditional recitation of the sentence 'blessed be the name of his glorious kingdom for ever and ever', which is a Temple response in origin, immediately after that verse [the *Shema'* verse], may be seen as confirming the authenticity of the claim about the *Shema'*'s use in the Temple" (p. 83). Alternatively, the insertion of 'blessed be the name of his glorious kingdom for ever and ever' may have been inserted after the *Shema'* verse upon it being conceptualized as the realization of divine sovereignty. Since, according to *Mishnah Berakhot* 2:2, this was the contribution of R. Joshua b. Korha, the interpolation may have been a second-century development[13] and thus not useful for authenticating

---

13. See Kimelman, "The Shema' and Its Rhetoric," 139.

the claim about the *Shema''s* use in the Temple. Be that as it may, the book remains the most up-to-date statement of Jewish liturgical history.

Another work that covers similar ground is that of Jeffrey Cohen, *Blessed Are You: A Comprehensive Guide to Jewish Prayer*. This 1993 updating of his 1986 *Horizons of Jewish Prayer* was published by Jason Aronson. Although Part One is similar to Reif's work, albeit in a lighter tone with less documentation, Part Two and Part Three discuss quite comprehensively issues of theology pertinent to prayer and elements of the synagogue. Although the *'Amidah* is discussed in a helpful manner, he repeats some of the standard comments which have been critiqued above. Peculiarly absent is any comprehensive discussion of the *Shema'* and its blessings despite the fourteen references to the *Shema'* in the index. In general, Cohen adheres to accepted scholarly positions though he is not adverse to offering his own speculations. Nonetheless, the work serves as a fine introduction to the liturgy in particular and to issues of prayer in general.

Last but not least of the harvest of 1993 is *Worlds of Jewish Prayer: A Festschrift in Honor of Rabbi Zalman M. Schachter-Shalomi* also published by Jason Aronson. It is hard to believe that anyone interested in contemporary liturgical expression will not find a piece to his or her liking. Although little is relevant to the "historical" meaning of the classical liturgy, there is hardly a moment in contemporary religious life that has not been liturgized in new or renewed forms here. The overall experience ("reading" is inadequate) of the book is downright Zalmanesque in honor of its honoree. Those who want to deepen their understanding of contemporary wrestlings with *davvening,* the *'Amidah,* the psalms, blessings, public prayer, women's rituals, ecology, *nigunim,* art, the environment, *inter alia,* cannot do better than start here.

Several earlier works of the nineties belong in such a survey. The first is that of Tzvee Zahavy, *Studies in Jewish Prayer,* published by University Press of America in 1990. This book is an interesting combination of solid historical research and idiosyncratic conclusions.[14] Zahavy has assembled in a systematic way the considerable evidence for the rabbinic input into both the prayers and rituals of the synagogue. He lists, document by document, the rabbinic rulings on liturgical matters for most of the major holidays along with the daily service. He shows that the rabbis also determined the blessings, the protocol, and the content of the Torah readings in the synagogue. Moreover, he notes that they made special rules for its administration and its sale, the obligation to build and attend it, the proper decorum, handling of donations, the role of synagogue officials, seating, direction of doors, and rules for eulogizing. Through this documentation he has laid to rest any doubts about rabbinic involvement in synagogue life.

Typical of a different approach to the liturgy, in the 90's, is that of Avrohom Chaim Feuer whose *Shemoneh Esrei: The Amidah / The Eighteen Blessings* forms part of the ArtScroll Mesorah Series. This work is a line by line commentary on the *'Amidah*. It integrates classical and more recent comment with didactic observation and anecdote with the purpose of "interpret[ing] its message in terms of our daily lives and individual needs." The goal of the book is clearly not so much history as, in the words of the conclusion, "the wish that our prayers bring Israel closer to God's favor and the restoration of the Temple service."

Mention must also be made of the considerable advances in liturgical research due to the discovery of the Dead Sea Scrolls. The most recent survey is that of Moshe Weinfeld, "Prayer and Liturgical Practice in the Qumran Sect," in *The Dead Sea Scrolls: Forty Years of Research*, published by Magnes Press and Yad Izhak Ben-Zvi in 1992, pp. 241-258. This valuable survey includes studies on the *Shema'*, the *Kedushah* and the Benediction of the Lights, prayers for the Sabbath and festivals, the morning benedictions, the prayer of supplication, prayer before setting forth on a journey, benediction on performing the marriage ceremony, grace after meals, *minyan*, the precedence of the priest in matters of holiness, the canon, and *tefillin* and *mezuzot*, along with an appendix of the Qumran prayers in Hebrew.

---

14. About which, see my review in the forthcoming *Critical Review of Books in Religion 1993* published by Scholars Press.

NEW APPROACHES

It is clear from this survey that historical-critical studies of the liturgy still have the lion's share of academic research. Nonetheless, as Reif noted in his aforementioned chapter new methods are beginning to make headway. One of the more interesting is that of Lawrence Hoffman whose *Beyond the Text: A Holistic Approach to Liturgy* was published by Indiana University Press in 1987. He self-consciously seeks to understand the liturgy in the context of current discussions of social studies and religious phenomenology. His stated goal is to "integrate the entire act of worship into the study of liturgy" (p. 15) and to understand the history of the sacred myths, as it were, as they are reflected in the development of the liturgy. His second chapter on the *Havdalah* service is destined to become a classic of this approach. Hoffman occupies the alternative pole of Elbogen. His analysis of "the *Avodah*" (pp. 108-113) illuminates exactly what such a methodology can contribute to the historical-philological approach so well represented by Zunz and Elbogen.

Besides Hoffman and a few others, most studies of the liturgy are characterized by either a historical or a literary orientation. Focusing on responses to internal needs as well as reactions to external events, historical studies tend to see the liturgy as a document of its time from which information external to its intention can be derived. Such studies are inclined to decompose texts and analyze them diachronically. Literary studies, seeking out the synthetic meaning of the text, prefer to see the meaning of the liturgy within a significating framework internal to its intention. Both classical and modern scholarship have primarily focused on philology, semantics, allusions to biblical and rabbinic literature, and the historical development of the liturgy. There is precious little work on the synthetic meaning of liturgical units as a whole and even less as complete pieces of literature. Even less extant are literary treatments of individual liturgical units or of the overall framework that incorporate the findings of the historical school and that of the classical commentaries.

The literary approach suited for understanding liturgy as liturgy is rhetorical criticism. The purpose of rhetorical

criticism is to point out how the liturgy makes its case. By
focusing on the rhetoric of the liturgy, the inquiry highlights
the persuasive strategies or rhetorical techniques deployed by
the liturgical narrative to enhance the worshiper's receptivity
to its position. In addition to remarks about modes of
argumentation, attention is focused on how language is
textured, how themes are concatenated, and how images are
contextualized. It is the convergence of these elements that
serves to orchestrate the subtle interplay between statement
and subtext in order to induce in the worshiper a new
perspective. By tracing the transformation of the worshiper's
outlook, the text is shown to be what it really is—liturgy.

Liturgical inquiry needs to follow the order of asking what
the worshiper is apprised of, how is he or she apprised, and
finally why. This what, how, and why, follows what Meir
Sternberg in his *The Poetics of Biblical Narrative* refers to as
the historiographic function, the aesthetic principle, and the
ideological principle respectively. Such an approach not only
allows for a focus on ideology in the form of theology but also
for a focus on new historical information, for when literary
studies precede historical inquiry, the historical inquiry itself
is affected. Nonetheless, since it is rare that the two can be
conducted effectively in isolation, there needs to be a constant
dialectic between literary and historical analysis, for what is
conceptually prior may not be so programmatically.

From this survey of liturgical works of the 90s, we can see
how well-positioned we are to advance an historical-literary
program in liturgical research.

JENNIFER BREGER

Women's Devotional Literature: an Essay in Jewish Bibliography

IF LITURGY HAS TRADITIONALLY been a neglected area of religious bibliography, women's prayers in particular have been viewed as unworthy of research and of the differentiation that can enhance our understanding of their history and meaning.[1] But as Jewish women have looked to their past for a clearer idea of their spiritual history, this neglect of their liturgy has begun to change.[2]

For the first time, scholars are beginning to ask such basic questions as: How did Jewish women of the past pray? What

---

1. The most important work of liturgical history is that of Ismar Elbogen, *Der jüdische Gottesdienst in seiner geschichtlichen Entwicklung*, 1913. This is now available in English as *Jewish Liturgy: A Comprehensive History*, tr. by Raymond P. Scheindlin (Jewish Publication Society and Jewish Theological Seminary, 1993). It basically deals with public liturgy and has no references at all to the prayers of Jewish women. See also S. Krauss, "Zur Literatur der Siddurim," in *Soncino-Blatter* II Band, (Berlin, 1927), 1-30.
2. The renewed interest has been shown by English translations of tkhines, such as Tracy Guren Klirs, *The Merit of Our Mothers: A Bilingual Anthology of Jewish Women's Prayers* (Cincinnati, 1992), Rivka Zakutinsky, *Techinas: A Voice from the Heart. As only a Woman Can Pray.* (Brooklyn, 1992), and a Hebrew translation of a few tkhines by Meir Wunder, *Ateret Rivka* (Jerusalem, 1992). For an English edition of an Italian manuscript see Nina Cardin, *Out of the Depths I Call to You: A Book of Prayers for the Married Jewish Woman* (Northvale, NJ, 1992). For a review of some recent translations, see J. Breger, "The Prayers of Jewish Women: Some Historical Perspectives," *Judaism*, 42 (Fall 1993), 504 -515.

prayers did they recite? When did they use vernacular languages like Yiddish, Ladino, Judeo–Arabic and Judeo–Italian? What of devotions in German, English, French, Italian, Dutch or Hungarian?

This essay is an attempt to bring together and compare prayers for Jewish women in different historical and cultural contexts, and to look at similarities and differences in scope, content and style. It will start with the Yiddish tkhines and then turn to the devotional literature in Western European countries that began as translations of the tkhines. Later it will look at the manuscript prayers of Jewish women in Italy; then see if there are any comparable prayers in Ladino or in Judeo–Arabic. Finally, the article will briefly explore contemporary liturgical writings of American Jewish women .

TKHINES

Taking their name from the Hebrew word "tehina" meaning supplication, tkhines are individual prayers in Yiddish that Ashkenazi women recited on different occasions.They were part of a wider grouping of Yiddish literature directed at women, including Tsene-renes, morality books and books of women's commandments.[3] Tkhines were first printed in the 16th century . The first known printed collection called *Tkhine Zu*, an eight–page pamphlet by Avrom Apoteker with five tkhines in both Hebrew and Yiddish, was printed in Prague in 1590, although an individual tkhine for recitation before entering the mikveh had already been published in *Seyder Mitsvos Nashim* in Cracow in 1577.[4]

In Western Europe, tkhines were printed mainly as collections, perhaps beginning with an Amsterdam collection entitled *Seyder Tkhines* in 1648. In some instances, the

---

3. For a review of these different categories, see J. Breger, "Jewish Women's Religious Literature," in *Antiquarian Bookman*, May 23, 1994. See also Dorothy Bilik, "Tsene-rene: A Yiddish Literary Success" in *Jewish Book Annual*, vol. 51 (1993) 96-111.
4. *Seyder Mitsvos Noshim*, Crakow, 1577, p.18. See C. Shmeruk, *Sifrut Yiddish, Perakim le-Toledoteha* (Tel Aviv, 1978), p. 51.

collection would be included at the end of various prayer books.[5] From the mid–18th century, longer collections entitled *Seder Tkhines u'Vakoshes,* containing about 120 tkhines were printed and reprinted in many German towns, like Sulzbach and Fuerth, and were later reprinted in Eastern Europe as well.[6] In Eastern Europe tkhines mainly appeared in pamphlet form, each pamphlet consisting of an individual tkhine, or of small groups of them.[7]

Although some individual manuscript copies of tkhines were written by hand, tkhines were a mass genre, aimed at large numbers of women. Thus most tkhines were printed, and with the development of cheaper and faster printing techniques, as well as cheaper paper, the numbers of volumes grew greatly. Until the beginning of the 19th century, a specific typeface, called "vaybertaytsh" was used.[8]

How did the tkhines develop? It seems likely that they began as paraphrased translations of Hebrew prayers into Yiddish, which were then turned into independent devotional prayers, perhaps by the *firzogerins,* (or *zogerkes*), who "led" the

---

5. These early collections were usually called *Seyder Tkhines, Taytsh Tkhines,* or simply *Tkhines.* For a listing of some of these early Western tkhine collections, see Devra Kay, "An Alternative Prayer Canon for Women: The Yiddish Seyder Tkhines," in *Zur Geschichte der jüdischen Frau in Deutschland,* ed. Julius Carlebach, (Berlin: Metropol, 1993) 86-88.
6. For an examination of the contents of the *Seyder Tkhines u'Vakoshes,* see Chava Weissler, "The Traditional Piety of Ashkenazic Women" in *Jewish Spirituality,* II, ed. Arthur Green (New York, 1986), 245-275.
7. The earliest extant East European tkhines date from the 18th century: it is likely that there were much earlier ones that were lost. Chava Weissler, *Traditional Yiddish Literature: A Source for the Study of Women's Religious Lives* (Cambridge, Mass.: Harvard University Library, 1988), p. 6. For a fine description and analysis of the East European tkhines, see Tracy Guren Klirs, *Bizkhus fun Sore, Rivke, Rokhel un Leye: The Tkhine as the Jewish Women's Self Expression.* (Rabbinical thesis, Hebrew Union College, 1984).
8. Dorothy Bilik,"Tsene-rene: A Yiddish Literary Success," op. cit., 100, and Max Weinreich, *History of the Yiddish Language,* tr. Shlomo Noble (Chicago: University of Chicago Press, 1980) 275.

prayers in the women's section of the synagogue.[9] It has been argued that the spread of tkhines was closely connected to the revival of Kabbalah in the 16th and 17th centuries, and the introduction of kabbalistic prayers into the prayer books, and that many are direct translations or adaptations of kabbalistic prayers and devotions.[10]

Tkhines cover a wide variety of subjects. While many relate to the regular prayer service, others are focused on the three positive women's commandments, candle–lighting, mikveh and hallah, on family and childbearing, and for recitation at visits to the cemetery. They often reflect the personal world of women.

Although there were definitely men who could not read or understand Hebrew, tkhines were published mainly for women. Presumably because of the male obligation of statutory communal prayer, men would have been embarrassed to recite them.[11]

---

9. Emily Teitz, "Women's Voices, Women's Prayers: Women in the European Synagogues of the Middle Ages," in *Daughters of the King: Women and the Synagogue,* ed. Susan Grossman and Rivka Haut (Jewish Publication Society, 1992) 66-68, and Shulamith Z. Berger, "Tehines: A Brief Survey of Women's Prayers)," in the same volume, 77. The introduction to *Seyder Tkhines*, printed in Amsterdam, 1648, describes the aim of the tkhines as making the prayers understandable to women. See Kay, op. cit., 49-50.

10. S. Freehof, "Devotional Literature in the Vernacular," *CCAR Yearbook*, 33 (1923) 375-424. In her analysis of individual tkhines, Weissler delineates the connections with kabbalistic sources, and the transformation and modification of these texts in the tkhines. See Chava Weissler, "Woman as High Priest: A Kabbalistic Prayer in Yiddish for Lighting Sabbath Candles," *Jewish History,* vol. 5 (1991) 9-26.

11. It is unclear what evidence there is to support Freehof's statement that although "originally the Tehinnoth may have been written chiefly for women, the use of them soon spread among all who could not read Hebrew fluently," (op. cit., 375-6) except that there are a few individual tkhines for men in *Seder Tkhines u-Vakoshes* and other collections. Most of the title pages say "for pious Jewish women," or something similar.

WOMEN AUTHORS

Some tkhines were written by women, particularly in Eastern Europe.[12] One of the most well known writers was the famous Sarah Bas Tovim, born in the Ukraine at the end of the 17th century to an important rabbinical family, who wrote the famous *Tkhine Shloyshe She'orim*.[13] All the women writers are identified as the daughters and wives of rabbis, such as Mamael, daughter of Rabbi Tsvi Hirsch and wife of Rabbi Yizhak, head of the Bet Din in Belz, composer of *Tkhine Tshuve u'Tfile u'Tsdoke*.

One of the most educated of the women composers of tkhines in the 18th century was Sarah Rebecca Rachel Leah Horowitz, daughter of the Rabbi of Brody. Her *Tkhine Imohes* (Tkhine of the Matriarchs) was written in Aramaic, Hebrew and Yiddish. In the introduction, she discusses issues of women's prayer and the role of the learned woman. In her view, women should go to synagogue twice a day. She argued that women's prayers are important and can bring about the

---

12. In Western Europe there were a few women who wrote liturgical works, such as Hannah Katz, the author of "A Prayer for the Sabbath," "A Prayer for the Month of Elul" and "A Prayer to Moses." See Shlomo Ashkenazi, *Dor Dor u'Minhagav* (Tel Aviv, 1977) 219. See also Shoshana Patel Zolty, *And All Your Children Shall Be Learned*. (Northvale, New Jersey, 1993) 213, and Meyer Waxman, *A History of Jewish Literature*, vol. 2, (New York: T. Yoseloff, 1960) 662. A tkhine for the month of Elul by Bella Horowitz was printed in Prague about 1705. For a description of some of the tkhines composed by women, see Israel Zinberg, *A History of Jewish Literature*, vol.7, *Old Yiddish Literature from its Origins to the Haskalah Period*, tr. Bernard Martin (New York and Cincinnati: 1975) 246-259.

13. For a translation of this by Norman Tarnor see "Three Gates Tehinno: A Seventeenth Century Yiddish Prayer by Sarah Bas Tovim," in *Judaism*, 40 (Summer 1991) 354-367. Although the tkhine gives many details about Sarah Bas Tovim's life, scholars have debated whether she was a real person or an imaginary composite figure, in that her name means "daughter of the good or notable people." See Weissler, "Prayers in Yiddish and the Religious World of Ashkenazic Women," in *Jewish Women in Historical Perspective*, ed. Judith Baskin (Detroit, 1991) 173-176.

Redemption.[14]

Many tkhines include such attributions as by a "groyse tsedeykes," by an "isha tsenua" or that "this tkhine was found in the possession of a righteous woman." At the end of the 19th century, maskilim and yeshiva students wrote tkhines as a way of supporting themselves, often using female pen names.

Tkhines can be distinguished from regular prayers in that they are written in the first person singular, in a personal and intimate tone, and very concrete in their subject matter and their requests. Some are quite sophisticated and full of textual allusions. Others are very simple and sentimental such as the prayer for lighting candles in which a woman prays that her children be pious and learned and continues:

> May they be fresh and healthy and whole in their organs. May they have no defects in their whole bodies, and may they be not too tall and not too short, not too pale and not too swarthy, not overly smart and also not big fools. They should only be wise as is proper to be, and they should find grace and mercy in Your eyes and in people's eyes.[15]

The tkhines are imbued with a strong and sincere piety. From the early West European collection, *Seyder Tkhines,* the following is part of a daily tkhine:

> Here I stand, poor woman, before You and Your holy name and acknowledge my sin and make great repentance for it and will never do it again. I beg you as a Father and one King, excuse my sin and grant eternal pardon and forgiveness.[16]

Research into printed tkhines is complicated by the fact that the same tkhines have been printed and reprinted. Earlier editions were incorporated into later ones, sometimes

---

14. Weissler, "Prayers in Yiddish and the Religious World of Ashkenazic Women," op. cit, 169-173. It is interesting that only early editions of this tkhine contain the Hebrew introduction and the liturgical poem in Aramaic.
15. *Shas Tkhine Khadoshe.*
16. From *Seyder Tkhines,* quoted in Kay, op. cit., 65.

with changes, sometimes without, and it is often difficult to
know which is the original text. Many tkhines were printed
without dates.[17] There are over one thousand tkhines in the
Jewish National University Library at the Hebrew University.
Often the same titles were used for different texts and the
same texts were printed under different titles.[18]

By the end of the 19th century, larger collections of tkhines
were printed in Eastern Europe, such as *Ayn Naye Shas
Tkhine fun a Gants Yor*,[19] and *Shas Tkhine Khadoshe Mekor
Dimeh*.[20] These collections are "vade mecums" for the religious
woman, aiming to cover every possible occasion. Most contain
groupings of tkhines to be said when the blessing for the New
Moon is recited, with a separate prayer for each month,
referring both to significant events considered to have
occurred in that month, as well as specific prayers and
wishes.[21]

Many of these collections were reprinted in America, such

---

17. For the identification by typography of a tkhine with no printed
    date or place of printing, in the collection of the J.N.U.L., which
    was probably printed in Prague about 1600, see Yitzhak Yudlov,
    "Sheyne Tkhine v'Orakh Khayim...Two Unknown Yiddish
    books..." *Kiryat Sefer* (1988/9) 457-458. The title of the tkhine is
    "Ayn gehr sheyne tkhine," and under its title it notes that it had
    been kept for a long time secretly among a group of righteous
    women who did not allow it to be copied, but had now changed
    their mind and had brought it to be printed.
18. For a discussion of some of the misattributions and confusions in
    identifying the writers of different tkhines, see H. Lieberman,
    "Tkhine Imohos u'Tkhine Shloyshe She'orim," in *Ohel Rahel* (New
    York, 1979-80) 432-454.
19. Pietrikov, 1881.
20. (Vilna: Rosenkranz and Schriftsetzer, 1911). This collection
    contains 248 tkhines, edited by Benzion Alfes with a commentary,
    in which he brought together many old tkhines and added new
    ones and includes many relevant halakhot. The 1927 Vilna
    edition contains 306 "new" tkhines. This was reprinted numerous
    times. For details about Alfes and his tkhines, see Shulamith
    Berger, op.cit., 77-82.
21. These tkhines for each month seem to have begun to appear in
    the second part of the 19th century, as in pamphlets of tkhines
    like *Tkhine Mikro Kodesh*.

as *Shas Tkhine Khadoshe,*[22] and *Shas Tkhine Rav Peninim.*[23] Collections of tkhines are still being reprinted in Israel and in New York for the Orthodox Yiddish speaking communities.[24]

The most interesting question, perhaps, is how the contents of the tkhines differ as to time and place. The early West European tkhines, containing about thirty-seven selections, followed a set pattern, with tkhines for every day of the week, for the three women's mitzvot, prayers for fast days, prayers for visiting of graves, and for Rosh Hashanah and Yom Kippur.[25] The larger collections of *Seder Tkhines u'Vakoshes*, with about 120 tkhines, include specifically liturgical prayers, for each day of the week, for the Sabbath and festivals, and for Rosh Hodesh which has traditionally been considered a holiday for women. Besides the liturgical prayers, there are tkhines for the three women's mitzvot, and many for pregnancy and childbirth. There is a cycle of penitential prayers for the period between Rosh Hodesh Elul and Yom Kippur, and for cemetery visits, and a number expressing personal family concerns such as for livelihood, for a husband who is traveling away from home, and for recovery from sickness.[26]

It is particularly interesting that in many of the East European reprints of this collection, the prayers for ritual immersion are not included. The women for whom they were printed obviously still went to the mikveh: was it for reasons of modesty that they were now omitted? Niddah is only included in one part of the famous *Shloyshe She'orim* tkhine of Sarah Bas Tovim mentioned earlier, and there is no specific devotion attached to the performance. The tkhines that were printed individually or in small groups in Eastern Europe are actually quite limited in subject: the majority are penitential

---

22. New York: Hebrew Publishing Company, 1916.
23. Brooklyn, New York; Ahron Flohr, n.d. Much of this collection is not specific to women.
24. See, for example, *Seyfer Tkhine Sore Rohel*, (Brooklyn, N.Y.: Kaftor va'Ferah, 1992).
25. For a detailed analysis of the 37 prayers in *Seyder Tkhines* (Amsterdam, 1648), see Kay, op.cit., 49-51.
26. See Weissler, 1986, cited in note 6 above.

prayers and those connected to parts of the synagogue or prayer service.[27]

In the collections at the end of the nineteenth century which cover vast ranges of occasions, again there are no prayers for "mikveh": this has continued to be the case for reprints and editions printed in America up till today.

There have been Yiddish tkhines printed in America which are specific to the immigrant experience. One such example is entitled "A new tkhine for America, when one hears bad news from the old country."[28] Other tkhines offer prayers relevant to World War 1; one marks the sinking of the "Titanic," including a special memorial prayer for Isadore and Ida Strauss among those who drowned;[29] still others focus on a particular stage of life such as going into a nursing home. But usually the collections returned to the old texts and themes.

SIDDURIM THAT INCLUDE TKHINES

Many siddurim (prayer books) were published with a collection of tkhines as an appendix, The favorite siddur for East European women in the nineteenth and early twentieth centuries was the *Korban Minhah* siddur, compiled at the beginning of the 18th century, and reprinted repeatedly.[30]

---

27. The titles that occur in many reprints include *Tkhine Mikro Kodesh, Tkhine Minkhas Erev, Tkhine Kol Bekhie, Tkhine Kodem Tfile,* and *Tkhine Moyde Ani.*
28. Chava Weissler, "American Transformation of the Tkhines," unpublished paper given at the conference *Across Boundaries: A History of Jewish Women in America* (University of Maryland at College Park, 1993), p. 16.
29. *Shas Tkhine Rav Peninim,* (New York: Hebrew Publishing Company, 1916) 256-258. I am grateful to Shulamith Berger for drawing my attention to this "memorial tkhine."
30. The first edition of the *Korban Minhah* siddur seems to be that printed by Proops in Amsterdam in 1724/5. Important 19th century editions included ones printed in Vienna by A. Schmid (1816, 1828, and 1839), and those printed in Vilna by Mann (Romm) and Zimel in 1838 and 1843. There were also *Korban Minhah* siddurim printed following the "Ari-Habad" rite (e.g., Vilna, Yehudah Leib Lipman Press, 1898, and Vilna, Romm, 1902).

In Western Europe this approach can be found in siddurim
such as those printed in Amsterdam in the 18th and 19th
centuries with tkhines for women and brides at the back.[31] If a
woman had one of these siddurim, would she also have had
separate books of tkhines? The distribution and use of these
volumes is unclear. There were many luxury editions of
siddurim and mahzorim with Yiddish translations, "Sivlonos
siddurim" that were given to brides as gifts by the bridegroom
in German communities,[32] as well as luxury decorated manuscript books of women's mitzvot from the 18th century.[33]
Again, there is a lack of information as to whether these were
just decorative or whether they were actually used.

31. See, for example, the siddur in Hebrew and Yiddish by Moshe
ben Abraham Mendes Coutinho (Amsterdam, 1704), which has a
title page depicting the three women's commandments. (Illustrated in M.H. Gans, *Memorbook*, 1971 ,p. 185.) A later siddur for
women has a title page illustrated with 8 scenes depicting biblical
women (Amsterdam, Shlomo Proops, 1730).
32. "Sivlonos" is the word traditionally used for gifts to the bride
from the bridegroom and his family, going back to mishnaic times
(*Bava Batra* 9:5). See, for example, *Siddur le-Sivlonos*, Hannover,
1840. The famous *Safah Berurah* siddur, printed with a German
translation, was also sometimes given as a Sivlonos siddur, and
would include psalms and tkhines at the back. (e.g. Rodelheim,
1841, 12th edition).
33. Some of these were put together with grace after meals and
prayers on retiring such as "Seder birchath ha-mazon...u-birkoth
ha-nehenin u-keriath shema u-birkath ha-levanah ve-seder hadla-
kah niddah hallah u-sefirath (ha-omer)," dated Fuerth 1793, for
Braindel, wife of Seckel Z'B' in the J.T.S. library. Another
decorated manuscript, with a velvet binding, in the library, dated
Mannheim, 1736, "for Fradche (?), wife of Jacob Kalman)," is
especially interesting because a section of tkhines was added in
"vaybertaytsh". See the richly detailed listing of Menahem
Schmelzer, "Decorated Hebrew Manuscripts of the Eighteenth
Century in the Library of the Jewish Theological Seminary of
America," in *Occident and Orient. A Tribute to the Memory of A.
Schreiber* (Akademiai Kiado, Budapest/Brill, Leiden, 1988)
331-351.

DEVOTIONS IN GERMAN AND
OTHER LANGUAGES

Under the influence of Moses Mendelssohn and the Enlightenment, Yiddish was disfavored in German lands, and considered as a major obstacle to the integration of Jews into the cultural and social life of their surroundings. Jewish women therefore at the end of the 18th century in Germany began to learn German.[34] They had available bilingual Hebrew and German prayer books.[35] This was moreover the period of the Reform revision of the prayer book.[36]

Jewish women also had available books of devotions in German which appeared first in Hebrew lettering,[37] and then in German in Latin letters, sometimes in Gothic type. Examples of these in Hebrew lettering include *Tkhines u'Vakoshes* edited by Joshua Heschel Miro, first printed in

---

34. For an excellent description of the transition from Yiddish to German as the written language of German Jews, see Steven M. Lowenstein, *The Mechanics Of Change: Essays in the Social History of German Jewry* (Atlanta, Georgia: Scholars Press, 1992) especially chapter 7, "The Yiddish Written Word In Nineteenth Century Germany," 183-199.
35. There were also specific bilingual mahzorim for women, e.g *Machzor Nashim* or *Frauen-Machzor*, tr. and published by Moritz Frankel and Dr. G. Kleefeld, with the approval of the Rabbinical Association of Berlin, 1841. (This is illustrated in Abraham J. Karp, *From the Ends of the Earth: Judaic Treasures of the Library of Congress*, 1991, 172.)
36. For the impact of the Reform movement on liturgy, see Ismar Elbogen, op. cit., 297-333, and Jakob Petuchowski, *Prayerbook Reform in Europe* (New York: World Union for Progressive Judaism, 1968).
37. According to Lowenstein, the writing of High German in Hebrew letters was sometimes called Jüdisch-Deutsch, and the writers of the texts were not uniform as to grammar and spelling. Some of the texts were close to Yiddish and included many Hebrew words. Lowenstein, op. cit, 184.

Breslau in 1829,[38] which was then revised by S. Blogg. Many of these books specifically stress on the title-pages that they were directed at "educated" and "cultured" women.[39]

One of the most famous of German devotions was the *Stunden der Andacht* (Hours of Devotion), first published in 1855 by an Austrian woman, Fanny Neuda, née Schmiedl (sister of a Viennese rabbi) as a memorial to her husband, a rabbi in Moravia.[40] This seems to have been the first book of prayers written by a woman. Some editions were printed in "vaybertaytsh" type in Hebrew lettering.[41] It was widely reprinted in

---

38. Later editions included: Breslau 1833, Altona 1837, Hannover 1836/7, Fuerth 1840, Rodelheim 1851 and 1879, etc. From the forewords it seems clear that the purpose of the editions was to make accessible to a German speaking public, Yiddish tkhines which although "almost completely forgotten," the editors felt still had much to say to 19th century women. The title page, which says the text is taken from "old-German" tkhines, is printed in pure German and it is dedicated by Blogg to "all the worthy women who live in the spirit of the true Israelite religion." The tkhines are attributed to "various people, mostly pious women, written at different times over thousands of years."

39. See, for example, Hermann Englander, *Enkat Bene Temutha....Hochdeutsche Gebethe für gebildete israelitische Frauenzimmer* (Prague, 1824). Unlike the Miro compilation, the author, in his introduction, states that he has composed these devotions because of the inapplicability of the content of the Yiddish tkhines (not because of the inaccessibility of the language). While "there are many prayer books for other nations, the daughters of our nation are without such a book," and the old-time tkhines do not express "what our hearts feel." Because of this, he took upon himself to fill the gap. Thus he presents himself as replacing the Yiddish tkhines rather than updating them. The subscription list at the end of the volume suggests that it was distributed mainly in Prague and in cities in Moravia.

40. The title "Stunden der Andacht" had already been used before for a devotional manual for young women. See *Stunden Der Andacht für Israeliten zur Befoerderung Religiosen Lebens und Hauslicher Gottesverehrung* (Dinkelsbuehl, 1833.)

41. For example, Prague, 1859, 1864, and 1876.

German lettering at least 29 times until the 1930's,[42] and translated into other languages including English.[43]

Many of the prayers and devotions relate to the regular prayer service; but there are also prayers for matrimonial happiness, prayers to be said on the wedding day of a child, as well as one for a child's confirmation. Even through the formal language, one gets a feeling for the hopes and fears of the women for whom they are written. In a prayer for a childless wife, there is an expression of great disappointment and sadness, and a plea for God to listen to her prayer as He listened to the biblical Hannah, but also for the strength to accept a denial of her request.

> May I then also always remember that though Thou hast denied me a mother's joys, there are yet manifold pleasures which Thou, in Thine endless goodness, hast granted me already and wilt yet grant me anew, every day.[44]

In a prayer to be said on a son's wedding day, after her wishes for his future, she expresses a personal fear:

> [G]rant, that his devotion for his consort of life may not weaken or deaden the feelings of those who gave him life, and educated him, that he may continue to be our joy and delight and preserve that love and reverence in his soul, for which Thou hast promised long life here on earth, and full divine reward in eternity." [45]

Later German devotional books for Jewish women included the very popular *Hanna: Gebet und Andachtbuch für israelitische Frauen und Mädchen,* edited by Jacob Freund, a

---

42. Most of the editions were issued in Prague, but a number were also printed in Breslau and New York. The last edition seems to have been that of Martha Wertheimer Landman (Frankfurt am Main, 1936).

43. It was first translated into English by M. Meyer in 1866 as *A Book of Prayers and Meditations for the Use of the Daughters of Israel during Public Service and at Home for all Conditions of Woman's Life* (New York, 1866.) There were many later editions.

44. Ibid., 83-4.

45. Ibid., 79-80.

teacher in Breslau, in 1867. This too was reprinted widely.[46]
Unlike the tkhines which were almost totally directed at the
married woman,[47] many of the devotions in German and other
languages include specific prayers for girls as well.

Jewish women in France also resorted to the vernacular for
their devotions. *Bat Yisrael. Recueil pour la Femme Israelite*
by G. Heumann was printed entirely in French in 1847 in
Hagenau, Alsace. The book contains devotions for each day of
the week, morning and evening, and has prayers for times of
prosperity and hardship. It includes prayers for taking hallah.
At the end, there is an appendix of "Prières specialement
désinees a l'épouse"– for infertility, for the beginning of
pregnancy, for before and after delivery, during circumcision,
when giving birth to a daughter, and when coming to
synagogue for the first time after birth. Once again there are
no prayers for the mikveh.

A volume that was to attain much greater popularity was
Imrei Lev: Prières d'un Coeur Israelite, published in 1848 by
the "Société Consistorale de Bons Livres," edited by Arnaud
Aron–Grand Rabbin of the consistoire of Bas-Rhin, in
Strasbourg. This was reprinted first in 1852, and many times
after that. It includes devotions for a mother before a son's
circumcision, and before a baby is named. Again, at the end of
the book there is an appendix for the married woman,
including prayers for infertility, for the beginning of
pregnancy, for before and after delivery, and for another
woman's safe delivery. A note in the book suggests that the
appendix can be detached from the rest of the text.

Imrei Lev was translated into Italian[48] and English soon
after its publication in French. The first English translation

46. Other German devotional volumes include Oscar Sachairiasohn,
    *Hadassa: Gebet und Andachtsbuch für israelitische Frauen und
    Mädchen* (Vienna, 1902), and Max Grunwald, *Beruria: Gebet und
    Andachtsbuch für jüdische Frauen und Mädchen* (Vienna, 1907).
47. The title-page of the early collection *Seyder Tkhines* does
    however state that the tkhines are presented for "frume vayber
    un meydlekh."
48. *Imrei Lev. Preghiere d'un Cuore Israelita, Raccolta di Preghiere e
    di Meditazioni per tutte le Circonstanze della Vita*, Asti, 1852. A
    second edition was issued in 1864 in Trieste.

was by Hester Rothschild in 1856 in London entitled *Prayers and Meditations*. It was revised by Isaac Leeser of Philadelphia in 1864. Leeser's aim was for it to serve as a manual of domestic devotion with extra prayers:

> It is only following examples of the great ones of former years to place in the hands of our females especially, a book which is, so to say a mirror of the soul, containing reflections and short formulae of petitions of thanksgiving adapted to the several circumstances of our existence, to serve as a constant companion in our life's journey, whether the incidents be of joy or sorrrow .

While there are some prayers for men as well, such as a bridegroom's prayer and a husband's prayer at a wife's grave, the majority were addressed to women.

Other English devotions were also translations of European works. *Hours of Devotion–Book of Prayer and Devotion for Israel's Women and Maids for Public and House Devotion as well as for all Circumstances of Female Life* by R. Vulture was printed in Budapest in English.[49] Some of the prayers are particularly interesting, including one by a mother for an unhappily married daughter, a prayer of a widow for her impoverished children, and prayers for times of scarcity and war.

One devotion is entitled " Prayer of the Happy":

> I live happy and without sorrow....Teach me to make proper use of what Thou hast given me. Lord, save me from haughtiness and pride, from supercilliousness and magnanimity(!), and from hard-heartedness.

Most of the Western and Central European devotions have a formal, less intimate tone than the Yiddish tkhines. It would be important to compare them with Christian prayers of the period in different countries. Did non-Jewish women have similar books of occasional prayers and devotions?

One clue as to the distribution of these devotional books is a list of subscribers at the end of a volume published in

---

49. Both the printing and the English translation are very poor. Why the book was published in English in Budapest is unclear.

Birmingham, England in 1852, entitled *Devotional Exercises for the Use of the Jewish Woman.*[50] The list includes names, mostly women and a few rabbis not only in England but also in New Orleans, Montreal, Curacao, and Gotheberg.[51]

ITALIAN PRAYERS

By the end of the 14th century, prayer books in Italian, or Judeo-Italian were written specifically for Jewish women in Italy.[52] One manuscript, now in the British Museum, was written in 1483 for a woman named Rivka, and another, a year later, was written in Florence for Gentile, daughter of a prominent banker and bibliophile, Isaac ben Emmanuel de S. Miniato.[53] The first edition of the Siddur in Judeo-Italian appeared in 1505, printed by Gerson Soncino in Fano,[54] to be

---

50. Tr. by Miriam Werthheimer, from the German of Wolfgang Wessely, a professor of criminal law in Prague, who also wrote widely on Hebrew literature .

51. As an example of devotions in Dutch, *Tachanune Bat Yehudah* by Meir Letteris, dedicated to Lady Judith Montefiore, was translated from the German into Dutch as *Gebeden voor Israelitische Vrouven*, (Amsterdam, 1853). For examples of Hungarian devotions, see Dr. Arnold Kiss, *Mirjam* (Budapest, 1901). In the introduction to the 9th printing in 1905, the author, the Chief Rabbi of Buda, notes that the fact that 15,000 copies had already appeared was evidence of the deeply rooted religious sentiment in the female population, adding that "it proves, too, that in our synagogues the sweet language of our native land has become holy." For Hungarian devotions for women that are less elaborately poetic and more rooted in the traditional liturgy, see Gabor Weisz, *Eszter* (Budapest, 1902).

52. Leonella Modona, *Il Vessillo Israelitico* (1887), 76-80, and 110-114. The implication is that this was so that the women would understand their prayers.

53. See Umberto Cassuto, "Les Traductions Judeo-Italiennes du Rituel," in *Revue des Études Juives* (1930) 265-268.

54. Later editions included *Tefillot Latini* (Bologna, 1538), one published by Giustiniani (Venice, 1547), and *Tefillot Vulgar*, (Mantua, 1561). See Cecil Roth, *Revue des Études Juives*, (1925) 63-65.

followed by others. These, too, were specifically directed at women.

We do not have any evidence of printed Judeo-Italian siddurim after the end of the 16th century.[55] What do exist, however, are manuscript prayers books in Hebrew that were commissioned in Italy for particular women between 1700 and 1850. Often these had captions in Italian as to when the prayers should be said in the context of the standard prayer service, for days on which "tahanun" is said and not said, at the end of the 'Amidah, and so on.

These manuscript prayer books seem to assume both a knowledge of Hebrew, and that the women for whom they were written prayed regularly. This is not surprising for, as Cassuto points out, women could clearly read Hebrew letters, as the Judeo-Italian was printed in Hebrew characters. The range of the prayers is much more limited than the Yiddish tkhines. They deal directly with a woman's experience – prayers connected with the three mitzvot for women and for the events surrounding pregnancy, childbirth and delivery. A few of the manuscripts have "segulot" (charms and remedies); some have the traveller's prayer, or the priestly blessing or a section of laws relating to the women's mitzvot. But they do not include prayers for a vast range of other occasions like the Yiddish tkhines.

The texts of these manuscripts combine psalms, blessings, prayers and biblical verses. The books are similar but not identical in content and order. Because the texts of the prayers are so similar in different manuscripts, one must assume that they have a common source, but if so, it is unknown to us. Clearly more research is needed, both to try to discover a common source, and to ascertain the origin of the variants.

Most of the prayers are petitions in the first person singular. In some books that were clearly written for specific women, the woman's name is inserted into the text at different points, e.g. "Lord our God and God of our ancestors, may it be Your will that I, ------ daughter of ------." In others a gap is left

---

55. Cassuto attributes this to the Edict of Clement VIII in 1596, prohibiting the printing of liturgy in any language other than Hebrew. Cassuto, op. cit., 275-6.

and the text will say "pelonit bat pelonit" (x daughter of y) for the reader to insert her own name.

In some manuscripts, the language is taken directly from the standard prayers, in others the texts are paraphrased or adapted. Sometimes there are exact parallels to the wording in the standard liturgy; sometimes when there are not, its derivation is clear.[56] Often there are kabbalistic interpolations with references for example to sufferings beyond the grave and the birth pangs of the Messiah. Like the tkhines, therefore, they are steeped in traditional sources and have an intimate tone. They also invoke the merits of the Matriarchs. The prayers very concretely distinguish between different periods of a woman's life, particularly as regards different stages of pregnancy.[57]

Many of these manuscripts were owned by wealthy women and have inscriptions or dedications. Some have decorated or embroidered covers or elaborate bindings, such as one in the library of the Jewish Theological Seminary which has a gold

---

56. As in the case of the tkhines, many of texts follow the language of the Selihot (the penitential prayers recited before Rosh Hashana). As one example, in a prayer to be recited on days Tahanun is said, the woman asks God to respond to her prayers, and gives a list of those in the past to whom God has responded favorably. This follows precisely part of Selihot based on the Mishnah in *Ta'anit* 2:4. The woman then returns to her specific requests.

57. One very important study of the volumes at the Hebrew Union College and the Jewish Theological Seminary has compared the manuscript books, focusing on prayers to be said during pregnancy and childbirth. It identifies 9 different prayers, ranging from ones to be recited throughout pregnancy, others for specific periods of a pregnancy. Other prayers occur occasionally, such as before a son's circumcision, but all the above occur in at least three of the twenty-nine manuscripts studied. Included in 13 manuscripts were prayers for the entire pregnancy, for the first 40 days and from the beginning of the 9th month until delivery. See Paula Feldstein, *Eighteenth Century Italian Women's Prayer Books*, Thesis Submitted in partial fulfillment of requirements for ordination (HUC-JIR, Graduate Rabbinic Program, New York, 1993).

imprinted green leather binding.[58] One in the Israel Museum from the 18th century has attached to one page, 7 ribbons of braided thread used for counting the 7 clean days of the menstrual cycle before going to the mikveh.[59] Obviously many of these were presentation copies, gifts to brides and wives. Were they used? It is hard to tell. How widespread was more than a basic knowledge of Hebrew? In that the instructions are written in Italian, can we assume understanding in both languages?[60]

MANUSCRIPT HOLDINGS

The listing of the Institute of Microfilmed Manuscripts at the Hebrew University shows about 90 of these manuscripts in public and private collections. The Jewish Theological Seminary Library in New York has 17 and the Klau Library of HUC-JIR in Cincinnati has 12. These are similar but not identical in content and in the order of the prayers.[61]

Some manuscripts list the names of the scribes, some have the name of the woman for whom the text was written on the title page, and some have her name specified in prayers in the text. Others have inscriptions of ownership. For example, one at the Jewish National and University Library in Jerusalem

---

58. This manuscript, dated 1786 and written by Guiseppe Coen for his wife Yehudit, has been translated and edited by Rabbi Nina Cardin (1992). See note 2 above.
59. Einhorn Collection, Tel Aviv, on loan to the Israel Museum.
60. For recent discussion of literacy and education among Italian women, see Howard A. Edelman, "The Educational and Literary Activities of Jewish Women in Italy during the Renaissance and the Catholic Restoration," in *Shlomo Simonsohn Jubilee Volume* (Tel Aviv University, 1992) 9-23. See also Zolty, op. cit., 155-169.
61. More work needs to be done on these manuscripts, on the different topics covered, the use of sources, and the variant texts. The Feldstein thesis (see note 56 above) is especially valuable in its detailed comparisons of the texts on pregnancy and childbirth. Yael Levine Katz of Jerusalem is currently preparing a volume of prayers for niddah and mikveh, that will include examples from the Italian women's prayer books.

has the name of the scribe – Yehezkel bar Moshe Barged and a
date. It was written for "Richetta Luzzatto di Trieste l'Anno
Corrente 1823," and also has inscribed the name of Annetta
Luzzatto di Gradisca.[62] One at Bar-Ilan University mentions
the owner of the manuscript, "Diamante bat Esther and her
husband Avraham ben Tzion bar Consuela."[63] Only in a few
cases do we know in which city-states they were used or
written, such as the one from Trieste mentioned above, or one
written in Venice in 1740 for Bathsheba, the wife of Shlomo
Ashkenazi by Nissim David Hacohen.[64] Thus it is hard to see
any geographical pattern. There is no internal or external
evidence that any of the texts were composed by women or
were the product of a female scribe or copyist.

No printed editions of these special prayer books for women
exist. This is surprising as Italian liturgical bibliography in
this period abounds with prayers that were printed for specific
occasions, such as cholera epidemics. Why were there no
printed prayers of Jewish women? Could it be because they
were only gift books? Or because the prayers that dealt with
ritual immersion and childbirth were deemed too intimate to
put in print?

PRAYERS OF SEPHARDIC WOMEN

There do not seem to be comparable prayers for women in
Ladino. In part, this is because Sephardic culture, while
sophisticated in many respects, was clearly less literate,
particularly for women.[65] This said, there might well have
been strong oral prayer traditions in different communities
that were not committed to writing, particularly as regards

---

62. J.N.U.L. 80873.
63. Bar-Ilan University Library 787. See p. 5a.
64. In H.U.C. Library (HUC 243).
65. There are a few ethical books about biblical women in Ladino,
    and also books on the women's commandments in Ladino and
    Judeo-Arabic. See J. Breger, "Jewish Women's Religious Litera-
    ture," op. cit., May 1994.

visits to holy tombs.[66]

There is evidence however, that Jewish women in 19th century Iraq were literate,[67] and we have knowledge of prayers of Iraqi women from an early twentieth century volume in Judeo-Arabic entitled *Kanaan Al Nissa* by Rabbi Yosef Hayim ben Elijah of Baghdad, the leading rabbi of that community, also known as "Ben Ish Chai." This is a book of ethical and legal writings for women that was very popular at the beginning of the century.[68]

Ben Ish Chai certainly assumes in his book that women do engage in prayer. In discussing candle lighting for Shabbat, for example, he rules that a woman should recite Minhah before lighting candles.[69]

One chapter of the book contains specific prayers for women. In the introductory lines, Ben Ish Chai says:

> The words that a person says, in a language he understands, express how the words come out of the heart, that they should be pleasing for God. Therefore I present a few necessary petitions and prayers, that each in its appropriate time you should say in

---

66. In a recent interview with three generations of Iranian women, it appeared that while, in the mother's generation, some women read Hebrew, in the grandmother's generation, none of the women could read but knew prayers by heart, especially the prayer of Hannah from I Samuel, ch. 2. See Susan Grossman and Rivka Haut, "From Persia to New York: An Interview with Three generations of Iranian Women," in *Daughters of the King*, 1992, 217-225.

67. Shoshana Zolty, op. cit., 144-5.

68. According to A. Ya'ari, the first edition was actually printed in Baghdad in 1906, even though the title-page says Livorno. Apparently it was forbidden to use the word "kanaan," meaning "canon," in Baghdad, where it was reserved exclusively for law books. See Ya'ari, *Ha-Defus ha-Ivri be-Artzot ha-Mizrah*, part 2, Jerusalem, 1940, 135. The book was reprinted in Jerusalem in 1926. A Hebrew translation was published under the title *Hukkei ha-Nashim* in 1979 by "Otzar Hamizrah" in Jerusalem.

69. There are also references in responsa by R. Yosef Hayim in which it is clear that women are involved in prayer as well as in Torah study. *Rav Pe'alim*, Kuntrus "Sod Yesharim," par. 9, cited in Zolty, 1993, op. cit., 144-5.

your language, from the depths of your hearts.[70]

He first presents a shortened general prayer in the first person, part paraphrase of regular prayers and part personal petitions as follows:

> Please Hashem, purify my heart.
> Please Hashem, help me to do Your will
> Please Hashem, strengthen me to fulfill Your commandments...
>
> My Lord, I am Your maidservant, and I have no mitzvot in the merit of which I can beg, and no good deeds that I can rely on, but I have begged for Your mercy and relied on Your great loving-kindness, and trusted in Your great name. You raise the lowly from the dust and lift the poor from the ground. Listen in your mercy to my prayer and supplication, answer me Lord , answer me.[71]

There are prayers to be said at gravesides, especially if the woman is pregnant, which are phrased as "I ----- daughter of -----," with gaps for a woman to insert her own name.[72] There are also prayers to be said every day by a woman who is subject to evil thoughts.

> I ----- daughter of ----- say and confess before my God, all the strange and bad thoughts, which are against Divine will, which have risen in my heart and brain, should be negated and should be without power and strength, and should be made nothing as if they never were.[73]

There are also specific prayers for the month of Elul, for Rosh Hashanah and for the 10 days of Penitence.[74]

Although *Kanaan Al Nissa* contains a chapter on going to the mikveh, it does not give specific prayers beyond the

---

70. The translation is from the Hebrew edition, 1979, op. cit, chapter
    48, 133.
71. Ibid.
72. Ibid, p. 134.
73. Ibid, p. 135.
74. Ibid, p. 136-146.

blessing.[75] But in another book, *Leshon Hakhamim*, Ben Ish Chai provides a prayer for a woman who has counted "seven clean days" and is therefore ready to go for ritual immersion.[76] In strongly mystical language, the woman invokes the union between God and Israel, between the upper and lower spheres, and prays that as she will purify her body in the mikveh, so God should purify her soul. She prays that her observance of all the laws of ritual purity will serve as a "repair" to the world, for defects both of her generation, and that of Adam and Eve, to return to a state of untainted holiness. The writer clearly attributes mystical importance to the woman's actions.[77]

CONTEMPORARY PRAYERS

There has been increased interest in recent years in prayers and rituals among Jewish women in America. Many women have wanted to connect Jewishly with events in their life cycle—including dealing with infertility, miscarriage,

---

75. Ibid, p. 106. He also says that before the blessing, the woman should recite three times Psalm 90, verse 17, which should also be said three times before the blessing for separating "hallah" (p. 109).

76. *Leshon Hakhamim*, 1st edition, Jerusalem, 1905 (reprinted 1990), part 2 , section 23, pp. 146-7.

77. This relates to the mystical view that the world is in a state of disrepair, and that we can act to "correct" this. This seems different from the notion of "niddah" and "mikveh" as being a punishment for the sin of Eve. It is particularly interesting that he talks of defects of Adam as well as of Eve, whereas many texts treat Adam as the victim of Eve. The different theological notions underlying the prayers relating to ritual purity cannot be dealt with here. For an analysis of the tkhine literature on this subject, see Chava Weissler, "Mitzvot Built into the Body: Tkhines for Niddah, Pregnancy and Childbirth," in *People of the Body: Jews and Judaism from an Embodied Perspective,* ed. Howard Eilberg Schwartz (S.U.N.Y., 1993) 101-115.

weaning, baby-naming, hysterectomy and menopause.[78] Many of these "life cycle" concerns such as those for the onset of menstruation, were not included in traditional tkhines, which were targeted at the married Jewish woman, not the single or divorced one.

Other prayers or rituals deal with modern family relationships, often much more complicated than in the past and for marking different stages and turning points, such as adult bat-mitzvah and mid-life transitions. Many people feel uncomfortable at the idea of specific prayers for the aftermath of a rape or following an abortion, but there is clearly what Chava Weissler calls a "therapeutic function" in these prayers.[79] As opposed to the tkhines of the past, which are based on individual petition and personal supplication, these have more of a ceremonial aspect, and more of a sharing with others. Time will tell the extent to which women will want to use the prayers composed by other women, as opposed to creating their own.

CONCLUSION

How much these books of women's liturgy were actually used is not definite, although there is significant external evidence that they were. One can look not only at the volume of tkhines printed, but also at the wear on those that have survived. While only a few collections of tkhines are personalized, or that have decorated bindings, many of the

---

78. See, for example, Susan Grossman, "Finding Comfort After Miscarriage," in *Daughters of the King*, op. cit., 1992, 284-290; Elizabeth Resnick Levine, ed. *A Ceremonies Sampler: New Rites, Celebrations, and Observances of Jewish Women* (Women's Institute for Continuing Jewish Education, San Diego, 1991); and Irene Fine, *Midlife, a Rite of Passage and the Wise Woman. A Celebration*, (Women's Institute, San Diego, 1988). For a collection of contemporary rituals organized around Rosh Hodesh, see Penina V. Adelman, *Miriam's Well: Rituals for Jewish Women Round the Year*, (New York; Biblio Press, 1986.)

79. See Chava Weissler, "The American Transformations of the Tkhines," op. cit., 32.

Italian prayer manuscripts were presentation copies, as were many of the printed books of devotion and many women's prayer books. Often they were bound in silver, mother of pearl, embroidered material or decorated "tooled" leather. But evidence of the use of these "fancy" editions is their employment as registers of birth and yortsayt reminders. Some books of devotions from the late nineteenth and early twentieth century indicate the locations of family graves on the inside covers.

Jewish women of the past obviously accepted prayers written by men as expressing their spiritual needs, since only some of the tkhines, a few of the devotions, and the modern prayers were actually written by women. As regards the nature of the prayers themselves, despite differences in content and in tone, there are common features. All the women's prayers are more personal and more concrete than the standard liturgy. Even the devotions in German and the other languages, which are more formal and less intimate than the Yiddish tkhines, are still personal. The Italian Hebrew prayers are intensely so, and distinguish vividly between different stages of pregnancy. All of the prayers, even those of the Iraqi women are in the first person singular.

The perception one has of traditional Jewish women's piety as exemplified by the recitation of psalms is probably accurate, and there is a sense that the "prayerfulness" of traditional Jewish women extended beyond the period of "Enlightenment" and religious reform, as shown by the popularity of the devotional literature. Indeed most, though not all, of the contemporary American Jewish ceremonies and rituals seem to be by or concerning women.

The past provides precedents as well as models for understanding Jewish women's liturgy. But our knowledge in this area is still limited. While we know something of the education of Jewish women from rabbinical and scholarly families, we know much less about the literacy levels of other women.[80] There is a need for more exploration of halakhic and literary sources, including memoirs, to ascertain the extent to which "ordinary" women actually engaged in regular and supplementary prayer.[81] There is now scholarly work being done on the oral traditions of the less literate, and the spiritual meaning invested in prayer-like activities.[82]

More study of available sources, and more bibliographic information will help us understand how women's liturgy fits into the general history of Jewish prayer. Exploring the individual prayers of Jewish women in different cultures provides us with windows into the lives of Jewish women of the past, as well as with help in filling out our knowledge of liturgy as a form of spiritual expression.

---

80. Shoshana Zolty, op. cit. Zolty uses a vast array of sources to trace the evolution of Jewish education for women, showing the high level of knowledge achieved by many women from scholarly families in different periods of Jewish history. For an important article on Eastern European Jewish women, including some quantitative data on women's education and literacy, see Shaul Stampfer, "Greater Differentiation and Education of the Jewish Woman in Nineteenth-Century Eastern Europe," in *Studies from POLIN: From Shtetl to Socialism*, ed. Anton Polansky (London and Washington: Littman Library, 1993) 187-211.

81. In his autobiography, Chaim Weizmann describes his mother as saying her prayers every day, as well as going to the synagogue every Sabbath during his childhood in Motel and Pinsk, and continuing to say them daily until her death in Haifa in 1939. See his *Trial And Error* (New York, 1949), 13-14. But what prayers did she say? Would she have said tkhines as well? While Weizmann specifies his father's reading material, and knowledge of volumes of Maimonides and Yosef Caro, he does not similarly specify in the case of his mother.

82. Susan Starr Sered, *Women as Ritual Experts:The Religious Lives of Elderly Jewish Women in Jerusalem* (Oxford University Press, 1992) and "The Synagogue as a Sacred Space for the Elderly Oriental Women of Jerusalem," in *Daughters of the King*, op. cit., 205-216. Among other aspects, Sered describes how illiterate women participate in the formal synagogue services through a series of gestures, kissing and bowing, such as rolling their hands, kissing their fingers and touching their foreheads with their fingertips.

MARC D. ANGEL

Rabbi Hayyim David Halevy: A Leading Contemporary Rabbinic Thinker

RABBI BENZION UZIEL, the late Sephardic Chief Rabbi of Israel, delivered an address in the winter of 1936 in which he called for the establishment of an authoritative rabbinic body along the lines of the Sanhedrin of old. He argued that the rabbinate had the responsibility of establishing true justice. This responsibility included issuing rulings on cases between contending individuals, and also extended to public issues, questions of taxation and communal needs. Rabbi Uziel suggested that one who simply knew how to rule concerning what is permitted and what is forbidden, or one who is guilty and who is innocent – such a rabbi is known simply as a *talmid hakham*, a wise student. To be a real decisor (posek) though, entails a greater responsibility and authority. A great decisor is one who has the wisdom and courage to apply Torah teachings to all aspects of life.[1]

In his generation, Rabbi Uziel exemplified the very ideal which he described. Rabbi Uziel was not only a brilliant scholar in all details of Jewish law and tradition, but he also had a transcendent vision which extended to all areas of Jewish life. Through his writings and teachings, he inspired his followers with a grand vision of rabbinic responsibility. Among his most significant disciples is Rabbi Hayyim David Halevy, the current Sephardic Chief Rabbi of Tel Aviv.

Born in Jerusalem in 1924, Rabbi Halevy served for a number of years as Rabbi Uziel's assistant. He then served as Chief Rabbi of Rishon Le-Zion 1950-72, and has been Chief Rabbi of Tel Aviv-Jaffa since 1972. He is a well known figure in Israel through his communal service, radio programs, frequent lectures and voluminous writings. Rabbi Halevy told me that he considers his books to be his yeshiva, and the readers of his books to be his students. Indeed, his writings

---

1. Benzion Uziel, *Mikhmanei Uziel.* Tel Aviv, 1939, pp. 358f. See especially pp. 371, 376, 382 and 391.

have enjoyed increasing popularity both in Israel and throughout the diaspora. He has written a code of Jewish law; a guide to the Zohar; volumes of responsa; a Torah commentary; and books dealing with specific issues such as the relationship of Israel and the nations, the nature of justice in Jewish law, and laws pertaining to Jewish women.[2]

Periodically, Rabbi Halevy has been quoted in the general press in the United States. He was among the first rabbinic authorities to issue a halakhic ruling forbidding cigarette smoking. Several years ago, he was widely quoted for an address he delivered in which he argued for the option of civil marriages in Israel. Recently, he also has been quoted in American newspapers for his ruling against wearing fur. Rabbi Halevy has never shied away from controversy. He is a gentle, modest scholar; and at the same time, he is a man of remarkable courage and forcefulness.

Rabbi Halevy has authored a nine volume set of responsa under the title *Aseh Lekha Rav* (Make For Yourself a Rabbi). In these volumes he covers a wide range of questions in Jewish law. The responsa are erudite, thoughtful, sensitive and clear. While the bulk of these volumes naturally deals with halakhah, there are also a number of significant essays and responsa relating to hashkafah (Jewish thought, ideology). This essay will consider a number of issues in the latter category.[3]

---

2. Among Rabbi Halevy's publications are: *Bein Yisrael la-Amim,* Tel Aviv, 1954; *Devar Mishpat,* 3 vols., Tel Aviv, 1963-65; *Mekor Hayyim* (a code of Jewish law), Tel Aviv, 1967-68; *Dat u'Medinah,* Tel Aviv, 1969; *Maftehot ha-Zohar ve-Rayonotav,* Tel Aviv, 1971; *Aseh Lekha Rav* (responsa), 9 vols., Tel Aviv, 1976-1989; *Mekor Hayyim li-Venot Yisrael,* Tel Aviv, 1977, *Kitzur Shulhan Arukh Mekor Hayyim,* Tel Aviv, 1975; *Mayim Hayyim* (responsa), Tel Aviv, 1991; *Torat Hayyim* (Torah Commentary, 2 vols., Tel Aviv, 1992. A number of these works have been reprinted in other editions as well.

3. All references in the text will be to *Aseh Lekha Rav,* indicating the volume and responsum number. For a discussion of Rabbi Halevy's treatment of halakhah see my article "A Study of the Halakhic Approaches of Two Modern Posekim," *Tradition,* Spring 1988, pp. 41-52. Rabbi Halevy deals with many issues in Jewish thought and ideology throughout his responsa. For this article I selected several major themes.

ISRAEL AND THE REDEMPTION PROCESS

Rabbi Halevy believes that the establishment of the State of Israel represents the beginning of the period of ultimate redemption for the Jewish people. He attributes profound religious significance to the State of Israel.

Yet, the question arises: If the State of Israel represents the beginning of the period of Messianic redemption, why were so many of Israel's founders and pioneers non-religious Jews? One would have imagined that a religious phenomenon such as the redemption would have been initiated specifically by the most religious Jews, not by secularists.

Rabbi Halevy offers several responses to this challenge. He notes that classical Jewish thought includes the notion that the Messianic era will be the result of a natural process of development among the Jewish people. Another approach is that redemption will be brought about in a miraculous, supernatural way. Through generations of oppression, many Jews gave up hope in achieving redemption through natural means. They came to rely entirely upon God's miraculous intervention to save them. While this attitude gave them hope during times of despair, it also contributed towards a sense of helplessness and passivity. Religious Jews, to a large extent, came to think that the ingathering of exiles to the land of Israel would have to wait for God's supernatural intervention.

But God's providence has preferred to initiate the ingathering of the exiles (the beginning of redemption) through natural means. Which Jews were ready to play a role in this redemptive process? None other than those who had rebelled against the passivity maintained by the bulk of religious Jewry! In other words, God's providence drew the non-religious and secular Jews into the Messianic redemption of Israel. Certainly, there were also a number of religious Jews involved in this process; yet, since God wants to redeem all of the Jewish people, it is necessary for all the Jewish people (religious and non-religious) to be engaged in this process (1:3).

Rabbi Halevy, thus, grants tremendous importance and dignity to non-religious Jews who have been chosen by God's providence to play so important a role in the unfolding of Jewish redemption. Instead of seeing the religious and non-religious Jews as antagonists, Rabbi Halevy sees them as each playing a vital role in the redemption of the Jewish people.

Rabbi Halevy draws an analogy between the ultimate redemption of the Jews and the original redemption of the Israelites from Egypt. He observes that the Torah describes the Exodus as an expulsion. Pharaoh and the Egyptians *expelled* the Israelite slaves! This appears to be an unusual use of language, since one would have expected the Israelites to have left eagerly, not needing to be expelled. Rabbi Halevy explains that apparently not all the Israelites wanted to leave their servitude. They were reluctant to break their pattern of life to enter into an uncertain future. Therefore, they virtually needed to be expelled, since they would not have left on their own volition. But the question arises: Why was it necessary for *all* the Israelites to leave Egypt? If there were those who were afraid of leaving, why not let them remain in slavery? To this, Rabbi Halevy answers that the nature of true redemption is to have all the Israelites become free, whether or not they themselves felt the need to go free. Redemption is total and all-encompassing. No one may be left behind. Likewise, in the future redemption, all Jews must be included. The future redemption will be complete and eternal. It will involve the total ingathering of exiles, even those who have assimilated, even those who have lost their Jewish identity (4:8).

Rabbi Halevy was asked: If this indeed is the beginning of the Messianic redemption, why has Israel been involved in so many wars? Why have so many lives been lost in battle? In responding to this question, he draws an analogy from the Exodus experience of the ancient Israelites. While they were enslaved in Egypt, God performed great miracles on their behalf. Indeed, the Israelites were passive in their own redemption; God brought the ten plagues on the Egyptians which led Pharaoh to send out the Israelites. Yet, once the Israelites left Egypt, they had to face military battle with Amalek. Why didn't God simply perform another miracle so that the Israelites would not have to engage in any battles? Rabbi Halevy notes that the battle with Amalek was an important lesson for the Israelites. God had redeemed them from slavery in Egypt. But if they were to obtain their own land with freedom and dignity, then they had to assume personal responsibility and risk. The Bible itself shows that Joshua led the people in various battles to conquer the land and establish Jewish sovereignty. In the process, lives were lost. So, too, in the current stage of our ultimate redemption, we should also expect to engage in war and make many sacrifices. The nation of Israel derives self-respect from earning national sovereignty, not from having it handed to them miraculously by God (1: 5).

NATURE OF PRAYER

What is the nature of Jewish prayer? Since God already knows all of our needs and thoughts, why do we go through the process of praying? How effective is prayer?

Rabbi Halevy sees prayer primarily as a spiritual experience for the one who is praying. When we petition God to help solve our various problems, we are not telling Him something that He does not already know. Rather, we are verbalizing our own dependence on Him. Our prayers are a way of reminding us of our own relationship with God. Rabbi Halevy cites the Talmud in *Berakhot* 25a, which states that one who elongates in his prayer and analyzes it – in the end will have a broken heart. Rashi comments: Such a person says in his heart that his wishes should be fulfilled because he has prayed with such devotion. This person will come to have a broken heart because his request will not be fulfilled. One has no right to expect that God will accede to his requests, simply because he has prayed with devotion.

Rabbi Halevy quotes Rabbi Bahya who used to conclude his prayer with his own private devotion in which he expressed his smallness in the presence of God. "For You are awesome and lofty, and I am too insignificant to ask help from You and to call out to You with praises and sanctifications to Your holy Name. But You have permitted me to do this. You have elevated me by commanding me to call out to You, and You have allowed me to praise Your Name most high according to my understanding of You, though I am fully aware of my smallness before You....I have not told You my needs in order to inform You about them, but rather so that I can feel the greatness of my lacks before You and express my trust in You" (1:29).

Rabbi Halevy suggests that the Divine influence can be compared to rain. Just as rain cannot make the earth flourish unless the earth had been prepared in advance through plowing and planting, so prayer and spiritual exercise cannot be satisfactory without prior preparation. For one to experience prayer properly, one must first develop a spiritual sense, the religious consciousness of being in the presence of God. One cannot pray for wisdom if his mind is not prepared to receive wisdom. A human being must develop himself, and then the Almighty will give His blessing on what the individual himself has begun (2:22).

Someone posed a question to Rabbi Halevy: When we petition God in our prayers to fulfill our various needs, why do we sing or chant? If we were to ask a government official for something, we would simply state our case; we certainly would not sing to the official.

To this, Rabbi Halevy responds that the bulk of our prayers are in the category of praising God, not petitions. However, even those sections which are strictly in the category of petitions are sung or chanted in a pleasant way. It is through song that a person is able to experience and reveal his deepest feelings. Rabbi Shelomo Alkabez, the famous sixteenth century mystic and poet, taught that music has very deep spiritual significance, so that even the angels on high sing their praises of God. Music can enable a person to transcend his physical senses; it is the language of the soul. It is clear, then, that we sing our prayers in order to elevate our own spiritual experience.

It is not music in general that elevates a person, but specifically the traditional music which is associated with specific prayers. For example, the special melodies of the prayers on the High Holy Days evoke an emotional response among the congregation. The melodies carry profound historical associations, echoing the voices of generations of our ancestors. The music and its memories add other dimensions of feeling to our prayers.

Rabbi Halevy reminds us that when we make a petition to a human being, our goal is to change that person's mind or to convince him to do what we request. It is suitable to explain our case in a logical, reasonable way. When we are praying to

God, though, we are not calling for any change in God's mind. Rather, we are really trying to create a change in our own selves, making us more receptive to God's will and compassion. And for this goal, music is an essential element (4:17).

JEWISH EDUCATION

A number of Rabbi Halevy's responsa deal with issues in Jewish education. Although they present halakhic decisions, they also reflect a philosophy of Torah education.

In several responsa, Rabbi Halevy discusses the permissibility of strikes by teachers of Torah studies. A number of teachers' strikes were called in Israel. The prevailing rabbinical opinion was that teachers of religious subjects were not allowed to strike. Rather, they were obligated to find other places in which to teach their students. Teaching children Torah is so important that it cannot be interrupted because of a labor dispute.

Rabbi Halevy ruled, in contrast, that teachers of religious studies did have the right to go out on strike. If they had engaged in legitimate negotiations and had tried their best to reach a settlement, then they could strike if management did not offer them a suitable contract. Teachers of religious studies have the right to proper compensation, just as any other people do.

Rabbi Halevy is quite aware of how important it is for children to study Torah. However, he points out that the responsibility to teach children Torah rests on the childrens' *parents*, not on others. If parents do not have the time or ability to teach their own children Torah, then they have the responsibility to hire someone else to do this. But the teacher thus engaged serves as an agent of the parents. The teacher is always free to decline to continue as the parents' agent. In that case, the responsibility to teach the children devolves back on the parents themselves. Thus, if there is a teachers strike, then it is up to the parents to assume personal responsibility for the Torah education of their children. If the children do not learn Torah during a teachers' strike, the fault does not lie with the teachers, but with the parents (3:23; 5:23).

In dealing with this issue, Rabbi Halevy underscores the personal responsibility of parents to see to it that their children receive proper Torah instruction. If parents want to delegate this responsibility to others, then they must meet the legitimate needs of those whom they would hire to teach their children. In placing the responsibility squarely on parents, Rabbi Halevy gives Torah teachers the opportunity to expect and demand proper compensation for their services. Torah teachers should not be considered any less worthy of making a decent living than any other teachers.

Rabbi Halevy's philosophy of Torah education can also be seen in several responsa dealing with a totally different issue. In 1985 a movie theater in Petah Tikvah opened for business on Friday nights. This provoked a response of outrage on the part of religious Jews. Demonstrations were organized in front of the movie theater each Friday night for quite a few months.

Rabbi Halevy viewed this controversy as symbolic of a deeper battle between religious and non-religious Jews over the character of Israeli society. Religious Jews want the State of Israel to reflect respect towards traditional Jewish law and custom. Non-religious Jews want to overthrow the influence of religious law and tradition. Rabbi Halevy believes unequivocally that the State of Israel must be a "Jewish" state, following and respecting halakhic norms.

In the issue at hand, though, one needs to evaluate the effectiveness of the demonstrations. Rabbi Halevy feared that these demonstrations only served to deepen the chasm between the religious and non-religious communities. There was no evidence whatsoever that any of the non-religious Jews had become more sympathetic to religion because of these demonstrations. Rabbi Halevy expressed his deep conviction that the proper way to deal with this controversy is not by means of public demonstrations on Friday nights. Rather, more will be achieved by following the "ways of pleasantness," by calm and civil discussions. If there were a genuine chance that these demonstrations would succeed in stopping the desecration of the Sabbath, then he would certainly favor continuing them. However, since he saw no chance at all of success, and since a continuation of the demonstrations only deepened the hatred between the religious and non-religious elements of society, it was preferable to find non-confrontational ways of dealing with the issue. The ways of the Torah are ways of pleasantness and peace (8:32-35). Religious values should be taught by setting an example of kindness, moral uprightness and sensitivity.

BETWEEN JEWS AND NON-JEWS

The Declaration of Independence of the State of Israel calls for complete equal rights for all citizens of Israel, regardless of religion or race. All citizens of Israel are entitled by right to equality before the law.

Some rabbinic scholars have argued that the basis of the Jewish relationship with non-Jews is the principle of "darkhei shalom," maintaining peaceful relationships in society. Thus, Jews are called upon to give charity to the non-Jewish poor, to visit and care for the non-Jewish sick, and generally to behave civilly towards non-Jews.

This reasoning implies that the Jewish responsibility to non-Jews is a matter of expedience, rather than ethical responsibility. Rabbi Halevy contends that the principle of "darkhei shalom" in relationships to non-Jews was applicable when the non-Jews were outright pagans and idolaters. However, the modern situation is far different. In respect to the set of rules based on "darkhei shalom," Rabbi Halevy states that neither Moslems nor Christians are in the category of idolaters. Therefore, the source of Jewish responsibility for the well-being of non-Jews does not stem from expedience, but rather from a firmly established ethical imperative (9:30 and 9:33).

Rabbi Halevy's position provides the religious framework for the Jewish State providing equal rights to all its citizens, Jewish and non-Jewish.

AFTERLIFE

Rabbi Halevy is not only an outstanding sage in Jewish law and thought, but he is also deeply imbued with the teachings of Kabbalah. He authored a guide to the study of the Zohar, and throughout his writings he refers to ideas found in the Zohar and other kabbalistic writings. He, of course, applies his kabbalistic wisdom to his halakhic decisions. But he also deals with metaphysical ideas relating to our faith.

In Volume 2 of *Aseh Lekha Rav*, he includes a lengthy essay (pp. 17-94) dealing with the topic of life after death. He refers to the work of an American researcher who studied individuals who had death experiences, i.e., their doctors had declared them to be dead, but they somehow returned to life. Dr. Raymond Moody of the University of Virginia interviewed a number of such individuals, finding common patterns in their death experiences. They reported seeing a dark tunnel which ended in an incredible light. They felt a certain presence which imbued them with a feeling of infinite love. This presence communicated with them through their thoughts. Relatives and friends who had previously died came to greet them. They witnessed clear flashes of pictures from their own lives. All individuals who experienced death said that they were aware that their souls were hovering above their bodies. They were able to see and hear everything which was happening around their bodies.

Dr. Moody found that people who had "died" and then returned to life were not at all afraid of death. On the contrary, they experienced death as an amazingly positive happening.

Rabbi Halevy sees in these findings a verification of knowledge which our sages have taught since antiquity – that there is life after death. Science has finally come to understand something which Judaism has been teaching for millenia. Rabbi Halevy demonstrates how the descriptions of those who had "died" are remarkably consistent with age-old rabbinic traditions.

The Zohar alludes to the fact that the death process involves passing through a dark tunnel. It states that the souls pass from this world to the world to come by going through the *me'arat ha-makhpelah*, the cave in which our forefathers and their wives are buried in Hebron. The experience of an overwhelming light infused with love has its roots in various rabbinic writings including the Zohar. The Zohar explains that at the time of death, one perceives a vision which he could not behold while still alive. The custom of closing the eyes of the dead is so that the eyes which saw this vision of holiness will no longer see any profane things. It further states that a person's soul does not depart until he first sees a vision of the glory of God. Then his soul leaves with a profound longing for the Divine Presence. Rabbi Halevy also cites the Zohar which indicates that upon death, one is greeted by relatives and friends who have died previously. The Zohar relates that all of a person's deeds pass before him at the time of death.

Those who have experienced "death" have consistently arrived at two conclusions: One must love others; one must learn as much as possible. Rabbi Halevy cites rabbinic passages which have conveyed the same ideas. (*Avot de-Rabbi Natan*, end of chapter 16; *Pesahim* 50a). Our soul's blessing in the world to come is directly correlated to our righteousness in this world. The great light which people experience at death continues for the righteous. But for others, it fades away. The ultimate punishment is experiencing this love-infused light, and then being deprived of remaining in its presence.[4]

Rabbi Halevy's treatment of this metaphysical topic reflects his conviction that human life transcends our mere physical being. Human beings have souls; they have spiritual needs; they have a life after death. To ignore this aspect of our being, or to fail to develop it properly is to do ourselves irreparable harm.

This essay has provided several examples of the richness and creativity of Rabbi Halevy's teachings. As the years go on, I believe that the corpus of his voluminous writings will be deemed to be among the great contributions to rabbinic learning of this century.

---

4. See also my article "Life After Death," in *Body and Soul in Judaism*, New York Region of the Orthodox Union, 1991, pp. 10-13.

ROBERT SINGERMAN

Bloch & Company: Pioneer Jewish Publishing House in the West

THE EARLY HISTORY of Bloch Publishing Company in the formative years from its founding in 1855 in Cincinnati until its removal to New York City in 1901 has never been adequately documented.[1] Business records of this major publisher of Judaica are no longer extant and Edward Bloch (1829-1906), the firm's founder, was not a literary man and never recorded his memoirs for posterity. Furthermore, Bloch was overshadowed by his illustrious brother-in-law and business associate,

---

1. Bloch celebrated its centennial in 1954 and throughout its history and early advertising has traced its year of founding to 1854 to coincide with the inception of Isaac W. Wise's weekly, *The Israelite* (since 1874, *The American Israelite*), for many years associated with the Bloch firm as its publisher. Wise's publisher, however, for the first year was Charles F. Schmidt; Bloch and Co., at 43 East Third St., only came into existence in 1855 with the *Israelite's* issue of July 27. For appreciations of Bloch Publishing Co., chiefly its twentieth century activity, see Solomon Grayzel, "A Hundred Years of the Bloch Publishing Company," *Jewish Book Annual* 12 (1953-55): 72-76; Isaac Rosengarten, "A Cultural Centennial," *Jewish Forum* 38:9 (Sept. 1955): 151-53; Bloch's *Book Bulletin* no. 111/12 (April/June 1955), containing the "Centennial Section;" and Charles A. Madison, *Jewish Publishing in America* (New York, 1976), pp. 74-77. For additional biographical information on Edward Bloch, see sketch on the occasion of his silver wedding anniversary with Henrietta Miller in *American Israelite* (henceforth cited as *AI*, including its previous title, *The Israelite*), Nov. 17, 1880, p. 166; "Das siebenzigste Wiegenfest," *Die Deborah*, 20 Juli 1899, p. 5 (compare with less complete English text in *AI*, July 20, 1899, p. 6), "Pioneer Hebrew Publisher," *American Hebrew*, Aug. 18, 1899, p. 477 (copied from Cincinnati *Enquirer*), and obituaries as follows: *AI*, March 29, 1906, p. 6, Cincinnati *Enquirer*, March 23, 1906, p. 7, and *Publishers' Weekly*, April 14, 1906, p. 1174.

110

Rabbi Issac Mayer Wise, the masterbuilder of Reform Jewish institutions (he established the Hebrew Union College, Union of American Hebrew Congregations, Central Conference of American Rabbis). Piecing together biographical data on Edward Bloch is a challenge but not an insurmountable one; source data for writing the firm's corporate history can be found deeply embedded and scattered throughout the Jewish press; namely the *American Israelite*, founded by Isaac M. Wise in 1854 and for many years published by Bloch, and other contemporary sources such as R. G. Dun and Company credit reports and accounts in rival Jewish newspapers. The study that follows is an attempt to document the business activities of Bloch Publishing Company in Cincinnati, its early struggles, and eventual prominence as the "American Hebrew Publishing House" and, interestingly enough, as a major specialty manufacturer of flags.

The son of Herman and Nannie Bloch (married 1818), Edward Bloch was born 1829 in Grafenried, Bohemia, and arrived in the United States as a teenager in 1845, settling in New York where he clerked in a clothing store. The Blochs were the only Jewish family in this town near the frontier with Bavaria and, as fate would have it, Theresa Bloch, Edward's sister, was a pupil of Isaac M. Wise, eventually marrying her teacher in 1844 after an extended courtship. When the young Wise, now Rabbi Wise, obtained his first American pulpit in Albany in 1846, Edward also removed to Albany where he and a partner, Arnold Kaichen, opened a lace and fancy goods store around 1851, this the year of Bloch and Kaichen's first listing in the Albany city directory. Bloch married Cilly Strauss and had one daughter in Albany; both the wife and child died in 1852 apparently in the same conflagration that also destroyed the business.[2]

Again following his brother-in-law, the widowed Bloch came to Cincinnati in 1854 when Wise assumed the pulpit of

---

2. Nannie Bloch's obituary, *AI*, Oct. 20, 1876, p. 6. The standard biographies of Isaac M. Wise are by James G. Heller, *Isaac M. Wise: His Life, Work and Thought* (New York, 1965) and Sefton D. Temkin, *Isaac Mayer Wise, Shaping American Judaism* (Oxford, 1992).

Congregation B'nai Jeshurun, the post he held with national
distinction until his death in 1900. It simply cannot be
determined with any certainty when and where Edward Bloch
learned the printing trade; Grayzel (note 1) writes that Bloch
"worked in a printing establishment in Albany" while Madison
(note 1) is less specific, only indicating that Bloch had worked
for a printer (the context clearly indicates this was in
Cincinnati) and Wise helped him to set up the shop in 1854
when no "cooperative printer" could be found for *The Israelite*.
Elsewhere (*American Israelite*, July 20, 1899, p. 6, on the
occasion of Bloch's seventieth birthday), it is stated that Bloch
clerked for a year in a jewelry store during his first year in
Cincinnati and prior to the establishment of the printing firm
that bears his name. Wise's *Reminiscences* reveal that the
Israelite lost $600 during its first year and Charles Schmidt,
the paper's original publisher, despite having his losses repaid
personally by Wise, wanted out of the unprofitable relationship. At this juncture (summer 1855), Bloch and Company
bought type, presses, and "all the printers' necessities" on a
$3,000 line of credit. To quote Wise, "Not satisfied with losing
money on the *Israelite*, we began to issue the *Deborah* also,
and bought enough Hebrew type to found the first Jewish
printing-house in the West."[3]

GETTING ESTABLISHED

It should be made clear, however, that Hebrew printing
made its appearance in Cincinnati as early as 1824 with
Martin Ruter's *An Easy Entrance into the Sacred Language,
being a Concise Hebrew Grammar*. Benjamin Levy, of New
Orleans, was active in 1822-41 and is regarded as "the first
American Jew to combine printing, publishing and selling"

---

3. Isaac M. Wise, *Reminiscences*. Ed. by David Philipson (Cincinnati,
   1901; reprint, New York, 1973), pp. 292-93. The history of *Die
   Deborah* has been studied by Joseph Gutmann, "Watchman on an
   American Rhine: New Light on Isaac M. Wise," *American Jewish
   Archives* 10 (1958): 135-44.

though his imprints were not Jewish ones.[4] Bloch's achievement, with Isaac Mayer Wise's publications, school books, liturgies, and hymnals of the Reform movement as a perennial high-demand stock offsetting other losses, was to create a sustainable Jewish publishing house in the United States where none existed for English and German Judaica. Philadelphia's Isaac Leeser, a severe critic of Isaac M. Wise, was constantly struggling to publish his own works and translations. "No publisher," writes Bertram Korn, "... would undertake the risk of issuing his books; Leeser had to be his own publisher, business manager, proof-reader, salesman, agent."[5] L. H. Frank, a New York publisher with a small but popular list of liturgies and *haggadot* initiated by his father, Henry Frank, was Bloch's only potential rival.[6] According to Jonathan Sarna, Bloch and the Jewish Publication Society of America of Philadelphia "held a virtual monopoly over American Jewish publishing" at the time of JPS's formation in 1888.[7]

Bloch's early years as a printer were a struggle and prospects for success were slight. Most subscribers of *The Israelite* simply did not pay their bills; the country suffered a financial panic in 1857, and the Civil War deprived the *Israelite* of fully one half of its subscriptions and readership in the South. Even as late as 1871, the constant struggle for existence precipitated a "To Delinquents" announcement in the *Israelite* revealing that it cost no less than $10,000 to publish the paper and its

---

4. Bertram Wallace Korn, *The Early Jews of New Orleans* (Waltham, 1969), p. 147.
5. Idem, "Isaac Leeser: Centennial Reflections." *American Jewish Archives* 19 (1967): 134.
6. Madeleine S. Stern, "Henry Frank: Pioneer American Hebrew Publisher." *American Jewish Archives* 20 (1968): 163-68. For a short period near the end of the Civil War, Bloch was the Cincinnati agent for L. H. Frank, per *Occident and American Jewish Advocate* 22: 9 (Dec. 1864), advertising section (repeated in issues of January and February, 1865).
7. Jonathan Sarna, *JPS: The Americanization of Jewish Culture, 1888-1988* (Philadelphia, 1989), p. 143.

German-language companion, *Die Deborah*.[8] Bloch quickly
learned from bitter experience with unpaid bills that a
no-exceptions policy requiring all advertising copy to be paid
in advance was called for; no credit was to be extended to
congregations, societies, or public bodies.[9] In 1856, and again
in 1857 and 1858, Bloch went on collecting trips in the east
while also drumming up new subscriptions and orders for
advertising.[10] In the *Israelite*'s fifth year of existence (1859),
fully two-thirds of the paper's subscribers were not paying
their bills and on at least one occasion, Bloch was plagued by a
travelling imposter posing as a collector for the paper.[11]

VARIED UNDERTAKINGS

Yet, despite all adversity, the firm staved off bankrupcy
and managed to diversify in order not to depend solely on the
Israelite's pitiful earnings and poor cash flow. Bloch solicited
book and job printing in English, French, German and
Hebrew; for added income, contemporary ads for the company
show that it took orders for coal and for book binding, sold
clothing tickets, *ketubot* blanks (100 for $5.00), *etrogim* from
Corfu, and Jewish calendars. It also printed patriotic envelopes during the Civil War, and routinely filled job printing
orders for "plain and fancy" bill heads, circulars, receipts, busi-

---

8. *AI*, March 31, 1871, p. 10. *The Israelite* was not above publishing
   in its pages lists of delinquent subscribers; e.g., Feb. 22, 1857, p.
   266, March 6, 1857, p. 278 . See also, "Pay for Your Papers," *AI*,
   Nov. 28, 1856, p. 166, indicating that it cost the publisher at least
   $5,000 a year to publish the two papers, and "On Finances," *ibid.*,
   May 14, 1858, p. 359, for reliance on a mercantile agency to collect
   unpaid bills. Crippling losses resulting from the Civil War and
   recurring problems of non-payment by deadbeat subscribers well
   into the 1870s were candidly recalled by Wise in *AI*, June 25,
   1875, p. 4, July 7, 1882, p. 6.
9. *AI*, April 4, 1856, p. 315 .
10. *AI*, May 23, 1856, p. 372, May 8, 1857, p. 347, Jan. 8, 1858, p.
    214.
11. *AI*, May 6, 1859, p. 351, Aug. 2, 1867, p. 6.

ness and visiting cards, invitations, programmes, checks, and labels for wine, brandy, and liquor bottles.[12] The earliest ad by Bloch for flags, later to be a profitable specialty of considerable magnitude, would seem to be the one in anticipation of the Fourth of July in 1858.[13] The jobbing office was now doing well, sufficiently so that Bloch moved in 1856 from 48 E. Third St. to enlarged quarters opposite the post office at 27-29 E. Fourth St. where Bloch announced he could execute large orders with precision and speed. Later in that year, the confident Edward Bloch bought at auction choice portions of the Columbian Job Office's equipment and stock enabling him to do color printing in five languages augmented by a full range of plain and ornamental cuts and borders.[14] With a large and expanding business, Bloch and the *Israelite* office moved again, this time in 1857 to a five-story building at 32 W. Sixth St. to better accomodate newspaper, book, and job printing.[15]

The earliest non-serial Bloch imprint known to this writer is an ephemeral little pamphlet of a mere fourteen pages, *Address Delivered before the Agricultural Society, of Ripley County, Indiana, at their Annual Fair, on the 20th Day of September, 1855* (Cincinnati: Printed by Bloch & Co.), by Stephen S. Harding, a leading abolitionist in Indiana and later to become Governor of Utah Territory and Chief Justice of the Colorado Supreme Court.[16]

Job printing for Jewish organizations resulted in the

12. See representative Bloch ads for printing and binding services, *AI*, Aug. 10, 1855, p. 39, Nov. 7, 1856, p. 142, July 31, 1857, p. 30, Dec. 17, 1858, p. 185, March 2, 1860, p. 278, April 18, 1862, p. 330, and Oct. 10, 1862, p. 110. For *ketubot* (*AI*, Dec. 7, 1855, p. 183); *etrogim* (*AI*, Sept. 25, 1863, p. 98); patriotic envelopes (*AI*, May 10, 1861, p. 354); clothing tickets (*AI*, July 18, 1856, p. 15); orders for coal (*AI*, Oct. 7, 1859, p. 111), and Jewish calendars (*AI*, Sept. 9, 1859, p. 79).

13. *AI*, June 25, 1858, p. 407.

14. *Ibid.*, April 11, 1856, p. 326, April 18, 1856, p. 334, May 23, 1856, p. 375, Nov. 21, 1856, p. 158.

15. *Ibid.*, Nov. 6, 1857, p. 140.

16. Only known copy located at Indiana State Library and not to be found in the Stephen S. Harding papers housed at the Indiana Historical Society.

Constitution and By-laws of the Young Men's Hebrew Literary Association of Davenport and Rock Island (1857) and the *Order of Prayers* printed for Chicago's Kehilat Anshe Mayriv (5618=1857 or 1858), both bearing the Bloch imprint and each known only on the basis of a single extant specimen. The long-recognized and pressing need for textbooks adapted to the needs of American Jewish youth, especially for but not limited to Reform congregations, resulted in the decision to issue Rabbi Emanuel Hecht's *Synopsis of the History of the Israelites* (1857), enlarged by Cincinnati's Rabbi Max Lilienthal. Works by two of Wise's rabbinical collaborators in the Reform movement also came off the press in 1857: Max Lilienthal's book of German verse, *Freiheit, Frühling und Liebe* and Isidor Kalisch's *Guide for Rational Inquiries into the Biblical Writings.* Bloch's relocation and expansion in 1857 may, in part, be explained by his involvement in the new *Minhag Amerika* liturgy project, the publishing cost of which was defrayed by Bloch, its publisher, according to Rabbi Wise. The comments of Isaac M. Wise on the travails of printing this landmark work, the standard American Reform prayerbook until its replacement in the early 1890s by the *Union Prayer Book*, are informative regarding the early years at Bloch & Co.: "The firm ... had but little money and scarcely any typesetters who were able to set Hebrew type. Yet the book appeared in Hebrew, English, and German; but, pray do not ask me how ..."[17] Opposition to Reform Judaism and its progress prompted Isaac Leeser, Wise's nemesis, to print an anonymous attack on Wise signed "Lawyers" in the pages of his *Occident* shortly after the appearance of *Minhag Amerika* in 1857; this anti-Reform rejoinder singled out Bloch & Co. for allegedly keeping its store open on the Jewish Sabbath and

---

17. Wise, *Reminiscences*, p. 345. Wise further indicates that Bloch's continued existence was very much in doubt as of late 1857 (*ibid.*, pp. 346-47). Typographical errors in a Hebrew text printed by Bloch at the Office of the Israelite & Deborah were noted by a forgiving Isaac Leeser, himself the victim of errant printers, in the specimen pages of Isaac Mayer's *Systematical and Practical Hebrew Grammar* (1856); see *Occident and American Jewish Advocate* 14:1 (April 1856): 39.

closing it on Sunday, the Christian Sabbath.[18] Attacks on Wise or Bloch as Sabbath desecrators by angered rivals continued to flare up from time to time, as in the case of the *Chicago Israelite* when it was launched three decades later.

FURTHER GROWTH

Despite suffering the loss of all its southern subscribers and the unpaid accounts owed by creditors throughout the Civil War totalling in the thousands of dollars, the firm endured and expanded.[19] Bloch enlarged its premises in 1867 by taking over the adjoining building at 34 W. Sixth St.; this was a few months after Solomon Friedman came on board as a copartner. Herman Moos, editor of the *Israelite*'s literary section and a former partner, rejoined in 1869. In 1869, the plant, with its nine steam presses and a storefront, moved into a "capacious building" at 150 W. Fourth St. Bloch's expanded operations and ability to print in English, German, and Hebrew were described in the announcement of the move as making the firm one of "largest of its kind in the country."[20] Keen to diversify, Bloch successfully bid on the contract for Cincinnati's municipal printing for the year 1870 and again in 1871; payments for city printing, including printing of the *Annual Reports of the City Departments of the City of Cincinnati*

18. Lawyers (pseud.), "A Rejoinder to 'Dixi' of the *Israelite*." *Occident and American Jewish Advocate* 15:9 (Dec. 1857): 452.

19. For a wealth of data on the *Israelite*'s coast-to-coast circulation, consult Rudolf Glanz, "Where the Jewish Press was Distributed in Pre-Civil War America," *Western States Jewish Historical Quarterly* 5 (1972 / 73): 1-16.

20. *AI*, March 15, 1867, p. 3, "Enlarged–Doubled," *AI*, Aug. 16, 1867, p. 4, "Consolidation, Enlargement and Improvement," *AI*, April 30, 1869, p. 4. For additional biographical material on Moos, later to become a distinguished Cincinnati lawyer, see "Death of Herman M. Moos," *AI*, Feb. 1, 1894, p. 4, William Coyle, ed., *Ohio Authors and Their Books* (Cleveland, 1962), p. 453.

in the 1870/71 fiscal year amounted to $6,853.66.[21]

It may be assumed that with more and more Reform congregations adopting the *Minhag Amerika* liturgy, profits from sales of this prayerbook helped sustain Bloch & Co., also the copyright holder, and covered other deficits. German-language printing, as in the case of *Die Deborah*, and the sale of imported novels, sermons, and orthodox prayerbooks such as the popular Rödelheim editions also brought in needed revenue while carving out a potentially profitable market niche.[22]

The 1870s represented new ventures as well as the beginning of a string of disasters; a list published in 1871 indicates that Bloch was printing or publishing William M. Corry's influential Cincinnati weekly, *The Commoner*, a business-oriented bulletin, *The Collector*, issued by Blanchard & Co., a local collection bureau, the monthly *Physio-Medical Recorder*, and the *Cincinnati Daily Register and Strangers' Guide*.[23] Herman Moos, the editor of the *Literary Eclectic* and the

---

21. Bloch's bids were reported in *AI*, Nov. 5, 1869, p. 7 (includes contracted rates for printing and advertising services), and *AI*, June 30, 1871, p. 10. For records of payments made to Bloch in the "City Auditor's Report," see *Annual Reports of the City Departments of the City of Cincinnati for the Year Ending February 28, 1870* (Cincinnati: Bloch, 1870), p. 73, and similar report for year ending February 28, 1871 (Cincinnati: Bloch, 1871), p. 82. Another surviving municipal imprint from this period is the *Report of the Investigation of the Committees on Law and Light, of the City Council of Cincinnati, on the Price of Gas. November, 1869* (Cincinnati: Bloch, 1869).

22. Bloch's grandson, Edward H. Bloch, told an interviewer that "Income from prayerbooks for both the Orthodox and Reform elements supplied deficiencies incurred from other types of books," in Rosengarten, "A Cultural Centennial," p. 151. For representative Bloch advertisements for liturgies, homiletics, rabbinica, and German Judaica, see *AI*, July 30, 1869, pp. 6-7, April 21, 1871, p. 7, Oct. 4, 1872, p. 12, June 30, 1882, p. 419. Interestingly, a letter to the editor of *The Israelite* in 1868 from one Moses Surgemus echoed a then familiar and characteristic business hallmark when he praised Bloch & Co. for having "published enough books that benefitted Judaism more than their own pockets . . ." (*AI*, March 13, 1868, p. 6).

23. *AI*, Dec. 8, 1871, p. 8.

American Law Record, retained his ties to Bloch by having his periodicals published by the firm. It is not without interest that two German-language Christian serials based in Cincinnati were then being printed by Bloch in 1875, the *Protestantische Zeitblätter* and the *Christliche Jugendfreund*.[24] Jewish interests were not overlooked in the decade of the seventies; Rabbi Max Lilienthal initiated the *Hebrew Sabbath School Visitor*, the first Jewish children's weekly in America, in 1874, so Jewish children would not be compelled to read Christian Sunday school magazines or, generally, be influenced by messages of proselytism.[25] Lodge printing for annual *Proceedings* of the B'nai B'rith (District No. 2) and Order Kesher Shel Barzel (District No. 4) district grand lodges naturally gravitated to the firm, as did substantial printing orders from the Reform movement's Union of American Hebrew Congregations, headquartered in Cincinnati; e.g., its massive *Proceedings*.

On the morning of July 20, 1875, a fire starting in a neighboring lithography firm led to the flooding of Bloch & Co. from water used to extinguish the fire; then, when the fire appeared to be under control, an explosion leveled the entire building with a number of firemen perishing in the collapsing ruins. Damage to Bloch & Co. totalled some $55,000, but insurance covered only $32,000 of Bloch's losses; a lifetime

---

24. *AI*, July 30, 1875, p. 1.
25. See Morton J. Merowitz, "Max Lilienthal (1814-1882)—Jewish Educator in Nineteenth-Century America," *Yivo Annual of Jewish Social Science* 15 (1974), pp. 57-58. The importance of publishing children's books for the American Jewish community was stressed very early in the *Israelite*'s existence by Rabbi Max Lilienthal, "We Want Good Books for Our Jewish Youth," *AI*, Sept. 29, 1854, p. 94. Bloch's pre-publication announcement of the children's weekly with the rationale for its inception is to be found in *AI*, Dec. 26, 1873, p. 6; a glimpse into the weekly's distribution and the positive influence it enjoyed in remote Jewish schoolhouses as far away as Eureka and Reno, Nevada, and Green Valley and Marysville, California, is offered by *AI*, Jan. 31, 1879, p. 5. A glowing review by a French rabbi of the *Hebrew Sabbath-School Visitor* and other recent Bloch publications appeared in the *Archives Israelites* (Paris) and was promptly translated for domestic consumption; see Isaac Levy's review in *AI*, March 26, 1875, p. 5.

accumulation of Isaac M. Wise's personal papers, letters, and book manuscripts perished, as did the entire mailing list for the *American Israelite* and *Die Deborah*.[26] Disaster in the form of $10,000 of water damage struck again in their rented building on Home Street later in the year when a fire broke out in the upper lofts directly above Bloch & Co.; damages, only partly insured, were said to be slight and unimportant.[27]

FLAG MANUFACTURE

The involvement of Edward Bloch in the manufacturing of flags was given prominent attention in 1876 with America's centennial when Bloch opened store outlets in Chicago and Philadelphia for the sale of flags, including those of all foreign nations, coats of arms, banners, and variegated bunting, as well as fancy paper lanterns, globes, and shields, directly from

---

26. "The Fire," *AI*, July 30, 1875, p. 1, also "A Card to the Subscribers . . ." *ibid.*, p. 5. Contemporary R. G. Dun and Co. credit report entries for 1875 and 1876 indicate that the firm indirectly benefited from the fire in that it replaced the old presses with new, improved ones. With a solid reputation for honesty in the community and rated an excellent credit risk, Bloch & Co. (Edward Bloch in partnership with Solomon Friedman) claimed about $50,000 in capital with very few liabilities (*Ohio*, vol. 87, p. 302, R. G. Dun & Co. Collection, Baker Library, Harvard University Graduate School of Business Administration). All contemporary entries in the R. G. Dun & Co. ledgers incorrectly refer to Block (sic) & Co.

27. "Washed Out." *AI*, Dec. 10, 1875, p. 6. On March 1, 1876, Bloch was again permanently re-established in a five-story building at 169 Elm St., per *AI*, March 3, 1876, p. 6, highlighting the presence of flags waving "conspicuously in front of the house, marking distinctly the locality, that none can possibly go amiss." An illustration of Bloch's Elm St. printing plant and store appears in *AI*, June 18, 1880, p. 8. A third disaster struck in March, 1881, reducing the *American Israelite*'s issue of April 1, 1881, to a single explanatory sheet; the headline of the surrogate issue told it all: "No Fire–But Water! . . . Inundated for the Third Time!"

"one of the largest flag manufactories in the world."[28] Although obituaries for Bloch declare that he was the inventor and the first manufacturer of printed flags in the United States, this family tradition is not subject to independent confirmation nor is it known who rightfully can claim to be the inventor of such flags. William E. Alcorn, a Cincinnati manufacturer of awnings, tents, circus canvass, and tarpaulins, was known to be making flags in 1853, but they were most likely produced by sewing judging by his other product lines.[29] In the 1880s, Bloch variously claimed that his was "The Oldest and Largest Flag Manufacturing House, West, South and North" or was "The largest Flag manufacturer in the U. S."[30] Bloch's flag business, along with three unrelated New York firms, subsequently merged into the American Flag Co., based in Troy, New York, in 1893, though Bloch and his son, Charles, successively acted as directors in the new firm, with branches apparently remaining in Cincinnati and Chicago at Bloch's

---

28. Bloch's obituary, *AI*, March 29, 1906, p. 6; for the Chicago and Philadelphia flag depots in 1876, see *AI*, March 3, 1876, p. 6, and more fully, "Flags, Emblems and Patriotic Decorations. A Sketch of the Enterprise of Bloch & Co., Cincinnati and Philadelphia," *ibid.*, May 19, 1876, p. 6, reprinted from the *Philadelphia Commercial and Manufacturers' Gazette.*
29. *Williams' Cincinnati Directory . . . Fourth Annual Issue* (Cincinnati, 1853), p. 112. If not the inventor of flag printing, Edward Bloch may nonetheless be responsible (in 1858?) for the first printed flags west of the Alleghenies; see profile on Charles E. Bloch, *Bloch's Book Bulletin*, no. 19 (Jan. 1932): 4, and "Pioneer Hebrew Publisher," *American Hebrew*, Aug. 18, 1899, p. 447 (copied from the Cincinnati *Enquirer*). A full column ad for Bloch & Co.'s Flag Manufactory geared to the presidential campaign and political conventions in the election year of 1872 makes direct reference to manufacturing flags at his steam printing house for the last eighteen years (*AI*, July 5, 1872, p. 15). Bloch was awarded the contract to furnish flags and banners to the tenth Cincinnati Industrial Exposition in 1882, per *AI*, Aug. 18, 1882, p. 55.
30. Bloch's ad in *American Jews' Annual* 5645 (1884/85), opposite p. 97, and *AI*, July 8, 1887, p. 3.

former locations during the 1890s.[31]

With its issue of July 3, 1874, the *Israelite* was renamed the *American Israelite* and within a few weeks, Bloch's advertising promoted the firm as the "American Hebrew Publishing House." Hebrew books were continually advertised as a specialty and Bloch, as a general agent for school books from all publishers, was attentive to the needs of Jewish sabbath schools for texts. Rabbis were courted with new releases such as Aaron Hahn's *The Rabbinical Dialectics* (1879) or *The American Jewish Pulpit; A Collection of Sermons by the Most Eminent American Rabbis* (1881). The growing market for Jewish music was tapped by Simon Hecht's *Zemirot Yisra'el* (1878). A juvenile series by and large devoid of Jewish themes (among them, *Dominic; or, A Good Action Always Has its Reward* and *The Lost Rifle*) was promoted in 1881 as Hanukkah presents. Manuscripts for novels were solicited in 1878; not less than $500 was being offered for a publishable novel on American Jewish life.[32] With Bloch as its publisher, the

---

31. E. Bloch's obituary, *Publishers' Weekly*, April 14, 1906, p. 1174, American Flag Company's *Catalogue No. 2, 1895* (text kindly provided by Dr. Whitney Smith, Executive Director, Flag Research Center, Winchester, Mass.); entry for Charles Edward Bloch in *Who's Who in American Jewry*, vol. 3 (1938/39), p. 102; obituary of Charles Bloch, *New York Times*, Sept. 13, 1940, p. 17; Stephen S. Wise, "Charles E. Bloch," *American Jewish Year Book* 5702 (1941/42): 382; corporation reference file card for American Flag Company, at New York Dept. of State, Division of Corporations and State Records, Albany, confirming firm's dissolution on Jan. 17, 1956.

32. *AI*, Aug. 7, 1874, p. 7, for first appearance of the "American Hebrew Publishing House" logo; Bloch's ads in *AI*, June 25, 1880, p. 8, and July 30, 1880, p. 40, promoting Hebrew books and school books, respectively; *AI*, July 8, 1887, p. 3, offering thirteen titles in Bloch's juvenile series; *AI*, Aug. 2, 1878, p. 5, seeking submission of a manuscript on American Jewish life. Bloch is mentioned as one of the pioneers in Jewish music publishing by A. W. Binder, "Jewish Music in America–Historical Outline," *Jewish Forum* 38:2 (Feb. 1955): 44. For a representative Bloch ad for temple music and liturgies, see *AI*, Aug. 21, 1885, p. 3; for European imports, *ibid.*, July 7, 1882, p. 3; for American Jewish novels, all of them Bloch imprints, *ibid.*, June 25, 1880, p. 3.

Rabbinical Literary Association of America launched the *Hebrew Review* in 1880. The *Holy Family Manual*, 770 pages in length and undoubtedly the most curious of all Bloch imprints because of its Catholic origin, came off the press in 1883, ordered and paid for by the Sisters of Notre Dame in Cincinnati. Among the most scholarly and enduring Bloch imprints must be counted Moses Mielziner's well-received *The Jewish Law of Marriage and Divorce in Ancient and Modern Times* (1884) and his *Introduction to the Talmud* (1894).[33]

Calendars, *sifre torah*, catechisms, confirmation certificates, New Year's cards, wedding invitations, and imported Hebraica solidified Bloch's reputation as a major publisher and supplier of religious goods to the growing American Jewish community in the mass immigration period; Bloch's reputation for a quality stock and mail order service to congregations everywhere would carry forward into the next century.

For reasons that remain unclear to this day but probably related to problems of cash flow and assignment of interest, Leo Wise, the son of Isaac M. Wise, and Edward Bloch alternated as publishers of the *American Israelite*; the issue of April 27, 1883 was the first one issued by Leo Wise & Co., but Bloch would replace Wise a year later with the issue of April 25, 1884. During this period, Wise also marketed his father's writings, formerly in the inventory of their original publisher, Bloch & Co. Accounts in the Jewish press reveal that Bloch's financial position was highly unsettled; on January 16, 1884, Bloch temporarily defaulted on his creditors; a terse paragraph in the *American Israelite* (Feb. 2, 1884, p. 4) merely stated that payments had been suspended but they resumed

---

33. See extensive worldwide list of reviews of *Jewish Law of Marriage and Divorce* in Ella McKenna Friend Mielziner, *Moses Mielziner, 1828-1903* . . . (New York, 1931), p. 47. One reviewer was especially complimentary of this work by a professor at the Hebrew Union College for having raised the status of Jewish scholarship in America. European rabbis and others who previously judged American scholarship to be "very low and insignificant" would now know that "on the other side of the Atlantic . . . Jewish learning, solid Jewish learning, has found a home." See *Occident* (Chicago), Nov. 7, 1884, p. 4.

in full a week later. The embarrassed firm emerged from this
episode as a stockholding company; creditors were to be paid
"100 cents of every dollar that is due them" over the next two
years.[34] Leo Wise again superseded Bloch as the *American
Israelite*'s publisher on Oct. 12, 1888, and the paper, associated with Bloch & Co. since 1855, never again reverted to Bloch
after that date. The final separation of Leo Wise and Edward
Bloch was never explained (but see note 41); there may have
been a personality conflict with Leo, the *American Israelite*'s
veteran business manager and a copartner, or Edward concluded that Cincinnati's Jewish community was rapidly being
overtaken by faster growing Jewish population centers such as
Chicago which offered better rewards as a homebase for
Jewish newspaper publishing.

NEW VENTURES

Having survived the default and perhaps gambling on a
westward shift in the American Jewish community, Bloch
bought the *Jewish Tribune* of St. Louis; the issue of April 4,
1884, is the first under the reorganized Bloch Publishing &
Printing Company's ownership. This attempt at expansion
was shortlived and the paper suspended publication with the
issue of April 18, 1884, this at least being the date of the last
extant issue.

Charles Edward Bloch (1861-1940) entered the firm in 1878
as a "printer's devil" and quickly mastered the business,
becoming plant superintendent while in his early twenties.
Charles, described as a "clever young journalist and businessman," established, with Leo Wise as editor, the *Chicago
Israelite* in early 1885, and also managed Bloch's flag and

---

34. "Our Cincinnati Letter," *Jewish Tribune* (St. Louis), Jan. 25,
    1884, p. 57; "Cincinnati News," *ibid.*, Feb. 8, 1884, p. 88; R. G.
    Dun/OH 87/p. 395, 499, with details of credit extension and reor-
    ganization as a capital stock company. Assets were estimated at
    $47,000, liabilities at $23,000. Officers are recorded in the R. G.
    Dun report dated March 1, 1884 as Edward Bloch, president;
    George C. Clements, secretary; E. H. Austerlitz, treasurer.

publishing affairs in the new Chicago branch.[35] The *Chicago Israelite* probably reverted to Leo Wise's ownership in 1888 at the same time he assumed control of the *American Israelite*, *Die Deborah*, and the *American Jews' Annual*. Charles Bloch, in partnership with Edward M. Newman, established a rival Jewish organ in Chicago, the *Reform Advocate*, in 1891, solely to disseminate the progressive views of Rabbi Emil G. Hirsch, its editor.[36]

Back in Cincinnati, Edward Bloch plotted new enterprises for the firm during the 1880s. Crayon portraits of England's Sir Moses Montefiore, a philanthropist and folk icon venerated by Jews worldwide and no less so in the United States, were produced in anticipation of the centenarian's birthday in 1884; orders for the portraits came in from as far away as Prague! A lithograph bearing the likeness of the recently deceased Rabbi Max Lilienthal appeared in 1882, while a portrait of Eduard Lasker, a liberal Jewish member of the German *Reichstag*, was marketed as a memorial tribute for home display following his death in 1884.[37] *The American Jews' Annual*, in part a

---

35. *AI*, Aug. 10, 1888, p. 1. Did Bloch's final separation from the *American Israelite* result from irreconcilable differences with Leo Wise? A contemporary source may not have been far off the mark: "Reasons assigned, something like those in a divorce case: incompatibility of temper, etc." See "Western Notes," *American Hebrew*, Oct. 26, 1888, p. 183 (signed "A Young American"). Rabbi Isaac M. Wise withdrew from the partnership with Bloch around 1870, per *AI*, "Seventieth Anniversary Supplement," July 24, 1924, p. 30, but a contemporary source (R. G. Dun/OH 80/p. 241) indicates he sold his interest in July of 1873. Biographical sketches of Leo Wise are to be found in *Menorah Monthly* 15:4 (Oct. 1893): 269, and *American Jewish Year Book* 5665 (1904/05): 207.

36. An overview of Bloch's operations in Chicago is provided by Morris A. Gutstein, *A Priceless Heritage: The Epic Growth of Nineteenth Century Chicago Jewry* (New York, 1953), pp. 387-89. On Edward Newman, later to gain a measure of fame as a world-traveller and lecturer, see Philip P. Bregstone, *Chicago and Its Jews* (Chicago, 1933), pp. 363-65. Representative ads for Bloch's bookstore and printing operations in Chicago appear in *AI*, Aug. 5, 1887, pp. 2, 3.

37. *AI*, Sept. 15, 1882, p. 90, Nov. 16, 1883, p. 3; for orders received from Prague, *ibid.*, Nov. 28, 1884, p. 7; ad for Montefiore and Lasker portraits, *ibid.*, July 31, 1885, p. 9.

literary almanac but also containing historical articles and discussions of current Jewish affairs with a pronounced bias toward equating all Jewish progress with the advancement of Reform Judaism, was an exceedingly attractive and well-designed Bloch venture inaugurated with the volume for 1884/85. The entire inaugural edition for that year, containing a poem by Emma Lazarus, "Maimonides," was quickly exhausted. Commenting on the new release for 5647, one eastern reviewer paid Bloch a faint compliment: "The cover is pretty, and the typography and the advertisements look as though it was a paying concern."[38] Cincinnati's Bloch and New York's Philip Cowen, it may be noted, co-published in 1888 the Jewish Ministers' Association of America's *Jewish Home Prayer Book*; joint ventures between Jewish publishers were conspicuously few and far between at the time. An example of Bloch co-publishing overseas would occur in 1910 with Leon Simon's *Aspects of the Hebrew Genius*, published by Bloch, then in New York, and the famous London firm of G. Routledge & Sons.

The quest by the American Jewish community for inexpensive editions of the Hebrew Scriptures was met by the Union of American Hebrew Congregations when it obtained from Montreal's Rabbi Abraham de Sola, Isaac Leeser's executor, permission to sell the Leeser Bible. Bloch was well-positioned to act as the UAHC's distributor and sole agent; by 1888, his firm obtained the copyright of this popular and frequently reprinted landmark text.[39]

---

38. *AI*, Sept. 26, 1884, p. 4, review by "C. A." in *American Hebrew*, Nov. 26, 1886, p. 35.
39. "A Cheap Bible," *Jewish Messenger* (N.Y.), March 19, 1869, p. 4; "The Cheap Bible," *AI*, Nov. 11, 1873, p. 4 "A Cheap Bible," *ibid.*, July 30, 1875, p. 4. See Bloch's ads for the Leeser Bible in *AI*, July 4, 1884, p. 3, and as "sole agents," *ibid.*, July 8, 1887, p. 3; Lance J. Sussman, "Another Look at Isaac Leeser and the First Jewish Translation of the Bible in the United States," *Modern Judaism* 5 (1985): 180.

ALLEGATIONS OF PIRACY

Two episodes involving the house of Bloch brought the firm momentary bad publicity in the eastern Jewish press in 1888. Angered by non-payment for his translation of Abraham Mapu's *Amnon: Prince and Peasant. A Romantic Idyll of Judea*, then running in the *American Israelite*, Frank Jaffe wrote from London to New York's *American Hebrew*, complaining bitterly and publicly of Bloch's literary theft, its "utter lack of moral rectitude and ... gross dishonesty ..." Not only was Jaffe not paid for his translation of Mapu's *Ahavat Tsiyon*, completed by him only after five years of "strenuous and unceasing toil," but he was never informed by Bloch that it was being serialized in the pages of the *American Israelite* and, to add insult to injury, the uncompensated Mr. Jaffe's name was nowhere in evidence alongside his text. The series, initiated on April 13, 1888, ended abruptly with chapter 25 in the issue of July 20, 1888, just a few days before Jaffe's open letter ran in the *American Hebrew*. No explanation was ever offered to confused readers by Isaac M. Wise as editor or Edward Bloch as publisher for the sudden cancellation of *Amnon: Prince and Peasant*, originally sent to Bloch only to ascertain his willingness to act as the North American distributor.[40] Another allegation of literary piracy surfaced in 1888 when Rebecca G. Jacobs, daughter of Philadelphia's Rev. George Jacobs, charged Bloch with dishonesty for the sake of a "small pecuniary gain" when it reprinted and sold without permission editions of her father's *Catechism for Elementary Instruction in the Hebrew Faith*. As it happens, the book never enjoyed copyright protection but Rebecca Jacobs was not shy about announcing to all the world her outrage over Bloch's

---

40. Frank Jaffe, "Dishonest Journalism," *American Hebrew*, Aug. 3, 1888, p. 200, *idem*, "A Question of Literary Honesty," *Jewish Exponent* (Philadelphia), Aug. 3, 1888, p. 12. See also the unsigned "Journalistic Ethics," *American Hebrew*, Aug. 3, 1888, p. 198, relating the Jaffe episode ("the *Israelite* has been guilty of a wanton, gross and unjustifiable breach of confidence, as well as of breaking the eighth commandment") to long-recognized violations of rights of foreign authors by American publishers in the absence of protection from an international copyright law.

violation of moral principles.[41]

New business came to Bloch with the creation of the Central Conference of American Rabbis, first with printing the CCAR's *Year Book* beginning in 1891, and then with the lucrative contract to distribute the *Union Prayer Book*, the new Reform liturgy supplanting Wise's *Minhag Amerika*. In 1905, the CCAR appointed Bloch & Co. sole agent for its publications, with Bloch receiving 30% of the list price for the *UPB* and *Sermons by American Rabbis*, and 40% of the list price for the *Union Hymnal*.[42] As a Jewish publishing history aside, unauthorized attempts to lift texts from the *Union Prayer Book* soon after its appearance were not unknown, with one infuriated rabbi-editor threatening a lawsuit against a rabbinical colleague.[43]

In 1893, Joseph Bloch, Edward's brother, was manager of the firm's retail store and at this time a durable new logo, "The Jewish Book Concern" was apparently adopted for the first time to enhance the corporate identity. A glowing obituary of Joseph Bloch (he was variously a peddler and a hotelkeeper in Santa Cruz, California, and lived at different times in Mexico, Texas, and San Francisco) is undoubtedly overly lavish when it opines that "it was due to his genius that the Jewish book trade was established in Cincinnati ..."[44]

By 1900, Isaac M. Wise passed away and with Edward

---

41. Rebecca G. Jacobs, "Disregarding Author's Rights," *American Hebrew*, Aug. 17, 1888, p. 20, *idem*, "The Bloch Publishing Company Again Called to Account," *Jewish Exponent* (Philadelphia), Aug. 10, 1888, p. 5. Is it merely a coincidence that the public complaints by Jaffe and Jacobs surfaced in the same month that Leo Wise wrested from Bloch final control of the *American Israelite*?
42. "Report of Recording Secretary," *Year Book of the Central Conference of American Rabbis* 15 (1905): 31-32.
43. Isaac S. Moses to Gustav Gottheil, Oct. 30, 1894, accusing New Haven's Rev. David Levy of pirating from the *Union Prayer Book*, in Richard Gottheil, *The Life of Gustav Gottheil: Memoir of a Priest in Israel* (Williamsport, Penn., 1936), pp. 110-11.
44. Obituary of Joseph Bloch, *AI*, July 4, 1895, p. 6; Wise, *Reminiscences*, p. 26; George J. Fogelson, "A Conversion at Santa Cruz, California, 1877," *Western States Jewish Historical Quarterly* 11 (1978/79): 138, 141; first appearance of ad for "Jewish Book Concern," *AI*, March 2, 1893, p. 2.

Bloch now advancing in years, thoughts were focused on the firm's future. New York, with its Jewish masses, overshadowed Cincinnati and, for that matter, Philadelphia for supremacy as the center of American Jewish life. Charles Bloch, with his father's encouragement, guided the move of Bloch's retail operations to New York in early 1901, and sold off his interest in the *Reform Advocate* to Edward M. Newman as part of the consolidation in New York Clty.[45] Some sort of a physical presence, perhaps the printing facilities, was maintained in Cincinnati since Edward Bloch remained the company's president until his death in 1906, the year of the last entry for Bloch Publishing Co. in *Williams' Cincinnati Directory*.

In writing this history of Bloch & Co. from its founding until the relocation to New York, very little has been gleaned about the personal life of Edward Bloch. The reminiscences by Rabbi Clifton Harby Levy, a rabbinical student at Hebrew Union College (class of 1890), mention that Bloch, as Rabbi Wise's brother-in-law, "was so generous to Rabbi Wise in all of his publishing enterprises as to impoverish himself," largely because Wise, a poor businessman, would pocket remittances for the *American Israelite* and *Die Deborah* without crediting the sender.[46] The slight mention of Edward Bloch and his

45. Bloch's final move to New York and not westward to Chicago is recounted by Edward H. Bloch, grandson of Edward Bloch, in an interview with Isaac Rosengarten, "A Cultural Centennial," p. 151, supplemented by *AI*, Feb. 28, 1901, p. 6, March 21, 1901, p. 7. Cincinnati, New York, and Philadelphia as "competing centers of nascent Jewish culture" are discussed by Sarna, *JPS*, pp. 16-20; Bloch Publishing Company is mentioned here (p. 16) as one of Cincinnati's primary Jewish assets. Cincinnati's Jewish population in 1900 is estimated to be only 16, 000 persons, an increase of just 1,000 over the figure for 1890, per Jonathan Sarna, " 'A Sort of Paradise for the Hebrews': The Lofty Vision of Cincinnati Jews," in Henry D. Shapiro and Jonathan D. Sarna, ed., *Ethnic Diversity and Civic Identity: Patterns of Conflict and Cohesion in Cincinnati since 1820* (Urbana, 1992), p. 157.

46. Clifton Harby Levy, "How Well I Remember," *Liberal Judaism* 18:1 (June 1950): 32. For Wise's confession of sloppiness with money affairs as contributing to the *American Israelite*'s lack of financial success, see *AI*, June 25, 1875, p. 5.

contributions in Leo Wise's *"Israelite* Personalities" penned for the paper's golden anniversary commemorative issue in 1904 was so egregious that an editorialist in the *American Hebrew* (most likely Philip Cowen) paused to reflect, "We miss, however, any reference to Mr. Edward Bloch, who, if we mistake not, was its original publisher, and retained his connection with it for over three decades."[47] As Wise's publisher, the unsung and overshadowed Edward Bloch was praised by one historian of American Jewish journalism for the "loyal, devoted and zealous service he rendered, often at a great sacrifice of time and money ... [he] probably kept the journal alive in its days of storm and stress."[48] The obituary of Edward Bloch appearing in the *American Israelite* hit squarely on the mark and an excerpt from it concludes this study of a Jewish publishing pioneer: "Out of this grew the Jewish publishing house which has put out more Jewish books and publications than all others in the United States combined ... He was a liberal contributor to all Jewish and unsectarian charities, and was a fine exemplar of the best type of citizenship. He was educated, refined, and modest."[49]

---

47. "Editorial Notes," *American Hebrew*, July 15, 1904, p. 223.
48. Albert M. Friedenberg, "Main Currents of American Jewish Journalism," *Reform Advocate*, May 27, 1916, p. 508.
49. Obituary of Edward Bloch, *AI*, March 29, 1906, p. 6; Leo Wise, *"Israelite* Personalities," *AI*, June 30, 1904, jubilee number extra, p. 14.

יעקב קבקוב
JACOB KABAKOFF

פעולתה המו"לית של ההסתדרות העברית
(סקירה ביבליוגרפית)

עוד בראשית דרכה הדגישה ההסתדרות העברית באמריקה את הפעולה למען
הספרות העברית כחלק מתפקידיה. בין המטרות שהתוותה לה ב"תקנות ההסתדרות
העברית באמריקה" (ניו יורק, תרע"ז-תרע"ח) היתה הקמת הוצאת ספרים לגדולים
ולבני הנעורים. היא שאפה אז לייסד קרן של מאה אלף דולר למטרה זו על יסוד
מניות ואף הבטיחה לתמוך בהוצאות ספרים פרטיות על-ידי רכישת ספריהן
והפצתם. שאיפת ההסתדרות העברית נתגשמה בשנת תרע"ח כשהונח היסוד
להוצאת הספרים "קדימה". לחברי ועד ההוצאה נבחרו: ראובן בריינין, ד"ר נחום
סלושץ, שעשה אז באמריקה, י.ז. פרישברג וקלמן וייטמן.

עוד לפני הקמת "קדימה" ראתה ההסתדרות העברית צורך לפתוח בהוצאת
סידרת חוברות לשם תעמולה למען התחיה העברית. בשנת תרע"ז הופיעו שתי
החוברות הראשונות. בחוברת הראשונה נכללו מאמריהם של בן-ציון מוסינזון על
"השפה והתחיה" ושל יצחק בן-צבי על "העברית בארצנו". בשנייה באו הרצאותיהם
של ראובן בריינין על "הספרות העברית ועתידותיה", מתוך נאומו בוועידה העברית
הראשונה שנתקיימה בשנת תרע"ז, ושל אליעזר בן-יהודה על "המבטא בלשון
העברית", שהכילה עיקרי הדברים שהשמיע באותה ועידה.

בשנת תרע"ח המשיכה ההסתדרות בהוצאת סידרת חוברות זו. קלמן וייטמן,
שהיה בין היוזמים לאיגוד האגודות העבריות השונות במסגרת ההסתדרות העברית,
היה מחברה של חוברת בשם "ההסתדרות העברית ושאיפותיה". בחוברת זו הטעים
את צורך השעה בהקמת תנועה עברית מאוחדת והביא את תקנות ההסתדרות שהופיעו קודם
בחוברת מיוחדת. וייטמן כלל גם עמוד של מידע על מטרות הוצאת "קדימה",
שהוחלט על הקמתה בוועידה העברית הראשונה. בשנת תרע"ח יצאו גם החוברות
"עברית ולעזים" לאליעזר בן-יהודה, שדנה בהתפתחות הלשון מימי קדם ועד
לתחייתה, ו"שפתנו" למנחם שיינקין, שכללה את דבריו של עסקן ציוני זה על ערך
הלשון שפורסמו קודם ב"התורן", שנה ה'. באותה שנה הופיעו גם שתי חוברות
תעמולה ביידיש: "דאס אידישע בוך" (על הספר העברי) לחיים נחמן ביאליק,
בתרגומו של ז. קוטלר, ו"וואס איז אידישע ערציהונג" (חינוך יהודי מהו) מאת י.ז.
פרישברג. האחרונה בסידרת חוברות התעמולה יצאה בשנת תרע"ט וכללה את דברי
צבי שרפשטיין על "הבית העברי". חוברת זו נועדה לשמש מעין מדריך למשפחות
שביקשו לבסס את אורח חייהן על יסודות עבריים.

כפי שיוצא מן הרשימה של חוברות התעמולה הסתייעה ההסתדרות באישים
שונים שנמצאו אז בארה"ב ושנתעכבו בה בימי מלחמת העולם הראשונה. אישים
אלה עזרו בידי העברים המקומיים ותרמו בכתב ובעל פה להפצת התרבות העברית
בין שדרות העם. ביחוד מצאו העברים סעד באליעזר בן-יהודה, ששימש להם סמל

ודוגמא. ההסתדרות העברית השתתפה ביחד עם הפדרציה הציונית בחגיגת יובלו
הששים, שחל בשנת תרע״ח. בין השאר הוגש לבן-יהודה ״ספר זכרון״ למלאות לו
ששים שנה, שנערך על-ידי ראובן ברייניין ויצא בהוצאת ההסתדרות העברית. בקובץ
באו מאמרים וזכרונות על בן-יהודה החוקר ומחייה הלשון מאת ארבעה-עשר
סופרים ואישים, מהם יושבי אמריקה ומהם אורחים לשעה.

הוצאת ״קדימה״

מפני ניתוקה של ארה״ב מאירופה בגלל המלחמה הורגש צורך להדפיס מחדש
את כתביהם הנבחרים של טובי הסופרים והמשוררים ולהגישם לקהל הקוראים
ב״ספריה עממית״, שתכיל ספרי כיס בכריכה רכה ובמחיר שווה לכל נפש. את
מטרות הוצאת ״קדימה״ שהוקמה לשם כך סיכם קלמן וייטמן בסוף חוברתו
״ההסתדרות העברית ושאיפותיה״, שנזכרה לעיל. בין השאר נאמר שם:

> הועידה העברית הראשונה, שנקראה על ידי ההסתדרות העברית, החליטה ליסד
> הוצאה, שמטרתה תהיה להפיץ את הספר העברי בין החוגים של יודעי עברית בארץ זו.
> בהסכם להחלטה זו נוסדה הוצאת הספרים ״קדימה״, והיא נגשה לעבודתה הראשונה,
> להוציא ספריה עממית זולה.
>
> הצורך בהוצאה, שתמציא את כל הטוב והמשובח שבספרותנו החדשה והצעירה בצורה
> נאותה ובמחיר זול, היה מורגש זה כבר בשוק הספרות העברית. ומיום שפרצה המלחמה
> גדל הצורך עוד יותר. משלוח הספרים מרוסיה פסק לגמרי וכל הספרים שנמצאו למכירה
> אצל מוכרי הספרים אפסו, ועתה אי-אפשר להשיג כל ספר עברי בארץ זו.
>
> מצב זה המריץ את חברת-ההוצאה ״קדימה״ לגשת תיכף לעבודה. המעשה הראשון
> הוא הוצאת ״הספריה העממית״...
>
> הוצאת הספרים ״קדימה״ הנה חברת מניות מאושרת מטעם הממשלה. מחיר כל מניה
> עשרה דולרים וחובה קדושה מוטלת על חברינו העברים וחובבי השפה עברית לבוא
> לעזרתנו, לקנות ולהפיץ בין מכיריהם את המניות של הוצאת הספרים ״קדימה״ (מוסד
> ההסתדרות העברית באמריקה).

בין הספרים שנמנו בקבוצה הראשונה היו לכתחילה גם ״סיפורים״ לדוד
פרישמן, ״נפש רצוצה״ לש. בן-ציון ו״שירים״ לח״נ ביאליק. אולם מפני הקשיים
בהשגת הסכמתם של סופרים אלה באו שינויים בתכנית. סידרת הספרים בקבוצה
הראשונה, שיצאה בשנת תרע״ח, כללה: יצחק ארטר - ״הצופה לבית ישראל״; פרץ
סמולנסקין - ״נקם ברית״; י.ל. פרץ - ״חסידות״; בוקי בן יגלי - ״ספורים ואגדות״;
ל.א. אורלוף (אריאלי) - ״אללה כרים״, דרמה מחיי הארץ; י.ח. ברנר - ״ספורים״;
י.ל. גורדון - ״פואמות״; מ. וילקנסקי - ״ספורים מחיי הארץ״; ומ.י. לבנזון -
״שירים״. לשבעה ספרים מתוך אלה נלוו הקדמות מאת ראובן ברייניין. במודעות
נאמר שסידרת הספרים כולה תישלח לחותמים בבת אחת במחיר 1.60$ כולל
המשלוח.

העובדה שרוב הספרים בקבוצה הראשונה היו הדפסות חוזרות של ספרים
קלאסיים עוררה ביקורת מצד אלה שדרשו לפרסם יצירות מקוריות וחדשות.
כשהודיעה ״קדימה״ על הקבוצה השנייה של ספריה נכללו בה ספריהם של בן-
יהודה (״עד אימתי דברו אבותינו עברית״); ברייניין (״משמורי התחיה״); י״ד
ברקוביץ (״ספורים״); ד״ר סלושץ (״באיי הים״); מ. שינקין (״ארץ ישראל
וישובה״); מ. ברנשטיין (״מחיי הארץ״); ותרגום ״פאן״ לקנוט האמסון מאת מרדכי
ליפסון. אחר-כך נוסף גם ״עיקר הלאומים״ לישראל זנגוויל בתרגום א״ש אורלנס.
״קדימה״ הודיעה גם על הוצאת כתבי שלום עליכם בחמישה כרכים בתרגומו של

ברקוביץ אבל כתבי הסופר ("חיי אדם" בשלושה כרכים) יצאו בהוצאת שטיבל, שהקימה סניף בניו-יורק ושמינתה את ברקוביץ לעורך.

מתוך רשימת הספרים בקבוצה ב' הושמטו לבסוף ספריהם של שינקין וברייניין ובמקומם נוסף ספרו של בן-ציון מוסינזון בשם "הנביאים". הספרים בסידרה זו הופיעו בכריכה קשה והוצעו לחברים בתשלום דמי מנוי של שלושה דולר. כפי שנמסר ב"התורן" נתמנה א"ש אורלנס כמנהל "קדימה". כשנוסד סניף הוצאת שטיבל, שפיתחה תכנית רחבה של תרגומים וספרי מקור, עבר אורלנס לשמש מנהל הוצאה זו.

גלגולים שונים עברו על הוצאת "קדימה". מלכתחילה נוסדה על-ידי ההסתדרות העברית. אחר-כך היתה לאגודה של מניות ומאוחר יותר לאגודה של חברים שנתיים. לבסוף היתה שוב מוסד של ההסתדרות. היא הצליחה במשך ימי קיומה להפיץ רבבות עותקים של ספרֶיה ועל-ידי כך למלא במקצת את החלל שנוצר בשדה הספר העברי בארה"ב בזמן המלחמה.

שנות העשרים

תחילת שנות העשרים היו שנות התעוררות לעבודה העברית באמריקה ונוסד אז "הדואר" היומי. כשנפטר דוד פרישמן הוספד מעל העתון על-ידי טובי הסופרים העברים. ההסתדרות העברית כינסה את הדברים בקובץ שנקרא "קומֵץ-עלים על קבר דוד פרישמאן (תרכ"ב-תרפ"ב)", בעריכת י"ט הלמן ומנחם ריבולוב. במנהג זה של הקדשת קבצים לסופרים נפטרים נהגה ההסתדרות העברית גם בשנים הבאות. בשנת תרצ"ד הופיע "ספר זכרון לב. נ. סילקינר". בשנת תש"א יצא "ספר זכרון לח. א. פרידלאנד" ובשנת תש"ו הופיע "ספר אברהם גולדברג", שכלל קובץ מאמריו בנוסף לדברי הערכה על חייו ופעלו.

עם חברי ועד הפועל של ההסתדרות העברית נמנו כמה וכמה מחנכים שדרשו שהארגון יטפל באופן סדיר בחינוך העברי. בשנת תר"ף נפתח על-ידי ההסתדרות משרד לחינוך ואחת מפעולותיו היתה הוצאת ירחון לחינוך ולהוראה בשם "תרבות". הירחון, שארבע חוברות ממנו הופיעו בחדשי חשון-שבט תר"ף, נערך על-ידי צבי שרפשטיין, ששימש גם מזכיר המשרד. בראש גליון א' של העתון באו דברי ברייניין תחת הכותרת "תרבותנו" כדלקמן: "הירחון שלנו, של ההסתדרות העברית, נוסד להיות לעזר לכל אלה העוסקים בעבודת החנוך העברי, שהוא לכל הדעות היסוד והבסיס של התרבות העברית".

עם הפסקת "הדואר" היומי והפיכתו לשבועון קיבלה עליה ההסתדרות העברית את האחריות למימון הוצאתו. במשך השנים הבאות הושקע רוב מרצה במשימה זו. לאחר פרישתו של מרדכי ליפסון מן העריכה המשיך מנחם ריבולוב לערוך את העתון כשבועון. הוא התמסר בלב ונפש למשימה זו וברבות הימים שימש הכוח המניע בהקמת מפעלים ספרותיים שונים ליד ההסתדרות.

נסיון צנוע להמשיך בהוצאה לאור היתה החוברת "ערבה" מאת המספר שמואל ליב בלאנק, שהופיעה בצירוף הקדמה של מנחם ריבולוב. סיפורו של בלאנק, שנדפס קודם בהמשכים ב"הדואר", נועד להיות הפרסום הראשון ב"ספרית אחיספר" של ההסתדרות. בין פעולות הארגון שנמנו בסוף החוברת היתה גם הוצאת ספרים. שם גם נתפרסמה מטעם ההסתדרות העברית ההודעה הבאה:

מתוך חפץ וכוונה ליסד הוצאת-ספרים באמריקה אנו מוציאים את הספור הזה.
מרגישים אנו בצורך הגדול שיש במוסד כזה לטובת הספרות העברית באמריקה - ונשתדל
למלא את החסר. הגדולות לא הצליחו - נתחיל מן הקטנות.

בדעתנו להוציא מזמן לזמן, עם כל יכולת שתנתן לנו, ספרים, קבצים וקונטרסים בכל
המקצועות - שירים, ספורים, בקורת ומדע - מיצירות סופרינו אשר פה.
תשמש "ערבה" התחלה.

בשנת תרפ"ו ערך ביאליק ביקור באמריקה ובהזדמנות זו הוציאה ההסתדרות
חוברת בשם "חיים נחמן ביאליק: תולדות ימי חייו לבני-הנעורים" מאת א.ר. מלאכי.
בשתי הזדמנויות אחרות שיתפה ההסתדרות העברית פעולה עם ועד החינוך היהודי
בניו-יורק בהוצאת חוברות לתלמידים על משוררים. בשנת תש"ד יצאה לכבוד
החודש העברי "חוברת לתלמידים לזכר שאול טשרניחובסקי". לקראת ביקורו של
ש. שלום בארה"ב יצאה "חוברת לתלמידים לכבוד ש. שלום", בעריכת חיים ליף
ויעקב קבקוב. חוברת אנגלית על המשורר, באותה הוצאה, נערכה על-ידי גבריאל
פרייל ויעקב קבקוב.

מנחם ריבולוב ראה תמיד בעתונות משום מנוף לפעולה ספרותית רחבה יותר,
שהתבטאה בהוצאת מאספים וספרים שבהם רוכז פרי-עטם של סופרי אמריקה.
למלאת חמש שנים לקיום "הדואר" בשנת תרפ"ז ערך ריבולוב את "ספר היובל של
הדואר", ובו כינס את מאמריהם ודברי היצירה של המשתתפים בעתון. בפתח הספר
עמד על הצורך בהוצאת ספר שנה והטעים כי "ספר היובל" בא למלא במקצת את
המחסור. הוא הדגיש את תפקידיה המיוחדים של הספרות העברית באמריקה
והצביע על כך שבקובץ הוקדש מקום נכבד למאמרים ורשימות על סופרי אמריקה.
ריבולוב המשיך במסורת של הוצאת גליונות וספרי יובל לציון תאריכים חשובים
בתולדות העתון. בעלי ערך מיוחד הם ספרי היובל של "הדואר" שיצאו למלאות לו
שלושים שנה (תשי"ב) ושלושים-וחמש שנה (תשי"ז).

הספר הראשון שיצא בהוצאת "עוגן" לאחר היווסדה על-ידי ההסתדרות
העברית, היה "ספר המסות" של ריבולוב, שבו כינס בשנת תרפ"ח את מאמרי
הביקורת הראשונים שלו. באותה שנה הופיע גם ספרו של צבי שרפשטיין בשם
"החינוך בארץ-ישראל", שהיה לו המשך בשנות הארבעים בשלושת כרכי "תולדות
החינוך בישראל בדורות האחרונים" (תש"ה; תש"ז; תש"ט). בשנת תרפ"ט פתחה
הוצאת "עוגן" בהוצאת כתבי אב. גולדברג ופירסמה תחילה את כרך ב', שהכיל
מסות על "ספרות ואמנות". שנה לאחר מכן יצאו גם כרך א' ("לקראת תקופה",
מסות ומאמרים) וכרך ג' ("שריגים", שירים ציורים, שרטוטים ופיליטונים). באותה
שנה הופיעה גם מסתו של גולדברג "לקראת אפקים חדשים" (לשינוי הכיוון
בציונות), שנדפסה בירושלים.

שנות השלושים

בשנות השלושים הגבירה ההסתדרות את פעולתה המו"לית וביצעה תכנית
שהיתה עד אז רק בבחינת משאלה בלבד - הוצאת "ספר השנה ליהודי אמריקה".
כרך א' של "ספר השנה" יצא בשנת תרצ"א בעריכת מנחם ריבולוב וצבי שרפשטיין.
במירווח-זמן של שנים אחדות הופיעו במשך שנות השלושים כרך ב' (תרצ"ה,
בעריכת ריבולוב וד"ר שמעון ברנשטיין), כרך ג' (תרצ"ח) וכרך ד' (תרצ"ט), שניהם
בעריכת ריבולוב. הוא ערך גם את חמשת ספרי השנה הנוספים שהמשיכו לצאת
בשנות הארבעים. כרכים אלה הכילו מיגוון עשיר של חומר ספרותי שהקיף מדורים

שונים, כולל ספרות יפה, מסה ומחקר ומאמרים וסקירות על בית ישראל מאמריקה.
ספרי השנה כולם שיקפו בנאמנות את מיטב היצירה הספרותית העברית באמריקה.

הוצאת "עוגן" התחילה משמשת בשנות השלושים המכשיר העיקרי לכינוס
פרי-עטם של סופרי אמריקה ולפירסומו ופעולתה התרחבה והלכה גם בעשור הבא.
לעיתים שיתפה פעולה עם הוצאות ספרים בארץ שקיבלו עליהם להוציא את כתביהם
של סופרי אמריקה. בעלת חשיבות ראשונה במעלה היתה הוצאת ה"אנתולוגיה של
השירה העברית באמריקה" בשנת תרצ"ח, בעריכת ריבולוב. אנתולוגיה זו, שכללה
מבוא רחב בצירוף תולדותיהם ותמונותיהם של המשוררים, הראתה בעליל שעיקר
תרומתה של הספרות העברית באמריקה בא לידי גילוי בשירה, שהיתה עשירה לא
רק במוטיבים כלליים אלא היתה בעלת ייחוד אמריקני משלה.

את ספרי "עוגן" בשנות השלושים ניתן לחלק לפי מקצועות שונים. המספר
הגדול היותר היה היה של ספרי שירה. אלה כוללו: ברוך כצנלסון - "לאור הנר" (תר"ץ);
א.א. ליסיצקי - "נפתולי אלהים" (תרצ"ד) ו"מדורות דועכות" (תרצ"ז); אברהם
סולודאר - "שירים" (תרצ"ט); וח.א. פרידלנד - "סוניטות" (תרצ"ט). עם ספרי
הפרוזה והביקורת נמנו: י.ז. פרישברג - "עם הדור" (תרצ"ב), קובץ מאמרים;
אברהם אפשטיין - "סופרים" (תרצ"ה), דברי מסה וביקורת; דניאל פרסקי - "לאלף
ידידים" (תרצ"ה), קובץ רשימות; מנחם ריבולוב - "סופרים ואישים" (תרצ"ו); א.ר.
מלאכי - "מסות ורשימות" (תרצ"ז); וח.א. פרידלנר - "סיפורים" (תרצ"ט). רבים מן
הספרים הנזכרים מהווים כינוס ראשון לפרי-עטם של סופרי הקבוצה האמריקנית
ובפעם הראשונה אפשר היה לעמוד על ייחודם הספרותי.

לבסוף יש להזכיר את שני המחזות לחנוכה מאת א.נ. פרלברג, שיצאו בשנת
תרצ"ב על-ידי הוצאת "נוער" שליד ההסתדרות העברית – "העוורת", שנדפס
בניקוד, ו"המנצחים", שנועד לנוער המבוגר. כדי להמציא לילדי ישראל באמריקה
חומר קריאה קל באופן סדיר פתחה ההסתדרות בשנת תרצ"ה בהוצאת "הדואר
לנוער", שהתמיד בהופעתו כמוסף של "הדואר" במשך עשרים-ושש שנה.

שנות הארבעים

בדין-וחשבון על פעולות ההסתדרות העברית שפורסם בכרך ו' של "ספר השנה
ליהודי אמריקה" לשנת תש"ג, נאמר שהארגון עיבד תכנית להוצאת שלושים ספרים
של כתבי ספורי אמריקה. בכך הוטעמה שאיפתה של ההסתדרות להפנות תשומת-לב
להישגי בני הקבוצה האמריקנית שעמדו על רמה ספרותית ראויה לשמה.

בשנות השלושים הודגשה ביחוד הספרות היפה והפעם ניתן היתרון לסיפורת על
השירה. עם המספרים שספריהם יצאו אז נמנו: ש. ל. בלנק - "אי הדמעות" (תש"א)
ו"ביד הגורל" (תש"ד); יוחנן טברסקי - "אחד העם" (תש"א); צבי סקלר - "הקשת
בענן" (תש"ח); ודב אייזיקס - "בין שני עולמות" (תש"ט). "עוגן" כלל בתכניתו גם
את מקצוע הדרמה והוציא את "ספר המחזות" (תש"ד) לסקלר ושני תרגומים
למחזות שקספיר: "הסערה" (תש"א) על-ידי ליסיצקי ו"המלט" (תש"ד) על-ידי
אפרת.

עם ספרי השירה שיצאו בשנות הארבעים נמנו: ח.א. פרידלנד - "שירים"
(ת"ש); "שירי יהודה הלוי" (תש"ה), הוצאה לעם בעריכת שמעון ברנשטיין; ישראל
אפרת - "אנחנו הדור" (תשי"ז); א.א. ליסיצקי - "אדם על אדמות" (תש"ז); ויצחק
זילברשלג - "עלה, עולם, בשיר!" (תשכ"ז). בשנת תש"ח עלתה בידי ההסתדרות

לבצע תכנית ספרותית חשובה שהיתה קשורה בביאליק והיא הוצאת מבחר שיריו
של המשורר בתרגום אנגלי. התכנית נתגשמה עם הופעת הכרך הראשון של
Selected Poems of Hayyim Nahman Bialik בעריכת ישראל אפרת ובצירוף
דברי מבוא ממנו. הספר זכה לתפוצה רבה ויצא במהדורה שנייה בשנת 1965.

בתחילת שנות הארבעים מילא ד"ר שמעון גינצבורג תפקיד נכבד במו"לות
העברית באמריקה. היו לו זכויות מרובות כאדם שתרם רבות לספרות ולתרבות
העברית כאן. הוא עלה לארץ בשנת תרצ"ג אבל כעבור חמש שנים חזר לאמריקה
בשליחות תרבותית על מנת לייסד את "קרן התרבות העברית בארץ-ישראל", שחלק
עיקרי בתכניתה היה הקמת הוצאת ספרים. בשיתוף עם ההסתדרות העברית הוקמה
הוצאת "ספרים" שהוציאה שבעה ספרים משנת תש"ב ואילך. בין הספרים היו שניים
מפרי-עטם של סופרי אמריקה, "זהב" (תש"ב), שיר אפי על בהלת הזהב באמריקה
מאת אפרת ו"מסתרי העבר" (תש"ג), קובץ מחקרים מאת שמואל י. פייגין. שאר
הספרים היו: "תחת שמי סרביה" (תש"ב) ו"ארצה" (תש"ו), שכללו סיפורים של
שלמה הלל'ס, ו"מסורת ומהפכה" (תש"ב) לאפרים שמואלי, "יחידים ברשות הרבים
(תש"ג) לצבי ויסלבסקי ו"כתבי בקורת היסטוריים" (תש"ד) לאהרן קמינקא. פעולת
ההוצאה נפסקה עם פטירתו של ד"ר גינצבורג בניו-יורק בשנת תש"ו.

מפעל מרכזי שבוצע בשנת תש"ב בעריכת שמואל ניגר ומנחם ריבולוב היה
הוצאת "אחיספר", מאסף לדברי ספרות, חקר הלשוננות בישראל ותרגומים מן
השירה היידית. המאסף יצא אמנם על-ידי "קרן לואיס למד לספרותנו בעברית
ובאידית" אבל ההסתדרות העברית היא שעסקה בהפצתו. כפי שהוצהר בפתח הספר
כל ההכנסה היתה מוקדשת למפעלי הספרות של ההסתדרות. בספר באו מדורים
שהוקדשו למסות ומחקרים, לסקירות על ספרותנו באמריקה בין שתי מלחמות עולם,
לסיפורים ולשירים. עיקר תעודתו של המאסף היה לחקור את הקשר את חזיון דו-הלשוניות
בתולדות ישראל ובספרותו, להעמיד את הקורא על מצבה והישגיה של ספרותנו
בשתי הלשונות באמריקה, ולהביא תרגומים לדברי-מופת מן השירה היידית הישנה
והחדשה.

בין ספרי המסה והביקורת שהוציא "עוגן" בשנות הארבעים היו אלה: "צללי
דורות" (ת"ש) מאת א.ר. מלאכי; "כתבים ומגילות" (תש"ב) מאת ריבולוב; "המוסר
והמשפט בישראל" (תש"ד) מאת שמעון פדרבוש; "עם, עולם וארץ" (תש"ו) מאת
שלמה גולדמן בתרגומו של שמעון הלקין; ו"עבר וערב" (תש"ו) מאת אברהם שלום
יהודה.

יש לציין שההסתדרות נהגה גם לסייע בידי סופרים שהוציאו את כתביהם
בהוצאות שונות. עם הסופרים שקיבלו סיוע נמנו: מ.ח. מייזלש - "מחשבה ואמת";
צבי שרפשטיין - "דרכי לימוד לשוננו" ו"החדר בחיי עמנו"; אברהם רגלסון -
"מלוא הטלית עלים" ו"שם הבדולח"; י.י. ואהל - "בשתי רשויות"; ש. גינצבורג -
"במסכת הספרות", אברהם וייס ולוי גינצבורג, עורכים - "קובץ מדעי לזכר משה
שור"; וניסן טורוב - "הערכות". בזמנים שונים תמכה ההסתדרות בהוצאת עתונים
פדגוגיים, כגון "החינוך העברי" (תרצ"ח-תרצ"ט) ו"שבילי החינוך" (תש"ב).

ההסתדרות לא הסיחה דעתה מבעיית פירסום ספרות לילדים. לאחר הכנות
מרובות יצא בסיוע ועד החינוך היהודי היהודי ספר המקרא "חגינו ומועדינו" (תש"ה),
בעריכת זאב חומסקי. שנתיים לאחר מכן שיתפה ההסתדרות פעולה עם ועד היובל
של זלמן שניאור בהוצאת קובץ שירי הילדים "לילדי ישראל". בסוף שנות הארבעים
פעל על יד ההסתדרות ועד להוצאת ספרי ילדים בשיתוף עם המוסדות החינוכיים

החשובים. הוועד יזם הקמת הוצאה נסיונית בשם "עוגן לילדים", שהוציאה שני
סיפורים מנוקדים לדור הצעיר: "אם השומרים" (תש"ח), סיפור על ראשוני
השומרים בארץ מאת עליזה חומסקי ו"חברים" (תשי"י), סיפור על-פי משה
סמילנסקי מאת בנימין ז. קמחי (זאב חומסקי). שתי החוברות הופיעו בצירוף תרגומי
המילים הקשות לאנגלית בשולי העמודים. לבסוף יש להזכיר גם את תרומת
"הדואר" להספקת חומר קריאה לדור הצעיר בהקמת ה"מוסף לקורא הצעיר".
המוסף, שהתחיל מופיע בשנת תש"ה, נערך על-ידי חיים ליף במשך תקופה של
ארבע-עשרה שנה.

שנות החמישים

בעשור זה עלה מספר ספרי המסה והמחקר על אלה שבספרות יפה. ריבולוב היה
מחברם של שני ספרי ביקורת - "עם הכד אל המבוע" (תשי"י) ו"מעולם לעולם"
(תשט"ו), שיצא שנה לאחר פטירתו. מותו של ריבולוב היתה מכה קשה לפעולה
המו"לית של ההסתדרות. בערוב ימיו הגה את הרעיון של הוצאת רבעון ספרותי
מדעי בשם "מבוע". הרבעון התחיל יוצא בשנת תשי"ג על-ידי חברת "הדואר",
בהשתתפות ההסתדרות העברית והברית העברית העולמית, ובו השתתפו גם סופרים
ממדינת ישראל. בפתח-דבר שכתב ל"מבוע" הביע ריבולוב את התקווה שהרבעון
יועיל "לבנות את בית ספרותנו פה על יסודות קבועים ומתמידים". אולם רק ארבעה
גליונות יצאו והגליון הרביעי (תשי"ד) כבר הכיל דברי הספד על מות העורך. ספרי
המסה והמחקר שיצאו בשנות החמישים כללו: מהדורה חדשה של "כתבים נבחרים"
(תשי"י) מאת מאיר וכסמן וקובץ מסות שלו בשם "גלות וגאולה בספרות ישראל"
(תשי"ב) ; "קטנות עם גדולות" (תשי"ד), קונטרס בעניני חינוך מאת צבי שרפשטיין
ליובלו השבעים ; "חיי היהודים באיטליה בתקופת הריניסאנס" (תשט"ו) מאת משה
א. שולוואס ; "קורות בתי-התפילה בישראל" (תשט"ו) מאת שמואל קרויס ; "רוחות
נפגשות" (תשי"ח), דברי ביקורת מאת הלל בבלי ; ו"בעקבי הדור" (תשי"ז),
רשימות, מסות וזכרונות מאת יעקב צוזמר.
בשדה הספרות היפה הופיעו: קובץ שהכיל שירים שנכתבו בגיטו על-ידי עקיבא
אגוזי בשם "אורות מאופל" (הוצאת ההסתדרות העברית בסט. לואיס, תשי"ב) ;
קובץ פואימות מאת ליסיצקי בשם "נגהות בערפל" (תשי"ז) ; וספר שירים של מ.ש.
בן-מאיר בשם "צליל וצל" (תשי"ח). בסיפורת יצאו קובץ סיפוריו של יעקב
טארקוב-נעמני בשם "רסיסי חיים" (תשי"ב) והרומאן "נחלת צבי" (תשי"ז) מאת
בנימין רסלר. לאחר פטירתו של טארקוב-נעמני הופיע גם "מבחר סיפורים"
(תשל"ה) שלו. "עוגן" גם הוציא מחזה היסטורי של יעקב כהן בשם "רבי מאיר
וברוריה" (תשי"א).
בשנות החמישים הורגש הצורך להנציח את תרומות יהדות אירופה שנספתה
בשואה והוקם ועד בשם "מורשה" להוצאת קבצים מיוחדים לשם כך. מפעל זה,
שבראשו עמדו ד"ר שמעון פדרבוש והרב שמואל ק. מירסקי, היה לו המשך גם
בעשור הבא. שני קבצים גדולים הוקדשו לתרומותיהם של מוסדות החינוך והתורה
השונים לסוגיהם. הקובץ "מוסדות תורה באירופה בבנינם ובחורבנם" (תשט"ז),
בעריכת הרב מירסקי, כלל את תולדות שלושים-ואחת מוסדות תורה מן המפורסמים
והחשובים ביותר באירופה. רוב המאמרים בשני הקבצים נכתבו על-ידי אנשים
שהכירו את המוסדות מקרוב ומובא בהם חומר היסטורי רב ערך. הקובץ "החינוך
והתרבות העברית בין שתי מלחמות העולם" (תשי"ז) נערך על-ידי שרפשטיין.

סידרה של שלושה ספרים, שיצאה בהשתתפותם של חוקרים שונים, הוקדשה
לחכמת ישראל. הסידרה כללה: "אישים ודמויות בחכמת ישראל באירופה
המזרחית" (תשי"ט), בעריכת הרב מירסקי; "חכמת ישראל במערב אירופה"
(תשי"ט) ו"חכמת ישראל באירופה" (תשכ"ח), בעריכת ד"ר פדרבוש.

בד בבד עם הפעולה למען הנצחת יהדות אירופה טיפחה ההסתדרות העברית גם
את העבודה המדעית בין מלומדי אמריקה. ביזמת הרב מירסקי נוסדה האקדמיה
העברית שליד ההסתדרות בשנת תשי"ד. האקדמיה ערכה כינוסים שונים שבהם
הושמעו הרצאות מדעיות בעברית וייסדה את הבמה המדעית "פרקים", שארבעה
כרכים ממנה יצאו בעריכת הרב מירסקי החל בשנת תשט"ז. השנתון "פרקים" הלך
ונתרחב מכרך לכרך וקבצים נוספים הופיעו בשנות הששים (תש"ך, תשכ"ג
ותשכ"ו).

פרשה בפני עצמה הייתה פעולתה של ההסתדרות העברית בשנות החמישים וכן
בעשורים הבאים בהוצאת ספרות ילדים בצורת חוברות. לרוב היו אלה חוברות
שיצאו לרגל מפעל "החודש העברי" במסגרת "ספרייה לילד" וחולקו בין תלמידי
בתי-הספר בקשר עם המפעל. כמה מן החוברות יצאו בשתי מהדורות, אחת לכיתות
הגבוהות ואחת לכיתות הנמוכות, וכמה מהן גם תורגמו אנגלית. רוב החוברות
נתחברו על-ידי אלחנן אינדלמן ובין המחברים האחרים היו ירחמיאל וויינגרטן, משה
פלאי ורחל וכסלר. החוברות כולן נכתבו בעברית קלה ובניקוד בצירוף ביאורי
המלים הקשות, והיו מאויירות בציורים וצילומים. חוברות מיוחדות הוקדשו
לאישים, בהם הרמב"ם, רש"י, הרב קוק, ישראל בעל שם טוב, הרצל, ביאליק, בן-
יהודה, שלום עליכם, לואי ד. ברנדייס, צבי שפירא, ש.ז. שזר וגולדה מאיר. חוברות
אחרות הוקדשו לנושאים מרכזיים כ"מדינת ישראל בת-עשר", "מדינת ישראל בת
כ"ה", "עברית בעולם החדש", "היסוד העברי בתרבות אמריקה", "העיירה",
ו"גיבורי הגיטו". אינדלמן גם תירגם מאנגלית את הסיפור "הסוד" (תשי"א) מאת
מירים. בתוך החומר החינוכי שהוגש לתלמידים היו גם מילוני כיס מצויירים לפי
נושאים ("המילון שלי") בעריכת דניאל פרסקי. בשנת תשכ"ו יצאה מהדורה שלישית
מתוקנת של מילון זה. הופיעו גם חוברות מצויירות בשם "השירון שלי" ו"ישראל
בתמונות".

בסוף שנות החמישים הוציא "עוגן" קטלוג מיוחד בשם "ספרייה עברית-
אמריקאית" (תשי"ט), שבו הכריזה על רשימה של ארבעים-ותשעה ספרים בחכמת
ישראל, ספרות יפה וספרות ילדים שיצאו בשנים האחרונות. בדברי ההקדמה אל
הקורא העברי נאמר: "ספרים אלה פרי יצירתם של סופרי ישראל וחכמיו בארץ זו,
ברכה רבה בהם - ברכת עונג ודעת - לכל קורא עברי, ותפארת הם לכל בית עברי".

שנות הששים ואילך

בעשור זה בא המשך למפעל "מורשה" להנצחת יהדות אירופה והופיעו על ידו
שלושה ספרים. אלחנן אינדלמן ערך את האנתולוגיה "אודים" בשני חלקים,
שהציב יד ושם לסופרי פולין, בכרך א' (תש"ך) ניתן לקט של שירים וסיפורת מאת
סופרים שניספו בשואה. בכרך ב' (תשכ"ה) בה אוסף של מסות, מחקרים, מאמרים
ורשימות של הסופרים. הספר השלישי שיצא על-ידי "מורשה" נקרא בשם "יצחק
שיפר" (תשכ"ז) וכלל כתבים נבחרים ודברי הערכה על חוקר ומלומד זה בעריכת
שלמה אידלברג.

בשנות הששים הופיעו ארבעה ספרי שירה וחמישה ספרי סיפורת. בשירה היו

מיוצגים ליסיצקי - "בימי שואה ומשואה" (תש"ך) , ח.א. פרידלנד - "שירי עם"
(תשכ"ג), ושני משוררים צעירים, אברהם בנד - "הראי בוער באש" (תשכ"ג) ויפה
אליאך - "אשת הדיג" (תשכ"ה). בסיפורת ראו אור קובצי הסיפורים הבאים: "חוטר
מגזע" (תש"ך) מאת ב. אייזיקס; "נרות דועכים" (תשכ"ו) מאת שמחה רובינשטיין;
"אנשים פשוטים בצוק העתים" (תש"ל) מאת יהודה פילטש; ושני רומנים
היסטוריים מאת ה. סקלר - "וסיפור הכוכבים" (תשכ"א) ו"הלולא במירון" (תשכ"ג).
ירידה נראתה במספר ספרי מסה ומחקר. בין אלה היו: קובץ מחקרים היסטוריים
בשם "בצבת הדורות" (תש"ך) מאת מ.א. שולוואס; "תולדות הספרות העברית
באמריקה" מאת יעקב ק. מיקליישנסקי; ו"נפילים במערב", על ראשיתה של
קליפורניה ועל החלוצים היהודים במערב, מאת ישראל ט. נעמני.

כפי שצויין לעיל המשיך מפעל "החודש העברי" להוציא חומר קריאה לילדים
והוברות שונות יצאו עד שנת תש"ב. לאחר הפסקה ארוכה יצאה החוברת "שלום"
(תש"ם) מאת משה פלאי, שהמשיכה במסורת המפעל. בשנת תשכ"ג פתחה
ההסתדרות בהוצאת הירחון המנוקד "למשפחה", שהיה מעין המשך ל"מוסף לקורא
הצעיר", שיצא קודם. הירחון התמיד לצאת בעריכת עורכים שונים ומופיע בקביעות.

בשנות השבעים חל צמצום בפעולה המו"לית של ההסתדרות. הופיעו רק שני
ספרים: "יהדות אמריקה במבחן" (תשל"ו), קובץ מסות ומאמרים מאת ישראל
הרבורג, ו"ילקוט מאמרים ורשימות" (תשל"ט) מאת יהודה פילטש.

לכבוד יובל השישים של שבועונה הוציאה ההסתדרות העברית אנתולוגיה בשם
"ספר הדואר" (תשמ"ב), שכלה מבחר מאמרים שהופיעו על דפיו מאז התחיל יוצא
כשבועון בשנת תרפ"ב. האנתולוגיה נערכה על-ידי יעקב ק. מיקליישנסקי ויעקב
קבקוב ויצאה בצורה אלבומית. החומר שנאסף בו חולק לפי מדורים אלה: בית
ישראל באמריקה, מחזון לתקומה, יהדות התפוצות, עיון והגות, מסה ומחקר
ובחינות והערכות. בראש האנתולוגיה בא פתח-דבר שסקר את תולדות העתון
והתפתחותו.

גלגולים שונים עברו על הוצאות הספרים של ההסתדרות וביחוד על "עוגן".
בזמן שגשוגה של הספרות העברית כאן נענתה ההסתדרות לצו השעה ומילאה
תפקיד מרכזי בעידוד כוחות ספרותיים לשם יצירת מרכז ליצירה העברית. היא
עשתה זאת לא רק על-ידי הוצאת עתונים והקמת במות ספרותיות שונות כ"ספר
השנה ליהודי אמריקה" אלא גם על-ידי הספקת מלאי ספרותי במקצועות ספרות
שונים. במשך הזמן התרכזה ההסתדרות יותר בהוצאת עתונות וצמצמה את פעולתה
המו"לית. סיבות שונות גרמו לכך. הדרישה לקיום הוצאת-ספרים פחתה והלכה עם
הירידה במספר הסופרים העברים. ברכות הימים קמו גם הוצאות וסוכניות אחרות
שעל ידיהן יכלו סופרי אמריקה הפעילים לפרסם את פרי עטם. והעיקר - מדינת
ישראל הפכה תלפיות בכל מה שנוגע למו"לות העברית וסופרים לא מעטים מצאו
הזדמנות להוציא את ספריהם בארץ.

טיפוח היצירה והמו"לות העברית היה תמיד לחם-חוקה של התנועה העברית.
יש לקוות שהההסתדרות העברית לא תוותר על תפקידה בשטח זה וכשם שמצאה
דרכים בעבר תמצא דרכים גם בעתיד להביא לפני הקהל הרחב ובני הנעורים ממיטב
הספרות העברית.

אבנר הולצמן
AVNER HOLTZMAN

על שני חוקרי ספרות מובהקים*

אם הפרופסור שמואל ורסס מייצג ברצף הדוברים כאן את דור המורים של גרשון שקד ודן מירון, וא"ב יהושע מייצג את בני דורם שנכנסו אל החיים הספרותיים בשנות החמישים ושינו את פני הספרות ואת פני הביקורת, הרי בחלקי שלי נפלה הזכות להשלים את המעגל ולומר כמה דברי הוקרה בשמם של בני הדורות הצעירים יותר של לומדי הספרות, מוריה וחוקריה, אלה שעמידתם מול שני חתני הפרס היא עמידת תלמידים בפני רבותיהם. נדמה לי שכל מי שנכנס בשלושים השנים האחרונות אל עולם הלימוד והחקר האקדמי של הספרות העברית הוא באופן כזה או אחר תלמידם של פרופ' גרשון שקד ופרופ' ודן מירון. בין אם חבש בפועל את ספסלי בית מדרשם וזכה בהדרכתם האישית, ובין אם ניזון בעיקר מספריהם וממאמריהם. אמרתי שלושים השנים האחרונות, מכיוון שב-1962 הופיע הספר 'ארבע פנים בספרות העברית בת ימינו' של דן מירון, וב-1963 ספרו של גרשון שקד 'על ארבעה סיפורים', שהם שני ציוני דרך בחקר הספרות העברית - הראשון בזכות הקריאה המבריקה שהוא מציע ביצירותיהם המרכזיות של אלתרמן, רטוש, יזהר ושמיר, והשני באופן שהוא מדגים מהי אינטרפרטציה של הטקסט הספרותי הבודד, במיטבה, באמצעות קריאה אנליטית למופת בסיפוריהם של ביאליק, ברדיצ'בסקי, ברקוביץ ועגנון.

לא אתיימר לתאר בדקות ספורות את מפעלם של מירון ושקד אפילו בראשי פרקים ובהכללות, וזה, ראשית, משום שמדובר בהיקף עצום של כתיבה: כעשרים ספרים בשפות אחדות ומאות מאמרים ורשימות שכל אחד מהם חיבר. שנית, משום שמדובר בכתיבה מגוונת ביותר בנושאיה ובשיטותיה, המתמודדת כמעט עם כל תופעה משמעותית בספרות העברית שנוצרה במאה וחמישים השנים האחרונות, וכן עם חטיבות רחבות מן הספרות היהודית שלא נכתבה בעברית. ושלישית, משום שכל הכללה תחטא לייחודו של כל אחד מהם, שהרי מדובר בשני אישים שונים כל כך זה מזה כמעט בכל היבט משמעותי: מן הרקע הביוגרפי, המזג האישי וההשקפות הפוליטיות והחברתיות, ועד תחומי המחקר המובהקים, המתודולוגיות הפרשניות וסגנון הכתיבה של כל אחד מהם.

ובכל זאת, עם כל המודעות לשוני ולהבדל, אין להתכחש לנטיה המקובלת, שבאה לידי ביטוי גם בהענקת הפרס המשותפת, לראות את דן מירון ואת גרשון שקד כמין צמד תאומי סיאם, כיכין ובועז של חקר הספרות העברית החדשה, ואולי כזוג נוסף במסורת הזוגות העתיקה של חיי הרוח היהודיים. אנסה, לכן, להשיב כאן רק

―――――――
*דברים במסיבה שנערכה באוניברסיטה העברית בירושלים לכבוד חתני פרס ישראל לחקר הספרות העברית, גרשון שקד ודן מירון.

140

על שאלה אחת, והיא: מהו היסוד המשותף להם המכונן בנו אותו סוג של קשב דרוך
לקולם בין כהיסטוריונים וכפרשנים של הספרות, בין כמבקרים ובין כמי שמשמיעים
את דברם גם בעניינים שעל סדר היום הציבורי?

את היסוד המשותף הזה אפשר לאתר כבר מראשית הדרך ממש. אולי ראוי
בשעה החגיגית הזו להזכיר דווקא בנקודת ההתחלה, ומסתבר שההתחלה היתה
משותפת לפחות מן הצד הכרונולוגי, משום שמאמריהם הראשונים של גרשון שקד
ודן מירון בביקורת הספרות הופיעו למרבה הסמליות באותה שנה עצמה, ב-1952
ביולי 1952 פורסם במוסף לספרות של 'הארץ' בעריכתו של יעקב הורוביץ מאמרו
הראשון של גרשון שקד בן ה-23, שהוא ניתוח הסיפור 'החצוצרה נתביישה' של
ביאליק (שהוא גירסה ראשונה של הנוסח המוכר של מאמר זה, הכלול בספריו של
שקד). כעבור חודשים אחדים, בשלהי אותה שנה פורסם בכתב-העת 'גזית' של
גבריאל טלפיר מאמרו הראשון של דן מירון בן ה-18, המנתח תבניות של ניגודים
ומשמעותן ביצירות השירית והפרוזאית של זלמן שניאור. מדובר, כמובן, בנסיונות
ראשונים של מי שהיו אז סטודנטים מתחילים בחוג לספרות עברית באוניברסיטה
העברית, אבל אפילו בהם אפשר כבר לאתר בגרעינו אותו סוג של ראייה שעשה את
שקד ומירון למה שהם. ראשית, בעצם הפנייה אל העבר בנסיון להאיר מחדש יצירות
מן הקלאסיקה של הספרות העברית החדשה. שנית, בעובדה ששני המאמרים
מתמקדים לכאורה בתיאור תופעות מבניות שונות ביצירות הנדונות ברוח 'הביקורת
החדשה' שעקרונותיה החלו להיקלט בארץ באותן שנים. אבל הם אינם נעצרים בכך,
אלא משתמשים בהבחנות הפואטיות כמנוף להבנה של עקרון נפשי או מחשבתי
רחב יותר בעולמו של היוצר. ושלישית, בחריגה מן התיאור אל ההערכה, אל קביעת
הטעם הברורה והבוטחת החותרת לשרטט את מפת הספרות על-פי הבדלי הערך
והמשמעות בין חלקיה. מאמר מוקדם אחר של גרשון שקד, 'צורות וראיית עולם
ביצירת ושל שופמן', שפורסם בירחון 'מבואות' ב-1953, ממחיש את המהלך הזה
כבר בכותרתו, המציגה את המצגתו של המחבר להפליג מן ההבחנות הצורניות אל
האחיזה בשורשי עולמו הרוחני של הסופר, וממנה אל ההערכה, שבמקרה זה אינה
מחמיאה ביותר.

מסתמן כאן מעין דגם האופייני בווריאציה כזו או אחרת לעבודתם של גרשון
שקד ודן מירון כל השנים. במרכז עומד הטיפול המיומן בטקסט הספרותי כשלעצמו,
אבל הטקסט הבודד נקשר ומשתלב במעגלי משמעות מתרחבים והולכים: עולמו של
היוצר, הז'אנר, התימה, הדור הספרותי, התקופה ההיסטורית, ועד המערכת
התרבותית והחברתית כולה שאותו טקסט מאיר אותו וחוזר ומואר מתוכה. אצל
שניהם ניכרת תפיסה רחבה של הספרות לא רק כמערכת של דגמים אסתטיים אלא
כחלל-קיום בעל ממדים היסטוריים, מוסריים ואנושיים. כך, למשל, ספרו האחרון
של דן מירון, 'מול האח השותק', בנוי כסידרת ניתוחים מדוקדקים של שירים
בודדים, שבאמצעותם הוא מבקש לפענח את לבטי הולדתה של הזהות הישראלית
מתוך מלחמת השחרור, ויש בו, כהגדרת המחבר, 'חקירה אמפאתית של התרבות
כפי שהיא מתגלמת בטקסטים שיריים'. על-פי אותו עקרון אפשר לתאר גם את ספריו
של גרשון שקד, כגון אחד האחרונים שבהם, 'פנים אחרות ביצירתו של עגנון'.
המפליג מנקודת-מוצא תבניתית אל אמיתות חברתיות וקיומיות גדולות המובלעות
בסיפורי עגנון.

אבל ההיבט המשותף המרתק ביותר בין מפעליהם הביקורתיים של מירון ושקד
הוא ההיבט האישי הסובייקטיבי, כלומר, האופן שכל אחד מהם ממש בכתיבתו את

המתחים הרוחניים המניעים אותו. תכונה זו, שהיתה מובלעת בכתיבתם מראשיתה,
נחשפת והולכת במפורש בשנים האחרונות במסות אוטוביוגרפיות כתובות ביד אמן
כגון ב׳אין מקום אחר׳ של שקד ובמבוא ל׳בודדים במועדם׳ של מירון. שקד הודה
בכך בגלוי במבוא לספרו האנגלי 'The Shadows Within', כשכתב כי הבחנותיו
ושיפוטיו כמבקר מותנים ברקע הביוגרפי, הפסיכולוגי והאידיאולוגי שלו, וכי כל
מה שהוא כותב משקף בדרך כלשהי את הטראומות שלו כמהגר, ולעניין זה אין
חשיבות להבחנה בין ביקורת לבין מחקר, וביניהם לבין הספרות היפה. אכן, קריאה
במכלול הביקורתי הדינמי שהעמידו מירון ושקד מגלה שני מסלולים של ביוגרפיה
נפשית ואינטלקטואלית שמתקיימת ביניהם, אם לתאר זאת באופן סכימאטי,
סימטריה ניגודית מובהקת. מצד אחד - מי שהחל את דרכו כילד אוסטרי ממוצא
גליצאי, קורא גרמנית, שהגיע לבדו בגיל תשע לארץ ישראל, ונעשה הציוני הלוהט
ביותר והישראלי הנלהב ביותר, ועם זאת בשנים האחרונות הוא שב ובוחן את שורשי
זהותו באמצעות התבוננות בספרות יהודית-גרמנית ויהודית-אמריקנית המשקפת
חוויות של הגירה, תלישות וקרע תרבותי. מצד שני - הצבר התל-אביבי שהחל את
דרכו כמבקר הבולט של הספרות הישראלית, שפרש כנפים והפליג אל מרחבי
התרבות היהודית שנוצרה בדורות האחרונים בלשונות שונות, בטריטוריות שונות
ובהקשרים אידיאולוגיים שונים, אך גם הוא חזר וממקד את מבטו בשנים האחרונות
במציאות שבה נטועות חוויות התשתית הביוגרפיות שלו - תקופת היישוב והמעבר
ממנה לתקופת המדינה, שהוליד ושעיצב את הספרות והתרבות הישראלית.

הקשר בין דראמת הזהות האישית של גרשון שקד ודן מירון לבין הדראמה של
החברה והתרבות היהודית והישראלית שהם בוחנים בכתביהם הוא, אולי, האחראי
יותר מכל לתו הגדולה הטבוע בעבודתם. אנחנו מודים להם היום על ארבעים שנה
של עבודה שקודה שהניבו שני מכלולים מפוארים של הערכת עצמנו בכרכים רבים,
ומאחלים להם ולעצמנו שנוסיף ליהנות עוד שנים רבות מן החוכמה, מן הקסם, מן
הנוכחות המפרה והמעוררת של שניהם במרכזם של חיי הרוח והתרבות שלנו.

לוי שאליט
LEVI SHALIT

איציק מאַנגער: דער זשעני-פּאָעט פֿון פּשטות
(צו זיין 25סטן יאָרצייט)

"נַהֲרָא, נַהֲרָא וּפַשְׁטֵהּ", יעדער טייך האָט זיין אייגנאַרטיקן גאַנג. און לויט
דער גמרא (חולין יח:) לאָזט זיך עס פֿאַרשטיין, וועגן דער באַזונדערער
השפעה, וואָס יעדער אָרט האָט אויף אירע איינוווינערס.
איציק מאַנגער (1969-1901) איז געבוירן געוואָרן אין טשערנאָוויץ,
בוקאָווינע – און אָט די געאָגראַפֿיע, פֿון זיין געבורט-אָרט און אנטוויקלונג,
איז אַן אנטשיידנדיקער פֿאַקטאָר אין זיין דיכטערישער ביאָגראַפֿיע. דערפֿאַר
איז וויכטיג זיך צו פֿאַרהאַלטן לענגער וועגן דעם.
ווען מען זאָל צונויפֿשטעלן, אַ קאַרטע פֿון אַלע געוועזענע
יידישע גלותן, וואָלט זיך באַקומען אַ פֿאַנטאַסטישע מאָזאַיק. יעדער חלק פֿון
דער מאָזאַיק מיט זיין באַזונדער פֿאַרב, נוסח און גאַנג. ווייל קיבוצים יידישע,
אפֿילו אין גאָר נאָענטע לענדער, זיינען אָפֿט געווען גרונט-אנדערש מיט
זייער אויסשפּראַך, קליידונג, הנהגה, און אויך אין זייער פֿיזישן אויסזען, ווי
זיי וואָלטן קוים געהערט צום זעלבן פֿאָלק. דאָס איז ניט זעלטן געשען אפֿילו
אין אידענטישן לאַנד, נאָר אין באַזונדערע לאַנד-שטחים.
צו פֿאַרשטיין, פֿאַרוואָס די יידישע מאָזאַיק איז אזוי פֿיל=פֿאַרביק,
דאַרף מען לערנען די קולטורעלע און סאָציאָלאָגישע אייגנשאַפֿטן פֿון די
פֿעלקער, צווישן וועלכע די באַזונדערע יידישע קיבוצים האָבן געלעבט. (דער
יידישער קאָנגלאָמעראַט אין צפֿון אַמעריקע און די אנדערע קיבוצים היינט
האָבן אנדערע אייגנשאַפֿטן און געהערן צו אַן אנדער באַטראַכטונג).
יידישע קיבוצים האָבן געלעבט, אין אַלע גלותן, באַזונדער, געצוווונגען
אָפּגעטיילט פֿון די ניט-יידישע באַוווינערס, אָפֿט אין באַליידיקנדיקער
איזאָלאַציע. און דאָך ווען זיינען געווען שטאַרקע קעגנזייטיקע שטראָמען פֿון
איינפֿלוס. און אָן צו לערנען אָט די קעגנזייטיקע באַוווירקונגען קען מען ניט
פֿאַרשטיין די ספּעציפֿישע תכונות און מנהגים פֿון די באַזונדערע יידישע
קיבוצים.
דאָס אַלע איז געזאָגט געוואָרן, ווי אַ נויטיקע הקדמה, וועגן איציק
מאַנגער. ווייל אים קען מען נאָר פֿאַרשטיין לויט דעם כלל: ווייל מען דעם
דיכטער קענען מוז מען אין זיין לאַנד גענענען.

---

*די נומערן אלע דא זיינען די זייטן, ווו די דערמאָנטע לידער זיינען געדרוקט, אין דאָס בוך וואָס איז
ארויסגעגעבן געוואָרן אין ישראל, פֿונעם איציק מאַנגער קאָמיטעט מיט דער באַטייליקונג פֿון "לעצטע
נייעס" (יאָר ניט אָנגעגעבן).

"ווּ עס זינגען ציגיינער און טרובאדורן"

איך האב אָנגעצײלט, אויף טשיקאוועס, פערציק לידער און באַלאַדעס
מאַנגנגערס, ווו געאגראַפישע נעמען ווערן בפירוש דערמאָנט און באַשריבן.
און נאָך דרייסיק מעגן אויך פאַרעכנט ווערן ווי אַזעלכע. דאָס זײַנען די
אויטאָביאָגראַפישע "סאַנעטן פאַר מיין ברודער נטע". נאָר אפילו אין לידער
און באַלאַדעס, ווו ערטער זײַנען ניט דערמאָנט, הערן מיר קלאָר אַרויס "פון
יעדן שטיין פון יעדן פעלז" (72) דעם עכא פון דער אָרטיקער מוזיק און זעען
דעם פאַרבן-קאָלאָריט פון דער לאנדשאַפט, ווו עס איז געשטאַנען דעם
דיכטערס וויג.

דאָס זײַנען די וויין-קעלערן פון דעם לאַנד, ווו-

אַ קעניגרײַך מיט לידער ווערן געבוירן
ווו עס זינגען ציגיינער און טרובאַדורן.

טשערנאָוויץ, יאַסי, די "קרוינשטאַט פון מאלדאַוויע", בראַד, קאַסעוו און
קיטעוו, צווישן סטאַפטשעט און קאָלאַמיי: "אַ שטילע פרײד פון מיינע
קינדער-יארן". (331)

אין אָט די ערטער, אין די לאַנד-שטחים ביים דניעסטער, איז געוווען די
אַטמאָספערישע מיליע וואָס עס זאל זיך אויסיעֶרן מאַנגערס פאַעטישער טאַלאַנט,
מיט אַ ביסעלע פרייד און אַ סך טרוייער.

דערפאַר אויך זײַנען אָט דאָ אויפגעקומען מאַנגערס פאַעטישע
פאַרגייֶערס, וועלכע ער האט אַזוי פאַעטיש פאַרטרעטירט אין:
"גאָלדפאַדיאַנע" (געמיינט דעם אויפקום דאָ פון טעאַטער אין יידיש);
"וועלוועל זבאַרזשער" (יידישע קלעזמער); "הערשעלע אָסטראפאָלער"
(דערצייֶלער פון לעגענדעם); און "בערל בראָדער", וואס אין זײַן נאמען
זאָגט מאַנגער, ווען דעם לאַנד דעם פון זײַער ליד און לעבן, וועגן בעמיש און
בראָד:

דאָ ווּ עס שפילט דער ציגיינער
און ייִדן טרינקען ווײַן. (206)

מאַנגער זעט זיך ווי דער יורש פון די בראָדער זינגער:

כ׳בין אַרויפגעשפרונגען אויפן וואָגן פון די בראָדער זינגער און בין מיט
זיי אַ מהלך וועגס אָפגעפאָרן,

עס איז מיר געוווען גרינגער,
מיט אָט די ערשטע פריילעכע ייִדישע אַקטיאָרן (385).

"געפאָרן" איז אָבער מאַנגער מיט זײַן אייגענער פור און אויף זײַן
אייגענעם וועג, וואָס איז געוווען - און געבליבן - אַזוי ניי, אַזוי אַנדערש, אַזוי
זעלטן אין פאַעטישן אויסדרוק.

פאַראַן אין מאַנגערס דיכטערישע פאַליטרע אלע פאַרב-ניוואַנסן. זײַן ליד

האָט שפּיל און חן, גראַמיט און גראַטעסק, טיפע מחשבה אויסגעשפּילט אויף
די דינסטע לירישע סטרונעס. און וווּנדערלעך: דאָס אַלץ איז אויסגעדריקט
מיט די סאַמע פּשוטסטע ווערטער. קיין אָנשטעל. קיין פאַלשער טאָן. אָפּט
אין די ראַמען פון פאָלקלאָר און מיט פּראָזאַישע ווערטער. די צאַרטסטע
פּאָעזיע, ״וווּ די שיינקייט ווייישט די טרערן אָף פון אלע צערן״ (384).

מאַנגער האַלט כּסדר פאַרהויבן די אויגן צו די שטערן. זיינע ביכער־
נעמען און לידער־ציקלען האָבן אַ סך שטערן. נאָר מאַנגערס שטערן פינקלען
אַרונטער צום מענטשן און צו זיין אייגענעם פּאָעטישן גמיט:

> מיטן נאַכט. די גלויבער אין די שטערן
> גייען מיט מידע טריט א היים. (166)

פאַראַן אָבער אויך אַ גלויבהאַפטיקער אַרויפקוק צו די שטערן:

> דו האָסט געזאָגט ״עס איז געוועןן״
> און איר ״עס וועט ערשט ווערן״,
> אַ סימן, זע, אין אונדזער שויב
> האָט אויפגעשײַנט אַ שטערן. (292)

פאַרהיימישט דעם תנ״ך

מאַנגער האָט ״אויפגעעוועקט די אבות״ אין זיין זעלטענעם ״מדרש
איציק״. געטאָן האָט ער עס מיטן זעלבן דרך. פון נוצן פאָלקלאָר מיט
פּשטות.

זיינע איבערגעדיכטעטע דערצייילונגען פון תנ״ך, בעיקר פון בראשית און
פון מגילת רות, האָבן אויך געבראַכט די אבות און די אַנדערע געשטאַלטן אין
דער סביבה פון היימישער נאָענטקייט.

חנה ווייגט איר בן־יחיד, דעם צוקונפטיקן שמואל הנביא, און זינגט אים צו
וועגן דריי יידן, וואָס -

> איינער איז פון יאַראָסלאַוו,
> דער צווייטער פון לובלין,
> דער דריטער דרייַ אַ פּאַפּיראָס
> פון טערקישן טוטין. (246)

און ווען אברהם אבינו מוסרט לוט, פאַר דעס וואָס ער שיכורט, דערציילט
עס מאַנגער שוין גאָר אינטים:

> לוט, איך מוז דיר זאָגן ס׳איז - פע !
> דו שיכורסט איעדע נאַכט.
> ערשט נעכטן האָסטו אין ״גאָלדענעם הערש״
> אַזאַ וויסטן סקאַנדאַל געמאַכט.

> ─────
> דאַס פּאַסט פאַר מאַנגער, דעם שניידערוק,
> אָבער אָסור נישט פאַר דיר. (215)

דאָס אַלץ איז נאָר סאַטיריש לויטן נוסח. אָבער אַזוי אַרום האָט מאַנגער

גענברעכט די תנ״ך דערציילונגען בילדעריש און מיט צייטיקן לשון.

מאַנגער האָט גרויס פיעטעט פאַר די געשטאַלטן פון תנ״ך, אַפילו ווען ער
שרייבט וועגן זיי מיט שאַרפן הומאָר. דאָס קומט אויך צום אויסדרוק אין
זיינע לידער וועגן בעל שם טוב, ווו עס איז פאַראַן נאָר פיעטעט. דער
"מתנגד" און, אין אַ פלוג, פרעמדער צו פראַקטישער, תורהדיקער יידישקייט,
האָט זיך פאַרחברט מיטן בעל שם, דורך דעם אַסאָציאַטיוון פאַעטישן געפיל.
דער הפקרדיקער פאָעט, ווי מאַנגער אַליין פאָרטרעטירט זיך אָפט, איז טיף
אַדורכגענומען מיט רעליגיעזע סענטימענטן, ווייל: "אַ ליד אָן אמונה איז
פאַרווויאַנעט גראָז" (481).

אַלע מענטשן זוכן גאָט. פאָעטן געוויס. יעדערע אויף זיין אופן. מאַנגער,
לויט זיין טיפער עמאָציע, האָט גאָט געפונען, "זוכנדיק מיט די פינגער גאָט
אין שטויב" (57).

ווייל:

טיף אין מיר
צינדן אָן שאָטנס גלויביקע פייערן.

———

כ׳האָב דיך דערקענט,
קיין רגע שיינקייט גייט נישט אויף דער ערד פאָרלוירן. (65)

נאָך שאַרפער קומט דער גאָט-זוכאַרישער מאָטיוו, אין אַפילו אמונה,
אין זיין ליד, וועלכן מיר קענען נישט פאַרבייגיין. דאָס ליד - פילאָסאָפיש -
מעג באַטראַכט ווערן ווי דער תמצית אין דער דעלעמע גאָט - אוישוויטש.
און דאָס ליד דריקט אויס אמונה דורך גערואַנגל מיט דער געטלעכקייט - און
קיין אַנדער אמתע אמונה איז דאָך נאָר נישטאָ. ער דערציילט וועגן די "אוהבי
ישראל" , די רבים פון גאַליציע, ביים טויטן-לאַגער בעלזשעץ. זיי זאָגן דאָ
אַלע אין איין קול:

באַשעפער פון די וועלטן,
דו ביסט מאַכטיק, מוראַדיק און גרויס,
נאָר מיר, די גאַליציאַנער, מעקן דיך אויס
פון דער עדה אמתע "אוהבי ישראל". (462)

זיך ניט געוואַלגערט אין דער חיים

מען קען ניט שרייבן וועגן מאַנגערן, אָן צו דערציילן וועגן זיינע לעצטע
יאָרן, אין ישראל. אויך דאָס איז געווען קלוגשאפט, פאָעטישער געפיל, וואָס
ער האָט אַזוי שטאַרק געוועלטעט אויסלעבן זיינע יאָרן אין ישראל.

עס דערציילט שלום ראָזנפעלד, וועלכער האָט געהאָלפן זיין קומען קיין
ישראל און אין אַלץ וואָס מיט אים איז דאָ געשען, אַז מאַנגער האָט אים
געזאָגט, אין אמעריקא: דאָ וועט דאָך קיינער אפילו ניט וויסן ווען איך וועל
שטאַרבן. (און דאָס איז כאַראקטעריסטיש: דער וועלכער האָט אַ גאַנצן לעבן
אויסגעלאַכט דעם טויט, ווייל "איך פייף אויף לעצטן ניגון און גיי מיט

פרייד אוועק" (427), האט, פונדעסטוועגן, ניט געוועלט שטארבן
אומבאקאנט און געזאָרגט אפילו פאַר זיין לויה....)

מאַנגער האט געשריבן :

איך האָב יאָרן זיך געוואַלגערט אין דער פרעמד,
איצט פאַר איך זיך וואַלגערן איך דער היים. (486)

אָבער אין דעם האָט ער זיך טועה געווען. ישראל האָט אים אויפגענומען
מיט גרויס כבוד און מיט ליבשאפט. יוגנטלעכע זיינען געקומען צום
דיכטערס קראַנקן בעט. זיי האָבן איבערגעזאָגט און איבערגעזונגען זיינע
לידער, און זיי טוען עס נאָך איצט, אין א שטאַמלדיקן יידיש מיט א
העברעאישן אקצענט.

זיינע מגילה־לידער זיינען דראָמאַטעזירט געוואָרן און טויזנטער האָבן עס
געזען, אין טעאַטער און אין טעלעוויזיע, געהאַט הנאה, און מען דערמאָנט
זיך, אין טעלעוויזיע, צו ווייזן עס אויך איצט.

תל אביב האָט ארויסגעשניטן אַ שטיק פון עטלעכע גאסן, מיט די נעמען
פון העברעאישע שרייבערס, און געמאַכט אַן אָרט , אין האָרץ פון שטאָט,
פאַר אַן אָנזעעווודיקן סקווער, מיטן נאמען: איציק מאַנגער.

"דער שניידער - געזעלן בראָדיאַגע און פאָעט" איז געקומען צו רו - ניט
לויט זיין עפיטאַף - נאָר באַגלייט פון טויזנטער, אויף דעם בית עולם פון תל
אביב אויף דעם חשובסטן ארט, - ווי דאָס האָט אים געקומט. און זיין נאמען
און זיין ליד זיינען ניט פארגעסן געוואָרן אין לאַנד.

MORRIS M. FAIERSTEIN

The Literary Legacy of Shneur Zalman of Lyadi

On the 250th Anniversary of His Birth

HABAD HASIDISM HAS ALWAYS seen itself as a distinct subgroup within the larger family of Hasidism. It is a commonplace within Habad[1] to speak of "Hasidism in general and Habad in particular." Central to any understanding of Habad and its unique place in the history of Hasidism is its founder, Rabbi Shneur Zalman of Lyady, one of the most important thinkers and charismatic leaders in the history of Hasidism. R. Shneur Zalman was not only the author of important works of hasidic thought, but also authored an updated version of the *Shulhan Arukh* and a Habad edition of the *siddur*. This essay will survey R. Shneur Zalman's literary legacy and consider recent scholarly evaluations of his thought.

R. Shneur Zalman ben Baruch was born in 1745. He received an excellent rabbinic education and his intellectual acumen was recognized at an early age. At the age of twenty, he sought a more spiritual path. He found his way to Mezhirech and became a disciple of the Great Maggid, R. Dov Baer. The Maggid recognized the intellectual abilities of his new disciple and asked him to tutor his son, R. Abraham, in Talmud and halakhah and in return R. Abraham would teach R. Shneur Zalman the esoteric teachings of Hasidism. The Maggid also asked R. Shneur Zalman to edit a new edition of

---

1. The Habad school of Hasidism is more popularly known as Lubavitcher Hasidism. Habad, an acronym for *Hokhmah, Binah*, and *Da'at*, the three upper Sefirot in Lurianic Kabbalah, is the official name of this school of Hasidism. It became known as Lubavitcher Hasidism only in the second generation, when R. Shneur Zalman's son and successor, R. Dov Baer, moved to the town of Lubavitch.

the *Shulhan Arukh*, bringing it up to date. He remained an intimate disciple of the Maggid until the latter's death in 1772. Afterwards, R. Shneur Zalman returned to White Russia where he was a disciple and junior colleague to R. Menachem Mendel of Vitebsk, a senior disciple of the Maggid. In 1877, R. Menachem Mendel and a group of followers migrated to Israel settling in Tiberias.[2] Eventually, R. Shneur Zalman became the dominant hasidic leader in White Russia.[3] He was, at the same time, the most successful and controversial leader in the third generation of hasidic leadership.[4] R. Shneur Zalman and his school bore the brunt of the attack on Hasidism launched by the Gaon of Vilna and his followers, the *mitnagedim*, who saw it as a new version of the Sabbatean heresy that had so recently been suppressed.[5] Some of R. Shneur Zalman's opponents among the *mitnagedim* went so far as to denounce him to the Russian authorities and accuse him of sedition.[6] The government arrested R. Shneur Zalman and brought him to St. Petersburg for interrogation. After an investigation he was freed from prison on the 19th day of Kislev, 1798. This day has become the central Habad day of celebration and is called the *"Rosh Hashanah* of Hasidism" by followers of Habad. He was arrested a second time on the same charges in

---

2. On the hasidic migration to Israel see I. Halpern, *Ha-Aliyot ha-Rishonot shel ha-Hasidim le-Eretz Yisrael* (Jerusalem, 1947) and more recently M. Wilensky, *Ha-Yishuv ha-Hasidi be-Teveriah* (Jerusalem, 1988).

3. See I. Etkes, "Aliyato shel R. Shneur Zalman mi-Lyady le-Emdat Manhigut," *Tarbiz* 54 (1985), pp. 429-441.

4. The leader of the first generation of Hasidism was the Baal Shem Tov, the founder. The second generation was led by the Maggid, R. Dov Baer. The third generation did not have a single leader, but consisted of the Maggid's disciples, each of whom became a leader in his own right.

5. E.g., the many references to R. Shneur Zalman in M. Wilensky, *Hasidim u'Mitnagedim* (Jerusalem, 1970), 2 vols., Index, s.v., R. Shneur Zalman mi-Liozna.

6. Y. Mondshein has uncovered much interesting material from Russian archives concerning R. Shneur Zalman's arrest and interrogation, which he has published in vols. 4 and 5 of *Be-Kerem Habad*. For a précis of his findings, see, D. Assaf, "The Rebbe was Framed," *Jerusalem Report*, December 17, 1992, pp. 46-47.

1801, and released shortly afterwards. This event marked a major turning point in R. Shneur Zalman's life. He moved from Liozna to Lyady for reasons that are not entirely clear and students of his writings have noticed a marked change in his teachings after his release. In 1812, when Napoleon invaded Russia, he strongly supported the Czar. He explained this seeming paradox by pointing out quite presciently that if Napoleon won, the material fortunes of the Jewish people will rise, but their spiritual status would decline. However, if the czar was victorious, the opposite would be true. R. Shneur Zalman was quite prepared to sacrifice the material wellbeing of his flock for their spiritual welfare. After his death in 1813, he was succeeded by his son R. Dov Baer who further developed and expanded R. Shneur Zalman's intellectual legacy.[7]

THE TANYA

The *Tanya*[8] is R. Shneur Zalman's best known and most influential work. First published in 1796, it was the end product of a long process. The basic teachings that are contained in the *Tanya* were taught orally by R. Shneur Zalman over a period of years. Beginning in 1792, he allowed handwritten copies of his teachings to be circulated among his disciples. Within a short time, discrepancies began to creep into the circulating manuscripts. Concern for the correct transmission of his teachings finally led R. Shneur Zalman to publish the first edition of the *Tanya,* as he states in the foreword. His name does not appear on the title page. Even after its publication the book underwent a further process of editing and expansion. The first edition only contained the first two parts of the *Tanya*, the *Book of the Intermediate Man*

---

7. The succession was marked by controversy. See R. Elior, "Ha-Mahloket al Moreshet Habad," *Tarbiz* 49 (1980), 166-186.
8. The original name of the book was *Likkutei Amarim* (Selected Teachings). It was only the Zolkiew, 1799 edition that first used the title *Tanya*, which is the first word of the book. However, this is the title by which it has become known and it is now the accepted usage for the book.

(Sefer shel Beinonim)[9] and the *Gate of Unity and Faith (Sha'ar ha-Yihud veha-Emunah).* Subsequent editions added additional sections and were revised. The Warsaw, 1814 edition, edited by R. Shneur Zalman's sons, was the first complete edition of the *Tanya* as it is known today. This was also the first edition where the author's name appears on the title page.

The Warsaw edition was the basis for all editions in the nineteenth century. By the end of the century, enough typographical errors had crept into the various editions that it was decided to re-edit the *Tanya*. The new edition, published in Vilna in 1900, was not only based on the earliest printed editions, but also referred back to earlier manuscripts which had been preserved in Habad archives.[10] This edition became the template for all subsequent editions of the *Tanya*.

The *Tanya* has always had a quasi–canonical status in Habad Hasidism. Even though the *Tanya* is divided into five parts, it is a Habad convention to count the last two parts as one. The "four" parts of the *Tanya* are thereby "equal" to the four parts of the *Shulhan Arukh*. However, the centrality and importance of the *Tanya* has grown significantly in the last two generations. The major turning point came at the end of 1942 when the former Rebbe R. Joseph Isaac Schneerson published a small booklet called *Ha-Yom Yom* in which R. Menachem Mendel Schneerson, the compiler, divided the *Tanya* into sections and instituted an order of daily study consisting of *Humash*, *Tehillim*, and *Tanya*. Each day, ideally after the morning prayers, each Habad Hasid was now expected to study the daily portion of the weekly Torah reading, recite the appropriate section of Psalms and review

---

9. The term "Intermediate Man" or *Beinoni* has a very specific meaning in Habad terminology. It does not mean an ordinary person, but refers to someone who is a person of significant spiritual stature, but has not yet attained permanent spiritual transformation (i.e., become a *zaddiq*).

10. In 1981, one of the more important manuscript copies of the *Tanya* was published. A comparison of this manuscript with printed editions shows some of the differences between the two versions.

the appropriate section of the *Tanya*.[11] The current *Rebbe* has continued the process of placing the *Tanya* at the center of Habad Hasidism in a number of ways. In the 1950's he published a series of indices and textual corrections which were added to subsequent printings of the *Tanya*. In 1973, he ordered that a special edition of the *Tanya* be printed to commemorate the Israeli Army's crossing of the Suez Canal. A printing press was put on a truck, driven across the Suez Canal into Egypt and a *Tanya,* Habad *siddur*, and *Tehillim* were printed. All of these items have since become collector's items. This presaged a decree by the Rebbe in 1978 that the *Tanya* be printed in as many places as possible. Until 1978, the *Tanya* had gone through approximately 80 editions since its first publication in 1796. Today there are close to 4,000 editions of the *Tanya* printed all over the world, including such centers of Jewish life as Yuma, Arizona, Seoul, Korea and even Ulan Bator, Mongolia.[12]

It is also noteworthy that the first Habad translation of the *Tanya* into a language other that Hebrew occurred as late as 1956 when it was translated into Yiddish.[13] Since then it has been translated into a number of languages, including English, French, Spanish and even Arabic.[14]

---

11. The idea of a daily study session of classic texts is not new. This tradition may be traced back to the *Hoq le-Yisrael.* attributed to R. Hayyim Vital, (first ed., Egypt, 1740), which laid out a daily routine of study of the classic genres of Jewish religious literature: Torah, Prophets, Writings, Mishnah, Talmud, and Zohar. Another, more recent inspiration may have been the *Daf Yomi,* the daily page of Talmud study instituted by Rabbi Meyer Shapiro of Lublin in the 1920's.

12. Every edition of the *Tanya* printed in the last 25 years contains a complete listing of all editions. A scholarly bibliography of all editions to 1981 is Y. Mondshein, *Torat Habad. Bibliographiah: Likkutei Amarim* (Kfar Habad, 1982).

13. Raphael Ben Zion translated the second part of the *Tanya, Shaar ha-Yihud veha-Emunah* (The Gate of Unity and Faith), in *The Way of the Faithful* (Los Angeles, 1945), pp. 88-128. To the best of my knowledge this work has no connection to Habad.

14. Habad, for example, has a yeshiva in Morocco and this edition was published there.

Even in translation, the *Tanya* is not a simple work to understand. It is written for an audience steeped in rabbinic concepts and at home with medieval Jewish ethical and kabbalistic writings. Though there have been many Habad commentaries and expositions of the ideas contained in the *Tanya*, they are not readily accessible to the outsider. Rabbi Adin Steinsaltz, best known for his new edition and translation of the Talmud, is also the author of a comprehensive commentary on the *Tanya*.[15] Abridged English translations of the first two volumes have been published.[16] Also noteworthy is Prof. Moshe Hallamish's *Netiv le-Tanya*,[17] a commentary on the first part of the *Tanya* written from a scholarly perspective.

OTHER HASIDIC WRITINGS

R. Shneur Zalman delivered discourses on hasidic thought throughout the years of his leadership like other hasidic leaders. These teachings were transcribed by several people, the most important of which were R. Dov Baer, his son and R. Menachem Mendel, his grandson. R. Dov Baer published some of the teachings in his book, *Be'urei ha-Zohar* and as a commentary to the second revised edition of R. Shneur Zalman's edition of the prayerbook.[18] The best known collections of R. Shneur Zalman's discourses were edited by R. Menachem Mendel (also known as the *Zemah Zedek*). They are *Torah Or* (Kopys, 1836) and *Likkutei Torah* (Zhitomir, 1848). These collections by no mean exhausted the materials available in manuscript. In 1958, the current Rebbe decided to initiate a program to publish the writings of R. Shneur Zalman still in manuscript. In 1978, a part of the former Rebbe's library which had been left behind in Warsaw during

---

15. *Beiur Makif le-Sefer ha-Tanya* (Jerusalem, 1989-). Thus far 5 volumes have appeared.
16. *The Longer Shorter Way* (Jason Aronson: Northvale, 1988) and *The Sustaining Utterance* (Jason Aronson: Northvale, 1989).
17. Tel Aviv, 1987. It deserves to be translated into English.
18. Both printed in Kopys, 1816.

World War II and was thought to have been lost was found
and acquired by the current Rebbe. Included in this new-found
collection were many important manuscripts of R. Shneur
Zalman's writings. The whole series has been published under
the title, *Ma'amarei Admor ha-Zaken*. To date almost twenty
volumes have been published in this series. Parallel with this
series, a second series of R. Shneur Zalman's letters has been
published entitled, *Iggerot Ba'al ha-Tanya*. In this series too,
over twenty volumes have appeared thus far.

R. Shneur Zalman was also an important halakhic scholar.
He began work on a new edition of the *Shulhan Arukh* shortly
after his encounter with the Maggid of Mezhirech. His son R.
Dov Baer, who published R. Shneur Zalman's partial edition of
the *Shulhan Arukh* (first edition, Kopys, 1814), states in the
foreword that he worked on this book more than thirty years.
However, he never completed the work. Only *Orah Hayyim*
and selected chapters from the other three parts of the
Shulhan Arukh were published. It is not coincidental that R.
Shneur Zalman's first published work was *Hilkhot Talmud
Torah*, a section of the *Shulhan Arukh*.[19] R. Foxbrunner, in
his recent study of R. Shneur Zalman's writings has called this
work "the most comprehensive treatment of the subject in six
centuries since Maimonides originated the rubric."[20]

R. Shneur Zalman, in his edition of the *Shulhan Arukh*, endeavored to update and synthesize the halakhic developments
that had occurred since Joseph Karo's original publication of
the work. For the most part, he did not innovate or argue with
the classic commentaries, but sought to decide between
differing perspectives and reach a conclusion. Where there
were differences between Ashkenazi and Sephardi authorities,
his inclination was to follow the Ashkenazi tradition. In differences between normative halakhic tradition and kabbalistic
tradtion, he follows the halakhic tradition in the *Shulhan*

---

19. Shklov, 1794. For a definitive bibliography of all of R. Shneur
    Zalman's halakhic writings see, Y. Mondshein, *Torat Habad.
    Bibliographiah: Sifrei Halakhah shel Admor ha-Zaken* (Kfar
    Habad, 1984).

20. *Habad: The Hasidism of R. Shneur Zalman of Lyady* (Tuscaloo-
    sa, 1992), p. 137.

Arukh, but will often take the opposite view and follow the halakhic and kabbalistic tradition in the notes to his edition of the *siddur.*[21]

His tendency in deciding halakhic questions was to follow the more stringent, conservative position and only on rare occasions does he follow the more lenient interpretation.[22] The second edition of the *Shulhan Arukh,* published in Zhitomir in 1847, was expanded by the addition of much new material drawn from manuscript sources and from R. Shneur Zalman's published responsa. Recently an edition of the *Kitzur Shulhan Arukh* was published which was based on R. Shneur Zalman's edition.

Though a number of kabbalistic *siddurim* were published under hasidic auspices,[23] the only specifically hasidic *siddur* was published by R. Shneur Zalman in 1803.[24] This edition contained no kabbalistic *kavvanot,* but did have halakhic annotations at appropriate points.[25] In 1816, R. Dov Baer published an edition of his father's *siddur* with an addition of Habad teachings drawn from R. Shneur Zalman's writings. This Habad version of the *siddur* differs in some respects from the *nusah Sefarad siddurim* used by other hasidic groups and is called *nusah Ari.*[26]

---

21. The discrepancies have been collected by R. Abraham Hayyim Noe, in *Sefer Piskei ha-Siddur* (Jerusalem, 1937).
22. M. Teitelbaum, *Ha-Rav mi-Lyady u'Mifleget Habad* (Warsaw, 1910), vol. I, pp. 10-15, 252f.
23. See N. Loewenthal, *Communicating the Infinite* (Chicago, 1990), p. 278, n. 91, for a thorough discussion of kabbalistic and hasidic prayerbooks prior to R. Shneur Zalman's edition.
24. Unfortunately, no copies of this editon has survived. Our knowledge. of its form and content is based on A.D. Lavat, *Siddur Torah Or* (Vilna, 1887).
25. As has been noted above, these halakhic annotations did not always coincide with R. Shneur Zalman's *Shulhan Arukh,* but often follow more stringent kabbalistic practices.
26. Ari is the acronym for Rabbi Isaac Luria. In contexts other than Habad, "*nusach Ari*" implies a *siddur* with the Lurianic *kavvanot.*

RECENT STUDIES

The hasidic movement is in the process of undergoing a major reassessment of many of the conventionally accepted ideas about the history and the methodological approaches to its study. The current generation of scholars of Hasidism question many of the basic assumptions of the Scholem-Tishby school and have begun to see Hasidism in a new light.[27] An important change has been to see Hasidism more as a continuation of earlier Kabbalistic ideas than as a revolt against traditional theological concepts. There is also a new perspective on the relationship between elites and the masses in Hasidism, both on the theological and social level. The great innovation of Hasidism was not that it abandoned elitist kabbalistic theological ideas and practices, but rather that it sought a way to make these ideas accessible to the masses and make the ordinary person a partner in the mystical activites of the elite.[28] The tension between elite theological ideas and their popularization is a central subtext of R. Shneur Zalman's thought. Naftali Loewenthal makes this process of communication the central theme of his study of early Habad thought.[29]

Loewenthal suggests that Hasidism has traditionally been studied from two very different perspectives, sociopolitically and as a continuation of the Jewish mystical tradition. The first method tries to locate the rise of Hasidism in terms of the social and political situation of Polish Jewry in the first half of the eighteenth century. Scholars who have used this approach tend to see Hasidism in terms of a social struggle between the

---

27. For recent surveys of the state of scholarship on Hasidism see, Z. Gries, "Hasidism: The Present State of Research and Some Desirable Priorities," *Numen* 34 (1987), pp. 97-108, 179-213; M. Faierstein, "Hasidism – The Last Decade in Research," *Modern Judaism* 11 (1991) pp. 111-124; Foxbrunner, pp. 203-220.

28. For example, the central theme in the writings of R. Jacob Joseph of Polonnoye, the Besht's most important disciple and the first great theologian of Hasidism, is the relationship between the elite (*talmidei hakhamim* or *anshei zurah* [men of form] in his terminology) and the masses (*anshei homer*). I hope to address this theme more fully in a forthcoming study.

29. *Communicating the Infinite* (Chicago, 1990).

elite centered on the traditional structures of Jewish society, and the *Hasidim* who were centered around a new type of charismatic leader, the *zaddiq*, who was a rallying point for the disenfranchised masses. The second approach is concerned purely with the teachings of Hasidism and its relation to its predecessors in the Jewish mystical tradition. Here the dominant theme is the creative tension between religious radicalism and the pitfalls of antinomianism, particularly as exemplified in Sabbateanism. When one considers these two types of research, the results diverge dramatically. One often gets the impression that two entirely different movements are being discussed. Loewenthal suggests that there is a third method which will bring together the two apparently divergent approaches to Hasidism. He suggests "early Hasidism was not simply a movement of radical mysticism. It was one in which men who could achieve *unio mystica* became not just mystics, but mystic leaders, who sought to transform the people around them. The aim was not an elitist community of ecstatics, but the general unification of society and the elevation of the daily life of the men and women in the mundane world."[30] This ethos of communication, as Loewenthal calls it, was most explicitly developed by the Habad school of Hasidism. The first important hasidic document which conveys this concept, according to Loewenthal, is the famous letter sent by the Besht to his brother-in-law concerning hus heavenly ascent to the palace of the Messiah.[31] This theme was continued by the Maggid of Mezhirech and reached its fullest development in Habad. R. Shneur Zalman created a structure which sought to disseminate Habad teachings in different ways to the diversity of followers attracted to the movement who ranged from simple people to scholars of the highest intellectual attainment. Already in the 1790's R. Shneur Zalman promulgated a series of regulations, the "Liozna Regulations," which laid out the duties and responsibilities for followers on

---

30. Ibid., p. 3.
31. This letter has been translated into English by Norman Lamm, "The Letter of the Besht to R. Gershon of Kuty," *Tradition* 14 (1974), pp. 110-125.

different intellectual levels. There is an explicit hierarchy of disciples based on intellectual attainment. When the number of followers grew large, he delegated responsibility to his son, R. Dov Baer, and his disciple, R. Aaron ha-Levi, to teach the new followers the basics of Habad spirituality. He also sent out disciples to various parts of White Russia to spread the teachings of Habad. These activities not only aroused opposition from the *mitnagedim*, as has been mentioned, but also from within the ranks of Hasidism. R. Abraham of Kalisk, R. Shneur Zalman's erstwhile colleague, was very angry with him for translating the esoteric teachings of Hasidism, which he felt were reserved for a small pneumatic elite, into terms that were accessible to the ordinary scholar. R. Abraham felt that simple faith in the pneumatic powers of the *zaddiq* was at the core of Hasidism. R. Shneur Zalman was creating a new type of Hasidism that differed from the teachings that he had received from his master, the Maggid of Mezhirech.[32] Loewenthal's study is important not only for understanding Habad as it developed in its first generations, but also for the contemporary activities of Habad which have their basis in the structures first established by R. Shneur Zalman.

NEW ANALYSES

R. Shneur Zalman's theology has been the subject of two recent books by Rachel Elior and Roman Foxbrunner. Elior, whose earlier work was on R. Shneur Zalman's disciple, R. Aaron ha–Levi of Staroselye, studies R. Shneur Zalman's teachings as part of an integrated school of Habad teachings which begins with him and continues with his disciples,

---

32. The term that should be emphasized is scholar. Even the *Tanya*, which is considered an introductory work in Habad theology, is not readily accessible to someone who does not have a strong rabbinic education. On the dispute with R. Abraham see, A. J. Brawer, "Al ha-Makhloket bein R. Shneur Zalman mi-Lyady – R. Abraham ha-Cohen mi-Kalisk," *Kiryat Sefer* 1 (1924), pp. 140-150, 226-238; Z. Gries, "Mi-Mitos le-Etos – Kavim li-Demuto shel R. Abraham mi-Kalisk," in S. Ettinger, ed. *Umah ve-Toledoteha* (Jerusalem, 1984), vol. 2, pp. 117-146.

children and grandchildren. Her goal is to present a synthetic overview of Habad teachings of the classic period of Habad creativity from R. Shneur Zalman through his grandson R. Menachem Mendel, the *Zemah Zedek*. Her audience is not the specialist interested in the fine points of Habad thought and the subtle differences between different thinkers in the first generations of Habad, but the non-specialist who is more interested in the major themes of Habad spirituality.[33] She is concerned with the ideas of Habad and does not concern herself with its social history and its relationship to other schools of Hasidism.

For Elior, there are two basic themes that underlie the Habad worldview. The first is the perception of "a dual reality of existence and a dialectical relationship between its two components." [34] The basic dialectic is between the concepts of *Ayin* (nothingness, or transcendance) and *Yesh* (existence or contraction), the two basic aspects of divinity. The implication of this theology for man is that his "ultimate aim is to perceive the dual existence of his essential being, which reflects the two aspects of the divine being, and, through this perception, to fulfill its ambivalence. Man's relation with the *Ayin* and his contemplation of the true essence of the *Yesh* require him to perform a twofold act of worship known a *ratso vashov* or ascent and descent, which actualizes his heavenly and earthly existence simultaneously in relation to its divine source." [35]

The second central motif is acosmism. "In the acosmic view, God is the only reality and all else is but a veil of illusions. The world does not exist independently, but rather, all being, in all its manifestations, is set on one entity that nullifies all independent existence of individual detail and their generality, leaving the divine essence as one and only true reality."[36] In Habad writings this concept is succinctly summarized in the motto, *ein od bilvado* (there is nothing but

---

33. A good summary of Elior's presentation of Habad is her article, "Habad: The Contemplative Ascent to God," in A. Green, ed. *Jewish Spirituality* (New York, 1987), vol 2, pp. 157-205.
34. R. Elior, *The Paradoxical Ascent to God* (Albany, 1993), p. 25.
35. Ibid., p. 43f.
36. Ibid., p. 49f.

Him). Elior developed these basic themes in Habad theology in
three central areas: the doctrine of divinity, the soul, and
divine worship. Each of these major areas is broken down into
series of small chapters, occasionally no longer than a page or
two where the constituent elements are clearly explicated. The
area that receives the most attention is divine worship, a
theme that is at the heart of Habad spirituality. There is more
to Habad teachings than what is covered in this work, but a
comprehensive study of the movement's ideology was not the
author's intention. As the subtitle of the author's book states,
this is a study of the kabbalistic theosophy of Habad
Hasidism.

Roman Foxbrunner's study is at the same time more
limited and more comprehensive than Elior's. He restricts
himself to R. Shneur Zalman's thought as it is developed in his
own writings without significant reference to the development
of his ideas in the writings of subsequent generations of
Habad thinkers. Rather than looking forward, Foxbrunner
looks backwards to the thinkers who influenced R. Shneur
Zalman and those classics of Jewish thought with whom he is
in dialogue. In his view, "R. Shneur Zalman was not content to
limit his speculative thinking to kabbalistic terms. He wanted
to incorporate rabbinic and philosophical assumptions and
terminology as well."[37] Foxbrunner sees himself as faced "with
a kaleidoscopic corpus that resists both facile and ingenious
attempts at harmonization."[38] His response is an attempt to
analyze the corpus on its own terms using the general rubrics
of Man in God's World; Ethical Ways and Means; Torah and
Commandments; and Love and Fear.

Foxbrunner concludes that "the outstanding features of R.
Shneur Zalman's hasidic thought are synecretism, tension,
and paradox."[39] He suggests that the reason for this is that R.
Shneur Zalman's "hasidic thought was articulated primarily
in a series of discourses spanning about two decades (to 1813)
and varying greatly in length, style, and content, depending
on the period, the audience, and the need of the hour. His pur-

37. Foxbrunner, p. 57.
38. Ibid.
39. Ibid., p. 196.

pose was to inspire, not to fashion a system of religio-ethical thought. It is unlikely that he ever intended all the discourses to be compared for the purpose of analyzing his view on any given theme."[40] The differences of approach and conclusion reached by Elior and Foxbrunner serve to underline the breadth of R. Shneur Zalman's teachings and the diversity of ideas to be found in the writings of this great polymath.

Another unusual characteristic of Habad is its interest in history. The many "historiographical" activities of Habad during the lifetime of the former Rebbe are a good example. These included the publication of his memoirs, which were in fact stories about R. Shneur Zalman, the Besht, and other figures in the early history of Hasidism, the periodical *Ha-Tamim*,[41] and the "discovery" of a *genizah* in Kherson.[42] All of these are part of the enduring Habad interest in history which can be traced back to R. Shneur Zalman. The recent publication of the many manuscripts of teachings and collections of letters, alluded to above, are also examples of this concern. The amount of manuscript material that has been preserved and the precision of the documentation, which even includes specific dates and places where teachings were first taught, is virtually unprecedented in the history of Hasidism.[43] Ada Rapoport-Albert had analyzed the role of historiography in Habad and has shown its central place

---

40. Ibid.
41. Originally published from 1935 to the end of 1938 in Warsaw, the complete series was reprinted in Kfar Habad, 1984. Many of the articles are of a historical nature.
42. For a summary of the controversy surrounding the historical authenticity of the materials from Kherson, see, I. Raphael, "Genizat Kherson," *Sinai* 81 (1977), pp. 129-150. The scholarly consensus is that these documents are not authentic.
43. The only other hasidic group that even comes close to Habad in its level of documentation is Bratzlav. A recent phenomenon worthy of note and study is the "invasion" of scholarly apparatus, i.e., footnotes and source documentation, into internal hasidic periodicals and the many editions of classic texts which have a scholarly veneer added to them through the addition of notes and indices.

throughout the history of the movement.[44] Her study is a major contribution to our understanding of Habad Hasidism.

It has long been known that the printer who published *Shivhei ha-Besht* (In Praise of the Baal Shem Tov) Israel Yaffe, was a follower of R. Shneur Zalman. Recently, Moshe Rosman[45] has shown that the Habad influence on this first "historical" work of Hasidism is even more central than has been supposed. Not only was R. Shneur Zalman the source of a group of traditions about the early stages of the Baal Shem Tov's activities, but Rosman has shown that important editorial decisions reflected the specific circumstances of the Habad community following the death of R. Shneur Zalman and the controversy surrounding the succession. The publication of *Shivhei ha-Besht* was part of an effort to legitimate the succession of R. Dov Baer in the face of a challenge from R. Aaron ha-Levi of Staroselye.

The publication of many new manuscript materials from Habad sources and the scholarly studies of recent years have added significantly to our understanding of R. Shneur Zalman and his thought. A groundwork has been laid, but the scholarly study of Hasidism is still at a relatively early stage. As it develops, our understanding of R. Shneur Zalman and his intellectual legacy will be enhanced.

---

*My thanks to Zalman Alpert for reading an earlier draft of this article and offering many helpful suggestions and valuable insights.

---

44. "Hagiography with Footnotes: Edifying Tales and the Writing of History in Hasidism," *Essays in Jewish Historiography*, ed. A. Rapoport-Albert, in *History and Theory*, Beiheft 27 (1988), pp. 119-159.
45. "Sefer *Shivhei ha-Besht* va-Arikhato," *Zion* 58 (1993), pp. 175-214.

EMANUEL S. GOLDSMITH

The National Poet of Yiddish Literature

On Abraham Lyessin*

THE ONE HUNDREDTH ANNIVERSARY of the American Yiddish literary monthly *Di Tsukunft* (The Future) affords us the opportunity to renew our acquaintance with one of the truly great Yiddish literary figures — Abraham Walt Lyessin, who edited the publication from 1913 until his death in 1938. Lyessin transformed *Di Tsukunft* from an instrument of socialist, anarchist and assimilationist propaganda into one of the most widely respected journals of critical thought, literary creativity and Jewish survivalism in the Jewish world. His editorials, articles and poems brought the journal and its readers into the mainstream of Jewish life and made it a respected platform for a wide variety of positions and opinions on Jewish and general issues. (The *Tsukunft* continues to be published and is in fact the oldest extant Yiddish publication in the world.)

Lyessin's reputation had preceded his arrival in America in 1897. Even before the establishment of the Jewish Labor Bund of Russia and Poland, the former yeshiva student established a dedicated organization of followers committed to a synthesis of radical socialism with Jewish nationalism. Lyessin actually came to America only because he had to escape the Czarist police. He also achieved fame in Russia as a young Yiddish poet whose revolutionary poems and social satires were well known among both workers and Jewish socialist leaders in the Pale of Settlement.

Despite his longing for old world Judaism, for his comrades in Russia, and for the chance to participate in the coming revolution, Lyessin found a fertile field for both political activism and his literary talents on New York's lower east side. Those were the years when assimilationism and cosmopolitanism were the regnant ideologies among the newly arrived Jewish

---

*Translations from Yiddish in this essay are by the author.

immigrants. Socialists, Anarchists and others vied in debunk-
ing Jewish tradition and dethroning the Almighty. In the
articles, editorials and poems which he published in the *For-
verts*, to which he became a regular contributor and sometime
editor, as well as in the *Tsukunft*, Lyessin became the
champion of Jewish history and tradition and the voice of
Jewish self-respect in Yiddish-speaking America.

Lyessin admonished the Jewish workers and intellectuals
who were joining the socialist ranks in ever greater numbers
to seek inspiration for their suffering and defiance in the
prophets and sages of Israel rather than in the writings of
Marx and Lasalle. He addressed the Jewish masses in the
spirit of the ancient Jewish dedication to morality, heroism
and sacrifice. He drew upon figures and events from Jewish
history to comfort, encourage, arouse and attack. He made
Judaism and the Jewish experience relevant and vital for
masses of Jews who were on the verge of abandoning their
Jewishness in the heat of their struggle for justice and dignity.

NATIONAL SIGNIFICANCE

Lyessin's role in Yiddish literature is not unlike that of
Hayyim Nahman Bialik in Hebrew literature. He may justly
be called the national poet of the Yiddish tongue. Together
with Yitzkhok Leybush Peretz and H. Leivick, Lyessin became
a major mentor to Yiddish writers and readers. Peretz,
Lyessin and Leivick together shaped the contours of modern
Yiddish literature by demonstrating how the four thousand
year-old Jewish historical, literary and religious heritage
might be utilized as a creative force in the Jewish present and
future. Although Peretz's modernized folktales and hasidic
stories deal with the past, they are actually oriented toward
the future. They seek to instruct modern Jews in how to
continue the traditions of the "sabbath and festival Jews," the
proud and spiritually powerful Jews of yesteryear. As B.
Rivkin notes, Lyessin's poetry, like Peretz's tales in the folk
spirit, bore the promise of a Yiddish literature that would be
different from other literatures, "a literature that would be
more than literature: it would through art produce moral

energy for direct usage in life."[1]

Leivick was in many respects an heir of Lyessin. In his quest for Jewish spiritual strength, Leivick finds it in the legends of the talmudic and medieval periods. In his dramatic works he introduces figures such as the Messiah, Rabbi Judah Loewe of Prague (*Maharal*), the Golem, Rabbi Meir of Rothenburg (*Maharam*) and the Eternal Jew. Leivick learned much from Peretz but even more from Lyessin. There is a direct line from Lyessin's poems of Jewish heroism and martyrdom to Leivick's Holocaust poems (*I Was Not in Treblinka*, 1945) and to many of his dramas, including *Miracle in the Ghetto, Maharam of Rothenburg* and *The Wedding in Fernwald*.

Lyessin was born on May 19, 1872 in Minsk and died in New York on November 5, 1938. Like many of his contemporaries, he made the transition from traditional Judaism to socialism and modernity in a relatively brief time. Although he became a pioneer of Jewish socialism and of Yiddish socialist poetry while still a youth, it was in the United States that he became a journalist and editor as well as one of the classical Yiddish poets.

EARLY ACCEPTANCE

Lyessin's early poems became popular among the Jewish workers in Russia because of their mellifluent language, classical prosody, revolutionary message, and directness. The poem "In the Distant North" (1896), for example, was set to music and sung throughout the Jewish world. It depicts the death-throes of a revolutionary exiled to Siberia and the suffering of his beloved far away.

> In the cold land where the mighty waters
> Of the Lena river flow,
> Stands a tiny cottage
> Hidden in eternal snow.
> A plaything of the storm,
> It stands abandoned in the field.
> There in icy loneliness
> Smarts a sick and dying heart.

---

1. B. Rivkin, *Grunt-Tendentsn fun der Yidisher Literatur in Amerike*, New York, 1948, p.113

Winter keeps on howling
In all its blind and roaring power,
Darkness keeps on shielding
A mute, eternal night.

His death-throes keep oppressing
With suffering, endless pain.
The pale martyr tosses and turns
In oppressive, painful sleep.

It is apparent that H. Leivick's famous poem "Somewhere Far" (*Ergets Vayt*) was influenced by Lyessin's "In the Distant North." Years later, when he was already in America, Lyessin recalled the revolutionary Jewish youth of Russia and proudly proclaimed: "They are all ours, I see them and recognize our sisters and brothers!"

Not like the folk hero of the Russian book,
Not like the poets' dream,
Not in slippers and not in fur cloaks
Do they come to save Russia;
These children of the ghetto,
These poorest of Jews, the mocked and the scorned,
The very last of the slave mass
Are the first in redemption!

As great as Lyessin's influence on Leivick's Siberian poems was the influence of his *musar* themes on Leivick and later on the *musar* poems and novels of Chaim Grade. Lyessin writes of

The happiness to also be able to renounce happiness,
The joy to also be able to renounce joy —
To passionately restrain passion
And proudly conquer pride in the ecstasy of suffering.

In his memoirs, Lyessin recalls that, as a boy, among the thick volumes of the Talmud and the Codes in his father's bookcase there were also little books in Rashi script which he loved to read. These were ancient Jewish historical chronicles like *The Vale of Weeping*, *The Tribe of Judah* and *The Remnant of Israel*. In these chronicles Lyessin discovered "burning streams of Jewish tears and blood, wrapped in ancient yellow leaves." Hidden in a corner of the house, by the light of a lamp, the poet read the tales of Jewish martyrdom as he wept and swore that he too would conduct himself like the martyrs.[2]

MARTYRDOM THEME

Early in his career he began to connect the tales of the religious martyrs of the past with the socialist martyrs of his own generation. Gradually Jewish history of all the ages became for him one great martyrdom and the Jewish people "a nation of Jesuses and the Jesus of the nations."

> The brothers and sisters of Jesus march,
> Bent beneath the heavy crucifix.
> Not one but all — a nation of Jesuses,
> Bloodied, mocked and spat upon.

> Unseen they bear the crucifix through the exile,
> Not the wood of a mute tree
> But the raging hatred of all humankind,
> A roaring world gone mad.

> This path of pain is not a few streets long
> And it does not take just a few minutes;
> Space itself echoes their march of woe,
> Eternity saps their very blood.

On placing a wreath of flowers on the grave of a contemporary martyr of the Jewish working class, Fruma Frumkin, the poet states that "the hangman's noose never strangled a more pious life."

> So did our mothers walk
> To their martyrdom as sacrifices,
> Reciting a prayer over the slaughterer's knife,
> Responding with "Amen" and dying.

According to Lyessin, the greatness of the Jewish people is to be found in its being a victim rather than a perpetrator; a

---

2. A. Lyessin, *Zikhroynes un Bilder*, New York, 1954 , p 14.

martyr rather than a persecutor.[3] In human suffering,
especially the suffering of an entire nation during the
millennia, he finds a spark of the divinity in people and a
source of beauty, purity and light.[4] The Jewish people knows
"the sanctity of life which is reflected in the sanctity of
death."[5] It proclaims, in the poet's words: "I die in my life and
live in my death."

The power of Lyessin's martyrological poetry may be traced
to the author's complete identification with the victims and his
deep desire to partake of their suffering. He speaks in one
poem about how as a child, upon reading of Jews burned at
the stake during the Inquisition, he placed his finger over a
candle flame in order to experience the pain of the fire.
Lyessin empathizes with his suffering people throughout
history, with the martyrs of the Babylonian exile, the Roman
persecutions, the medieval ghetto, the Inquisition, the
pogroms of early modern and modern times. The long list of
martyrs depicted in his poems covers major and minor
personalities of the whole range of Jewish history. He writes of
the martyred rabbis of the Hadrianic era as well as of Jewish
cobblers and blacksmiths in the Russia of his day who
performed acts of remarkable courage in testimony to their
hopes and ideals. For Lyessin all of these heroes and martyrs
constitute manifestations of the Eternal Jew who marches
throughout the world down the centuries "through sand and
thorns, through stones and bones." Standing an anti-Semitic
image on its head, Lyessin speaks of the Eternal Jew making
a covenant with the devil so that the elements cannot harm
him nor natural disasters nor time itself destroy him!

> I feel I am stronger than all sufferings,
> All human malice and strife,
> And stronger than water, fire and storm
> And even stronger than time.
> Through the millennia, before my eyes,

---

3. Y. Mark, "Abraham Lyessin," *Di Goldene Keyt*, no.49, Tel Aviv,
   1964, p. 113.
4. M. Ribalow, "Abraham Lyessin: Poet fun Yidisher Geshikhte," *Di
   Tsukunft*, April 1936, p. 313.
5. A. Lyessin, *Lider un Poemen*, New York, 1938, vol. III, p. 104f.

The greatest kingdoms disappeared,
The strongest peoples were annihilated,
Major cities were plowed into salt,
Gigantic mountains disintegrated long ago,
Eternal forests rotted and were trampled,
Mighty rocks were softened into mud —
But I live and still exist!

I live and I live and I will yet go on living
Through millennia of strife,
I will continue to live and struggle and strive
And dull is the tooth of time!

The mission of the Jewish people, as Lyessin conceives it, is expressed in his celebrated ode on the Yiddish language.

Carry forward, my child, the teaching of the ages,
Even if in an altered light —
To live and die for sacred teachings
And to be a stiffnecked people of martyrs.

ROLE OF LANGUAGE

For Lyessin the significance of Yiddish lies in its dual role as the language in which the sacred teachings of the nation were transmitted orally from generation to generation and as the language of suffering and martyrdom. At a time when most speakers of the language in America lacked even a basic respect for its historical and contemporary significance, Lyessin's words constituted an ideological as well as aesthetic breakthrough.

I come to you, my child, from the silent exile,
From crowded, sealed-off ghettos.
I possess only the beauty of pious prayers,
I have naught but the loveliness of martyrdom.
And if I have no lightning flashes that blind one
Or flaming sun-like words that perform miracles,
I do have the sparkle of starry legends,
The precious moonlight of the spirit.
From Worms, from Mainz, from Speyer,
From Prague

and Lublin to Odessa,
One fire continued to burn,
One miracle continued to glow.
Wherever mortal enemies lay waiting
And death was ready nearby —
There, alone and in sorrow,
I accompanied your parents.
For hundreds of years together
We faced every danger.
I absorbed all the anger
And I took in all the pain.
I forged through the generations
The wonder of will power and woe:
To live for sacred teachings
And die for them with strength.
If pure holiness
Be reflected in suffering,
Then, my child, I am yours,
I am your most sacred one.

Hand in hand with Lyessin's glorification of the Jewish past went his concern with its present. Though most of his colleagues and comrades refused to identify themselves in any way with the Zionist enterprise, Lyessin supported the resettlement of Palestine and eagerly followed the development of the *yishuv*. He won the admiration and appreciation of a number of Zionist luminaries including Yosef Hayyim Brenner, Berl Katzenelson and Zalman Shazar. Shazar wrote of Lyessin that "Just as his heart was drawn to the Jewish revolutionary in Russia, so was his Jewish heart drawn to the Jewish pioneer in Eretz Yisrael. One distant example of loveliness sparkled and united with another distant example of loveliness and both nourished his internal opposition to the reality around him."[6]

Many of Lyessin's poems also convey the poet's profound anxiety over the Jewish future.

When I think, my people, of the fears of the past,
I'm caught and obsessed with your sorrow —
The glory of your thorn-wreath amid the nations,
Your three thousand year-old sentence.

---

6. Z. Shazar, *Opshatsungen un Eseyen*, Tel Aviv, 1976, p. 103.

When I think, my people, of your better future,
I become so sad and gloomy.
Will you vanish in happiness? For what then
Your sufferings of thousands of years?

It is difficult to think of another poet as inspired by love of his people as Lyessin. His *ahavat Yisrael* is much more than a literary theme or political program. In his poetry, the silent prayers uttered every year on the night of Tisha b'Av, were fulfilled.

Would that I were for my nation
A little ray of the light
That will drive away the cloud
Of thousands of years of pain.

Would that I were for my nation
A little spark of the flame
That will melt a path through the hatred
It will meet on its wanderers' way.

Would that I were for my nation
A speck of the dust on the road
On which it will finally march in joy
Toward the dawn of a better day.

IMPACT OF AMERICA

Lyessin's poetry bears the influence of several sources but primarily that of the American Yiddish press and literature in the early decades of the twentieth century. When Lyessin arrived in the United States in 1897 he was hardly more than a beginner as a poet. "As a person athirst, Lyessin made his way to our press, which was then already flourishing, and to our literature, which was then in its ascendancy. He devoured them and used them to brightly color his language and style."[7]

Lyessin's poems affect the reader principally with their directness and intimacy. H. Leivick saw in the poet's intimate

---

7. Y. Entin, "Abraham Lyessin," *Di Tsukunft*, February-March 1953, p. 105.

tone the key to his personality and creativity. Lyessin does not simply sing of afflictions and martyrdom. We often get the feeling that he is actually participating in torture and death himself. His choice of historical themes is never an escape from the present but rather an attempt to make the past live in the present.[8] Lyessin always chooses decisive events in Jewish history as well as seminal figures who achieve immortality by willingly accepting death through martyrdom. Aaron Zeitlin characterizes Lyessin's finest poems as achieving an authenticity which elevates them to a level beyond literature. "On the one hand they are documents, on the other — music. In those poems is accumulated all the energy of his word which is filled with fear and prayer, hope and disillusionment, all the conflicts of a modern Jew."[9]

Another key to Lyessin's poetry can be found in the personal tragedies of his own life: the death of his wife Libe Ginzburg in 1912 and the terrible illness of their only child, Rokhele. Rokhele was born with a hydrocephalic head which grew larger and more deformed with the passing years while her body shrank and grew weaker. Lyessin had to guard the deformed child as the apple of his eye since without him she could not function.[10]

Lyessin's personal tragedy affected and purified his writing and he became "the singer of sadness, pain and sorrow, a wrestler with mirages of hope. This almost turned Lyessin into the loveliest, most anguished and heavy laden of poets."[11] There was a wonderful harmony between Lyessin's ethical personality and his poetic calling. "The ethical personality aroused and spurred the poet to give the personality full and salient expression." [12]

---

8. H. Leivick, *Eseyen un Redes*, New York, 1963, p. 171.
9. A. Zeitlin, *Literarishe un Filosofishe Eseyen*, New York, 1980, p. 45.
10. R. Ayzland, *Fun Undzer Friling*, New York, 1954, p. 201.
11. Y. Entin, *op. cit.*, p. 107.
12. A. Tabachnik, *Dikhter un Dikhtung*, New York, 1965, p. 82.

FACTUAL UNDERPINNING

As noted above, Lyessin's historical poems are suffused with the hot breath of contemporary events. Lyessin often provides his poems with historical notes and comments. In the note on "The Young Apostate" he compares Hitler's persecutions of the Austrian Jews with the persecution of the Jews of Vienna in the 15th century. "Just as has recently been done with the Jews of Burgundy, so long ago were certain Viennese Jews packed into vessels full of holes, without oars, and shoved off on the blue waves of the Danube. An additional number of Jews — men, women and children, who were imprisoned in a synagogue, slaughtered themselves because they had heard that their children would be taken away from them and baptized. The remaining Jews were dragged from all of the prisons and burned on a pyre. The story tells that they all went to their fiery death as to the marriage canopy... A certain number of children were nevertheless kidnapped. Since they stubbornly refused to be baptized, they were sold into slavery. Among the few who were baptized was a young man, handsome and talented, who pleased the Baron very much. He was taken to the palace and was finally made an adjutant. But despite all the wild pleasures of the rakish life which the well-placed knights lead, the young man could nevertheless not suppress his gnawing longing for the Jewish faith and for his murdered brothers and sisters."[13]

> The baron searches for him,
> Surprised that he rides alone.
> And in exaltation the knight shows him the spot:
>
> "This is where they brought them together
> In the hundreds, and before the idols there,
> As a whole offering, threw them into the flames —
> I still hear the sacred songs
> Ascending in the flames."

---

13. A. Lyessin, *Lider un Poemen*, vol. III , p. 123.

The excited, angry baron warns him:
"Though I pity your young life,
You are a Christian now, sprinkled with holy water,
And I must convey you to the Church tribunal:
Oh, blind one, like your accursed people,
You will certainly not avert the flames!"

The knight bends lower:
"Yes, my lord,
Though I thank you for your kindness and goodwill,
I would thank you even more deeply
If you would fulfill my glorious wish.
Permit me, like my brothers, to
Even now burn for the name of God!"

Lyessin wrote epic and narrative poems in Yiddish before these forms had been really mastered by any other Yiddish poets. His Yiddish poems exhibited the classical literary possibilities of the language long before the *Yunge* or young rebels headed by Zishe Landau, Mani Leib and M. L. Halpern did their work. The critic A. Tabachnik marvels at the musical qualities of a poem like "Shine, My Lantern" which is so close to the spirit of Yiddish folk song and possesses all the qualities of a rhythmicized prayer or supplication.[14]

Shine, my lantern, a little bit longer,
Home is near now, rest close at hand,
I'll soon be there and close my weary eyes.
As I fall into sleep, into very deep sleep,
And I sink, far from all, into blissfulness,
Angel Michael guards me on the right,
Angel Gabriel guards me on the left
And all my anxieties are eased —
Shine, my lantern, a little bit longer.

Lyessin's achievements transcend the parameters of his period and his generation. They constitute pinnacles in the history of Yiddish culture and Jewish continuity. Lyessin remains unique in having been the only Yiddish poet to have singlemindedly devoted all of his talent to giving expression to

---

14. A. Tabachnik, *op. cit.*, p. 84.

the history and sufferings of the Jewish people. "The reader who loves the rhythm, sound and enchantment of poetry appreciates the poetic beauty revealed to him in Judaism, and the reader who is enthralled by the grandeur and divinity of Judaism is grateful for this Jewish light which radiates to him from the poetry."[15] Lyessin's legacy lives on in the annals of the Jewish spirit and in the treasury of Jewish creative expression.

15. M. Ribalow, op. cit., p. 313.

EZRA SPICEHANDLER

The Achievement of T. Carmi
On the Occasion of His 70th Birthday

T. CARMI OCCUPIES a unique position in Israeli poetry. Like the works of his close friend, the late poet Dan Pagis, his writing defies categorization. Neither belonged to the dominant schools of poetry which prevailed in Israel since Carmi's arrival there in 1947, yet both are major figures in contemporary Hebrew literature.

As a young poet, Carmi was part and yet not part of the so-called Palmach generation. Like them, he was a product of the Hebraist-Zionist movement and served as a soldier during Israel's war of independence (for a short time he was even a member of a Palmach unit). Like them, he was politically associated with the Zionist left and was among the young poets encouraged and cultivated by Abraham Shlonsky, the *eminence gris* of Israel's literary left. Early in his career, he was appointed as the editor of *Masa* the literary supplement which for many years served as a major vehicle for the Palmach writers. They and their senior mentors welcomed Carmi with open arms attracted by his live intelligence and his amiable personality.

Yet he was also not part of them. Unlike them, he is a native American Jew, born in New York in 1925 to a Hebraist-Zionist family. His father was a modern Orthodox rabbi who became a prominent Hebrew educator. The Carmis belonged to a handful of American Hebraists who had decided to raise their children in Hebrew. Carmi's parents even saw to it that he and his brother would spend three years in pre-state Eretz Yisrael in the early 1930's.

American Hebraists sought to integrate their Zionist commitment within the American cultural milieu. In alliance with neo-Orthodox elements, they founded Hebrew day schools which were designed to transmit traditional Jewish values and Zionist ideals together with a general American

176

education to their children.

The Jewish education of the young Carmi differed in three respects from the secular curriculum which most of his Israeli contemporaries had received either in pre-state Palestine or in the *Tarbut* schools of pre-World War II Eastern Europe. In American day schools, Jewish subjects were religiously orientated. Then too all secular subjects were taught in English, not mostly in Hebrew as they were overseas. Finally, while in the Yishuv and in Eastern Europe the non-Jewish literary influences were either Eastern or Central European, in American Jewish day schools they were decidedly Anglo-American.

Like a number of the graduates of the Hebrew day school system, he continued his secondary education at the Teachers' Institute of the Yeshiva University. Here and in several similar schools (The Teachers' Institute of the Jewish Theological Seminary and Herzliah) a group of students organized the Histadrut Hanoar Haivri (The Hebrew Youth Organization), one of whose major activities was the founding of *Niv,* a literary magazine, which became the organ for a new generation of American trained Hebrew writers. Carmi, the youngest member of the Niv group had his earliest poems published in its pages.

Carmi is a prolific poet and translator. Since 1958, he has published thirteen volumes of original verse, Hebrew translations of five plays by Shakespeare (*Midsummer Night's Dream*, 1964, 1978; *Measure For Measure*, 1979; *Hamlet*, 1981; *Much To Do About Nothing*, 1983 and *Othello*, 1991); several French plays (by Ghelarode, Giraudoux and Rostand), a comedy by Berthold Brecht and *Antigone* by Sophocles. Almost all of these have been presented on the Israeli stage and were widely acclaimed. His poems have been translated into English, French and German. A list of the main works which have been translated is appended to this article. In addition, many of his poems have appeared in leading European and American literary journals. Some of them were translated by leading contemporary poets: Ted Hughes, Dom Moraes and Stephen Mitchell.

Carmi is a distinguished member of the faculty of the Jerusalem School of the Hebrew Union College which has awarded him an honorary doctorate. He has also served as a visiting poet at several universities. Among them are: Tel Aviv University, New York University, Harvard, Yale, Oxford and Berkeley. He has represented Israel at many international literary conferences. In 1992, he received the prestigious Bialik Prize in recognition of his important contribution to Hebrew literature.

LITERARY BEGINNINGS

Carmi's early literary efforts in the United States have all the characteristics of a budding young poet's effort to master his medium. Only after his return to Eretz Yisrael, where he settled in 1947, did he develop his own voice and even then he did not find it until the late 1950's with the publication of *Ha-Yam ha-Aharon* (The Last Sea, 1958) for which he was awarded the distinguished Brenner Prize. When he published his *Selected Poems* in 1970, he himself included very few poems from his first book *Mum ve-Halom* (The Wound and the Dream, 1951). Yet he did include the title poem of this book which already contained the seed of what he would fully develop later as his views on the *ars poetica*.

> My left hand is under your head
> And my right grates the scratch:
> I've betrothed you with a wound and a dream,
> With neither mercy nor loving kindness.

In the poem, the speaker explains the betrayal of his beloved as being a result of his inability to sustain his love for her. His dream is spoiled by his wound.

> Our Spring was aflame,
> Our Summer tainted by Fall:....
>
> Our tent was folded and was silent,
> Our melody rotted in the leaf fall:
> We were betrothed with a wound and a dream
> With neither mercy nor loving kindness.

(Selected Poems, p. 60)

The addressee, at first reading, is a woman but she also represents the poet's muse. The poetic act is simultaneously an embrace and a scratching at the wound. (In Hebrew, *Mum* denotes blemish, defect, handicap).

The dream, which is the creative imagination of the poet, cannot be fully realized because of the blemish–the detachment which art demands from the artist. The dream is not only impaired by this wound but also by the artist's painful awareness that the translation of the dream into words always falls short of the thing in itself. The "wound" may also echo the well-known remark by Yeats, a poet very much admired by Carmi: "People become writers in the first place by those things which hurt you."

Carmi's profound knowledge of Hebrew sources, a product not only of his intensive religious education but of his constant studying of the many facets of a long literary tradition, is an enriching element in his poetry (One of the side products of his erudition is his splendid *Penguin Anthology of Hebrew Poetry,* which includes selections from more than two millennia of Hebrew verse). His own poetry is replete with allusions to biblical, rabbinic and kabbalistic texts and links his *oeuvre* with an ancient literary tradition. Like many secular modern Hebrew poets, his frequent use of the tension between the sacred subtext and the secular text affords him opportunities for ironic play. In this early poem, the allusions are mainly biblical. In *Song of Songs* II:6, the beloved woman declares: "His left hand is under my head; his right hand embraces me." Here Carmi reverses the roles. The speaker is a man. He also replaces the second part of the biblical text with a *surprise:* "And my right hand grates the scratch." Perhaps this recalls Job's disease (Job I:8) which is then followed by the bitter scolding of Job's wife (verse 9), "Do you still hold on to your innocence (naiveté)?" The speaker then shifts to another biblical allusion: "I shall betroth thee to me in righteousness and in judgement and in loving-kindness and in mercy" (Hosea XII:19) – words which the prophet lovingly declares as he renews his love for his once adulterous wife. In the refrain which closes both the first and final stanza of the poem, the betrothal is rather "with a wound and a dream, with neither mercy nor loving kindness."

In another poem, "To...", the superscription is a quotation
by Robert Graves: "The muse is the perpetual other woman."
The speaker addresses the muse as "The enemy, (Hebrew
tsarah = second wife, enemy, trouble), the other, the stranger
who lifts me with her in a storm. / The desirable, the calmer,
the hand of refuge,/ who closes my eyes/ slowly. /The beloved,
the betrayer.../Who covers my voice (my inspiration)/ With a
goat's pelt. The harlot, the peddler, my possession,/ Who
waves the scarlet thread/ in her window." (*Selected Poems*,
p.124)

The allusion to the goat's pelt is to the disguise which Jacob
used in order to deceive Isaac into believing that he was Esau
(Genesis XXVII:16). Perhaps the speaker is expressing his fear
that the unbridled, wild animal passions he voices are merely
a disguise covering his more controlled scholarly detachment.
The call of the muse remains overbearing. As the temptress, it
ultimately destroys all other emotional relationships or
commitments.

POETIC CREDO

Carmi's view of poetry may be described as being in the
classical anti-romantic mode. He has argued that modern
Hebrew poets must relate to what Eliot had called the
tradition. Carmi is indeed at home in the wide range of Jewish
literature from the earliest fragments of biblical poetry to the
latest works of his own generation. Like Eliot, he views the
literary tradition not as a restrictive code but as a rich
resource on which the modern Hebrew writer may draw to fit
the needs of his individual talent. In 1974, he stated in an
interview: "I live within a specific tradition and I am
permitted, even obliged to utilize it. I wish that the
relationship between what is written today in poetry and our
poetic tradition be like the relationship between Bartok and
Beethoven."

A second characteristic of his poetry, particularly his works
written in the 1960's and 1970's, is his recourse to the
concrete—a technique he learned from both the British and
American imagists and from several Hebrew poets (David

Fogel and to some extent Lea Goldberg). Thus, for example, "Love Poem" is an imagist poem reminiscent of the early Pound.

> You are slippery (the original Hebrew line reads: My
>   slippery one) –
> You slide through my fingers
> Like a cake of soap
> Into the drain (eddy) of the tub.
> I grope and fumble in vain.
> Only after the many waters run out
> I find you at the bottom,
> Pure and shining,
> White (or a moon) in the white sky.

Into Another Land, p. 19)

The white, shimmering, evasive cake of soap reminds the lover who is taking a shower while in a hotel in a distant city, of his evasive, white rounded love. The vain groping after the soap reminds him of her mystery, her charm, and physical beauty. The many waters allude to her elusiveness as well as to the sea which separates them.

An example of "the dry hardness" of Carmi's later verse can be found in part I of a poem called *Landscapes.*

> A white bird on a green river, two,
> And afterwards three.
> One electric-pole,two,
> Three bushes.
> More than that, roofs
> And clouds and stalks of grass.
> It's hard to count on a train,
> And therefore I don't mention them.
> Actuality I think I'll jot down (record, sketch)
> Only a single bird,
> And perhaps just its wings.

(*The Unicorn Looks at the Mirror,* pp. 34-35)

The speaker is on a train hurtling through a scenic countryside. The rapidity of the train's motion affords him only a fleeting glimpse of the passing landscape. Even the number of objects becomes blurred. In line three, for example, is the speaker referring to two electric poles or to two or three bushes? "It's hard to count on a train." We may presume that the poem deals with the problem of artistic conception. Is life a speeding train ride in which the observer cannot focus upon every object that fleets by him and even express its significance? The speaker narrows his range down to a simple bird and maybe merely to a single anatomical detail – its wings. The choice of the wings perhaps is a metonymy indicating the artistic imagination. The eye of the reader is fixed upon the wings and it is up to the reader to construct the meaning of the image.

Another aspect of Carmi's *ars poetica* is expressed in the poem "First I will Sing."

> First I will sing (say poetry). Then perhaps I will speak.
> And repeat the words I already said
>
> Like a person who studies his features (the marks on his
>   face) at dawn.
> I shall return to my silences
>
> As the moon decreases.
> I shall publicly brandish the bird of weeping
>
> As a child draws his sword on Purim.
> I will return to (woo) your closed hands
>
> Like a lamp shade ceaselessly turning black.
> So I shall return, keep silent and weep
>
> And I will sing. First I will sing. Wrap my words
> In paper bags like pomegranates.
>
> And then, perhaps we will speak.
>
> (*Selected Poems,* p. 126)

The image of the poetic word being a pomegranate – red and bursting with juice and seed – which must be wrapped in paper bags against the buffeting of the weather is powerful and central to the poem. Art is a private matter, too delicate and vulnerable. The poet must wrap his words "in paper bags." He may partially bare his soul and completely "brandish his bird of weeping" – his hidden pain (his wound – but only "like a child draws his sword on Purim." Purim is the time of masquerading and the child's sword is a cardboard sword. The real pain, the real sword cannot be fully revealed.

PAINFUL REACTIONS

From time to time, Carmi deals with social and political themes but even on such occasions he shuns placard verse. His second volume of verse, for example, is a dramatic poem in several voices which reflects his painful encounter with children who survived the Holocaust. He had served as a volunteer counselor at an orphanage established for such children in northern France in 1946-47. *Ein Perahim Sheho-rim,* (There Are No Black Flowers, 1953) telescopes the tragedy of the Shoah into a series of dramatic monologues spoken by four boys and three adult women. Their agony, their sense of loss mixed with feelings of guilt, is projected against the background of the indifference of society (here embodied in a French bureaucracy which in polite officialese orders that the children's home be evacuated and moved to another locale so that it could be replaced by an atomic installation). A bamboo tree transplanted from the Far East looms as a recurrent image of alienation and homelessness. The poem closes on an optimistic note despite the indifference of society to human life and to the portentous threat of a second *Shoah* of atomic annihilation. Rene, one of the survivor–children hears the wind blowing music through the bamboo shoots and sees "how suddenly the almond tree runs along (the director's) window in the perfumed snow and bursts into (her) room with its amazing abundance invading (her) heart with its white buds – there are no black flowers." (*Selected Poems*, p. 54)

Carmi is a well-travelled poet and has returned to France several times. In 1937, for example, he wrote a moving poem called "A Story" while in Paris.

When the woman in the fishermen's village told me
About her missing husband
And the sea which dies over and over again
      at her doorstep evening after evening,
I was silent.
I could not say to the shells of her eyes
Your lover shall return, or
That the sea will live again.

(There are days when I cannot find
Even a single word
To say to you.)

(*Selected Poems*, p. 79)

Women young and old – wives, lovers, widows, beggars—populate many of Carmi's poems. In an interview, he once spoke of the difficulties which a lyric poet has to escape in order to enter the skin of the "the other." Carmi's poetical voice ripens in *The Last Sea*. the volume in which this poem appears. It is that of a very meticulous artist in full control of his medium. His works show a keen but ambivalent sense of parent-child, husband-wife, lover-beloved relationships. In an essay discussing his poem "In Two Voices," he describes how he conceived one of his poems on the theme of parenthood:

"I happened to be sitting in a Parisian café next to a table at which a father and his son were sitting. They seemed to enjoy each other's company. Then the father placed the open palm of his hand on the table. Without uttering a word, the child put his hand into his father's. The father began to smile and the smile broadened until it faded. At that very second the child withdrew his hand, as if he wanted to rescue it. Something in this scene gripped me and I tried to turn it into a poem... Finally I got the idea of combining both the first person voice with the second expressing them simultaneously... that of the father and that of the observer's eye... The father's voice is in the first person and given in short sentences, the observer's is in the third person and in longer narrative segments":

"My eldest son—first of my strength"
When the boy's hand rested in his father's
"Put your hand in my hand"
Light of the deep floods the spring of my eyes
"Flesh of my flesh"
Bathing the smiling face like dew
"How can I contain the compassion"
The boy's small hand, the father's big hand
"Which overflows the banks of my fingers"
The jaw-bones break into a smile
"My son, my son"
The child retrieves his lost hand (the loss of his hand)
"Do not pull your hand back!"

(*Selected Poems,* p. 83)

The father's compassion of love had reached a level which frightened him; the child, too, instinctively defends himself by withdrawing to his self. In such poems, Carmi finds his true voice, whether they deal with father-child relationships (Carmi is a father of three sons and his relationship with his own father was complex), relationships between lovers, marital love, infidelity and divorce.

POLITICAL AWARENESS

Although, as indicated above, he never shunned writing social or political verse, he did so infrequently. His poem "Model Lesson," written before 1970, reminds us of "A Grammar of Practical Hebrew," a poem by Dan Pagis, a poet whom he very much admired:

In Biafra this year a million and a half died–
As the phrase goes:
Men, women and children–
Or, following the traditional order on a sinking ship:
Women, children, and men.

The plural is really not "number."
Its cheek, you might say, has no scratch
Nor are its ears inflamed.
So, too, are red or black toys.

Let's remember the colors: Red, Black
Likewise, the past tense has no time. (*Zeman* in
    Hebrew means both time and tense) ...
Therefore, show a bit of courtesy (lit.: the way of the earth).
We must rephrase every thing once more
In the singular and in the present:
In Biafra a child is dying and/or and/or.

Is it clear?
Now that I have handed out the forms,
Let's fill them out.
And then in the present and singular
Let's each go home
The way all the earth goes.

(Selected Poems. p. 195)

Allowing for all differences in setting, the poem about the
widowed fisherwoman in an English village could have been
written about an Israeli war widow. References to Israel's
constant awareness of the threat of war abound in poems
written after 1967. As, for example in the opening poem
"Order of the Day" in *Writer's Apology,* 1974:

Make the children happy!
Make the children happy!
Make the children happy!

So that they won't hear the throttled cries in our throat
So that they won't see the forest of antennas which
    sprout from our heads
So that they not hear the sounds of rending which
    rises on every side:
Clothing, paper, bed sheets, skies...
So they not see the camouflaged colors under the
    skins of our faces
So they not hear the communications net-work burning in
    our body.

We have to devise a code for adults:
"Distant Bell" (killed)
"Green Pine" (missing in action)
"Little Cloud" (taken prisoner)
"Bird's Nest" (wounded)

This is your commander
The bird's nest was carried away by a little cloud,
Rested on the green pine, at the sound of the distant bell.
Good night. End of dispatch.

To make the children happy!
To make the children happy!

Perhaps the most poignant expression of the tension generated by the situation of constant war which permeated Israeli society is found in "Something Different," the Hebrew title of Carmi's *Selected Poems,* p. 17.

They all say poetry:
Think one thing,
And say another;
Say one thing,
And think.

The winter scene is full of clocks.
A man wears his smile like a coat.
Don't look at the lining.

The noise (Ra'ash) is a gate (Sha'ar).
The fear (Pahad) is a spur (Dahaf).
The blast (Nefets) is a code (Tsofen).
There's nothing which does not compel (Kofeh)
its opposite (Hefko).

The grammar of terrors.
The rules – are very sudden
It's hard to talk.

One thing is clear:
They're all playing (a game).
And another thing:
You are no exception.

This segment is from the closing section of a dramatic monologue in four parts. The first part depicts the Jerusalem landscape which is repeatedly described as different (*aher*). "There's nothing like Jerusalem/ in which this distance says something very opaque (indifferent, unclear)/ and specific."

The second part focuses on the speaker's son and the father's scrupulous concern for his safety.

"Even when the sun shines,/ don't walk on the roadside. When the lamp is before us,/ Put your shadow in mine;/ When it is behind us, put your hand in mine.../ I will teach you games of hide-and-seek." The third part is an erotic interlude. "The sirens drain our blood out of us.... Undress/ 1 must touch you/ at this moment." The power of the poem is in its capturing of the worried tension of a city in danger. But it can be read as a depiction of the fear of death which clouds all human experience and the universal pretense of the living that life is quite normal. The poem's diction is taut and precise. The untranslatable punning in the third stanza of part four reinforces the idea that all is pretense–the hidden meanings of the words are imbedded in their sound. Reversing a few vowels or consonants crack its coded message: *ra'ash* (noise) contains *sha'ar* (gate - the gates) of Jerusalem. *Pahad* (fear) contains *dahaf* (compulsion), *nefets* (blast) contains *tsofen* (code).

INVOLVEMENT AND DETACHMENT

Carmi's poems about human relationships are usually similar to those expressed in "Wound and Dream." His speaker, whether lover or friend, cannot avoid the distancing which the artistic mind must undertake. Often there is a splitting of the personality of the speaker and the art of love becomes a *roman à trois*. This is not always the case. Certainly it is less frequent during a depiction of an early phase of a love affair when the speaker loses his objectivity in the heat of passion. However, as the ardor cools and the relationship becomes routine, the discerning consciousness of the speaker reappears and begins to mar the relationship.

The speaker–poet is always seeking new modes of expression, new experiences, new subjects. This, is the motif of the superb poem "To the Pomegranate" (1962).

Go, go away.
Go to other eyes.
I've already written about you yesterday.

I said green
To your leaves bowing in the wind
And red, red, red
To the drops of your fruit.
I called light to
Your moist, dark, stubborn root.

Now you are no more.
Now you block the day (from my sight)
And the moon which has not yet risen.

(Selected Poems, p. 127)

The coda of the poem is addressed to the speaker's lover. He tells her of the experience with the pomegranate tree but that although "I wrote about you the day before yesterday/ Your young memory inflames my hand like nettle." But he returns to "the peculiar pomegranate,/ Whose blood (guilt) is on my soul, my heart, my hand,/ And it still stands in its place."

In his last two volumes of verse: *Shirim min ha-Azuvah* (1988) (Poems of the *Azuvah*), which because of the ambiguity of the last word of the title was given the rather pale English title *Monologues and Other Poems,* and *Emet ve-Hovah,* translated as *Truth and Consequence* (1993), Carmi demonstrates an even more remarkable control of his medium and rises to an even higher level of poetic achievement. "Ha-Azuvah" is a double entendre. In Hebrew it has two meanings: 1) forsaken, i.e. desolation and 2) the forsaken one, i.e. the abandoned wife. The two central themes of *Shirim min ha-Azuvah* are: 1) the desolation felt by the speaker as he ages and as he suffers the loss of friends. And 2) the theme of his latest divorce – the abandonment of his wife and their home. The volume is dedicated to the memory of his close friend Dan Pagis, a poet whom he admired as an artist and mentor. It opens with a eulogy whose controlled emotion sharpens his grief at Pagis' untimely death. Two of its eight stanzas are in prose (stanzas

1,5). "If these were the usual days, I would have shown him
these lines and he would have passed a slow finger through
them, like a mine detector, and halt at a dangerous crossing,
suggesting a by-pass which might lead to the straight road."
(p. 13)
    Toward the end of this long poem, the speaker says:

> When a good friend dies
> You lose something of your (own) reflection
> From here on
> You always will be missing (lacking). (p. 14)

The lament sets the mood for a series of poems about aging
and death: "Those who remember me are disappearing....."

> I look at the palms of my hand
> And see desolation (Azuvah);
> No shadow, no echo, no voice (bat-kol = divine voice).
> How did they wrench the lines
> From my clenched fists? (p. 17)

In another poem the speaker ruminates:

> Without my sensing it,
> The time has come,
> Escorting me like a shadow.
> We are twins of the ending,
> Two who are one.
> I fool everybody:
> Speak in the singular
> And buy a single bus ticket. (pp. 18-19)

Almost all of the remaining poems in the volume are poems
on the theme of the 'abandoned' one." The speakers are either
the male or female partner.

> When you get a divorce, you are born anew.
> But the angel in charge of forgetting
> (This is your punishment)
> Maliciously forgets to slap you.
> And you are born crippled forever,
> Hard with years. You remember. (p. 39)

The allusion is to the Jewish legend that before its birth a baby was taught all the wisdom of the human experience. But as it emerges from the womb the angel of forgetfulness slaps the baby and causes it to forget everything it had learned.

RECENT WORK

In his latest book of poetry published in 1993, *Truth or Consequence* (literally Truth and Obligation) a title taken from a popular Israeli television show, Carmi returns to the problem of authentic art. On the frontispiece, he quotes both Moses ibn Ezra, the Spanish Hebrew poet, and Charles Baudelaire. Ibn Ezra wrote, "lf a poem were free of lying, it would be no poem." Baudelaire exclaimed: "Hypocrite reader, my double, my brother."

Carmi's speaker elaborates this motif:

> Please don't complain to me
> That I am pretending.
> Who doesn't?
> The queen of the night pretends
> That her reign lasts forever.
> The child pretends that
> There are no pronouns.
> The shed skin pretends
> It will again pretend.
> The spring, the tide, the abacus
> Pretend
> That they will last forever.
>
> Only these words
> Do not pretend. (p. 20)

In "the Whole Truth." the poem which opens the volume, the speaker contends: "I am the liar/ And I search for the truth)," and closes with "But if you would tell me/ That I am a liar,/ I would be very much insulted (offended)."

The speaker's narcissism is boldly assented in "A Letter to the Lyrical Ego":

Dear ego,
What would I do without you?

You are my meal, my clothing.
And when her voice is silent–
My conjugal rights as well...

Because of you I can
Silently ignore my mother,
Curse my sire and father,
Torment my wife.

Because of you I can
Carry, marry, roll in the dust, get divorced,
Plot, kiss, choke,
Grate, ingratiate, grow thin or fat,
Deny, beat my breast and confess–
And it's all true!

Because of you – O my Lyric –
I could distribute my estates
And spit out syllables
At the wind and the dark.

P.S. My dear ego, I forgot the main point.
Because of you I can even ask:
What would I do without you? (pp. 22-23)

The phrase "meal, clothing and conjugal rights" is taken
from a rabbinical listing of the duties husbands owe their
wives. Here the narcissism is blatant.

Of course, like sons and lovers neither mother nor father
are "silently ignored" in this volume. Several poems in part
deal with the death of a father (The death of Carmi's father
may have prompted them, [pp. 69-74]). "On the Death of
Father" is a guilt-ridden poem. The son visits his Orthodox
father lying on his death bed in a hospital:

Oxygen mask on his mouth
And pipes branching out
from his body in all directions

The father's dimming eyes reprimand the agnostic son. "Even now you dare stand at my bed-side bare headed?"

In the poem "Identification" he writes:

> The presider over the dead said: identify!
> Is this your father who sired you? the man
> Who ordered you to say kaddish?
> The man whose order you will violate?

And the reaction of the son:

> Yes, this is the man, and this is his face,
> And where (can I flee) from his face, mouth and eyes?...
> The water did not wash away the voices.

The last line alludes to the ritual washing of the body of the deceased. "This is the man" perhaps echoes *ecce home*, and if so is one of the few christological allusions in Carmi's poetry. The trauma of the father's death may have prompted the inclusion of "On Mother's Death" (an excerpt):

> I saw the moment,
>
> What did you see?
>
> A dried out women,
> Like a Fall leaf,
> Gold and copper on a grey road.
> Veins sparkling in the dew
> And shriveling in the sun.
>
> Paper-leaf,
> Where edges suddenly rise
> In fiery contortions.
>
> A space ship. (p. 75)

Mourning for parents is often a mourning for one's self. The volume contains a series of poems on death opening with a eulogy to the memory of Amir Gilboa, a fellow poet and intimate friend. Readers familiar with Gilboa's poetry will recognize how skilfully Carmi interweaves images of Gilboa's famous poem "Joshua's Face" into his own poem.

Carmi's recent illness may have also led to his focusing on his own mortality. In "To Him Who Is Far and to Him Who Is Near" he writes:

> In the distance–
> A train's whistle is heard
> Like the wail of a baby;
> The note on the wall dangles
> Like burnt-out hyssop;
> The cancerous (Hebrew *sartan* also means crab) line
>   in the damp sand
> Looks like a secret code
> Of a submarine agent.

The view is from a hospital sick bed. The note on the wall is the diagnostic chart, but it conjures up an association with the notes placed in the Western Wall petitioning for heavenly mercy. The cancer works as an undercover agent, or a crab leaving its traces on the sands of time. The poem focuses in closer on the patient: the train and, then, on the wall, on the reality of the medical chart, and finally on the patient himself and his life threatening illness:

> Close by–
> The malignant growth
> (radius 2.7)
> Looks like a malignant growth.
> Shalom I say,
> Shalom to near and far. (p. 81)

The play is on the ambiguous *shalom* which means peace but is more frequently a greeting meaning both goodbye or hello. It emphasizes the uncertainty faced by the patient conscious of his possible death and yet hoping for his survival. But *shalom* meaning peace introduces a calming strain. The critically ill often attempt to reassure themselves that everything will in the end be all right. A controlled despair is expressed in the deceptively simple "Last Instructions":

Kiss her on the mouth,
Lightly, quickly.
Don't tell her
With moving lips
That the night
Devoured your sleep,
That you writhed in terror
And the lamp-shade over your eyes
Edged closer, bit by bit
Like a whispering oxygen mask.

Kiss her gently,
Make it short.
Don't fill her breath (lit. resuscitate her)
with your darkness.

(p. 82)

Near the close of the volume Carmi writes:

Most of the people I see
Lately
Look like people I've already seen
In days past.
A sign that the sentence's end is drawing close;
And I wonder wanting to know
Whether or to whom it would be the same. (p. 84)

As he reaches his seventieth year, he remains the same
fascinating lover of ambiguities. Still delighted by the mirror
of life, he is deeply aware of the darkness which lines its
backside. His sure pen knows the consequences of both the
truth behind the lie and how to discover the delicate balance
between what one says and what one thinks.

I. A Selected Bibliography of Poems of T. Carmi
Translated Into English

The Brass Serpent. Translated by Dom Moraes.
    Andre Deutsch, London; Ohio University Press, 1964
Somebody Like You. Translated by Stephen Mitchell.
    Andre Deutsch, London, 1971
T. Carmi and Dan Pagis / Selected Poems. Translated by Stephen

Mitchell. Penguin Modern European Poets, 1976
At the Stone of Losses. Translated by Grace Schulman.
Jewish Publication Society and University of California Press;
Carcanet Press, Manchester, 1983

II. English Translations of Hebrew Poetry
Edited by T. Carmi

The Modern Hebrew Poem Itself, edited by Stanley Burnshaw,
T. Carmi and Ezra Spicehandler. Holt Rinehart and Winston,
1965/ Harvard University Press, 1989
The Penguin Book of Hebrew Verse, edited and translated by
T. Carmi. Penguin books/Viking Press, 1981

SOL LIPTZIN

Heine and the Yiddish Poets

HEINE'S INTERNATIONAL VOGUE exceeded that of any German poet except Goethe. Upon Yiddish literature his impact was even greater than that of Goethe.

Though Heine hoped to be remembered primarily as a warrior of the pen, a warrior for the liberation of man, posterity remembers him more often as the symbol of the Jew in literature. In the land of his birth, he has been a controversial figure and attitudes toward him have been colored by German reactions toward the Jews. Upon Yiddish literature, however, he exerted only a benign influence. His apostasy has been brushed aside as the regrettable aberration of a young person who saw in Christianity a necessary ticket of admission to society and who atoned for this aberration by the intensely Jewish poems of his later years, the "Hebräische Melodien" of *Romanzero*.

The pioneers of Yiddish poetry, who in the closing decades of the nineteenth century supplanted the *Badkhonim* and Yiddish folksingers, were more original in their poems of social protest, inspired by Heine, than in their love lyrics that followed in his wake.

Yiddish poetry of preceding centuries, reflecting the reality of Jewish life in Eastern Europe, the heartland of Yiddish, was not as rich in love lyrics as were other European literatures. Parents, often with the help of *Shadkhonim,* (matchmakers), arranged marriages for their children. Folksongs of budding desires, frustrated longings, and unhappy marriages did well up from the folksoul. The dramas of Abraham Goldfaden and the sentimental novels of Jacob Dineson did champion the demands of the heart as against the conventions of tradition in the imposed choice of mates. The Yiddish writers who pioneered with love poems had no tradition to guide them. Hence, they turned to Heine for models.

197

The Heine-tone is all too evident in the comparatively few love poems of a century ago. They do not, however, equal the poems of social protest based on Heine. Two of the most popular poets of the 1880s may serve as illustrations: David Edelstadt and S. S. Frug.

Edelstadt was born in 1866 and died at the age of twenty-six. His birthplace Kaluga in the heart of Russia was far from the Jewish Pale. But when at 14 he visited his brothers in Kiev, he heard pogrom-hordes crying for Jewish blood. He felt degraded and dreamed of escape from the land where he was not wanted to a land that welcomed the huddled masses yearning to be free. He later embodied this dream in a lyric based on Heine's "Ein Fichtenbaum." Heine sings of a fir tree that stands lonely in the icy north and that dreams of a palm tree in a distant land warmed by the sun. By means of these tree symbols, Heine gives expression to a lover's frustrated love for his beloved, who is far beyond his reach. Edelstadt, however, in his recasting of this poem, saw mirrored in it his own desolate fate and that of his suffering Jewish people. In his poem, "Der Zelner," a Jewish sentinel stands lonely on guard in Russia, covered with snow and shivering with frost. He dreams of his brothers who live in a free world under a warm sun and amidst green fields. To the two stanzas based on Heine, however, Edelstadt added a third stanza which contradicts Heine's pessimistic mood. The Jewish sentinel stands proudly amidst the storm, gun in hand. He does not despair. A free land beckons to him.

Among the poems in which Edelstadt acknowledges his indebtedness to Heine is the hymn which begins with the words: "I am the sword. I am the flame." He awakens his people to battle against the unjust establishment. All battles demand sacrifices and he sees about him the blood of warriors. But there is no time for tears. The war must go on until the world is cleansed of enslavement. Though we may fall in the struggle, mankind will be liberated. Edelstadt's poem "Di Hungrign un di Zatn," in which the hungry cry out for bread while the sated philosophize, is reminiscent of Heine's "Die Wanderratten."

Edelstadt's most famous poem "Mayn Tsavoe" (My Testament), inscribed on his tomb and sung by Jewish workers for decades, resounds with the rhythm and throbs, with the feeling of Heine's "Die Grenadiere." It concludes with his message to posterity: "When I die, carry to my grave the flag reddened with toilers' blood and sing my free song of the enslaved Christians and Jews. I shall bear it in my grave and shed tears for them. But, when there resounds the clash of swords in freedom's final battle, I'll sing from my grave and inspire the people's hearts."

EDELSTADT'S SUCCESSOR

Upon Edelstadt's death in 1892, Joseph Bovshover, who had exchanged Russia for America during the preceding year at the age of eighteen, composed an elegy lamenting the loss of the warrior-poet of the working class, an elegy which immediately established him as Edelstadt's successor.

In a dream-vision, entitled "Likht und Shatn," he conjured up Heine from the grave and walked with him through the streets of New York, the only city which had erected a monument to the much maligned poet. Through the lips of Heine, Bovshover voiced his own anti-religious bias, his own hedonist philosophy, his own cynical approach to the existing order.

In recasting the opening poem of Heine's "Die Harzreise," Bovshover does not end, as does his model, with the traveller's desire to climb up to the mountains and look down with laughter upon the polished but heartless ladies and gentlemen below. The Yiddish poet rather climbs the barricades, gun in hand. and fires bullets at the stony-hearted philanthropists, with their black frock coats and lacquered shoes, who dance at charity-balls.

In Bovshover's essay on Heine, he contrasts him with Goethe. He finds Heine's love poetry less healthy for youth. On the other hand, Heine is far superior as a warrior for human freedom.

Edelstadt and Bovshover were followed by other immigrant poets, radicals, anarchists, and socialists, who aroused Jewish sweatshop workers to unite against economic exploitation and who inspired them with militant songs during strikes and on the picket lines. For many of them Heine was the model of a revolutionary poet. In the free political atmosphere of America, a poet could denounce in strident verses the land which had lured them from far off Russia with golden visions and which had entrapped them in abysmal tenements and enslaved them to the heartless machines. Their contemporaries in Russia, however, had to be more circumspect in denouncing the oppressive Czarist regime. This can best be illustrated by the case of Frug, the most popular Yiddish poet of the pogrom years that followed the reign of Czar Alexander III.

Frug was a trilingual poet who began with Russian and ended with Hebrew, but who reached the summit of his fame with his Yiddish lyrics of the 1880s. The satirical Heine was the model for Frug's ironic ballads and his bitter songs of disillusionment. This is illustrated by a comparison between Heine's ribald "Disputation" and Frug's milder poem by the same name, which owes its inspiration to the German poet. Heine's "Disputation" (1851) was the last and most vitriolic of his "Hebräische Melodien." It depicts a verbal tournament in medieval Toledo between Caputian monks led by Brother José and Jewish champions led by Rabbi Judah of Navarre. The question to be decided is whether the Trinitarian God of the Christians or the Unitarian God of the Jews is the true one. If the Christians win the debate, the Jews are to accept baptism. If the Jews are declared the victors, the monks are to undergo circumcision. The king and queen and a large audience attend the disputation, which Brother José opens by exorcizing the devils who are invisibly helping the Jews. He then continues with vituperations against the obstinate Jews, who still do not accept the loving son of God. Rabbi Judah counters with an affirmation of the might and majesty of the one and only God who created heaven and earth and who on Judgement Day will reward his followers with slices of delicious Leviathan. The monks, however, are not tempted and the rabbi then also resorts to maledictions. The dispute goes on for twelve hours with neither side gaining the upper hand and finally nauseating the delicate queen.

FRUG'S VERSION

Frug's "Disputation," composed a generation later and under a more oppressive regime, is a much milder satire. He dares not echo Heine's ribald verses which calumniate Christianity, the religion of the Czar, and he does not want to present the Jewish faith in an unfavorable light. He therefore subtitles his poem a "Phantasy," a tale of long, long ago told by a grandfather to entertain children, a story of events that did not really happen. The adversaries confronting each other are the Catholic monk Diego and the Jewish rabbi Joseph, each a leader of his community. They apparently lived as good neighbors, except when they discussed religious questions about which so much blood has been shed throughout the ages. Then a gulf would open up between them.

In the course of time, both aged and died. Their disembodied souls winged their way to heaven. There they expected final answers to religious questions. Each was certain that his belief would be vindicated. En route to heaven, Fra Diego readies arguments that will annihilate his opponent, while Rabbi Joseph expects to land in "Gan Eden," paradise, where God, freedom, and peace prevail, and where the most learned sages, inspired by the "Shekhine," interpret the Torah and give final answers to troublesome questions.

At heaven's gate a stroke of lightning dazzles and confuses both disputants. Fra Diego is the first to recover and he asks God to hurl the lightning of his wrath upon the accursed Jew, who regards himself as belonging to a Chosen People, preferred by God because it was the first to receive the Torah. Perhaps this was once so, but now, and ever since the exodus from Egypt, all mankind can testify that Jews have become wicked and hence accursed unto eternity. Though they are comparatively few and weak, they cause much damage: so much fuel has been expended for their burning at autos-da-fé, so many prisons had to be built to confine them! Judges, jailors, hangmen, and free graves had to be provided for them, as well as convents to lodge their widows and orphans. Instead of thanks for such kindness in trying to save their souls, the Church has had to endure their curses. Fra Diego continues his long discourse, raging and thundering before the heavenly

Seat of Judgment. When he concludes, the Supreme Judge turns to Rabbi Joseph to present his side, but all that the rabbi replies is "Shma Yisrael, Hear, O Israel, the Lord is One." The decision of the Court is that the monk be repaid and with interest for the faggots, whips, chains, and instruments, which he used for torturing and burning others. As for the rabbi, he is to be reembodied and returned to earth, there to continue his wandering and to keep on proclaiming "God is One, eternally One."

Unlike Heine, Frug sensed the immediate danger to himself, were he to voice a single complaint against the spokesmen of Christianity. In his poem, he mirrored not only Jewish sorrow and enforced silence, but also his own personal tragedy. He had the misfortune to fall in love with and marry the daughter of a Greek Orthodox priest. Czarist regulations forbade her conversion to Judaism, and he did not want to become an apostate. His bitter sorrow was compounded when his efforts to implant in his only daughter a love for the Jewish people were frustrated by her priestly grandfather, who often took her to church for indoctrination and, after Frug died had her interred according to Christian ritual.

Frug's indebtedness to Heine was exceeded by that of his contemporaries David Frishman and Y. L. Peretz. Frishman had been persuaded by Sholom Aleichem to use not only Hebrew but also Yiddish as his poetic medium. He published his longest Yiddish poem, "Ophir," in the annual *Yidishe Folksbibliotek* for 1888, the same annual in which Peretz's "Monish" appeared and which established the reputation of both as outstanding Yiddish writers.

Frishman's "Ophir" paralleled Heine's "Bimini." In subject-matter and structure both poems developed along similar lines the search for the fountain of eternal youth. Heine's adventurer Ponce de Leon and Frishman's scholar Reb Getzel grew older and older as they continued their quest. Finally, Heine's hero found the island of Bimini and its river Lethe, whose waters bring forgetfulness and release from the burden of existence. Frishman's Reb Getzel also concluded his lifelong search for fabled Ophir, when he finally closed his enfeebled eyes and entered into the true Ophir, the eternal realm beyond life.

Frishman, in his Yiddish translations of Heine, gave preference to the political poems, introducing some of them by referring to their enduring relevance. Thus, the anger and the protests of the Silesian weavers, as embodied in Heine's poem, applied also to the weavers of Lodz, Frishman's native city, and to those of Bialystok, as well. Similarly, Heine's "Die Wanderratten" applied with even greater cogency to the communists of the twentieth century than to those of Heine's day.

Peretz's lyrics, even as those of Frishman and Frug, are also replete with echoes of Heine. Peretz's "Romanzero" reveals its indebtedness in its very title. Heine's "Lyrisches Intermezzo," in which the young man voices his longing for the girl and his frustration in being unable to win her, is, however, reversed by Peretz in his cycle of love poems, as the longing of the girl for the young man and her frustration because of her feelings carry little weight with her parents, who make the decision as to whom she is to marry. Her heart weeps within her when she is forced to part from him who is the center of her life; she will cherish her love until her last breath. When her mother tries to comfort her that there are other grooms for a girl so young and so beautiful, she replies that life without her beloved will always be joyless and only death will be sweet. The young man, rejected by her parents, roams far and wide but finds no happiness anywhere. He returns to her, alas, too late. She has been already married off.

In the Heinesque ballad entitled "In the Grave," Peretz returns to the theme of a boy and a girl who love each other. However, the boy is poor and the girl has a rich father who will not accept a poor mate for her. A Jewish girl has to obey her father. When she is led to the wedding canopy, the lovelorn youth in his cellar-dwelling pines away. She hears of his death and makes her way to his grave. It opens up and she is drawn into it. She kisses the dead eyes of her beloved. His dead hand embraces her and the grave closes over both of them.

Though Peretz's poem, "Er und Zi," is supposedly based on an old Spanish tale, Peretz prefaces it with the Heine-verses: "Es ist eine alte Geschichte. Doch bleibt sie immer neu" (It's an old story. Yet it remains ever true).

In the poem "An Edom," Peretz acknowledges his indebtedness to Heine's lyric with the same title. Edom, brother of Jacob, is the symbol for the hostile non-Jewish world. Edom accepts the fact that the descendants of his brother still draw breath, while   accepting Edom's insane rages. Sometimes, Edom is friendly and massages his brother's wounds. At other times, he uses Jewish fat to light his lamps and flays Jewish veins as wicks. But the friendship is becoming stronger, and Edom's brother, too, is learning to develop such insane rages, perhaps even greater ones.

REISEN AND YEHOASH

Peretz's disciples, especially Abraham Reisen and Yehoash, also follow Heine as a model in their lyrics, and they also rework these models to accord with the Jewish reality of their generation at the end of the nineteenth century.

For example, Reisen's Jewish "Azra," like Heine's "Asra," also turns pale and paler every evening when seen at the fountain. However, he is dying not of unrequited love, but of hunger. In his early lyrics, Reisen, following in the path of Frug, Peretz, Frishman, and numerous other Yiddish poets, also succumbed to the spell of Heine's *Buch der Lieder,* but he soon realized the falseness of presenting the budding love of a Jewish boy or girl in a flirtatious or ironic vein. Jewish reality demanded a different approach, because love was still a fresh experience for the Yiddish lyric. A cynical tone was most inappropriate. The imagery of the Song of Songs could better serve as a starting point. Hence, Reisen avoids sophistication. The melody of love that floats between his timid lads and chaste maidens is the same melody that angels sing in heaven's tents, and God is its composer. Of each kiss a new angel is born. A single caress is like a ray of sunshine breaking upon a dreary day or like a refreshing oasis in a parched desert. A moment of love is a moment of relief from the silence and loneliness that are ultimately inescapable. The mature Reisen, therefore, emancipates himself from Heine's cynicism and buries his individual sorrow in the sorrow of his people.

The impact of Heine upon Yehoash was far stronger than upon Reisen. He follows the trail of the German poet, not only in his love lyrics, but also in his ghostly ballads, in his nature poems, and in his versified legends.

In an essay on Jewish demonology, Yehoash, like Walter Pater in England, appropriates Heine's idea, expressed in *Götter im Exil* (Gods in Exile), that the demons who peopled Christian imagination were pagan gods exiled from their original shrines and degraded in rank by their successors in the Christian pantheon. Hence, some Christian demons still retain beautiful and helpful characteristics. Elves and dwarfs are especially helpful to man. Yehoash points out that since Jews worshipped only a single God, and have until now remained faithful to him, friendly demons could not develop. Jewish demons were in their origin wicked spirits and not dethroned Olympians. They can hurt but not help, with the single exception of the Golem, who is, however, only a temporary creation and without a will of his own.

Adoration of Heine reached its peak among the poets of "Di Yunge," the literary movement that burst upon the American Yiddish scene in 1907 and that dominated it for more than a decade. Its leading poets participated in a complete translation of Heine's works in eight volumes. These poets, many born in the 1880's, were not political or social revolutionaries, for they had been disillusioned by the failure of the abortive Russian uprising of 1905 and by the pogroms that followed and from which they sought refuge in the New World.

COMPLETE WORKS IN YIDDISH

New York received these young, romantic, dream-drenched immigrants and fed them into sweatshops and cavernous tenements. But, their vitality seemed inexhaustible. Their hunger for intellectual activities after a day's hard physical work was insatiable. They used their few free hours for literary expression and their last pennies to publish their lyrics in collections and ever new periodicals in which translations of Heine were numerous. In 1918, these translations were included in the complete edition of Heine's works. The chief participants in this enterprise among "Di Yunge" were Mani Leib, Reuben Iceland, Zisha Landau, Moshe Leib Halpern, Naftali Gross, I. J. Schwartz, Mark Scheid, Joseph Rolnick, and Lilliput. Of older poets, Bialik contributed a translation of "Prinzessin Sabbat," Pinski a translation of "Disputation," David Frishman translations of many of the "Zeitgedichte," and Abraham Reisen most poems of "Lamentation" and "Lazarus."

Nachman Syrkin, ideologue of Socialist Zionism and an American leader of the "Po'alei Zion," wrote the lengthy introduction to the complete works. He portrayed Heine as perhaps the most tragic Jewish poet of all generations, tragic even when he laughed at God, the world, and himself. Syrkin stressed Heine's Jewishness and dismissed Heine's baptism as having occurred in a moment of weakness, need, and despair, and as having been followed by a lifetime of regret and atonement. In analyzing Heine's Jewish poems and polemics in great detail, Syrkin sought to convince readers that apostasy weighed heavily upon the poet's soul and that all his twisting and turning, blasphemies and reconciliations with God and the Jewish people, stemmed from the deepest layer of his being, the Jewish layer, and that he deserved to have "Kaddish" said for his lacerated soul.

Among "Di Yunge," Moshe Nadir, in his life, poetry, and "Weltanschauung" shared the most affinity with Heine. His youthful poems, filled with "Weltschmerz," were already reminiscent of his adored German poet and his final volume, entitled *Mode Ani* (I confess), has much in common with Heine's *Bekenntnisse*. Early on, he mastered Heine's technique of reversing the flow of emotions in the course of a single short lyric, of shocking trusting readers with sobering irony, just as they were succumbing to sweet sentimentalism. This mixture of gentle lyricism and biting sarcasm remained with him throughout the four decades of his creative career. He acted the clown, the lover, the intoxicated idealist, the despairing cynic, and all his poses were assumed to be genuine. In the deepest reaches of his soul, however, he found life empty, barren of meaning, a vanity of vanities. From abysmal loneliness and nihilistic moodiness, he fled to communism, even as Heine, after personal disappointments, had fled to the utopian socialism of St. Simonism. For a time, communism brought him relief from deepest pessimism. But, when his idealized communists entered into a pact with Nazi Germany, he recognized late in life that he had been led astray by a utopian will-o'-the wisp, and, in his confessions, he pleaded for an understanding of his predicament: "For every drop of blood that I drew with my pen, I paid with two drops of my heart's blood. This is no excuse for all those I attacked with such blind fanaticism and my heart weeps because of my deeds." His last poems echoed those of the disillusioned, dying German poet to whom he had repeatedly paid tribute and whose fate he likened to his own. Like Heine, this penitent Yiddish poet also sought to make his peace with the God of Israel, from whom he had been estranged. He realized in the hellish flame of a world conflagration that force, bloodshed, revolution, and dictatorship of right or left could not create a better society, but that only through a long process of education in democracy, humanism, and tolerance could man ascend to a higher stage of civilization.

NADIR ON HEINE

Broken-hearted, the most talented humorist and satirist among "Di Yunge" bade farewell to God and man in his last poems, including the poem entitled "Heinrich Heine." In this poem, Nadir hails the German poet, whose book of gold and gall accompanied him since his boyhood and whose dreams he shared. He claims that he, too, was seared in freedom's battle and now weeps for a shattered world. He also gave his heart to hangsmen's daughters and fat Mathildas, and he now experiences hours in a mattress-grave, hours that drain his brain. As for his final resting place, he does not know whether it will be in a desert, in the deep sea, or in Brooklyn. A decade earlier he stood at Heine's grave, and he still hears the lyric cooing of Heine's doves. Generations come and go and each kisses the songs of this, his most beloved poet.

While most poets of "Di Yunge" spent their formative years in Russia, Nadir stemmed from a Galician townlet, but emigrated from it in 1900 at the age of fifteen, too early to

participate in the literary circle of the Galician Neoromanti-
cists, whose most productive years began in 1904. The central
figure of this circle was Shmuel Jacob Imber, nephew of the
Hebrew-Yiddish poet Naphtali Herz Imber, author of the
"Hatikvah." S. J. Imber translated Heine and often imitated
him in lyrics that abounded in doves and nightingales,
reluctant damsels and lovelorn knights, but the profundity of
the martyr of Montmartre eluded him.

David Koenigsberg referred to Imber as the head of "Young
Galicia" and to himself as its heart. His translation of *Buch
der Lieder* remained unpublished; he, as well as Imber and
other members of the Lemberg Circle, were murdered in the
Nazi purge of Galicia's Jews. Still, Heine's influence upon him
was as powerful as upon Imber, especially in his first volume,
simply entitled *Lieder* (1912).

Another member of the Lemberg Circle was young Melech
Ravitch, who roomed with Imber, hungered with him, and was
stimulated by him to aim at lyric perfection. Ravitch's early
verses betray the influence of Heine, Imber's own master.
They overflow with "Weltschmerz," sweet melancholy, and
sentimental love for all mankind.

As Yiddish literature matured beyond the pioneering
generation and its flowering that began in the 1880's and
ended with the death of its classical triumvirate during the
first World War, it threw off the hegemony of Heine. Besides,
greater dispersion of its writers and contacts with ever new
literary currents enriched it immeasurably with new themes
and new stylistic possibilities. The "Khaliastra," led by Uri Zvi
Greenberg, Peretz Markish, and Melech Ravitch in Warsaw,
the "Insikhism" of Jacob Glatstein, Glanz-Leyeles and N.B.
Minkoff in New York, and the Soviet poets centered in Kiev,
Minsk, and Moscow sought to give new structures to the
multiplicity of ever changing social and cultural phenomena.
Heine was accepted as the great poetic exponent of the world
of yesteryear with a remarkable prophetic insight into a
revolutionary order, which would shatter the beauty so dear to
his heart, uproot the lilies, fell the laurel, and plant potatoes
therein.

LASTING INFLUENCE

The Heine vogue ebbed, but it did not fade away. The finest Rumanian Yiddish poet, Itzik Manger, still wrote in the 1920s ghostly ballads in the style of Heine. In Minsk, Moshe Kulbak completed in 1933 his "Disner Childe Harold," a satire on the degenerate German bourgeoisie. It owed its title to Byron, but was more closely modelled after Heine's "Deutschland. Ein Wintermärchen." In Moscow, Shmuel Rossin translated Heine's lyrics, and in booklets of the 1920s sang of love's longing, of tears and kisses, of the blossoming of lips in spring and the pain of parting in autumn. But, he was a rare exception among Soviet Yiddish poets. In Warsaw and Bialystok, Zysman Segalowitch, who began to write under the spell of Heine with verses about nymphs, the great God Pan, and the loveliness of dew-drunk flowers, changed his tone when bombs rained down upon his readers. In the "Elegies of Dorten" (1944), he depicts with nerve-wracking intensity the hell in which his Jews, yellow-badged and branded like cattle, were being burned, not figuratively but literally, by other human beings, fashioned not in the image of God, but in the image of devils. In New York, Eliezer Greenberg, after the Holocaust, spoke in a poetic monologue through the voice of the dying Heine, who asks his Jewish friend Karl Marx: "0, Marx, how could we flee from our own stricken people and purchase our safety with baptism?"

The Heine wave spent its force after the First World War and has been ebbing away, as Yiddish poetry became more preoccupied with such themes as the visions and carnage of the Russian Revolution, the pogroms that followed in the wake of militant communism, the upheaval of the shtetl culture, the Stalin purges, and, above all, the Holocaust and the rise of Israel. Yet, Heine remains a world classic and is likely to experience a revived vogue as we near the bicentennial of his birth before the end of the present decade.

Germans may have regarded their finest nineteenth-century poet, their wittiest prose writer, as a stepchild. But, the Jews, with rare exceptions, have tended to view him, despite his aberrations, as their son, flesh of their flesh and soul of their soul. When Heine lamented that no mass will be sung for him and no "Kaddish" will be said for him, he was only half right. No mass is being sung for him. However, every Jew who has survived the lure of alien hearths and who has come home to his ancestral fireside recalls with poignant sorrow this early victim of a mirage that dazzled millions of Jews throughout two centuries, the mirage of Germanization, Russification, Polonization, or assimilation to Anglo-Americanism – a mirage from which Heine emerged, crippled in body, wounded in his pride, but clear in thought.

On his "Yortseit," Kaddish ought to be said for Heinrich Heine, this son of Israel, who, despite temporary alienation, atoned by the creation of literary masterpieces that are treasured as supreme products of Jewish genius and that will continue to inspire Jewish poets and thinkers in Yiddish, Hebrew, and other tongues.

THEODOR E. WIENER

Jewish Literary Anniversaries, 1995

THREE MAJOR AMERICAN Jewish writers celebrate this year their eightieth birthday. Saul Bellow, Arthur Miller, and Herman Wouk belong to the long list of Jewish authors who flourished after World War II, when the American-born generation, the children of the immigrants, came into its own. Saul Bellow relives the internal struggles of various Jewish characters on different levels of society, Arthur Miller in his plays explores the psychological needs of men to be accepted, as they struggle to face their weaknesses, whereas Herman Wouk is more interested in entertaining his readers, while at the same time putting forth positive Jewish images.

This year we also remember two outstanding American Jewish scholars, Salo W. Baron and Louis Finkelstein. The former blazed new paths in the analysis of Jewish history, paying greater attention to the economic and social backgrounds in which Jewish communities lived, the latter deepening our knowledge of rabbinic literature, while at the same time editing a popular anthology on Jewish history and civilization. Another Jewish historian, Cecil Roth of England, specialized in the history of the Jews in his native land, as well as those of Italy and Spain. He rendered also great service as the editor-in-chief of the Encyclopaedia Judaica and several editions of a one-volume Jewish encyclopedia.

Israeli writers are now writing for an ever-increasing Hebrew public. Shmuel Yosef Agnon, the Nobel laureate, and the younger Leah Goldberg and Nathan Alterman have become part of the Israeli literary tradition, the latter dealing also with Israeli themes, rather than looking back to the Diaspora. In order to transform the Hebrew language from a language of prayer into a modern language of communication on all levels great service was rendered by translators, such as Joseph Lichtenbaum, Saul Phinehas Rabbinowitz, and Alexander Siskind Rabinovitz.

From the more distant past we recall Jacob Abendana, a 17th century rabbi with contacts in the Christian community, and in marked contrast Shneur Zalman, of Lyady, the founder of Habad Hasidism, which has proved extremely resilient in recent years.

One of the forerunners of modern Zionism was Zevi Hirsch Kalischer. Our generation has seen the fulfillment of the dream furthered by Henrietta Szold, Levi Eshkol, and Abba Eban.

The spirit of Jewish creativity manifests itself in traditional Jewish learning, in scholarly exploration of our heritage, and in new creative writing in all languages spoken by Jews. The possibilities are endless.

CHRONOLOGICAL LIST

Without special date: MICHAEL LEVI RODKINSON.

January: 2, HERBERT J. GOLDSTEIN; 14, LEAH GOLDBERG; 22, ELSE LASKER-SCHUELER; 29, NATHAN SHAHAM; 31, BENNO JACOB.

February: 10, JOSEPH MAGIL; 13, HENRIETTA SZOLD; 16, JULIUS LEWY; 17, SHMUEL YOSEF AGNON, ABBA EBAN, MENACHEM RIBALOW.

March: 1, JOSEPH B. SCHECHTMAN; 3, ELIEZER RAPHAEL MALACHI; 8, FALK HELPERIN; 12, BERNARD DRACHMAN; 17, ISAAC RIVKIND; 28, NATHAN ALTERMAN.

April: 1, ZEVI HIRSCH KALISCHER; 8, SAUL PHINEHAS RABBINOWITZ; 20, JOSEPH HEIMANN CARO.

May: 20, AARON SAMUEL LIEBERMANN; 23, JOSEPH LICHTENBAUM; 27, HERMAN WOUK.

June: 10, SAUL BELLOW; 14, LOUIS FINKELSTEIN; 20, CECIL ROTH.

July: 4, SOLOMON SIMON; 17, LOUIS JACOBS.

August: 2, MORITZ GOTTLIEB SAPHIR; 8, AHARON MEGGED; 25, HERBERT C. ZAFREN; 28, FRANZ WERFEL; 29, BERL BOTWINIK.

September: 2, JOSHUA HESCHEL SCHORR; 6, ALEXANDER SISKIND RABINOVITZ; 7, YIZHAK GRUENBAUM; 15, SHNEUR ZALMAN, of Lyady; 16, JACOB ABENDANA; 25, JACOB H. SCHIFF; 26, RICHARD BEER-HOFMANN, MARCUS BRANN; 28, JEHIEL MICHAEL KITTSEE.

October: 10, LEVI ESHKOL; 17, ARTHUR MILLER; 20, DOV NOY.

November: 6, JOEL MUELLER; 8, S. ANSKI, SOLOMON SIMON; 20, ABRAHAM A. NEUMAN; 22, CHAIM RABIN; 24, SHRAGA ABRAMSON.

December: 1, DAVID DE SOLA POOL; 9, ERNST DANIEL GOLDSCHMIDT; 14, SALO W. BARON; 22, ABRAM S. ISAACS.

ALPHABETICAL LIST

JACOB ABENDANA. 300th anniversary of death. Born probably in Spain in 1630, died in London, England, September 16, 1695. A scholar who eventually became chief rabbi of the Great Synagogue, he had contacts with Christian Hebraists, such as Buxdorf, who tried to convert him to Christianity. To fortify the faith for himself and others, he published a Spanish translation of Judah ha-Levi's defense of Judaism, *Kuzari*. He also wrote a supercommentary on a medieval Torah commentary. In manuscript remained a Spanish translation of the Mishnah.

SHRAGA ABRAMSON. 80th birthday. Born in Ciechanowiec, Poland, November 24, 1915. In Eretz Israel since 1936, he continued his rabbinic as well as his university studies, concentrating on medieval Jewish thought and literature. For a number of years he taught at the Jewish Theological Seminary in New York, but he returned to Israel to become professor of rabbinics at the Hebrew University in Jerusalem. While his principal interest is the geonic period, he has also edited major works of medieval Hebrew poetry. He has likewise edited several talmudic tractates from hitherto unknown manuscripts.

SHMUEL YOSEF AGNON. 25th anniversary of death. Born in Buczacz, Galicia, in 1888, died in Jerusalem, February 17, 1970. One of the major Hebrew novelists, the first to win the coveted Nobel Prize for literature in 1966, he was a prolific writer of stories, especially about the life of East European Jewry in his youth. A large number of his works have appeared in English translation, among them *The Bridal Canopy* (1937, 1968), *A Guest for the Night* (1968), *Selected Stories* (1970), *Twenty-one Stories* (1970), *A Simple Story* (1985), and *Shira* (1989).

NATHAN ALTERMAN. 25th anniversary of death. Born in Warsaw, Poland, in 1910, died in Tel Aviv, Israel, March 28, 1970. In Eretz Israel since 1925, he became one of the major Israeli poets whose themes and moods changed over the years. Under the British domination he composed biting satires that had to be distributed secretly. After the Six-Day-War he opted for the larger Israel, but his horizon was not limited to politics, as the personal vicissitudes common to all poets engaged him also. In English translation there appeared *Selected Poems* (1978) and *Little Tel Aviv* (1981).

S. ANSKI (Solomon Rappoport). 75th anniversary of death. Born in Chashnik, White Russia, in 1863, died in Warsaw, Poland, November 8, 1920. Originally affiliated with the populist Russian movement, he worked among the peasants and wrote in

Russian. Later he turned to Yiddish and wrote the play, which
in English is entitled *The Dybbuk* (1926, 1974) and was
performed on stages throughout the world in many translations.
A Jewish folklorist who undertook an expedition throughout
Ukraine and western Russia to collect Jewish ethnographic
materials, he had them preserved in St. Petersburg.

SALO W. BARON. 100th anniversary of birth. Born in Tarnow, Galicia,
December 14, 1895, died in New York in 1989. He received his
early education in Vienna, graduating from the university and
also being ordained by the Jewish Theological Seminary there.
For a number of years he taught at a Hebrew teachers college
before coming to the United States to teach at what is now the
Hebrew Union College, New York School. From 1930 he was
professor of Jewish history at Columbia University. His major
work, *A Social and Religious History of the Jews,* appeared first
in three volumes in 1937. A revised and enlarged edition was
begun in 1952, and by 1983 18 volumes had appeared, carrying
the story through the Middle Ages. *The Jewish Community, Its
Story and Structure to the American Revolution* (1942; 1972)
emphasized his interest in the social history of the Jews. There
appeared several collections of his essays, and he edited himself
many conference publications on Jewish themes.

RICHARD BEER-HOFMANN. 50th anniversary of death. Born in Vienna,
Austria, in 1866, died in New York, September 26, 1945. An
Austrian poet who was part of the Young Vienna movement that
included many other Jewish writers, he tried to express in his
writings man's obligation to serve others. In an incomplete
trilogy of biblical plays, the first and only in English translation,
Jacob's Dream (1947) he recreates the scene where Jacob
wrestles with God at Beth-El and accepts His charge to lead His
people. In the second play on the young David, service to family,
nation and humanity is stressed as leading to true fulfillment. In
an early novel a self-centered person who is confronted with his
Jewishness throws himself into the struggle for his people.

SAUL BELLOW. 80th birthday. Born in Lachine, Quebec, Canada, June
10, 1915, to a Yiddish speaking family that moved to Chicago, he
became a writer and teacher of fiction who combined a general
exploration of the underlying psychological problems of his
characters with an analysis of their particularly Jewish
concerns. One of his first novels, *The Victim* (1947), dealt with
anti-Semitism. *The Adventures of Augie March* (1953) delineated
the struggles of a young Jew from a poor family. *Herzog* (1964)
explored the tribulations of a Jewish professor. *Mr. Sammler's
Planet* (1970) described the life of a Holocaust survivor in New
York. His trip to Israel is recorded in *To Jerusalem and Back*

(1976). He also edited an anthology, *Great Jewish Stories* (1963). In 1976 he was awarded the Nobel Prize for Literature, the first Jew writing in English to be so honored.

BERL BOTWINIK. 50th anniversary of death. Born in Rakov, Belarus, in 1885, died in New York, August 29, 1945. Beginning his career as a sign painter in his native land he joined the Socialist Bund and was frequently arrested for distributing illegal pamphlets. After coming to America in 1909, he eventually joined the staff of the *Jewish Daily Forward* as its theater editor. He also wrote Yiddish plays, which were performed in New York and elsewhere in this country. He published several collections of his stories. In English translation there appeared long after his death *Lead Pencil, Stories and Sketches* (1984).

MARCUS BRANN. 75th anniversary of death. Born in Rawitsch, Germany, in 1849, died in Breslau, Germany, September 26, 1920. After officiating for a number of years as a rabbi he became successor to Heinrich Graetz, the great Jewish historian, at the Jewish Theological Seminary in Breslau. In addition to scholarly monographs he published several popular histories of the Jews, one of which was adapted by Simon Dubnow and incorporated into his great historical work. He also helped prepare a new edition of Graetz's *History of the Jews*. For many years he was editor of the major scholarly periodical of German Jewry.

JOSEPH HEIMANN CARO. 100th anniversary of death. Born in Slupca, Posen district, in 1800, died in Wloclawek, Poland, April 20, 1895. A rabbi who commanded both German and Hebrew speaking facility, he served in Wloclawek for many years. He published a collection of sermons and an edition of *Pirke Avot* with a German translation and his own commentary in Hebrew. He was a friend of Zevi Hirsch Kalischer and supported his efforts on behalf of Jewish settlement in Palestine.

BERNARD DRACHMAN. 50th anniversary of death. Born in New York in 1861, died there March 12, 1945. The first American Orthodox rabbi to preach in English he was a leader in traditional Judaism, teaching first at the Jewish Theological Seminary and later when he disagreed with its religious orientation at the Rabbi Isaac Elchanan Rabbinical Seminary of Yeshiva University. In 1899 he published an English translation of Samson Raphael Hirsch's first work on modern Orthodoxy under the title, *The Nineteen Letters of Ben Uziel* (reprinted 1942). *From the Heart of Israel, Jewish Tales and Types* (1905; 1970), is a collection of Jewish stories. His autobiography, *The Unfailing Light* (1948), reviewed a busy and eventful life.

ABBA EBAN. 80th birthday. Born in Cape Town, South Africa, February 17, 1915. Educated in Great Britain, he came to Eretz Israel as a British Army officer during World War II. He eventually joined the staff of the Jewish Agency and was among the leading negotiators for the establishment of Israel. He held various high offices in the new state, such as ambassador to the United States and the United Nations as well as foreign minister. As an outstanding orator and English stylist he gained popularity also in his writings. His addresses before the United Nations appeared as *Voice of Israel* (1957; 1969). About Israel's history he wrote *My Country* (1972; 1973; 1975). Jewish history was covered by *My People* (1968, 1978). He wrote two autobiographies, *Abba Eban* (1977) and *Personal Witness* (1992). *Heritage–Civilization and the Jews* (1984) was a companion volume to a very well received television series on the history of the Jews.

LEVI ESHKOL. 100th anniversary of birth. Born in Oratova, Ukraine, October 10, 1895, died in Jerusalem in 1969. In Eretz Israel since 1914, he was an agricultural worker and founder of Deganya Bet and eventually became one of its leaders. Throughout his career he endeavored to advance the economic position of the Jewish community by broadening opportunities particularly in agriculture. Every aspect of life interested him and he soon became a leader of the Mapai Party, then the ruling party in the government coalition. He succeeded Ben-Gurion as prime minister in 1963 and served until his death in 1969. Especially critical was his leadership during the Six-Day-War in 1967. Over the years he gave many speeches which were gathered in several Hebrew volumes. In English there appeared *The State Papers* in 1969.

LOUIS FINKELSTEIN. 100th anniversary of birth. Born in Cincinnati, Ohio. June 14, 1895, died in New York in 1991. Ordained as a Conservative rabbi at the Jewish Theological Seminary of America in New York. he devoted his career to this institution. as a professor of rabbinics and eventually as its Chancellor. An early work was *Jewish Self Government in the Middle Ages* (1924; 1972). He also edited *The Commentary of David Kimhi on Isaiah* (1926). A popular work was *Akiba, Scholar, Saint, Martyr* (1936; 1990; 1993). A work on the origin of Rabbinic Judaism was *The Pharisees* (1938; 1962). A multi-volume work edited by him was *The Jews, Their History, Culture And Religion* (1949; 1955; 1960; 1971). He also was co-editor of *The Cambridge History of Judaism,* begun in 1984.

LEAH GOLDBERG. 25th anniversary of death. Born in Koenigsberg, Germany, in 1911, died in Israel, January 14, 1970. Her early years she spent in Lithuania, but later attended German universities. In Eretz Israel since 1935. she was first a teacher, then an editor of literary magazines, and finally a teacher of literature at the Hebrew University. Her Hebrew poetry is characterized by naturalness of form, almost in a conversational style and dealing with universal themes of nature and love, rather than with specific Jewish topics. In English translation there appeared *Little Queen of Sheba* (1959), a story for young people about Holocaust survivors coming to Israel, collections of poetry, *Light on the Rim of a Cloud* (1972), *Selected Poems* (1976), *and On the Blossoming* (1992), also a drama, *Lady of the Castle* (1974) and a work of literary history, *Russian Literature in the Nineteenth Century* (1976).

ERNST DANIEL GOLDSCHMIDT. 100th anniversary of birth. Born in Koenigshuette, Germany, December 9, 1895, died in Jerusalem in 1972. A senior official at the Prussian State Library in Berlin, he was one of the editors of the incomplete union catalogue of incunabula, sponsored by that institution. When the Nazis came to power, he emigrated to Israel and joined the staff of the Hebrew University Library. Just as his expertise in medieval Latin had served him well in Germany, his profound knowledge of Jewish liturgy manifested itself in many works, including editions of the siddur and mahzor. In Germany he had published a Haggadah with a new historical commentary. This appeared in an English edition, under the title, *The Passover Haggadah*, in 1953. His Hebrew essays on prayer and religious poetry were published posthumously in *On Jewish Liturgy* (1978).

HERBERT S. GOLDSTEIN. 25th anniversary of death. Born in New York in 1890, died there January 2, 1970. A leader in the Orthodox rabbinate in the United States he authored *Between the Lines of the Bible* (1959), an exposition of the 613 Commandments of traditional Judaism. He also compiled a biography of his father-in-law, Harry Fischel, who was a leader in the New York building trade and who paid his Jewish workers for the Saturdays that he relieved them of work. He was known for his extensive gifts to Jewish institutions here and in Jerusalem, where he endowed the institute of talmudic research named after him.

YIZHAK GRUENBAUM. 25th anniversary of death. Born in Warsaw, Poland, in 1879, died in Israel, September 7, 1970. A leader of Polish Jewry and an active Zionist, he wrote for the Hebrew and Yiddish press in Poland and also in Polish and Russian. After World War I, he served for a number of years in the Polish parliament, representing Jewish constituencies. After settling in Eretz Israel in 1932 he was a senior executive of the Zionist Organization and became minister of the interior in the first Israeli government. He wrote a number of books in Hebrew and Polish on contemporary Jewish problems in Poland.

FALK HEILPERIN. 50th anniversary of death. Born in Nesvizh, Russia, in 1876, died in Tel-Aviv, March 8, 1945. A Yiddish educator in Eastern Europe, who promoted the teaching of Yiddish to children since it was the language of their home, he wrote Yiddish stories for adults and children. He was the author of Hebrew and Yiddish textbooks and also translated two plays by Schiller. Later as teacher in Poland and editor in Eretz Israel, to which he emigrated in 1938, he wrote both in Hebrew and Yiddish.

ABRAM S. ISAACS. 75th anniversary of death. Born in New York in 1852, died in Patterson, New Jersey, December 22, 1920. His father had emigrated from Holland in the early part of the century, and many members of his family achieved much in the general and Jewish communities. Isaacs had studied for the rabbinate in Germany and combined rabbinic service with academic teaching throughout his life. He taught at New York University and served a congregation in Patterson. A scholarly work was *The Life and Writings of Moses Chaim Luzatto* (1878), at present being reprinted. A book on Judaism and contemporary Jewish life was *What is Judaism* (1912). Various collections of stories are: *Stories From the Rabbis* (1893, 1911, 1972), *Step By Step* (1910), about Moses Mendelssohn, *Under the Sabbath Lamp* (1919), and *The Young Champion* (1913), a novel about Grace Aguilar. He also edited *The Jewish Messenger*, an important Jewish weekly for many years.

BENNO JACOB. 50th anniversary of death. Born in Breslau, Germany, in 1869, died in London, England, January 31, 1945. A Liberal German rabbi, who served for many years in Dortmund, he retired in 1929 to devote himself to biblical studies, settling in London in 1939. Throughout his life he fought against the modern critical understanding of the Torah, and although not a fundamentalist believer, he maintained the unity of the biblical text. Of his massive commentaries on Genesis and Exodus, an abridgment of the former appeared in English in 1974, *The First Book of the Bible, Genesis*, and a full translation of the latter, *The Second Book of the Bible, Exodus*, in 1989.

LOUIS JACOBS. 75th birthday. Born in Manchester, England, July 17, 1920. A prominent London rabbi he has met opposition for his views on traditional Jewish doctrines by the Orthodox religious establishment as represented by the British chief rabbi. In *We Have Reason to Believe: Some Aspects of Jewish Theology Examined in the Light of Modern Thought* (1965) he maintained that there was some human input in the composition of traditional texts. *Theology in the Responsa* (1975) examines this very important part of rabbinic literature, which played such a large part in the life of the Jews in ages past. He also wrote *Hasidic Prayer* (1972, 1973, 1993) and *Hasidic Thought* (1976).

The Palm Tree of Deborah (1960) is a translation of a 16th century Kabbalistic work by Moses Cordovero.

ZEVI HIRSCH KALISCHER. 200th anniversary of birth. Born in Lissa (Lezhno), province of Posen, Prussia, April 1. 1795, died in Thorn, Germany, in 1874. A traditional Jewish scholar, who wrote several works on halakhah, he is best remembered as a forerunner of the Zionist movement. In *Derishat Zion* (1862) he advocated settlement in Palestine with particular emphasis on farming the land. so that the new immigrants would be independent of charity from the Diaspora, known as halukah, and thus hasten the coming of the Messiah and bring redemption to the suffering Jews. His efforts were opposed by many Orthodox leaders as impractical and were applauded by Moses Hess, who in his work, *Rom und Jerusalem* (1862), translated portions of Kalischer's work.

JEHIEL MICHAL KITTSEE. 150th anniversary of death. Born in Hungary in 1775, died in Bratislava, Slovakia, September 28, 1845. A learned businessman, who was admired by Moses Sofer, the Hungarian spiritual leader and scholar, he published several rabbinic works in his lifetime.

ELSE LASKER-SCHUELER. 50th anniversary of death. Born in Elberfeld, Germany, in 1869, died in Jerusalem January 22, 1945. An eccentric poet, who came from an assimilated background, she was nevertheless attracted to the strangeness of East European Jews. During the 1930's she settled in Jerusalem. In English translation there appeared *Hebrew Ballads and Other Poems* (1980), *Your Diamond Dreams Cut Open My Arteries* (1982), and *Concert* (1994) .

JULIUS LEWY. 100th anniversary of birth. Born in Berlin, Germany, February 16, 1895, died in Cincinnati, Ohio, in 1963. Before 1933 he was professor of Assyriology at the University of Giessen, Germany. Later he joined the faculty of the Hebrew Union College in Cincinnati, where he taught Bible and Semitic languages. In his teaching he stressed the relationship between the ancient Semitic civilizations and that of the Bible. In an earlier work in Germany he had dealt with the chronology of the kings of Israel and Judah, since the dates given in the Bible for the respective dynasties of the two kingdoms do not come out correctly.

JOSEPH LICHTENBAUM. 100th anniversary of birth. Born in Warsaw, Poland, May 23, 1895, died in Israel in 1968. In Eretz Israel since 1920 he published many children's stories, also anthologies of modern Hebrew prose and poetry. He rendered great service to the Hebrew reader in Israel through his translations from world literature, such as Goethe's *Hermann und Dorothea* and

Remarque's *Der Weg Zurueck*, as well as selected poems by the Polish Jewish poet Julian Tuwim.

AARON SAMUEL LIEBERMANN. 150th anniversary of birth. Born in Lunna, Lithuania, May 20, 1845, died in New York in 1880. First a teacher in a Jewish school in Russia, he later became involved in illegal Socialist activities, for which he finally had to leave Russia. He spent several years in England as a typesetter for Russian Socialist emigré magazine. In his Hebrew writings, he was among the first to champion Socialism for the Jews, although most Russian Socialists at the time could not accept Jews as Socialists since they regarded them as exploiters. Among his fellow Jews there was also little support, until the Labor Zionist movement in Eretz Israel recognized him as a forerunner.

JOSEPH MAGIL. 50th anniversary of death. Born near Kovno, Lithuania, in 1870, died in Philadelphia, Pennsylvania, February 10, 1945. A Hebrew teacher who came to Philadelphia in 1892, he published textbooks for the Jewish religious school. The unique feature of his bilingual, Hebrew-English and Hebrew-Yiddish Bible texts was the interlinear translation to facilitate the learning of the Hebrew vocabulary for the English and Yiddish reader respectively. Thus he published various parts of the Bible, the Pentateuch, *School Bible* (1915), *Book of Joshua* (1918), *Book of Judges* (1928), *Books of Samuel* (1928/29); also *Magil's Linear Haggadah for Passover* (1904). He also prepared *Linear Children's Companion* (1906), a selection from the prayerbook with the same principle.

ELIEZER RAPHAEL MALACHI. 100th anniversary of birth. Born in Jerusalem March 3, 1895, died in New York in 1980. In 1912 he came to live in New York after having published his first article at age 15. Most of his writings were in Hebrew and dealt with Hebrew bibliography, chiefly of modern writers, particularly American Hebrew authors. He also prepared an extensive survey of Hebrew lexicography as an appendix for a new edition of Solomon Mandelkern's *Concordance to the Hebrew Bible*.

AHARON MEGGED (Meged). 75th birthday. Born in Wloclavek, Poland, August 8, 1920. In Eretz Israel since 1926, he first joined a kibbutz, but later edited literary magazines in Tel Aviv. A popular novelist, he has been translated into English in quite a few volumes, such as *Fortunes of a Fool* (1962), *The Short Life* (1980), and *The First Sin* (1982). *Living on the Dead* (1971) is considered a major work as it deals with the disappointment of the Zionist settlers who realize that the ideal they hoped to find in the new land has eluded them in spite of all their efforts.

ARTHUR MILLER. 80th birthday. Born in New York October 17, 1915. A major American dramatist, who twice won the Pulitzer Prize, he remained in his writings somewhat at the periphery of American Jewish life. An early novel about anti-Semitism was *Focus* (1945). In the short story collection *I Don't Need You Anymore* (1967), the title story deals with a boy who is jealous of his older brother because he can fast on Yom Kippur. The play, *The Price* (1968) includes a Jewish character. In general he has been lauded for the profundity and sympathy of his characterizations.

JOEL MUELLER. 100th anniversary of death. Born in Moravia in 1827, died in Berlin, Germany, November 6, 1895. First a rabbi in his native region, he eventually became an instructor at the liberal rabbinical seminary in Berlin. He edited many rabbinic texts particularly from the geonic period. Among others he edited a work of Saadia Gaon. An important service to Jewish scholarship is his "Index" to geonic responsa, offering abstracts of their decisions, which has proved invaluable to scholars.

ABRAHAM A. NEUMAN. 25th anniversary of death. Born in Brezan. Austria, in 1890, died in Philadelphia, November 20, 1970. Growing up in New York, he became a Conservative rabbi who eventually joined the faculty of Dropsie College for Hebrew and Cognate Learning in Philadelphia, now the Center for Judaic Studies of the University of Pennsylvania. His field was medieval Jewish history, concentrating on Spanish Jewry. as evidenced by *The Jews in Spain* (1942). He also wrote a biography of his predecessor as president of Dropsie College, Cyrus Adler (1942). A collection of his articles was entitled *Landmarks and Goals* (1953). He served as editor of *The Jewish Quarterly Review*, American Jewry's major scholarly journal, from 1940 to 1966.

DOV NOY. 75th birthday. Born in Kolomea, Galicia, October 20, 1920, he came to Eretz Israel in 1938, and studied at the Hebrew University and later at the University of Indiana. His field is Jewish folklore and he has established a museum devoted to this subject in Haifa, where many collections of Jewish folk stories from various Diaspora communities have been published. In English translation several such collections, edited or coedited by him have appeared, such as *Moroccan Jewish Folktales* (1966); *Studies in Aggada and Folk-Literature* (1971); *Studies in Biblical and Jewish Folklore* (1973); *Studies In Marriage Customs* (1974); and *Studies in Jewish Folklore* (1980). In 1991 he reissued *Yiddish Folksongs in Russia*, originally published in St. Petersburg in 1901.

DAVID DE SOLA POOL. 25th anniversary of death. Born in London, England, in 1885, died in New York, December 1, 1970. In 1907 he became rabbi of Congregation Shearith Israel, New York, the oldest Jewish synagogue in North America, to whose history he devoted several books. *Portraits Etched in Stone: Early Jewish Settlers*, 1682-1831 (1952), which includes epitaphs from its Chatham Square Cemetery, and *An Old Faith in the New World: Portraits of Shearith Israel*, 1654-1954 (1955), marking the tercentenary of American Jewry. He also wrote *The Kaddish* (1909; 1964) and edited several prayerbooks for the traditional synagogue as well as specifically for the Sephardic ritual. His *Haggadah* with English translation passed through numerous editions.

SAUL PHINEHAS RABBINOWITZ. 150th anniversary of birth. Born in Tauroggen, Lithuania, April 8, 1845, died in Frankfurt am Main, Germany, in 1910. A Hebrew writer and teacher in Russia, he had been ordained by the famed Israel Salanter, but inclined toward Haskalah. His major contribution to Hebrew literature was his translation of Graetz's *History of the Jews* from German into Hebrew. It not only widened the horizons of East European Jewry, but also enriched the fledgling Hebrew literature. He likewise wrote Hebrew biographies of the German Jewish scholars, Leopold Zunz and Zacharias Frankel.

CHAIM RABIN. 80th birthday. Born in Giessen, Germany, November 22, 1915. In Eretz Israel since the 1930's he eventually became professor of Hebrew at the Hebrew University in Jerusalem. He specialized both in Hebrew and Arabic studies, publishing textbooks for both languages. In English there appeared *Qumran Studies* (1957, 1975). He also prepared translations of important Jewish classics, such as an abridged edition of *The Guide of the Perplexed* by Maimonides (1952) and *The Zadokite Documents* (1954; 1958), an early sectarian Jewish work.

ALEXANDER SISKIND RABINOVITZ. 50th anniversary of death. Born in Lyady, Russia, in 1854, died in Tel-Aviv, September 6, 1945. A teacher in his native land with pupils such as Ber Borochov, the leading Jewish Socialist theorist, and Yitshak Ben-Zvi, the future president of Israel, he became active in the Zionist movement, was a delegate to the First Zionist Congress in Basel in 1897 and settled in Eretz Israel in 1906. He was a prolific Hebrew writer, writing not only on Jewish history and biblical studies, but also translating works by prominent scholars, such as Wilhelm Bacher and David Hoffmann, from German into Hebrew. He also wrote popular studies on Islam and biographies of Rousseau and Joseph Hayyim Brenner.

MENAHEM RIBALOW. 100th anniversary of birth. Born in Chudnov, Russia, February 17, 1895, died in New York in 1953. In the United States since 1921, he edited the only Hebrew weekly for many years. His primary interest was literary criticism of Hebrew poetry, and several volumes of his essays originally published in his magazine and elsewhere made their appearance.

He also promoted the Histadruth Ivrith, the society advancing the Hebrew language and literature among American Jews. Posthumously an English translation of some of his writings appeared under the title *The Flowering of Modern Hebrew Literature* (1959).

ISAAC RIVKIND. 100th anniversary of birth. Born in Lodz, Poland, March 17, 1895, died in New York in 1968. Before coming to America in 1920 he had heen active in the Zionist movement in Poland. In New York he eventually became head of the Hebrew department of the library of the Jewish Theological Seminary of America, where he assisted many scholars in their bibliographic quests. He wrote a wide variety of articles in Hebrew and Yiddish on many subjects. His books dealt with the history of Bar Mitzvah, Jewish money and the struggle against gambling in the Jewish community.

MICHAEL LEVI RODKINSON. 150th anniversary of birth. Born in Dubrovno, Belarus, in 1845, died in New York in 1904. An editor of Hebrew and Yiddish magazines in Russia, he eventually came to the Ynited States. Here he published *History of Amulets, Charms, and Talismans* (1893) and *The History of the Talmud* (1903). His largest work, however, was a *New Edition of the Babylonian Talmud, English Translation* (1896-1903) in 20 volumes, which was generally rejected by experts as incorrect and carelessly put together.

CECIL ROTH. 25th anniversary of death. Born in London, England, in 1899, died there June 20, 1970. Trained as a historian at Oxford, he eventually became reader in Jewish studies at his alma mater. He produced an enormous amount of work on Jewish history, his bibliography listing nearly 600 items, primarily on England, Italy, and the Sephardim. An early work was *Venice* (1930), a part of the Jewish community series of the Jewish Publication Society. *A History of the Marranos* (1974, 1992) was one of many works dealing with the Sephardim. *Anglo-Jewish, Letters* (1158-1917), published in 1938, is an important contribution of source material to Anglo-Jewish history. In addition he served as editor-in-chief of the monumental *Encyclopaedia Judaica* (1971), whose completion he did not witness and which is carried on in his spirit through several yearbooks up to the present time. He also edited several editions of a one-volume encyclopedia, *Standard Jewish Encyclopedia,* beginning in 1958, and latest edition as *New Standard Jewish Encyclopedia* (1977).

MORITZ GOTTLIEB SAPHIR. 200th anniversary of birth. Born near Budapest, Hungary, August 2, 1795, died in Vienna, Austria, in 1858. The son of an Orthodox Yiddish–speaking family, he attended yeshivot in his younger years. He turned to popular

German feuilleton and satire later, leading to expulsions from several German states. After he converted to Christianity he did not anymore attack the authorities but managed to entertain the public with his biting wit, which made him very popular. For years his witticisms were quoted throughout Germany.

JOSEPH B. SCHECHTMAN. 25th anniversary of death. Born in Odessa, Russia, in 1890, died in Doylestown, Pennsylvania, March 1, 1970. Active in Russian Jewish life after World War I, he eventually became associated with Vladimir Jabotinsky in the Revisionist Zionist movement. He published *The Vladimir Jabotinsky Story* (1956-1961) and *The Life and Times of Vladimir Jabotinsky* (1986). *On Wings of Eagles* (1961) dealt with the immigration of Jews from Arab countries to Israel. His extensive travels were reflected in *Star in Eclipse: Russian Jewry Revisited* (1961). *The Mufti and the Fuehrer* (1965) showed the collaboration between the two during World War II. After coming to this country in 1941 he was active in population research and wrote *European Population Transfers* 1939-1945 (1946; 1971).

JACOB H. SCHIFF. 75th anniversary of death. Born in Frankfurt am Main, Germany, in 1847, died in New York, September 25, 1920. In the United States since the 1860's, he became a prominent financier, accumulating a large fortune, which he utilized to support a variety of causes, particularly within the Jewish community. Although a Reform Jew he supported the Conservative Jewish Theological Seminary of America, as well as the Hebrew Union College, and Orthodox institutions. Largely owing to his beneficence *The Jewish Encyclopedia,* the great achievement of American Jewish scholarship in the early part of this century, was made possible. The Jewish Publication Society of America received also many gifts from him, among them the endowment of the English Bible translation published in 1917 and the Schiff Library of Jewish Classics, producing traditional Hebrew works with facing English translations. He also presented several major collections of Hebrew books to the Library of Congress and the New York Public Library.

JOSHUA HESCHEL SCHORR. 100th anniversary of death. Born in Brody, Galicia, in 1818, died there September 2, 1895. A prosperous businessman, he had strong interest in reforming East European Jewish life and was willing to take on the uphill struggle against the traditionalists. A maskil, who wanted to recast Jewish life and thought somewhat in the manner of the German reformers, he attacked Rabbinic Judaism head-on. He applied the modern critical method to both Bible and Talmud, but found little support among the broad masses, except for some writers like

Moses Leib Lilienblum and Judah Leib Gordon. He founded his own Hebrew periodical, but many of his articles were published in translation in German Jewish periodicals.

NATHAN SHAHAM. 70th birthday. Born in Tel-Aviv, January 29, 1925. The son of the well-known writer Eliezer Steinman he is the author of plays and stories, some also for children. In English translation there appeared *They'll Be Here Tomorrow* (1957), a play, *The Other Side of the Wall* (1983), *The Rosendorf Quartet* (1991), and *Bone to the Bone* (1993). He also wrote the text to two picture albums, *Journey in the Land of Israel* (1966) and *Israel Defense Forces, the Six Day War* (1968; 1969).

SHNEUR ZALMAN of Lyady. 250th anniversary of birth. Born in Liozna, Belarus, September 15, 1745, died in Piena, Russia, in 1813. He is considered the founder of the Habad or Lubavitch movement in Hasidism. His two major works are a new *Shulhan Arukh*, a code of Jewish law, based on the work by the same title of Joseph Karo, and *Tanya* (teachings), an exposition of the hasidic message. He differed from other hasidic leaders, in that he stressed traditional Jewish learning more so than some of the others. Both of his works are characterized by a fine Hebrew style. A selection of the latter work in English translation appeared in Nissan Mindel's *Philosophy of Chabad* (1973; 1985).

SOLOMON SIMON. 100th anniversary of birth and 25th anniversary of death. Born in Kolikovichi, Belarus, July 4, 1895, died in Miami, Florida, November 8, 1970. In this country since 1913, he eventually became a dentist, but always remained interested in Yiddish literature and Jewish education, editing a Yiddish periodical for children, and writing on Bible in Yiddish. In English he coedited *The Rabbi's Bible* (1966), a selection of biblical texts with commentaries. His reminiscences of life in Europe were entitled *My Jewish Roots* (1956). Collections of stories were *In the Thicket* (1963) and *More Wise Men of Chelm and Their Merry Tales* (1965).

HENRIETTA SZOLD. 50th anniversary of death. Born in Baltimore, Maryland, in 1860, died in Jerusalem, February 13, 1945. The daughter of a rabbi she always took an interest in Jewish life, establishing Americanization classes for immigrants in Baltimore. Later she hecame associated with the Jewish Publication Society of America, editing the *American Jewish Year Book* from 1904-1908. She also translated important works hy Moritz Lazarus and Simon Dubnow for the Society. In 1892 she had translated Ahad Ha-Am's reaction to Pinsker's *Autoemancipation* into English. A new horizon opened for her to do practical Zionist work. In 1912 she went to Palestine to do nursing work and she established Hadassah, the Women's Zionist Organization of America to back up the health needs of the Yishuv. In 1915 she wrote *Recent Jewish Progress in Palestine* (reprinted 1977). *Henrietta Szold, Life and Letters*, edited hy Marvin Lowenthal, appeared in 1942; *Henrietta Szold and Youth Aliyah*, a collection of letters written between 1934 and 1944, appeared in 1986. It testifies to her ingenuity in starting this important movement at the crucial time of the beginning of the Nazi period.

FRANZ WERFEL. 50th anniversary of death. Born in Prague, Czech Republic, in 1890, died in Hollywood, California, August 28, 1945. A prominent Austrian writer, who came close to converting to Christianity, but never quite took the final step, he was preoccupied with religious questions all his life. Of some Jewish interest are *Paul Among the Jews* (1928; 1943), *The Eternal Road* (1936), a biblical play, staged by Max Reinhardt in New York, and *Jacobowsky and the Colonel* (1944). This comedy deals with the relationship of a Polish colonel and a resourceful Jew in flight during the invasion of France.

HERMAN WOUK. 80th birthday. Born in New York City, May 27, 1915. A World War II veteran, he first served as a television writer and then utilized his experience in the Navy in *The Caine Mutiny* (1952), which was an extremely successful novel, winning the Pulitzer Prize, and also a popular play and motion picture. *Marjorie Morningstar* (1955) was one of the first novels with a Jewish background that won wide acclaim by the general reading public. It was also made into a film. Other novels, *Winds of War* (1971) and *War and Remembrance*, (1978) had Jewish characters and dealt with the Holocaust, also becoming a television mini-series. *Inside, Outside* (1985) is a fictional treatment of the Watergate Affair, but also includes Jewish characters. His latest novel, *The Hope* (1993), deals with life in Israel and was on the best-seller list. A committed Orthodox Jew he expressed his faith in *This Is My God* (1959, and reprinted several times thereafter).

HERBERT C. ZAFREN. 70th birthday. Born in Baltimore, Maryland, August 25, 1925. Librarian of the Hebrew Union College in Cincinnati since 1950, he has also served as director of the libraries of the other branches of that institution in New York, Los Angeles, and Jerusalem in recent years. In 1953 he inaugurated the bibliographic journal *Studies in Bibliography and Booklore*, which serves the specialized needs of the Jewish bibliographer. He also has served as the editor of the series *Bibliographica Judaica* which has published important bibliographical monographs. The American Jewish Periodical Center, associated with the HUC Library endeavors to preserve a complete run of American Jewish periodicals, particularly from the early period, on microfilm.

SUZANNE M. STAUFFER

American Jewish Non-Fiction Books, 1993-1994

ART AND LITERATURE

BALABAN, ABRAHAM. *Between God and Beast: an Examination of Amos Oz's Prose.* Univ. Park, Pa.: Pennsylvania State Univ. Press, 1993. 258 p. Bibliog., index.

CITRON, STERNA. *Why the Baal Shem Tov Laughed: Fifty-Two Stories About Our Great Chasidic Rabbis.* Northvale, N.J.: Aronson, 1993. 301 p. Bibliog.

   Retells legends of remarkable hasidic rabbis, including the Baal Shem Tov, the Mezhirecher Magid, and Reb Zusha of Annapoli.

DESSER, DAVID AND LESTER D. FRIEDMAN. *American-Jewish Filmmakers: Traditions and Trends.* Urbana: Univ. of Illinois Press, 1993. 318 p. Bibliog., index.

The Field of Yiddish: Studies in Language, Folklore, and Literature: Fifth Collection. Ed. by David Goldberg. Evanston, Ill.: Northwestern Univ. Press; New York: YIVO Institute for Jewish Research, 1993. 327 p. Bibliog., index.

GLATSTEIN, JACOB. *I Keep Recalling: the Holocaust Poems of Jacob Glatstein.* Tr. from the Yiddish by Barnett Zumoff, with an intro. by Emanuel S. Goldsmith. Hoboken, N.J.: Ktav, 1993. 289 p.

HAKAK, LEV. *Equivocal Dreams: Studies in Modern Hebrew Literature.* Hoboken, N.J.: Ktav, 1993. 195 p. Bibliog.

Hebrew Literature in the Wake of the Holocaust. Ed. by Leon I. Yudkin. Rutherford: Fairleigh Dickinson Univ. Press, 1993. 131 p. Bibliog.

Holocaust Literature: a Handbook of Critical, Historical, and Literary Writings. Ed. by Saul S. Friedman; foreword by Dennis Klein. Westport, Conn.: Greenwood Press, 1993. 677 p. Bibliog., index.

227

Israeli Writers Consider the "Outsider". Ed. by Leon I. Yudkin. Rutherford: Fairleigh Dickinson Univ. Press, 1993. 143 p. Bibliog.

KAUVAR, ELAINE M. *Cynthia Ozick's Fiction: Tradition & Invention.* Bloomington: Indiana Univ. Press, 1993. 264 p. (Jewish Literature and Culture) Bibliog., index.

PENSKY, MAX. *Melancholy Dialectics: Walter Benjamin and the Play of Mourning.* Amherst: Univ. of Massachusetts Press, 1993. 281 p. (Critical Perspectives on Modern Culture) Bibliog., index.

RUSH, BARBARA. *The Book of Jewish Women's Tales.* Northvale, N.J.: Aronson, 1994. 305 p. Bibliog., index.
    Jewish women's folktales retold by Barbara Rush.

SABA, UMBERTO. *Stories and Recollections of Umberto Saba.* Tr. by Estelle Gilson. Riverdale-on-Hudson, N. Y.: Sheep Meadow Press, 1993. 222 p.

SCHWARTZ, HOWARD. *Gabriel's Palace: Jewish Mystical Tales.* New York: Oxford Univ. Press, 1993. 414 p. Bibliog., index.
    A compilation of 150 rabbinic, cabalistic, hasidic, and other mystical tales.

SHERMAN, JOSEPHA. *Rachel the Clever and Other Jewish Folktales.* 1st ed. Little Rock: August House, 1993. 171 p.
    Forty-six tales from all over the Jewish world; highly recommended.

Summoning: Ideas of the Covenant and Interpretive Theory. Ed. by Ellen Spolsky. Albany: State Univ. of New York Press, 1993. 272 p. (SUNY Series in Modern Jewish Literature and Culture) Bibliog., index.

The Visual Dimension: Aspects of Jewish Art. Ed. by Clare Moore. Westview Press, 1993. 184 p. Index.
    This collection of scholarly articles on synagogue architecture and Jewish art in the Middle Ages belongs in every serious academic library.

WEISSBREM, ISRAEL. *The World of Israel Weissbrem: Novels.* Tr. by Alan D. Crown. Boulder, Co.: Westview Press, 1993. 171 p. (Modern Hebrew Classics)

BIBLE STUDIES

BROWN, WILLIAM P. *Structure, Role, and Ideology in the Hebrew and Greek Texts of Genesis 1:1-1:3.* Atlanta: Scholars Press,

1993. 268 p. (Dissertation Series [Society of Biblical Literature], no. 132) Bibliog.

COHEN, JONATHAN. *The Origins and Evolution of the Moses Nativity Story.* New York: Brill, 1993. 205 p. (Studies in the History of Religions, vol. 58) Bibliog., indexes.

GOTTWALD, NORMAN K. *The Hebrew Bible in Its Social World and in Ours.* Atlanta: Scholars Press, 1993. 425 p. (Semeia Studies) Bibliog., index.

GRAY, REBECCA. *Prophetic Figures in Late Second Temple Jewish Palestine: the Evidence from Josephus.* New York: Oxford Univ. Press, 1993. 238 p. Bibliog., index.

GREENSPAHN, FREDERICK E. *When Brothers Dwell Together: The Preeminence of Younger Siblings in the Hebrew Bible.* New York: Oxford Univ. Press, 1994. 193 p. Bibliog., indexes.

GUNN, DAVID M. AND DONNA NOLAN FEWELL. *Narrative in the Hebrew Bible.* New York: Oxford Univ. Press, 1993. 263 p. (Oxford Bible Series) Bibliog., index.

HarperCollins Study Bible: New Revised Standard Version, with the Apocryphal/Deuterocanonical Books. General ed., Wayne A. Meeks; associate eds., Jouette M. Bassler, et al.; with the Society of Biblical Literature. 1st ed. San Francisco: HarperSanFrancisco, 1993. 2355 p. Index.

Presents new introductions by biblical scholars to each book; annotations give chronology, location, explanations of wordplay and the interplay between books. For academic and special libraries.

Hebrew and the Bible in America: the First Two Centuries. Ed. by Shalom Goldman. Hanover: Univ. Press of New England for Brandeis Univ. Press and Dartmouth College, 1993. 259 p. (Brandeis Series in American Jewish History, Culture and Life) Bibliog., index.

Fifteen scholars document the impact of the Hebrew language and Bible on American cultural and intellectual life. For academic libraries.

HIMMELFARB, MARTHA. *Ascent to Heaven in Jewish and Christian Apocalypses.* New York: Oxford Univ. Press, 1993. 171 p. Bibliog., index.

KAMESAR, ADAM. *Jerome, Greek Scholarship, and the Hebrew Bible: a Study of the Quaestiones Hebraicae in Genesim.* New York: Oxford Univ. Press, 1993. 221 p. (Oxford Classical Monographs) Bibliog., indexes.

KNOPPERS, GARY N. *Two Nations under God: the Deuteronomistic*

History of Solomon and the Dual Monarchies. Atlanta: Scholars Press, 1993. Vol. 1: The Reign of Solomon and the Rise of Jeroboam. (Harvard Semitic Monographs, no. 52) Bibliog., index.

LEVENSON, JON DOUGLAS. *The Death and Resurrection of the Beloved Son: the Transformation of Child Sacrifice in Judaism and Christianity.* New Haven: Yale Univ. Press, 1993. 257 p. Bibliog., index.

LINDSAY, DENNIS R. *Josephus and Faith: [Pistis] and [Pisteuein] as Faith Terminology in the Writings of Flavius Josephus and in the New Testament.* New York : E.J. Brill, 1993. 212 p. (Arbeiten zur Geschichte des antiken Judentums und des Urchristentums, Bd. 19) Bibliog., index.

MALONE, JOSEPH L. *Tiberian Hebrew Phonology.* Winona Lake, Ind.: Eisenbrauns, 1993. 204 p. Bibliog.

MURPHY, FREDERICK JAMES. *Pseudo-Philo: Rewriting the Bible.* New York: Oxford Univ. Press, 1993. 322 p. Bibliog., index.
    Includes a concordance to Pseudo-Philo's *Liber Antiquitatum Biblicarum.*

NEUSNER, JACOB. *Ancient Judaism: Debates and Disputes : Third Series.* Atlanta: Scholars Press, 1993. 311 p. (South Florida Studies in the History of Judaism, no. 83). Index.

NEW, DAVID S. *Old Testament Quotations in the Synoptic Gospels, and the Two-Document Hypothesis.* Atlanta: Scholars Press, 1993. 140 p. (Septuagint and Cognate Studies Series, no. 37) Bibliog., index.

NIDITCH, SUSAN. *War in the Hebrew Bible: a Study in the Ethics of Violence.* New York: Oxford Univ. Press, 1993. 180 p. Bibliog., index.

PERRY, T. A. *Dialogues with Kohelet: the Book of Ecclesiastes: Translation and Commentary.* University Park, Pa.: Pennsylvania State Univ. Press, 1993. 210 p. Bibliog., indexes.

PERRY, T. A. *Wisdom Literature and the Structure of Proverbs.* University Park, Pa.: Pennsylvania State Univ. Press, 1993. 134 p. Bibliog., index.

REED, WALTER L. *Dialogues of the Word: the Bible as Literature According to Bakhtin.* New York: Oxford Univ. Press, 1993. 223 p. Bibliog., index.

SARNA, NAHUM N. *Songs of the Heart: an Introduction to the Book of Psalms.* 1st ed. New York: Schocken Bks.; distr. by Pantheon Bks., 1993. 298 p. Bibliog., indexes.

A literary and historical analysis of ten representative psalms.

SAWYER, JOHN F. A. *Prophecy and the Biblical Prophets*. Rev. ed. New York: Oxford Univ. Press, 1993. 180 p. (Oxford Bible Series) Bibliog., index.

Rev. ed. of: *Prophecy and the Prophets of the Old Testament*.

Scrolls From the Dead Sea: an Exhibition of Scrolls and Archaeological Artifacts From the Collections of the Israel Antiquities Authority. Ed. by Ayala Sussmann and Ruth Peled; Library of Congress, Washington, in association with the Israel Antiquities Authority. New York: George Braziller, 1993. 143 p. Bibliog., index.

SHULMAN, DAVID DEAN. *The Hungry God: Hindu Tales of Filicide and Devotion*. Chicago: Univ. of Chicago Press, 1993. 157 p. Bibliog., index.

Shulman, a professor of Sanskrit at the Hebrew Univ., compares and contrasts the Hindu tales of Tamila and Telugu with the biblical akedah. For academic and special libraries.

SNELL, DANIEL C. *Twice-told Proverbs and the Composition of the Book of Proverbs*. Winona Lake, Ind.: Eisenbrauns, 1993. 146 p. Indexes.

A Song of Power and the Power of Song: Essays on the Book of Deuteronomy. Ed. by Duane L. Christensen. Winona Lake, Ind.: Eisenbrauns, 1993. 428 p. (Sources for Biblical and Theological Study, 3) Bibliog., indexes.

The Song of Songs in the Targumic Tradition: Vocalized Aramaic Text with Facing English Translation and Ladino Versions; Aramaic Concordance, Aramaic-English, Ladino-English Glossaries. Tr. and ed. by Isaac Jerusalmi. Cincinnati: Ladino Bks., 1993. 506 p.

In Aramaic, English and five versions of Ladino, one of which is that of the editor. With introductions, remarks, bibliography and other aids to study of the texts.

SPIEGEL, SHALOM. *The Last Trial: On the Legends and Lore of the Command to Abraham to Offer Isaac as a Sacrifice : the Akedah*. First paperback ed. Tr. with an intro. by Judah Goldin. Woodstock, Vt.: Jewish Lights Pub., 1993. 162 p. (Jewish Lights Classic Reprint) Bibliog., index.

STEUSSY, MARTI J. *Gardens in Babylon: Narrative and Faith in the Greek Legends of Daniel*. Atlanta: Scholars Press, 1993.

226 p. (Dissertation Series (Society of Biblical Literature),
no. 141) Bibliog., indexes.

STIREWALT, M. LUTHER. *Studies in Ancient Greek Epistolography.*
Atlanta: Scholars Press, 1993. 87 p. (Resources for Biblical
Study, no. 27) Bibliog.

*To Each Its Own Meaning: an Introduction to Biblical Criticisms
and Their Application.* 1st ed. Ed. by Stephen R. Haynes
and Steven L. McKenzie. Louisville: Westminster/John
Knox Press, 1993. 251 p. Bibliog.

TOEWS, WESLEY I. *Monarchy and Religious Institution in Israel
Under Jeroboam I.* Atlanta: Scholars Press, 1993. 197 p.
(Monograph Series (Society of Biblical Literature), no. 47)
Bibliog., index.

*2 Peter, Jude: a New Translation with Introduction and
Commentary.* Ed. by Jerome H. Neyrey. New York:
Doubleday, 1993, 287 p. (The Anchor Bible, 37C) Bibliog.,
indexes.

WILDAVSKY, AARON B. *Assimilation Versus Separation: Joseph the
Administrator and the Politics of Religion in Biblical Israel.*
New Brunswick: Transaction Pubs., 1993. 236 p. Bibliog.,
index.

BIOGRAPHY

ARCANA, JUDITH. *Grace Paley's Life Stories: a Literary Biography.*
Urbana: Univ. of Illinois Press, 1993. 269 p. Bibliog., index.

BERROL, SELMA CANTOR. *Julia Richman: a Notable Woman.*
Philadelphia: Balch Institute Press, 1993. 153 p. Bibliog.,
index.

BROWNSTEIN, RACHEL M. *Tragic Muse: Rachel of the Comédie-
Française.* 1st ed. New York: Knopf, 1993. 318 p. Bibliog.,
index.

CHAFE, WILLIAM H. *Never Stop Running: Allard Lowenstein and
the Struggle to Save American Liberalism.* New York: Basic
Books, 1993. 556 p. Bibliog., index.

CHERNOW, RON. *The Warburgs: the 20th Century Odyssey of a
Remarkable Jewish Family.* New York: Random House,
1993. 820 p. Bibliog., index.

Disraeli, the Jew: Essays by Benjamin Cardozo & Emma Lazarus.
Ed. and with an intro. by Michael Selzer; preface by Donald
Mopsik. 1st ed. Great Barrington, Mass.: Selzer & Selzer,
1993. 73 p.

"Was the Earl of Beaconsfield a Representative Jew?"
by Emma Lazarus, orig. pub. Century Magazine, 1882; "The
Earl of Beaconsfield: a Jew as Prime Minister" by Benjamin
Cardozo, previously unpublished.

ETKES, IMMANUEL. *Rabbi Israel Salanter and the Mussar
Movement: Seeking the Torah of Truth.* 1st English edition.
Tr. by Jonathan Chipman. Philadelphia: Jewish Publication
Society, 1993. 389 p. Bibliog., index.
    Translation of: *R. Yisra'el Salanter ve-reshitah shel
tenu`at ha-musar.*

EVANS, ELI N. *The Lonely Days Were Sundays: Reflections of a
Jewish Southerner.* Jackson: Univ. Press of Mississippi,
1993. 357 p.

FROMER, REBECCA. *The Holocaust Odyssey of Daniel Bennahmias,
Sonderkommando.* With an intro. by Steven B. Bowman.
Tuscaloosa: Univ. of Alabama Press, 1993. 151 p. (Judaic
Studies Series) Bibliog., index.

GHOSH, AMITAV. *In an Antique Land.* New York: Knopf, 1993.
393 p. Bibliog.,
    The story of the author's lifelong obsession with, and
research into, the life of Abraham Ben Yiju, a 12th century
Jew, and his Indian slave.

ISH SHALOM, BINYAMIN. *Rav Avraham Itzhak Hacohen Kook:
Between Rationalism and Mysticism.* Albany: State Univ. of
New York Press, 1993. (SUNY Series in Judaica) 357 p.
Bibliog., index.

JOSEPHY, ROBERT. *Taking Part: a Twentieth-Century Life.* Foreword
by Albert E. Stone. Iowa City: Univ. of Iowa Press, 1993.
225 p. (Singular Lives)

KLUKOWSKI, ZYGMUNT. *Diary from the Years of Occupation, 1939-
44.* Tr. by George Klukowski; ed. by Andrew Klukowski and
Helen Klukowski May; foreword by Monty Noam Penkower.
Urbana: Univ. of Illinois Press, 1993. 371 p. Index.

KORNBERG, JACQUES. *Theodor Herzl: From Assimilation to
Zionism.* Bloomington: Indiana Univ. Press, 1993. 240 p.
(Jewish Literature and Culture) Bibliog., index.

MATT, HERSHEL JONAH. *Walking Humbly with God: the Life and
Writings of Rabbi Hershel Jonah Matt.* Ed. by Daniel C.
Matt. Hoboken, N.J.: Ktav, 1993. 300 p. Bibliog.

MICHEL, ERNEST. *Promises to Keep.* Foreword by Leon Uris. New
York: Barricade Bks.; distributed by Publishers Group West,
1993. 298 p.

The story of his experiences in Auschwitz, his life in America, and his involvement with the Jewish Appeal Federation.

Moses Maimonides: Physician, Scientist, and Philosopher. Ed. by Fred Rosner and Samuel S. Kottek. Northvale, N.J.: Aronson, 1993. 281 p.

A collection of papers presented at the symposium "Maimonides as a Physician, Scientist and Philosopher," held in Jerusalem, Oct. 19-31, 1990.

PATTERSON, DAVID. *Pilgrimage of a Proselyte: From Auschwitz to Jerusalem.* Middle Village, N.Y.: Jonathan David, 1993. 207 p. Index.

An eloquent testimony to Judaism and the conversion experience.

PEYSER, JOAN. *The Memory of All That: the Life of George Gershwin.* New York: Simon & Schuster, 1993. 319 p. Index.

REINHARZ, JEHUDA. *Chaim Weizmann: the Making of a Statesman.* New York: Oxford Univ. Press, 1993. 536 p. (Studies in Jewish History) Bibliog., index.

Sequel to the author's 1985 biography, *Chaim Weizmann: the Making of a Zionist Leader.* This covers from World War I to the summer of 1922; it is a basic historical statement of the period.

ROSENFELD, NANCY. *Unfinished Journey: Two People, Two Worlds ... From Tyranny to Freedom.* Lanham, Md.: Univ. Press of America, 1993. 276 p. Index.

The biography of Yuri Tarnopolsky and Nancy Rosenfeld.

SCHACK, HOWARD H. WITH H. PAUL JEFFERS. *A Spy in Canaan: My Life as a Jewish-American Businessman Spying for Israel in Arab Lands.* New York: Carol Pub. Group, 1993. 246 p. Index.

SCHULMAN, AVI M. *Like a Raging Fire: a Biography of Maurice N. Eisendrath.* Foreword by Albert Vorspan. New York: UAHC Press, 1993. 108 p. Bibliog., index.

SILBERMAN, NEIL ASHER. *A Prophet from Amongst You: the Life of Yigael Yadin: Soldier, Scholar, and Mythmaker of Modern Israel.* Reading, Mass.: Addison Wesley, 1993. 423 p. Bibliog., index.

SLATER, ROBERT. *Rabin of Israel.* Rev. ed. New York: St. Martin's Press, 1993. 486 p.

Telling the Tale: a Tribute to Elie Wiesel on the Occasion of his

65th Birthday: Essays, Reflections, and Poems. Ed. by Harry James Cargas. 1st ed. St. Louis, Mo.: Time Being Bks., 1993. 169 p. Bibliog.

The tributes in this volume are uneven, making the work a marginal purchase.

WASKOW, HOWARD AND ARTHUR WASKOW. *Becoming Brothers.* New York: Free Press, 1993. 218 p.

WEINTRAUB, STANLEY. *Disraeli: a Biography.* New York: Truman Talley Bks./Dutton, 1993. 717 p. Index.

HISTORY

ALEXY, TRUDI. *The Mezuzah in the Madonnna's Foot: Oral Histories Exploring Five Hundred Years in the Paradoxical Relationship of Spain and the Jews.* New York: Simon and Schuster, 1993. 316 p. Index.

ARMSTRONG, KAREN. *A History of God: the 4,000-Year Quest of Judaism, Christianity, and Islam.* 1st American ed. New York: Knopf; distr. by Random House, 1993. 460 p. Bibliog., index.

This rather one-sided, humanistic overview of the changing idea of God throughout history may offend some conservative readers.

The Beilis Transcripts: the Anti-Semitic Trial that Shook the World. Ed. and tr. by Ezekiel Leikin. Northvale, N.J.: Aronson, 1993. 241 p. Bibliog., index.

Bits of Honey: Essays for Samson H. Levey. Ed. by Stanley F. Chyet and David H. Ellenson. Atlanta: Scholars Press, 1993. 335 p. (South Florida Studies in the History of Judaism, no. 74). Bibliog., index.

DIASPORAS IN ANTIQUITY. Ed. by Shaye J. D. Cohen and Ernest S. Frerichs. Atlanta: Scholars Press, 1993. 130 p. (Brown Judaic Studies, no. 288) Bibliog., index.

ELBOGEN, ISMAR. *Jewish Liturgy: a Comprehensive History.* Tr. by Raymond P. Scheindlin. Philadelphia: Jewish Publication Society; New York: Jewish Theological Seminary, 1993. 501 p. Bibliog., index.

The first English translation of: *Jüdische Gottesdienst in seiner geschichtlichen Entwicklung.* "Based on the original 1913 German edition and the 1972 Hebrew edition

edited by Joseph Heinemann, et al." An important addition
to most libraries.

EPPERSON, STEVEN. *Mormons and Jews: Early Mormon Theologies
of Israel.* Salt Lake City: Signature Bks., 1993. 237 p. Index.
    A carefully documented Mormon intellectual
history.

EL-KODSI, MOURAD. *The Karaite Communities in Poland,
Lithuania, Russia and Crimea.* Lyons, N.Y.: Wilprint, 1993.
79 p. Bibliog., index.

FELDMAN, LOUIS H. *Jew and Gentile in the Ancient World:
Attitudes and Interactions from Alexander to Justinian.*
Princeton: Princeton Univ. Press, 1993. 679 p. Bibliog.,
indexes.

FUNKENSTEIN, AMOS. *Perceptions of Jewish History.* Los Angeles:
Univ. of California Press, 1993. 390 p. Bibliog., index.

HADAS-LEBEL, MIREILLE. *Flavius Josephus: Eyewitness to Rome's
First-Century Conquest of Judaea.* Tr. by Richard Miller.
New York: Macmillan, 1993. 269 p. Bibliog., index.
    An attempt to define Josephus' place in Jewish
literature, as well as interpret his behavior.

HAGY, JAMES WILLIAM. *This Happy Land: The Jews of Colonial
and Antebellum Charleston.* Tuscaloosa: Univ. of Alabama
Press, 1993. 450 p. (Judaic Studies Series) Bibliog., index.

HARSHAV, BENJAMIN. *Language in Time of Revolution.* Los Angeles:
Univ. of California Press, 1993. 234 p. Bibliog., index.
    The history of the revival of the Hebrew language.

Hebrew in Ashkenaz: a Language in Exile. Ed. by Lewis Glinert.
New York: Oxford Univ. Press, 1993. Bibliog.

*Hostages of Modernization: Studies on Modern Antisemitism,
1870-1933/39.* Ed. by Herbert A. Strauss. New York:
W. de Gruyter, 1993. 2 vols. (Current Research on
Antisemitism, vols. 3/1-3/2) Bibliog.
    Vol. 1 - Germany, Great Britain, France; vol. 2 -
Austria, Hungary, Poland, Russia.

Interpreters of Judaism in the Late Twentieth Century. Ed. by
Steven T. Katz. Washington, D.C.: B'nai B'rith Bks., 1993.
423 p. (The B'nai B'rith History of the Jewish People)
Bibliog., index.

KATZ, JACOB. *Tradition and Crisis: Jewish Society at the End of the
Middle Ages.* Tr. with a bibliographical appendix and
afterword by Bernard Dov Cooperman. New York: New York
Univ. Press, 1993. 392 p. Bibliog., index.

LANDAU, DAVID. *Piety and Power: the World of Jewish Fundamentalism.* 1st American ed. New York: Hill and Wang, 1993. 358 p. Bibliog. index.

LASSNER, JACOB. *Demonizing the Queen of Sheba: Boundaries of Gender and Culture in Postbiblical Judaism and Medieval Islam.* Chicago: Univ. of Chicago Press, 281 p. (Chicago Studies in the History of Judaism) Bibliog., index.

LEVINE, ROBERT M. *Tropical Diaspora: the Jewish Experience in Cuba.* Gainesville: Univ. Press of Florida, 1993. 398 p. Bibliog., index.

MILLER, PHILIP E. *Karaite Separatism in Nineteenth-Century Russia: Joseph Solomon Lutski's Epistle of Israel's Deliverance.* Cincinnati: Hebrew Union College Press, 1993. 252 p. (Monographs of the Hebrew Union College, no. 16) Bibliog.

Includes annotated text and translation of: *Igeret Teshu'at Yisra'el.*

MOORE, DEBORAH DASH. *To the Golden Cities: Pursuing the American Jewish Dream in Miami and L.A.* New York: Free Press, 1994. 358 p. Bibliog., index.

A solidly documented, seminal work that details the factors and trends that led to fundamental changes in the American Jewish community after the Second World War.

MOSSE, GEORGE L. *Confronting the Nation: Jewish and Western Nationalism.* Hanover: Univ. Press of New England for Brandeis Univ. Press, 1993. 220 p. (Tauber Institute for the Study of European Jewry Series, 16) Bibliog., index.

A Museum of Faiths: Histories and Legacies of the 1893 World's Parliament of Religions. Ed. by Eric J. Ziolkowski. Atlanta: Scholars Press, 1993. 366 p. (Classics in Religious Studies, no. 9) Bibliog., index.

NICHOLLS, WILLIAM. *Christian Antisemitism: a History of Hate.* Northvale, N.J.: Aronson, 1993. 499 p. Bibliog., index.

POGONOWSKI, IWO. *Jews in Poland: a Documentary History: the Rise of Jews as a Nation from Congressus Judaicus in Poland to the Knesset in Israel.* New York: Hippocrene Bks., 1993. 402 p. Bibliog., index.

RABINOWITZ, STANLEY. *The Assembly: a Century in the Life of the Adas Israel Hebrew Congregation of Washington, D.C.* New York: Ktav, 1993. 592 p. Index.

SCHWARZFUCHS, SIMON. *A Concise History of the Rabbinate.* Cambridge, Mass.: Blackwell, 1993. 179 p. (Jewish Society and Culture) Index.

A serious and scholarly, yet accessible, history of the rabbinate from its origins in the talmudic period to the present day.

TENENBAUM, SHELLY. *A Credit to Their Community: Jewish Loan Societies in the United States, 1880-1945.* Detroit: Wayne State Univ. Press, 1993. 204 p. (American Jewish Civilization Series) Bibliog., index.

TULCHINSKY, GERALD. *Taking Root: the Origins of the Canadian Jewish Community.* Hanover: Univ. Press of New England for Brandeis Univ. Press, 1993. 341 p. (Brandeis Series in American Jewish History, Culture, and Life) Bibliog., index.

When Philadelphia Was the Capital of Jewish America. Ed. by Murray Friedman. Philadelphia: Balch Institute Press, 1993. 191 p. (Sara F. Yoseloff Memorial Publications in Judaism and Jewish Affairs) Index.

HOLOCAUST

Auschwitz: a History in Photographs. Comp. and ed. by Teresa Swiebocka; English ed. prepared by Jonathan Webber and Connie Wilsack. Bloomington: Indiana Univ. Press for the Auschwitz-Birkenau State Museum, 1993. 295 p. Bibliog.

Insightful information and history is provided by the essays and captions which accompany the photographs. Recommended for all libraries.

CARGAS, HARRY J. *Voices From the Holocaust.* Lexington: Univ. Press of Kentucky, 1993. 164 p.

A collection of interviews with Holocaust survivors and bystanders.

The Collective Silence: German Identity and the Legacy of Shame. Ed. by Barbara Heimannsberg and Christoph J. Schmidt; tr. by Cynthia Oudejans Harris and Gordon Wheeler. 1st ed. San Francisco: Jossey-Bass, 1993. 254 p. (Gestalt Institute of Cleveland Publication) Bibliog., index.

Different Voices: Women and the Holocaust. 1st ed. Ed. and with introd. by Carol Rittner and John K. Roth. New York: Paragon House, 1993. 435 p. Bibliog., index.

ELLIS, MARC H. *Ending Auschwitz: the Future of Jewish and Christian Life.* 1st ed. Louisville, Ky.: Westminster/John Knox, 1994. 162 p. Bibliog.

FOGELMAN, EVA. *Conscience & Courage: the Rescuers of the Jews*

During the Holocaust. New York: Anchor Bks., 1994. 393 p. Bibliog., index.

In addition to biographical information, the work examines the psychology and motivations of the rescuers.

GEORG, WILLY. *In the Warsaw Ghetto: Summer 1941.* Comp. by Rafael F. Scarf. New York: Aperture, 1993. 112 p.

This compilation of photographs taken by a German soldier on assignment from 1939 through 1943 depicts a chilling semblance of normalcy. The accompanying text includes diary excerpts, extracts from the Polish Underground Press, and notices posted in the quarter.

GOLUB, JENNIFER L. AND RENAE COHEN. *What Do Americans Know About the Holocaust?* New York: The American Jewish Committee, Institute of Human Relations, 1993. 62 p. (Working Papers on Contemporary Anti-Semitism)

LIPSTADT, DEBORAH E. *Denying the Holocaust: the Growing Assault on Truth and Memory.* New York: Free Press, 1993. 278 p. Bibliog., index.

MOORE, JAMES F. *Christian Theology After the Shoah.* Lanham, Md.: Univ. Press of America, 1993. 189 p. (Studies in the Shoah, vol. 7) Bibliog., index.

The Nazi Elite. Ed. by Ronald Smelser and Rainer Zitelmann; tr. by Mary Fischer. New York: New York Univ. Press, 1993. 159 p. Bibliog., index.

OWINGS, ALISON. *Frauen: German Women Recall the Third Reich.* New Brunswick, N.J.: Rutgers Univ. Press, 1993. 494 p. Bibliog., index.

A highly recommended compilation of oral histories collected from, among others, a countess, a camp guard, women who hid Jews, Germans, Jews, Nazi supporters, and Communists.

SEGEV, TOM. *The Seventh Million: the Israelis and the Holocaust.* 1st ed. Tr. by Haim Watzman. New York: Hill and Wang, 1993. 593 p. Bibliog., index.

SHAW, STANFORD J. *Turkey and the Holocaust: Turkey's Role in Rescuing Turkish and European Jewry from Nazi Persecution, 1933-1945.* New York: New York Univ. Press, 1993. 424 p. Bibliog., index.

STERN, KENNETH. *Holocaust Denial.* New York: American Jewish Committee, 1993. 193 p. Bibliog., index.

TEC, NECHAMA. *Defiance: the Bielski Partisans.* New York: Oxford

Univ. Press, 1993. 276 p. Bibliog., index.
YOUNG, JAMES EDWARD. *The Texture of Memory: Holocaust Memorials and Meaning.* New Haven: Yale Univ. Press, 1993. 398 p. Bibliog., index.
ZUCCOTTI, SUSAN. *The Holocaust, the French, and the Jews.* New York: Basic Books, 1993. 383 p. Bibliog., index.
ZUCKERMAN, YITZHAK. *A Surplus of Memory: Chronicle of the Warsaw Ghetto Uprising.* Ed. and tr. by Barbara Harshav. Berkeley: Univ. of California Press, 1993. 702 p. Bibliog., index.

ISRAEL AND ZIONISM

ABURISH, SAID K. *Cry Palestine: Inside the West Bank.* 1st American ed. Boulder, Colo.: Westview Press, 1993. 205 p.
BEN-YEHUDA, NACHMAN. *Political Assassinations by Jews: a Rhetorical Device for Justice.* Albany: SUNY Press, 1993. 527 p. (SUNY Series in Deviance and Social Control)(SUNY Series in Israeli Studies) 527 p. Bibliog., index.
COHEN, ELIEZER "CHEETAH." *Israel's Best Defense: the First Full Story of the Israeli Air Force.* Tr. by Jonathan Cordes. 1st American ed. New York: Orion Bks., 1993. 504 p. Index.
        Although far more historical than Yonay's *No Margin for Error* (1993), this work lacks a central theme and an insightful conclusion.
KATZ, SAMUEL M. *Israel versus Jibril: the Thirty-year War Against a Master Terrorist.* 1st ed. New York: Paragon House, 1993. 285 p. Bibliog., index.
KOOK, ABRAHAM ISAAC. *Orot.* Tr. and with an introd. by Bezalel Naor. Northvale, N.J.: Aronson, 1993. 302 p. Bibliog.
NETANYAHU, BENJAMIN. *A Place Among the Nations: Israel and the World.* New York : Bantam, 1993. 467 p. Bibliog., index.
With Friends Like These: the Jewish Critics of Israel. Ed. by Edward Alexander; preamble by Cynthia Ozick. New York: S.P.I. Bks., 1993. Bibliog.
YONAY, EHUD. *No Margin for Error: the Making of the Israeli Air Force.* 1st ed. New York: Pantheon, 1993. 426 p. Bibliog., index.
        This compilation of anecdotes and episodes from 1948 to the 1981 raid on the Osirah Nuclear Reactor in Iraq is more adventure story than historical study.

JEWISH WAY OF LIFE

BAYAR, STEVEN AND FRANCINE HIRSCHMAN. *Teens & Trust : Building Bridges in Jewish Education.* Los Angeles: Torah Aura Productions, 1993. 171 p.

BLECH, BENJAMIN. *More Secrets of Hebrew Words: Holy Days and Happy Days.* Northvale, N.J.: Aronson, 1993. 214 p.

BRENER, ANNE. *Mourning & Mitzvah: a Guided Journal for Walking the Mourner's Path Through Grief to Healing : with Over 60 Guided Exercises.* Woodstock, Vt.: Jewish Lights Pub., 1993. 248 p.

BULKA, REUVEN P. *More of What You Thought You Knew About Judaism: 354 Common Misconceptions About Jewish Life.* Northvale, N.J.: Aronson, 1993. 444 p. Bibliog., index.

BULKA, REUVEN P. *More Torah Therapy: Further Reflections on the Weekly Sedra and Special Occasions.* Hoboken, N.J.: Ktav, 1993. 198 p. Indexes.

Celebration & Renewal: Rites of Passage in Judaism. Ed. by Rela M. Geffen. Philadelphia: Jewish Publication Society, 1993. 277 p. Bibliog., index.

DANAN, JULIE HILTON. *The Jewish Parents' Almanac.* Northvale, N.J.: Aronson, 1993. 367 p. Bibliog., index.

DIAMANT, ANITA. *The New Jewish Baby Book: Names, Ceremonies, Customs: a Guide for Today's Families.* 1st paperback ed. Woodstock, Vt.: Jewish Lights Pub., 1993. 288 p. (Jewish Lights Classic Reprint) Bibliog., index.

FINKEL, AVRAHAM YAAKOV. *The Essence of the Holy Days: Insights From the Jewish Sages.* Northvale, N.J.: Aronson, 1993. 267 p. Bibliog., index.

FINKLE, ARTHUR L. *The Shofar Sounders' Reference Manual.* Los Angeles: Torah Aura Productions, 1993. 32 p.

FREEDMAN, SHALOM. *Life as Creation: a Jewish Way of Thinking About the World.* Northvale, N.J.: Aronson, 1993. 139 p.

Great Jewish Speeches Throughout History. Collected and ed. by Steve Israel and Seth Forman. Northvale, N.J.: Aronson, 1994. 298 p. Bibliog., index.

GREENSTEIN, GEORGE. *Secrets of a Jewish Baker: Authentic Jewish Rye and Other Breads.* Freedom, CA: Crossing Press, 1993, 368 p. Index.

  Contains dozens of recipes for breads, rolls, and muffins, including challah and sour rye.

GRISHAVER, JOEL LURIE. *And You Shall be a Blessing: an Unfolding*

of the Six Words that Begin Every Brakhah. Northvale, N.J.:
Aronson, 1993. 190 p. Index.

GRISHAVER, JOEL LURIE. *40 Things You Can Do to Save the Jewish
People.* Los Angeles: Alef Design Group, 1993. 245 p.

"Some really practical things for parents who want to
raise 'good enough' Jewish kids to insure that the Jewish
people last at least another generation."

The Haggadah for Passover. Ed. by Elie Wiesel; ill. by Mark
Podwal. New York: Simon & Schuster, 1993. 144 p.

HAMMER, REUVEN. *Entering Jewish Prayer: a Guide to Personal
Devotion and the Worship Service.* 1st ed. New York:
Schocken Bks., 1994. 350 p. Bibliog., index.

A broad work, which examines the forms and
history of Jewish prayer, as well as the siddurim and the
order of Sabbath and holiday prayers. It includes Orthodox,
Conservative, and Reform options, and addresses such
issues as sexist language and the exclusion of women.

ISAACS, RONALD H. *Becoming Jewish: a Handbook for Conversion.*
New York: Rabbinical Assembly, 1993. 79 p.

ISRAEL, RICHARD J. *Jewish Identity Games: a How-to-do-it Book.*
2nd ed. Los Angeles: Torah Aura Productions, 1993. 86 p.
Bibliog.

ISRAEL, RICHARD J. *The Kosher Pig: and Other Curiosities of
Modern Jewish Life.* Los Angeles: Alef Design Group, 1993.
160 p. Bibliog.

KAY, ALAN A. *A Jewish Book of Comfort.* Northvale, N.J.: Aronson,
1993. 332 p. Bibliog., index.

KERTZER, MORRIS N. *What is a Jew?* New and completely rev. ed.
Rev. by Lawrence A. Hoffman. New York: Collier Bks., 1993.
306 p. Index.

Highly recommended for all public and school
libraries; this will appeal to the young and the old, the Jew
and the non-Jew.

KING, ANDREA. *If I'm Jewish and You're Christian, What are the
Kids?: a Parenting Guide for Interfaith Families.* Foreword
by Alexander M. Schindler. New York: UAHC Press, 1993.
145 p. Bibliog.

KOLATCH, ALFRED J. *The Jewish Mourner's Book of Why.* Middle
Village, N.Y.: Jonathan David, 1993. 412 p. Bibliog., index.

KUSHNER, HAROLD S. *To Life!: a Celebration of Jewish Being and
Thinking.* 1st ed. Boston: Little, Brown, 1993. 304 p.

KUSHNER, LAWRENCE. *The Book of Words: Talking Spiritual Life,*

Living Spiritual Talk. Woodstock, Vt.: Jewish Lights Pub., 1993. 138 p. Bibliog.

KUSHNER, LAWRENCE AND KERRY M. OLITZKY. *Sparks Beneath the Surface: a Spiritual Commentary on the Torah.* Northvale, N.J.: Aronson, 1994. 276 p. Bibliog., index.

MIRON-MICHROVSKY, ISSACHAR. *Eighteen Gates of Jewish Holidays and Festivals.* 1st ed. Foreword by Elie Wiesel; ill. by Arthur Szyk; *From My Angle* by Hayim Hefer; epilogue by Irving Greenberg. Northvale, N.J.: Aronson, 1993. 241 p.

NUSSBAUM, CHAIM. *The Essence of Teshuvah: a Path to Repentance.* Northvale, N.J.: Aronson, 1993. 191 p. Bibliog., index.

OLITZKY, KERRY M. AND RONALD H. ISAACS. *The How-To Handbook for Jewish Living.* Hoboken, N.J.: Ktav, 1993. 165 p. Bibliog.

OLITZKY, KERRY M. *Recovery From Codependence: a Jewish Twelve Steps Guide to Healing Your Soul.* Woodstock, VT: Jewish Lights, 1993. 126 p. Bibliog.

REUBEN, STEVEN CARR. *Raising Ethical Children: 10 Keys to Helping Your Children Become Moral and Caring.* Rocklin, Ca.: Prima Pub., 1994. 246 p. Bibliog., index.

ROZWASKI, CHAIM Z. *Jewish Meditation on the Meaning of Death.* Northvale, N.J.: Aronson, 1994. 213 p. Bibliog., index.

SAGE, LINDA SEIFER. *The Complete Bar/Bat Mitzvah Planner.* New York: St. Martin's Press, 1993. 160 p.

Includes charts, checklists, and other forms as well as advice on planning the non-religious aspects of a bar/bat mitzvah celebration.

SCHACHTER-SHALOMI, ZALMAN. *Paradigm Shift: From the Jewish Renewal Teachings of Reb Zalman Schachter-Shalomi.* Ed. by Ellen Singer. Northvale, N.J.: Aronson, 1993. 322 p. Index.

Worlds of Jewish Prayer: a Festschrift in Honor of Rabbi Zalman M. Schachter-Shalomi. Ed. by Shohama Harris Wiener and Jonathan Omer-Man. Northvale, N.J.: Aronson, 1993, 358 p. Bibliog., index.

PHILOSOPHY

BENIN, STEPHEN D. *The Footprints of God: Divine Accommodation in Jewish and Christian Thought.* Albany: State Univ. of New York Press, 1993. 327 p. (SUNY Series in Judaica) Bibliog., index.

BLUMENTHAL, DAVID R. *Facing the Abusing God: a Theology of Protest.* 1st ed. Louisville: Westminster/John Knox Press, 1993. 318 p. Bibliog., index.

BURRELL, DAVID B. *Freedom and Creation in Three Traditions.* Notre Dame, IN.: Univ. of Notre Dame Press, 1993. 225 p. Bibliog., index.

Examines the similarities and difference among Jewish, Christian, and Islamic teachings on creation.

ELIOR, RACHEL. *The Paradoxical Ascent to God: the Kabbalistic Theosophy of Habad Hasidism.* Tr. from the Hebrew by Jeffrey M. Green. Albany: SUNY Press, 1993. 279 p. (SUNY Series in Judaica) Bibliog., index.

GREEN, KENNETH HART. *Jew and Philosopher: the Return to Maimonides in the Jewish Thought of Leo Strauss.* Albany: State Univ. of New York Press, 1993. 278 p. (SUNY Series in Judaica) Bibliog., index.

SCHATZ UFFENHEIMER, RIVKA. *Hasidism as Mysticism: Quietistic Elements in Eighteenth Century Hasidic Thought.* Tr. from the Hebrew by Jonathan Chipman. Princeton: Princeton Univ. Press, 1993. 398 p. Bibliog., index.

RABBINICS

BUXBAUM, YITZHAK. *The Life and Teachings of Hillel.* Northvale, N.J.: Aronson, 1994. 376 p. Bibliog., indexes.

HOENIG, SAMUEL N. *The Essence of Talmudic Law and Thought.* Northvale, N.J.: Aronson, 1993. 220 p. Bibliog., index.

The Holy Letter : A Study in Jewish Sexual Morality. Tr. and with an intro. by Seymour J. Cohen. Northvale, N.J.: Aronson, 1993. 187 p.

Translation of: *Igeret ha-Kodesh,* ascribed to Nahmanides. Previously published: New York: Ktav, 1976.

MAIMONIDES, MOSES. *Sefer Hamitzvoth: the Book of Mitzvoth.* Tr. by Shraga Silverstein. New York: Moznaim, 1993. 2 vols.

Midrash Aleph Bet. Ed. by Deborah F. Sawyer. Atlanta: Scholars Press, 1993. 344 p. Bibliog., index. (South Florida Studies in the History of Judaism, no. 39)

The Midrashic Imagination: Jewish Exegesis, Thought, and History. Ed. by Michael Fishbane. Albany: State Univ. of New York Press, 1993. 296 p. Bibliog., index.

NEUSNER, JACOB. *Abo Addresses: and Other Recent Essays on*

Judaism in Time and Eternity. Atlanta: Scholars Press, 1994. 273 p. (South Florida Studies in the History of Judaism, no. 22) Bibliog., index.

NEUSNER, JACOB. *Formative Judaism: Religious, Historical, and Literary Studies: Seventh Series: the Formation of Judaism, Intentionality, Feminization of Judaism, and Other Current Results.* Atlanta: Scholars Press, 1993. 222 p. (South Florida Studies in the History of Judaism, no. 94) Bibliog., index.

NEUSNER, JACOB. *From Text to Historical Context in Rabbinic Judaism: Historical Facts in Systemic Documents.* Atlanta: Scholars Press, 1993 (South Florida Studies in the History of Judaism, no. 93) Index.

Contents: Vol. 1– The Mishnah, Tosefta, Abot, Sifra, Sifre to Numbers, and Sifre to Deuteronomy.

NEUSNER, JACOB. *The Judaism Behind the Texts: the Generative Premises of Rabbinic Literature. I, The Mishnah.* Atlanta: Scholars Press, 1993-1994. 3 vols. (South Florida Studies in the History of Judaism, nos. 89-90, 97) Bibliog., index.

Contents: A. The Division of Agriculture. B. The Division of Appointed Times, Women, and Damages (through Sanhedrin). C. The Division of Damages (from Makkot), Holy Things, and Purities.

NEUSNER, JACOB. *The Judaism Behind the Texts: the Generative Premises of Rabbinic Literature. II, Tosefta, Tractate Abot, and Earlier Midrash Compilations: Sifra, Sifre to Numbers, and Sifre to Deuteronomy.* Atlanta: Scholars Press, 1994. 246 p. (South Florida Studies in the History of Judaism, no. 98) Index.

NEUSNER, JACOB. *Purity in Rabbinic Judaism: a Systematic Account: the Sources, Media, Effects, and Removal of Uncleanness.* Atlanta: Scholars Press, 1994. 217 p. (South Florida Studies in the History of Judaism, no. 95) Bibliog., index.

Pesahim. Tr. by Jacob Neusner. Atlanta: Scholars Press, 1993. 5 vols. Indexes. (The Talmud of Babylonia, vol. 4)(Brown Judaic Studies, no. 282-)

WINK, WALTER. *Cracking the Gnostic Code: the Powers in Gnosticism.* Atlanta: Scholars Press, 1993. 66 p. (Monograph Series [Society of Biblical Literature], no. 46) Bibliog., indexes.

YERUSHALMI, SHMUEL. *The Book of Samuel II: Me'am Lo'ez.* Tr. and adapted by Moshe Mykoff. Brooklyn: Moznaim, 1993. 537 p.

(The Torah Anthology) Indexes.
The biblical text is in Hebrew and English; the
commentary is in English.

REFERENCE

AHARONI, YOHANAN AND MICHAEL AVI-YONAH. *The Macmillan Bible
Atlas.* 3rd, rev. ed. Ed. by Anson F. Rainey and Ze'ev Safrai.
New York : Macmillan, 1993. 215 p. Index.
BEIDER, ALEXANDER. *A Dictionary of Jewish Surnames From the
Russian Empire.* Teaneck, N.J.: Avotaynu, 1993. 760 p.
Bibliog.
COHN-SHERBOK, DAN. *Atlas of Jewish History.* New York:
Routledge, 1994. 218 p. Bibliog., index.
Includes 100 maps, as well as city plans, from
antiquity to the Intifada.
*A Comprehensive Bilingual Concordance of the Hebrew and Greek
Texts of Ecclesiastes.* Ed. by John Jarick on the basis of a
computer program by Galen Marquis. Atlanta: Scholars
Press, 1993. 291 p. (Septuagint and Cognate Studies Series,
no. 36) (CATSS—Basic tools, vol. 3)
CUTTER, CHARLES AND MICHA FALK OPPENHEIM. *Judaica Reference
Sources: a Selective, Annotated Bibliographic Guide.* 2nd ed.
Juneau, AK.: Denali Press, 1993. 224 p. Indexes.
Rev. ed. of : *Jewish Reference Sources* (1982).
GRIBETZ, JUDAH, EDWARD L. GREENSTEIN, AND REGINA STEIN. *The
Timetables of Jewish History: A Chronology of the Most
Important People and Events in Jewish History.* New York:
Simon & Schuster, 1993. 808 p. Index.
ISAACS, RONALD H. *The Jewish Information Source Book: a
Dictionary and Almanac.* Northvale, N.J.: Aronson, 1993.
295 p. Index.
*The Jewish Traveler: Hadassah Magazine's Guide to the World's
Jewish Communities and Sights.* Ed. by Alan M. Tigay. New.
ed. Northvale, N.J.: J. Aronson, 1994. 574 p. Index.
KAUFMAN, STEPHEN A. AND MICHAEL SOKOLOFF. *A Key-Word-In-
Context Concordance to Targum Neofiti: a Guide to the
Complete Palestinian Aramaic Text of the Torah.* With the
assistance of Edward M. Cook. Baltimore: Johns Hopkins
Univ. Press, 1993. 1494 p. (Publications of the Compre-
hensive Aramaic Lexicon Project) Bibliog., index.

KNAPPERT, JAN. *The Encyclopedia of Middle Eastern Mythology and Religion.* Rockport, Mass.: Element, 1993. 309 p. Bibliog.

Includes Islam, Baha'ism, Judaism, Christianity, and Zoroastrianism; highly recommended for public and academic libraries.

MELTON, J. GORDON. *National Directory of Churches, Synagogues, and Other Houses of Worship.* Ed. by John Krol. Detroit: Gale, 1993. 4 vols.

More than 350,000 houses of worship are organized in four volumes by city within state; indexes provide access by denomination and by congregation name. Highly recommended for all libraries.

The New Encyclopedia of Archaeological Excavations in the Holy Land. Ed. by Ephraim Stern. New York: Simon and Schuster, 1993. 4 vols. Index.

The Oxford Companion to the Bible. Ed. by Bruce M. Metzger and Michael D. Coogan. New York: Oxford Univ. Press, 1993. 874, [28] p. Bibliog., index, maps.

Aims to "trace the Bible's ongoing significance in such areas as the arts, law, politics, and literature."

Reform Judaism in America: a Biographical Dictionary and Sourcebook. Ed. by Kerry M. Olitzky, Lance J. Sussman, and Malcolm H. Stern. Westport, Ct.: Greenwood Press, 1993. 347 p. Bibliog., index. (Jewish Denominations in America)

Scriptures of the World. Ed. by L. Lupas and E. F. Rhodes. 14th ed. New York: American Bible Society, 1993.

This biennial publication provides statistical information on Bible publication for 1992/93, presented alphabetically by language, chronologically, and geographically.

STEINBICKER, EARL. *Daytrips in Israel: 25 One Day Adventures by Bus or Car.* Mamaroneck, N.Y.: Hastings House, 1993. 205 p. Index.

SOCIAL AND CULTURAL STUDIES

BAKER, ADRIENNE. *The Jewish Woman in Contemporary Society: Transitions and Traditions.* Preface by Susie Orbach; consultant ed., Jo Campling. New York: New York Univ. Press, 1993. 234 p. Bibliog., index.

BILSKI BEN-HUR, RAPHAELLA. *Every Individual, a King: the Social and Political Thought of Ze'ev Vladimir Jabotinsky.* Washington, D.C.: B'nai B'rith Bks, 1993. 303 p. Bibliog., index.

BRESLAUER, S. DANIEL. *Judaism and Civil Religion.* Atlanta: Scholars Press, 1993. 269 p. (South Florida-Rochester-Saint Louis Studies on Religion and the Social Order, no. 3) Bibliog., index.

BRONER, E. M. *The Telling.* 1st ed. San Francisco: Harper San Francisco, 1993. 216 p.

This story of the activities of a feminist group includes the 1992 *Women's Haggadah* by E. M. Broner and Naomi Nimrod, which emphasizes the role of women whose names do not appear in the traditional haggadah.

Builders and Dreamers: Habonim Labor Zionist Youth in North America. Ed. by J. J. Goldberg and Elliot King. New York: Herzl Press, 1993. 362 p.

COOPER, JOHN. *Eat and Be Satisfied: a Social History of Jewish Food.* Northvale, N.J.: Aronson, 1993. 259 p. Bibliog., index.

FISHMAN, SYLVIA BARACK. *A Breath of Life: Feminism in the American Jewish Community.* New York: Free Press, 1993. 308 p. Bibliog., index.

Highly recommended.

GILMAN, SANDER L. *The Case of Sigmund Freud: Medicine and Identity at the Fin de Siècle.* Baltimore: Johns Hopkins Univ. Press, 1993. 298 p. Bibliog., index.

GILMAN, SANDER L. *Freud, Race, and Gender.* Princeton: Princeton Univ. Press, 1993. 277 p. Bibliog., index.

GINSBERG, BENJAMIN. *The Fatal Embrace: Jews and the State.* Chicago: Univ. of Chicago Press, 1993. 286 p. Bibliog., index.

Discusses current events within contemporary America.

Hebrew in America: Perspectives and Prospects. Ed. by Alan Mintz. Detroit: Wayne State Univ. Press, 1993. 337 p. (American Jewish Civilization Series) Bibliog., index.

Jewish Fundamentalism in Comparatiue Perspective: Religion, Ideology, and the Crisis of Modernity. Ed. by Laurence J. Silberstein. New York: New York Univ. Press, 1993. 248 p. (New Perspectives on Jewish Studies) Bibliog., index.

Jewish Identity. Ed. by David Theo Goldberg and Michael Krausz. Philadelphia: Temple Univ. Press, 1993. 344 p. Bibliog., index.

KAUFMAN, MICHAEL. *The Woman in Jewish Law and Tradition.* Northvale, N.J.: Aronson, 1993. 326 p. Bibliog., index.

KEPEL, GILLES. *The Revenge of God: the Resurgence of Islam, Christianity, and Judaism in the Modern World.* Tr. by Alan Braley. Univ. Park, Pa.: Pennsylvania State Univ. Press, 1994. 215 p. Bibliog., index.

LEVINE, AARON. *Economic Public Policy and Jewish Law.* Hoboken: Ktav; New York: Yeshiva Univ. Press, 1993. 285 p. (Library of Jewish Law and Ethics, vol. 19) Bibliog., index.

MENDELSOHN, EZRA. *On Modern Jewish Politics.* New York: Oxford Univ. Press, 1993. 168 p. (Studies in Jewish History) Bibliog., index.

New Visions: Historical and Theological Perspective on the Jewish-Christian Dialog. Ed. by Val Ambrose McInnes. New York: Crossroad Pub. Co., 1993. (A Tulane Judeo-Christian Studies edition) (Tulane Chair of Judeo-Christian Studies series; vol. 3) 165 p. Bibliog.

SHEPHERD, NAOMI. *A Price Below Rubies: Jewish Women as Rebels and Radicals.* Cambridge, Mass.: Harvard Univ. Press, 1993. 336 p. Bibliog., index.

SKLARE, MARSHALL. *Observing America's Jews.* Ed. and with a foreword by Jonathan D. Sarna; afterword by Charles S. Liebman. Hanover: Univ. Press of New England for Brandeis Univ. Press, 1993. 302 p. (Brandeis Series in American Jewish History, Culture, and Life) Bibliog., index.

WERTHEIMER, JACK. *A People Divided: Judaism in Contemporary America.* New York: Basic Books., 1993. 267 p. Bibliog., index.

The Writer in the Jewish Community: an Israeli-North American Dialogue. Ed. by Richard Siegel and Tamar Sofer. Rutherford, N.J.: Fairleigh Dickinson Univ. Press, 1993. 155 p. (Sara F. Yoseloff Memorial Publications in Judaism and Jewish Affairs) Index.

ZOLTY, SHOSHANA. *And All Your Children Shall be Learned: Women and the Study of Torah in Jewish Law and History.* Northvale, N.J.: Aronson, 1993, 339 p. Bibliog., index.

CAROLYN STARMAN HESSEL

American Jewish Fiction Books 1993-1994*

ALMOG, RUTH. *Death in the Rain*. Tr. from the Hebrew by Dalya Bilu. Santa Fe, NM: Red Crane Books, 1993. 204 p.

In a tale of love and death, set in Greece and Israel, the lives and reflections of four protagonists unfold through dramatic intersecting narrations. The central character, Elisheva, is a sensitive writer whose account of her untimely tragedy sometimes diverges from that of the three others.

APPLEFELD, AHARON. *Unto The Soul*. Tr. from the Hebrew by Jeffrey M. Green. New York: Random House, 1994. 213 p.

In the pre-industrial revolution days on a bleak mountaintop in the Ukraine, an orphaned brother and sister are bequeathed an uncle's position as caretakers of the remote Jewish martyr's cemetery. Over the years they forget their obligations and Applefeld illustrates in simple prose the price of forgetting the past.

ARI, MARK. *The Shoemakers Tale*. Tucson, AZ: Zephyr Press, 1993. 245 p.

A novel about Jewish life in 18th century Poland. A young shoemaker's search for the meaning of life, brings him into contact with the Baal Shem Tov.

BLAU, ERIC. *The Beggar's Cup*. New York: Knopf, 1993. 352 p.

A Holocaust survivor yearns to make a movie about Theodor Herzl. Along with a Hollywood producer he travels to Israel and encounters a wide array of characters who influence his life and work.

BLUMENTHAL, MICHAEL. *Weinstock Among the Dying*. Cambridge, MA: Zoland Books, 1993. 303 p.

A Harvard academic finds himself confused and lost in mid-life. In time he learns that humor and seriousness, life and death can coexist and help him find redemption.

BOGEN, NANCY. *Bobe Mayse, a Tale of Washington Square*. New York: Twickenham Press, 1993. 319 p.

A historical novel portraying a strong woman who breaks out from the typical Jewish home at the time of the Great Shirtwaist

---

*A number of translations are included.

Strike of 1910. Interesting characters who inhabit Greenwich Village emerge to make this a very contemporary story of the ways of human nature.

BUECHNER, FREDERICK. *The Son of Laughter*. New York: Harper-Collins, 1993. 274 p.

A fictional retelling of the biblical story of Jacob. The author dramatizes the dynamics in Jacob's life, including his struggles with Esau, the sojourn to Egypt, and the end of his life.

COHEN, FLORENCE CHANOCK. *The Sea of Stones*. Wainscott, NY: Pushcart Press, 1993. 322 p.

On a canvas that sweeps from Chicago to Jerusalem, this is a novel about participants in the Arab-Israeli dilemma. It goes to the heart of war and peace and love between peoples and countries as it chronicles one woman's desperate attempts to find her son in the slaughter of war.

COHEN, MARTIN S. *The Truth About Marvin Kalish*. Port Angeles, WV: Ben Simon, 1993. 228 p.

Set in World War II Munich, New York and Rome, the story's protagonist, a young Jewish stand-up comic in Queens, NY, poses a complex riddle about survival in ancient times and the present. The book combines themes of Jewish mysticism, Holocaust survivors, relationships between parent and child and the practice of contemporary Judaism.

DA'EHU, B.D. *With All My Heart, With All My Soul*. New York: Bosworth Press, 1993. 327 p.

A love affair between Joshua, a brilliant and charismatic ultra-Orthodox Jew, and Christine, a striking and gifted Gentile. The novel explores the world of Orthodox Jewry, its appeal to outsiders and its reasons for forbidding an interfaith relationship.

DANDEKAR, B.B. *David Rahabi*. Lawrence, KA: A.B. Literary House, 1993. 177 p.

A historical novel, based on Bene Israel legend, about the discovery of Jews in India in the twelfth century by an Egyptian trader in precious stones.

GOLDBERG, ED. *Served Cold*. Portland, OR: West Coast Crime, 1994. 177p.

A detective novel whose major theme is the effect of the Holocaust on some of its survivors.The main character has to struggle with his own rather complete assimilation while he addresses the beauty of the ceremonies he left behind.

GOLDBERG, MYRA. *Whistling: And Other Stories*. Cambridge, MA: Zoland Books, 1993.

The difficulties of love and marriage among people who are both New Yorkers and Jewish form the subtext of these eleven stories.

GOLDREICH, GLORIA. *That Year of Our War*. New York: Little, Brown, 1994. 356 P.

The profound consequences of World War II for a young Jewish woman and her family on the homefront in Brooklyn in 1944. For Sharon Grossberg it was a year of death and a year of birth. D-Day would always be remembered as death day but new life followed.

GRAY, JOAN CAROL. *The Francesca Diaries*. Huntington, WV: University Editions, 1993. 106 p.

From the arm of the Inquisition in Seville to Lisbon and beyond to the new world, a Jewish woman travels outward as well as inward as she struggles for faith and survival, personal freedom and dignity in the 15th century.

GUR, BATYA. *Literary Murder: A Critical Case*. Tr. by Dalya Bilu. New York: HarperCollins, 1993. 357 p.

The second of Gur's mystery novels to appear in English, it finds the familiar Jerusalem police chief faced with a murder in the sacred halls of academia. Investigation into the literature department turns up scandals and rivalries which force the questioning of profound ethical issues and social problems in Israel.

HEGI, URSULA. *Stones From The River*. New York: Poseidon Press, 1994. 507 p.

The setting is a small German community before, during and after World War II. Its protagonist is Trudi Montag, the dwarf who is often cruel, yet proves to be surprisingly sane as the world around her falls to madness. As Hitler comes to power, Trudi is a woman who protects those who have been kind to her including two Jewish families.

ISLER, ALAN. *The Prince of West End Avenue*. Bridgehampton, NY: Bridge Works Publishers, 1994. 246 p.

A comedy about old-age, love and loss, among the residents of a retirement home narrated by a Holocaust survivor whose life spans the 20th century in Europe and America.

KANTOR, HERMAN I. *The Merchant of Groskie: And Other Tales My Great-Grandfather Might Tell About Life in a Ghetto of Russia in the Time of the Czars*. Santa Barbara, CA: Fithian Press, 1993. 174 p.

27 short stories are presented as the fictionalized experiences of the author's forefather, Shmul. The tales are narrated by Shmul and include colorful Russian characters he meets on his travels from villiage to village in 19th century Eastern Europe.

MANEA, NORMAN. *Compulsory Happiness*. Tr. from the French by Linda Coverdale. New York: Farrar, Straus & Giroux, 1993. 259 p.

Four novellas that constitute a biography of a generation

ravaged by the Holocaust, by revolution and by social change. The stories present a picture of everyday life in the police state of Communist Roumania.

OSTROVSKY, VICTOR. *Lion of Judah.* New York: St. Martin's Press, 1993. 313 p.

A thriller of unsettling realism describing Mossad (Israel's famed military intelligence unit) machinations that link apparently unrelated events throughout Europe, the Middle East and America.

OZ, AMOS. *Fima.* Tr. from the Hebrew by Nicholas de Lange. New York: Harcourt Brace, 1993, 322p.

The closing years of Israel's first half century are examined through the life of a dreamer who is approaching fifty. He looks back at broken relationships and failed marriages and ponders Israel's corruption of the present. The anti-hero is a symbol of a generation in Israel.

PALEY, GRACE. *The Collected Stories.* New York: Farrar, Straus & Giroux, 1994. 386 p.

Brings together in one volume three previous collections published between 1959-1985. They record a redeeming strain in the life of the much lamented 20th century as reflected primarily through the character of American immigrant daughters.

PARKER, THOMAS TREBITSCH. *Anna, Ann, Annie.* New York: Plume/ Penguin, 1994. 325 p.

The novel traces one woman's life from pre-World War II Vienna to wartime London to postwar America. Anna Moser's journeys in her quest for survival and the changes in her circumstance and identity are reflected in her changing name.

RAGEN, NAOMI. *Sotah.* New York: Crown, 1993. 457 p.

A story of love among Jerusalem's ultra-orthodox community. Dina begins a flirtation with a married man and soon finds herself marked with the label "sotah," scandalized woman.

ROSENBERG, DAVID. *The Lost Book of Paradise.* New York: Hyperion, 1993. 192 p.

A different approach to the creation story in which the poet and essayist presents a story of equality between the sexes and a crucial connection between all of humankind.

ROSENBERG, ROBERT. *The Cutting Room.* New York: Simon & Schuster, 1993. 320 p.

Detective Cohen comes to the U.S. from Israel to solve the mysterious death of a Hollywood director whose last film about his escape from Dachau was pulled from release. The investigation turns up more mysterous deaths and leads to another ghostly survivor of Dachau.

ROTH, HENRY. *Mercy of a Rude Stream: Vol. I: A Star Shines Over Mount Morris Park*. New York: St. Martin's Press, 1994. 324 p.

The novel chronicles the adventures of Ira Stigman and his immigrant family from World War I through the early 1920's. It tells of Ira's adventures in New York as he searches for meaning in his life.

ROTH, PHILLIP. *Operation Shylock: A Confession*. New York: Simon & Schuster, 1993. 399 p.

A spy story and political thriller finds Roth being impersonated by a stranger, who could pass for an identical twin and who wishes to persuade all Jews to return to Europe. In the course of the story Roth reveals the complicated biography of his look-alike.

SERWER-BERNSTEIN, BLANCHE L. *In the Tradition of Moses and Mohammed*. Northvale, NJ: Jason Aronson, 1994. 298 p.

Forty Arabian and Jewish folktales that represent the experiences of the cultures out of which they emerged. The twenty-two Jewish tales taken from literary and oral sources also include stories told by immigrants to Israel from around the globe. The Arabian tales reflect humor and entertainment and a array of human characteristics.

SHAHAM, NATHAN. *Bone to the Bone*. Tr. from the Hebrew by Dalya Bilu. New York: Grove Press, 1993. 345 p.

Avigdor Berkov, age 70, arrives in Tel Aviv from Soviet Russia after having been to Palestine once before in the 1920's as a starry eyed idealistic youth who left for the sake of his passionate political faith.

SHAPIRO, GERALD. *From Hunger*. Columbia, MO: University of Missouri Press, 1993. 168 p.

Nine short stories about idiosyncratic characters who reveal the hunger and the hope in all of us. Lenny is drawn to "The Community Seder" in his father's hometown, where a mysterious synagogue is filled with faces of his past. There Lenny finds that what is missing from his life is a sense of community.

SHOMER, ENID. *Imaginary Men*. Iowa City, IA: University of Iowa Press, 1993. 152 p.

Short stories where family is the mold we break out of as well as the lap we seek comfort in. For the unappreciated Harry Goldring, tormented by his label of family mensch, wildness is first expressed in panic attacks, then day dreams. Other stories of colorful characters follow.

SINGER, ISAAC BASHEVIS. *Meshugah*. New York: Farrar, Straus & Giroux, 1994. 232 p.

The third posthumously published novel by Singer is set in the early fifties and tackles the Holocaust, God and paranormal phenomena. Its characters, despite their high spirits and constant gab, are haunted by stories that can't be forgotten and can't be told.

SPEILBERG, ELINOR. *Uninvited Daughters*. New York: St. Martin's Press, 1993. 224 p.

Odessa Levin, a Jewish woman in her thirties, flees to Vermont to escape her family and her commitment. Here she gains insight into her own past influenced by her Jewish upbringing.

STAVENS, ILAN. *Short Stories by Jewish Latin-American Writers*. New York: Holmes and Meier, 1993. 275 p.

Stories of adventure, cultural alienation, tradition, and exoticism make up this anthology of 21 stories by Jewish writers living in six countries from 1910 to the present. The stories focus on themes of alienation and present an ethnic diversity with roots in Spain and Eastern Europe.

STEINFELD, J.J. *Dancing at the Club Holocaust*. Charlottetown, Canada: Ragweed, 1993. 281 p.

Stories about the North American Jewish experience explore the psychological fall-out of the Holocaust in the second generation.

STERN, STEVEN. *A Plague of Dreamers*. New York: Scribners, 1993. 267 p.

Three novellas set in a comic Memphis backwater Jewish community. The stories focus on a mama's boy, a would-be succesor to Harry Houdini and a perpetual outcast with a traveling carnival whose baggage is the memory of three generations.

STEVENS, SERITA and RAYANNE MOORE. *Bagels for Tea*. New York: St. Martin's Press, 1993. 264 p.

A sixtyish widow and grandmother who, with the help of a Mossad agent, attempts to solve a mystery of her granddaughter and the friend, who was murdered after the granddaughter was expelled from school.

SZCZYPIORSKI, ANDRZEJ. *A Mass for Arras*. Tr. from the Polish by Richard Lourie. New York: Grove Press, 1993. 188 p.

A novel that explores the personal and political consequences of fear, fanaticism and fascism. A profound allegory of life for a young man coming of age in an emergent totalitarian state.

SZEMAN, SHERIE. *The Kommandant's Mistress*. New York: HarperCollins, 1993. 288 p.

Centering upon a concentration camp Kommandant and his Jewish prisoner-mistress, the novel tries to portray a complex relationship that inhabits the twilight world between love and hate. The events are narrated by each of these characters.

THOMAS, D.M. *Pictures at an Exhibition*. New York: Scribner's, 1993. 277 p.

The poetry of horror and eroticism, intermingles with images of Munich during the Holocaust. Nine separate canvases are presented; the first is set in Auschwitz where the death camp is evoked in stomach turning detail.

VOLAVKOVA, HANA and U.S. HOLOCAUST MUSEUM. *I Never Saw Another Butterfly* ....expanded 2nd. ed. New York: Schocken, 1993. 105 p.

The second edition of this acclaimed book includes additional poems and illustrations not found in the original edition. Also new is the translation of a personal diary which records specific events at Terezin remembered by all its surviving inmates.

WAGMAN, FREDRICA. *Peachy*. New York: Soho Press, 1993. 230 p.

A story of a middle-aged recently divorced American Jewish woman of the late 20th century who seeks her own identity. She is an honest, funny, and heroic Jewish woman of our times.

WOUK, HERMAN. *The Hope*. New York: Little, Brown, 1993. 693 p.

An epic historical novel set in Israel amid major battles, disasters and victories between 1948-1967. The novel focuses on four Israeli military men and the women they love.

ZWI, ROSE. *Safe Houses*. North Melbourne, Australia: Spinifex Press, 1993. 200 p.

The story of three Jewish families in a timely novel of hope and betrayal in South Africa. When the children of two of the families fall in love they are bound not to repeat the mistakes of their parents in the area of apartheid.

MARCIA W. POSNER

*Jewish Juvenile Books**
1993-1994

APELBAUM, SHIFFY. *Moshe Mendel and the Mitzva Maven and His Amazing Mitzva Quest.* Illus. by Shiffy Apelbaum. Spring Valley, NY: Feldheim, 1993. unp. (6-11)

Each page in this "Where's Waldo" type book has a myriad of mitzvah activities connected with Jewish holidays,values and halakhah for the children to identify. Answers are in the back.

ARONER, MIRIAM. *Kingdom of Singing Birds.* illus. by Shelly O. Haas. Rockville, MD: Kar-Ben, 1993. unp. (5-9)

Rabbi Zusya, known for his love of nature, explains to the king that if he truly wants to hear his captured birds sing, he must set them free. Poetic text and dreamlit illustrations. Wonderful for storytelling.

BAMBERGER, DAVID. A *Young Person's History of Israel.* rev., illus. with photos. West Orange, NJ: Behrman House, 1994. 192 p. (10-14)

A welcome updating of this history of Israel from biblical to modern times including the recent agreements with neighboring Arab states.

BENJAMIN, ALAN. *Chanukah.* illus. by Ellen Appleby. New York: Little Simon/Simon & Schuster, 1993. 16 p. (1- 4)

Single sentences and cheery full-color illustrations describe this family's Hanukkah. Glossary.

BOGOT, HOWARD I. My *First 100 Hebrew Words: A Young Person's Dictionary of Judaism.* illus. by Giora Carmi. New York: UAHC Press, 1993. unp. (5-8)

A fine book that teaches Hebrew words used in the observance and practice of Judaism. It may also be used as a children's dictionary of Judaism. Carmi's magic marker and colored pencil illustrations do not measure up to his usually outstanding work.

BREDMAN, CARMEN. *Jonas Salk: Discover of the Polio Vaccine.* illus. with photos. Hillside, NJ: Enslow Publishers, 1993. 112 p. (9-14)

Discusses the life and accomplishments of Jonas Salk, including his family's Jewishness.

BRINN, RUTH ESRIG. *Jewish Holiday Crafts for Little Hands.* illus. by

---

*Outstanding titles.

Katherine Janus Kahn. Rockville, MD: Kar-Ben Copies, 1993.
127 p. (4-8)

A craft book with six or more easy craft projects—most new to
this volume—for eleven Jewish holidays. Directions are clear;
materials are scrap items. Background information, games, and
snacks are included for each holiday. Lively black and white
illustrations.

BRODMANN, ALIANA. *The Gift.* illus. by Anthony Carnabuci. New York:
Simon & Schuster, 1993. 28 p. (5-8)

A recollection of the narrator's childhood in Germany when
she was given a 5-mark piece for Hanukkah and instead of
choosing a gift for herself, gave the money to a street musician
who in return, taught her to play. Fully realized romantic
paintings capture the nostalgic mood.

*BURSTEIN, CHAYA M. *The Jewish Kids Catalog.* 8th rev. illus. by
Chaya M. Burstein. Philadelphia, PA: Jewish Publication
Society, 1993. 224 p. (8-12)

A compendium of Jewish information and lore. Includes
chapters on holy and secular books; stories; how to be Jewish;
Jews around the world; history; languages of the Jews; holidays
with plans for parties and crafts; cooking; music; dance; song;
travel; bibliographies and a mini-encyclopedia.

*COHEN, BARBARA. *Make a Wish, Molly.* illus. by Jan Naimo Jones.
New York: Doubleday, 1994. 38 p. (6-10)

The companion volume to *Molly's Pilgrim* finds Molly
struggling with the problem of how to keep Passover while
attending a secular birthday party—her first in America—and
not eating the birthday cake which is *hametz.*

COUSINS, LUCY. *Noah's Ark.* illus. by Lucy Cousins. Cambridge, MA:
Candlewick Press, 1993. unp. (24)

Cousin's simple, brief sentences and childlike figures in bold
gouache colors will appeal to young children hearing the tale for
the first time.

CYTRON, BARRY AND PHYLLIS CYTRON. *Myriam Mendilow: Mother of
Jerusalem.* illus. with photos. Minn., MN: Lerner, 128 p. (10-14)

An inspiring biography of Myriam Mendilow, founder of Yad
L'kashish—Lifeline for the Old in Jerusalem and Meals on
Wheels, demonstrates the maxim, "Every great work at first
appears impossible." The writing is conversational and
anecdotal.

DANIEL, FRANK. *Chanukah.* illus. by Frank Daniel. New York:
Macmillan/First Aladdin Books, 1993. unp. (2-4)

A square-shaped board book about Hanukkah with a square
hole in its middle that stands for something different in each
illustration. Easy to hold.

DRUCKER, MALKA. *Jewish Holiday ABC.* illus. by Rita Pocock. New York: Harcourt/Gulliver, 1992. 40 p. (4-7)

Uses the first letter of highlighted words within sentences about Jewish holidays and symbols to teach the English alphabet. The holidays are not presented in calendar order. Illustrations are of brightly colored paper collages. Glossary and appended explanation of the holidays.

ELIAS, MIRIAM. *Special Days Are Wonderful: A Guessing Game Book.* illus. by Tova Leff. Brooklyn, NY: HaChai, 1993. unp. (2-4)

A novel guessing-game book about holidays that has a page of questions opposite a foldover two-page spread with holiday symbols and answers. Airbrushed illustrations.

EPSTEIN, SYLVIA B. *How the Rosh Hashanah Challah Became Round.* illus. by Hagit Migron. Hewlett, NY: Gefen, 1993. 28 p. (3-8)

Here is an imaginative explanation of how the Rosh Hashanah challah became round. By accident! Age appropriate text and cartoon illustrations.

FALK, RABBI AARON. *Torah for Children: Sefer Bereishis,* Vol. 1. illus. by Norman Nodel. Brooklyn, NY: Judaica Press, 1993. 28 p. (7-11)

Brief Bible stories are combined with Rabbi Falk's analysis, encouraging readers to think about the moral lessons that are found in the Torah. Illustrations resemble a well-drawn "comic book" with strident colors.

*FLUEK, TOBY KNOBEL. *Passover As I Remember It.* illus. by Toby Knobel Flueck. New York: Knopf, 1994. unp. (8 up)

The author of *Memories of My Life in a Polish Village: 1930-1949* recreates her family's preparations for and celebration of Passover in Czernica, Poland before most of the Jews of that town perished at the hands of the Nazis. Soft water-colors create images long stored in Fluek's memory. A jewel of a book.

FRIEDMAN, CHANIE. *Bat-'em Benjie (Art Scroll Middos Book).* illus. by Norman Nodel. Brooklyn, NY: Mesorah, 1993. unp. (6-10)

Benjie sacrifices a homerun to do a mitzvah, as he has learned that when one puts off doing a mitzvah, the time for doing it may pass. A kosher tall tale told in rhyme.

GANZ, YAFFA. *Yana and Marina Come Home.* illus. by Liat Binyamini Ariel. New York: American Friends of Shvut Ami, 1993. 33 p. (5-10)

A charmingly written book about two Russian Jewish little girls and their family who, yearning for more Yiddishkeit in their life, decide to emigrate to Israel despite their happy life in Moscow. In three languages—English, Russian, and Hebrew. Gracefully illustrated in fluid line with pen and ink by Ariel.

260 JEWISH BOOK ANNUAL

*GERAS, ADELE. *Golden Windows and Other Stories of Jerusalem.*
New York: HarperCollins/Willa Perlman, 1993. 148 p. (8-12)

Five captivating stories about the widow Genzel and her
seven children give readers much to think about. Set in
Palestine during the first half of the twentieth century.

GIKOW, LOUISE. *Kippi and the Missing Matzah: A Sesame Street
Passover.* illus. by Tom Brannon. New York: Comet International /Children's Television Workshop, 1994. unp. (3-6)

Kippi the Porcupine, on a visit from Israel's "Shalom Sesame"
invites all of his Sesame Street friends to a Passover Seder, but
first they have to find the matzos stolen by Oscar the Grouch. A
delight for the pre-school crowd.

*GOLDIN, BARBARA DIAMOND. *The Magician's Visit: A Passover Tale (by
I.L.Peretz).* illus. by Robert Andrew Parker. New York: Viking,
1993. 32 p. (5-8)

A mysterious magician comes to town and asks a poor pious
Jewish couple to be a guest at their Seder table, and then
magically supplies the feast. Goldin's telling and Parker's dark
swirling watercolors culminate in an outstanding version of this
story.

*GOLDIN, BARBARA DIAMOND. *The Passover Journey: A Seder Compan-
ion.* illus. by Neil Waldman. New York: Viking, 1994. unp. (7-11)

The story of the Exodus is followed by an explanation of the
traditions of the Passover seder. Goldin's commentary includes
midrashim. Her suggestions to children for reliving the Exodus
experience enrich the seder. The illustrations are superb—pages
washed in pastels from deep to pale. Stylized two-dimensional
borders recall Egyptian art. An outstanding book.

GORDON, RUTH. *Feathers.* illus. by Lydia Dabcovich. New York:
Macmillan, 1993. 32 p. (7-10)

The wise men of Chelm exchange the money collected for a
new bathhouse for feathers and wait in vain for the feathers to
reach Chelm. Sketchy, colored pencil illustrations.

*GREAVES, MARGARET. *The Naming.* illus. by Pauline Baynes. New
York: Harcourt Brace Jovanovich, unp. (4-8)

Adam names all the animals, finishing with the secret and
beautiful unicorn. Magnificent illustrations styled after a
300-year-old Rajput manuscript.

*GREENE, JACQUELINE DEMBAR. *One Foot Ashore.* New York: Walker,
1994. 208 p. (10-14)

A compelling sequel to *Out of Many Waters.* Maria and Isobel,
having escaped from the monks who kidnapped them, stow away
in separate ships bound for Amsterdam, but only Maria reaches
there. Befriended by Rembrandt van Rijn, she searches for her
family. The sense of time, place, and characters is utterly

convincing. The next sequel may be Maria and her parents' search for Isobel. Wonderful, really.

GREENE, PATRICIA BAIRD. *The Sabbath Garden.* New York: Lodestar, 1993. 214 p. (12 up)

Old Solomon Leshko, last Jew in the building in a neighborhood now filled with Afro-Americans and Puerto Ricans, changes the neighborhood with young Opal Tyler when they organize a community garden. A worthwhile read.

GREENFELD, HOWARD. *The Hidden Children.* illus. with photos. New York: Ticknor & Fields, 1993. 118 p. (10-14)

Greenfeld laces together excerpts of autobiographical description with background narrative, dividing the book into the children's early exposure to Nazi persecution, the events of their hiding, and the aftermath of liberation. Reading list of adult literature; index.

*GRONER, JUDYTH AND MADELINE WIKLER. *Thank You, God! A Jewish Child's Book of Prayers.* illus. by Shelly O. Haas. Rockville, MD: Kar-Ben Copies, 1993. unp. (3-6)

A lovely first prayerbook for children presents everyday blessings and prayers in simple English and Hebrew with transliterations. Pastel watercolors evoke the beauty and wonder of the world we live in.

HALPERN, CHAIKY. *Secret of the Seashell.* Brooklyn, NY: Tamar/Mesorah, 1993. 112 p. (12-16)

Staying with cousins in England when her mother becomes ill, lonesome Miri follows the path she sees in her dream and finds a seashell and an ancient door. The shell gives her insights that help her to adjust, and later to save her friends.

HANDLER, ANDREW AND SUSAN V. MESCHEL. *Young People Speak: Surviving the Holocaust in Hungary.* illus. photos. New York: Franklin Watts, 1993. 160 p. (12 up)

All eleven contributors survived in Hungary during the Nazi occupation by hiding or posing as gentiles. They lost family, friends and homes and yet their memoirs show the humor and resilience of the children they were during those horrible years. Just unbelievable!

HESSE, KAREN. *Poppy's Chair.* illus. by Kay Life. New York: Macmillan, 1993. 32 p. (5-8)

On her first visit to her grandmother after the death of her grandfather, a child is saddened by his absence, but her grandmother helps her to remember him with joy.

HURWITZ, JOHANNA. *Leonard Bernstein: A Passion for Music.* illus. by Sonia O. Lisker. Philadelphia, PA: Jewish Publication Society, 1993. 80 p. (10-14)

From childhood through his brilliant career, Bernstein cherished his Jewish roots.

ILLIONS, YEHUDIS. *Things I Like to See on Shabbos; on Hanukah;.* illus. by Yehudis Illions. Spring Valley, NY: Feldheim's Young Readers Division, 1993. unp. (2-4)

Two board books about Jewish holidays show Jewish symbols and traditions for the youngest child. Attractively illustrated and designed.

*JAFFE, NINA. *The Uninvited Cuest and Other Jewish Holiday Tales.* illus. by Elivia. New York: Scholastic, 1993. 72 p. (8-12)

The stories in this excellent collection are drawn from the rich folklore and legends surrounding the holidays of Rosh Hashanah, Yom Kippur, Sukkot, Hanukkah, Purim, Passover and the Sabbath.

*JAFFE, NINA AND STEVE ZEITLIN. *While Standing on One Foot: Puzzle Stories and Wisdom Tales from the Jewish Tradition.* illus. by John Segal. New York: Henry Holt, 1993. 80 p. (8-12)

Stories from various lands and periods in Jewish history give the reader a chance to match wits with the oppressor, and to think fast like the heroes and heroines in this book whose solutions follow on the next page. Charming.

KIMMEL, ERIC A. *Asher and the Capmakers: A Hanukkah Story.* illus. by Will Hillenbrand. New York: Holiday House, 1993. 32 p. (5-7)

Asher goes out in a snowstorm to borrow an egg to make latkes and ends up with Jewish fairy capmakers. Adventures follow. Munchian-like virtuoso illustrations, but nothing much about Hanukkah except a recipe for latkes.

KONDEATIS, CHRISTOS. *Bible Stories from the Old Testament in Three Dimensions.* illus. by Christos Kondeatis. New York: Simon Schuster, 1993. unp. (4-8)

A spectacular pop-up book of the Bible includes scenes from the Garden of Eden, Noah, Tower of Babel, the Crossing of the Red Sea, and Daniel in the Pit of Lions.

*KUSKIN, KARLA. *A Great Miracle Happened There: A Chanukah Story.* illus. by Robert Andrew Parker. New York: HarperCollins, 1993. 32 p. (4-8)

Parker's pen and ink watercolors suggest panoramic historical scenes, while illustrations of the child's home are kept to a single page facing a white page of text about the holiday. The mother philosophizes as she lights her grandmother's hanukkiah, that past history and present meaning are what makes a holiday meaningful.

LAKIN, PATRICIA. *Don't Forget.* illus. by Ted Rand. New York: Tambourine, 1994. 32 p. (6-10)

While each shopkeeper gives Sarah a baking tip, playfully warning her "not to forget," Mrs. Singer, a Holocaust survivor, has a more serious injunction: *"No one* should forget." A light-hearted story that suddenly turns serious. Realistic watercolors.

*LAMM, MAURICE. *Living Torah in America.* illus. with photos. West Orange, NJ: Behrman House, 1993.182 p. (12-18)

Relates the historical roots of halakhic practice and contemporary examples. It also discusses peer and family relationships, describing a beautiful, ethical Judaism. A handsome book in format and content written in a conversational tone, suitable for all denominations.

LEPON, SHOSHANA. *Hillel Builds a House.* illus. by Marilynn Barr. Rockville, MD: Kar-Ben, 1993. 32 p. (3-5)

Hillel, a little boy who loves to build houses, has his house-building interrupted by every holiday, except for Sukkot.

LEPON, SHOSHANA. *Noah and the Rainbow.* illus. by Aaron Friedman. Brooklyn, NY: Judaica Press, 1993. 32 p. (4-8)

A fine retelling in verse of the Noah story with humorous insights into how difficult it was for Noah and his family to care for all those animals. Appended are interesting thoughts about Noah taken from Rashi and a blessing that is said when we see a rainbow. Cartoon figures in garish colors.

*LEVINE, ARTHUR. *Pearl Moscowitz's Last Stand.* illus. by Robert Roth. New York: Morrow/Tambourine, 1993. 32 p. (5-8)

All the neighbors join Pearl in fighting the electric company that wants to remove the last gingko tree on the block. Bright watercolors show real people—wrinkles and all. A cheerful version of a changed neighborhood.

LEVINSON, NANCY SMILER. *Sweet Notes, Sour Notes.* illus. by Beth Beck. New York: Lodestar/Dutton, 1993. 54 p. (7-10)

Disappointed by the dreary sounds he makes, David resumes his violin studies after *Zayde* encourages him with a story. He is later rewarded by being able to play a song for *Zayde* when he falls ill. Humorous, but poignant.

LEVINSON, RIKI. *Soon, Annala.* illus. by Julie Downing. New York: Orchard, 1993. 32 p. (6-10)

Anna teaches her two younger brothers how to count stars in English the night of their arrival in New York. A sequel to *Watch the Stars Come Out* (Dutton, 1985), but more Jewish. The 2 books are illustrated by different artists, thus interrupting continuity.

*LEVITIN, SONIA. *Escape from Egypt.* Boston: Little, Brown, 1994. 267 p. (12 up)

The story of the Exodus is given new life by its focus on one family and as told from the perspective of teenage Jesse, a Hebrew slave, and Jennat, a lovely Egyptian-Syrian slave who loves him. Strong characterizations in an involving story that poses many questions. An outstanding book.

LEVITIN, SONIA. *The Golem and the Dragon Girl.* New York: Dial, 1993. 192 p. (10-14)

When twelve-year-old Jonathan, his mother and stepfather move into the house that the Wang family is vacating, Laurel Wang worries about the spirit of her deceased great-grandfather whom she feels inhabits the house, while Jonathan invokes a golem. Teenage angst.

*LINNÉA, SHARON. *Raoul Wallenberg: The Man Who Stopped Death.* illus. with photos. Philadelphia, PA: Jewish Publication Society, 1993. 168 p. (10-14)

A biography of the man who saved countless Hungarian Jews describes early influences upon his character, why he was asked to do this daring work, and who supplied the credentials and the money. An exciting and necessary biography that redefines "hero."

*MATAS, CAROL. *Sworn Enemies.* New York: Bantam, 1993. 132 p. (12 up)

Two sworn enemies are forced to cooperate as they struggle to survive after escaping from the Czar's army. Excellent historical fiction that poses provocative questions.

MAYER-SKUMANZ, LENE. *The Tower.* illus. by Janusz Stanny. Woodmere, NY: Yellow Brick Rd. Press, 1993. unp. (7-10)

A story inspired by the Book of Daniel about three Jewish slave boys in Babylonia. Striking sand, ombre, rust and green watercolors lend an illusion of grand scale and drama.

*MCDONOUGH, YONA ZELDIS. *Eve and Her Sisters: Women of the Old Testament.* illus. by Malcah Zeldis. New York: Greenwillow Books, 1994. 32 p. (6-10)

One-page stories about fourteen women of the Bible retold to highlight the feminine, more personal human aspects of the powerful biblical narratives. Illustrated in the naif style.

MINER, JULIA. *The Shepherd's Song: The Twenty-Third Psalm.* illus. by Julia Miner. NY: Dial, 1993. unp. (5-8)

The twenty-third psalm illustrated with elegaic scenes of a shepherd family and their flock. Magnificent, sweeping illustrations in pastel chalks.

OBERMAN, SHELDON. *The Always Prayer Shawl.* illus. by Ted Lewin. Honesdale, PA: Boyds Mills Press, 1994. unp. (6-10)

A prayer shawl, often mended, with its fabric replaced, is handed down from one generation to the next to boys named

"Adam," named for their *living* relatives, as well as to honor those deceased. Lewin's realistic watercolors are magnificent.

*ORLEV, URI. *Lydia, Queen of Palestine.* Boston: Houghton Mifflin, 1993. 168 p. (10-14)

A hilarious tale laced with bittersweet moments about a feisty 10-year-old girl growing up in Romania during World War II, and her adventures in Palestine.

PETERSEIL, TAMAR AND DANA PORATH. *Zap It!* illus. photos etc. Woodmere, LI: Yellow Brick Rd. Pr., 1993. 32 p. (8-12)

An attractively illustrated kosher microwave cookbook for children with easy-to-follow safety rules and recipes—many with funny faces.

PETIT, JAYNE. *A Place to Hide: True Stories of Holocaust Rescues.* illus. with photos. New York: Scholastic/Apple, 1993. 114 p. (8-12)

Tells of those who defied the Nazis to help Jews during the Holocaust.

*PORTNOY, MINDY. *Matzoh Ball.* illus. by Katherine Janus Kahn. Rockville, MD: Kar-Ben Copies, 1994. unp. (6-10)

Forbidden to eat from the snack stands at the ballfield during Passover, Aaron remains behind talking to a mysterious Passover observant stranger, with miraculous results!

POTOK, CHAIM. *Tree of Here.* illus. by Tony Auth. New York: Knopf, 1993. unp. (7-10)

Jason's sense of dislocation at his family's move to a new home is lessened by the small tree given to him by a gardening friend.

RANSOM, CANDICE. *So Young to Die: The Story of Hannah Senesh.* New Young: Scholastic/Apple, 1993. 98 p. (8-12)

Simpler version of the life and death of Hannah Senesh, who had escaped from Nazi-occupied Hungary to the safety of Palestine and volunteered to return to Europe to rescue others.

*RAY, JANE. *The Story of Creation.* illus. by the author. New York: Dutton, 1993. unp. (4-8)

A folksy depiction of the biblical tale of Creation with words from Genesis (King James version) and marvelous illuminations from Ray.

REUTER, ELISABETH. *Best Friends.* illus. by the author. Woodmere, LI: Yellow Brick Rd., 1993. unp. (7-10)

Lisa never gets a chance to apologize for her anti-Semitic putdown of her Jewish friend Judith, because Judith and her family are taken away on Kristallnacht. Tr. from the German.

RICHARDS, JEAN. *God's Gift.* illus. by Norman Gorbaty. New York: Doubleday, 1993. 32 p. (3-7)

A joyous presentation of the Creation with large sylized illustrations.

ROJANY, LISA. *Story of Hanukkah: A Lift-the-Flap Rebus Book.* illus. by Holly Jones. New York: Hyperion, 1993. 16 p. (3-8)

This story of Hanukkah has rebus flaps covering words and four pages of attractive pop-ups in realistic watercolors. Most fascinating is the pop-up where the boy's hand holding the lit *shamash* moves down to light the *hanukkiah* when the page is turned.

ROSEMAN, KENNETH D. *Gates of Prayer for Young People.* New York: CCAR, 1993. 228 p. (9-12)

Provides a bridge between pre-school liturgies and the adult Siddur. Includes evening and morning services for weekdays and Shabbat, ranging from the early primary grades into adolescence. Gender sensitive. Reform.

ROSEMAN, KENNETH. *On the Other Side of the Hudson.* New York: UAHC, 1993. 140 p. (9-12)

A "Do it-yourself adventure" invites the reader to choose between two options as if he had emigrated to the United States between 1850-1880, the time of the Civil War and Gold Rush.

ROTH-HANO, RENÉE. *Safe Harbors.* New York: Four Winds, 1993. 256 p. (12 up)

A sequel to Roth-Hano's *Touch Wood* in the form of a diary recording the trials and tribulations, as well as the joys of her stint as an *au pair* in the United States in 1951-52.

ROUSS, SYLVIA. *Sammy Spider's First Hanukkah.* illus. Katherine Janus Kahn. Rockville, MD: Kar-Ben, 1993. unp. (3-6)

A spider receives a holiday surprise, or eight of them.

SAGAN, MIRIAM. *Tracing Our Jewish Roots.* illus. by Beth Evans. Santa Fe, New Mexico: John Muir, 1993. 48 p. (8-12)

A children's history of Jewish life in Eastern Europe covering the 19th century and the ensuing emigration, through the establishment of the State of Israel. Illus. with black and white photographs and cartoon illustrations. Reading list.

SAMSON, SMADAR. *Ophir.* illus. by Smadar Samson. North Pomfret, Vermont 05053: Bodley Head/Trafalgar Square, 1993. unp. (5-7)

Relates the legend of how King Solomon obtained his wealth by a journey to the mysterious land of Ophir. The mystical mood is reflected in delicate controlled spatter over water-colors with tones of pink, rust and turquoise to gold-spattered maroon and inky navy.

SIEGEL, DANNY. *Tell Me a Mitzvah: Little and Big Ways to Repair the World.* illus. by Judith Friedman. Rockville, MD: Kar-Ben, 1993. 64 p. (8-12)

Twelve profiles of people who have contributed to making the
world a better place. Each story is followed by a brief page
entitled: "What can I do?" with specific suggestions for young
people.

*SILVER, NORMAN. *Python Dance.* New York: Dutton, 1993. 242 p.
(12 up)

Ruth, a Jewish South African teenager who hates her
obnoxious stepfather and may have inadvertantly caused her
mother's death, is made aware of her country's oppressive
system of apartheid by a politically active friend. Quite a book.

SMEE, NICOLA. *Noah's Ark Board Books.* illus. by the author. Boston:
Little, Brown, 1993. unp. (6 mos.-3 yrs.)

An innovative set of six tiny board books that relate the Noah
story with a sentence or two and illustrations. They and four
bookmarks with animals atop, fit into a Noah's Ark-shaped box
with a removable center cabin. Cute.

SNYDER, CAROL. *God Must Like Cookies, Too.* illus. by Beth Glick.
Philadelphia, PA: Jewish Publication Society, 1993. unp. (4-6)

The promise of three cookies at the Oneg Shabbat helps a
little girl get through the long service at her Grandmother's
Reform Temple, but she decides that sweet as the cookies are,
going to Temple with Grandma is sweeter.

STEINBERG, SARI. *... And Then There Were Dinosaurs.* illus. with
claymation. Woodmere, LI: Yellow Brick Rd, 1993. unp. (4-8)

A claymation depiction of a Jewish legend: "Six Worlds Were
Created Before Our World." The sixth, the world of dinosaurs,
ended when they became destructive. The last page shows God's
huge clay hand creating Adam in a jungle diorama.

STERN, SARA. *A Smile for Sammy.* Brooklyn, NY: Tamar/Mesorah,
1993. 93 p. (8-12)

After Avi befriends dyslexic Sammy, Sammy begins to im-
prove socially and excel in their Jewish boys' school. Frequently
touching, and with just enough adventure to keep the reader
turning pages.

STRONG, STACIE. *Big Book of Noah's Ark with 25 Peek-a-Boo Lift-Up
Flaps.* illus. by Franscec Mateu. Cincinnati, OH: Standard
Publishing Co., 1993. 8 p. (2-4)

Simple retelling of Noah's Ark story with bright, colorful art
and lift-up flaps in an oversize ark-shaped board book.

TECHNER, DAVID AND JUDITH HIRT-MANHEIMER. *A Candle for Grandpa.*
illus. by Joel Iskowitz. New York: UAHC, 1993. unp. (5-8)

Jewish funeral practices are explained from the perspective of
an eleven-year-old boy on the first anniversary of his grandfather's death. Each step is thoroughly detailed. Glossary and
notes to parents about handling death with children are

enclosed. For all Jewish denominations.

TELLER, HANOCH. *Welcome to the Real World.* illus. by Nachum Oseroff. Spring Valley, NY: Feldheim, 1993. 88 p. (10-14)

Deena, a *frum* teen who has strayed, reforms when she realizes how unhappy it would make her beloved ill grandmother should Deena become a superficial, irreligious person like the ones she observed on the train. Illus. in cross-hatch pen and ink.

*TOBIAS, TOBI. *Pot Luck.* illus. by Nola Langer Malone. New York: Lothrop, 1993. unp. (4-8)

Gram spends the rest of the day cleaning, shopping and cooking in preparation for her old friend, Sophie's visit after promising her "pot luck." A delightful, humorous story about human nature with apt illustrations.

*TOLL, NELLY S. *Behind the Secret Window: A Memoir of a Hidden Childhood During World War Two.* illus. by Nelly S. Toll. New York: Dial, 1993. 161 p. (10-14)

An illustrated diary of an 8-year-old child hiding with her mother in Nazi-occupied Ukraine, records the bleak news and her sadness about her lost father and brother. Also contains happy optomistic paintings about an imaginary childhood filled with joy and normalcy.

TOMASELLI, CECILIA MACAGNO. *Noah's Family.* illus. by Cecilia Macagno Tomaselli. Woodmere, NY: Simcha Publishing Co., 1993. unp. (2-4)

A spiral-bound die-cut board toy book that forms a carousel, not an ark, shows living conditions aboard the ark.

*VERHOEVEN, RIAN AND RUUD VAN DER ROL. *Anne Frank, Beyond the Diary: A Photographic Remembrance.* illus. with photos. New York: Viking, 1993. 113 p. (10-14)

In addition to telling the Anne Frank story and beyond, this excellent resource includes: a chronology of the Frank family and the families in the secret annex; notes on different versions of the *Diary of Anne Frank;* sources of quotations and photographs; and an index of people and places. Prepared by the Anne Frank House.

VOIGEL, EVA. *A Weed Among the Roses.* Spring Valley, NY: Feldheim, 1993. 237 p. (12-15)

When students disappear from an English high school for Jewish girls, both faculty and students begin to investigate a possible kidnapping. High melodrama in the English countryside.

WADDELL, MARTIN. *Stories from the Bible: Old Testament Stories Retold.* illus. by Geoffrey Patterson. New York: Ticknor & Fields, 1993. 76 p. (7-12)

Patterson's bright naive acrylic paintings of varying sizes are framed by borders, but there are no women in these seventeen simplified tales.

*WALDMAN, SARAH. *Light: The First Seven Days.* illus. by Neil Waldman. New York: Harcourt Brace Jovanovich, 1993. unp. (4-8)

A magnificent kaleidoscope of brilliantly colored paintings on a black background extend the simple words used to describe the Creation. A book to treasure.

WAX, WENDY. *Hanukkah, Oh, Hanukkah! A Treasury of Stories, Songs, and Games to Share.* illus. Spiers, John. New York: Bantam, 1993. 64 p. (6-9)

Highlighting this collection of games, songs, activities, chapters from books, poems, and stories set during Hanukkah, are recollections of the holiday by four well-known authors and performers. Dramatically hued illustrations. A much needed resource.

WEILERSTEIN, SADIE ROSE. *K'tonton's Sukkot Adventure.* Rev. Ed. illus. by Joe Boddy. Philadelphia, PA: Jewish Publication Society, 1993. unp. (4-8)

An updated, improved K'tonton story in a picture book format. Lively illustrations. Glossary.

*WEISS, NICKI. *Stone Men.* illus. by Nicki Weiss. New York: Greenwillow, 1993. unp. (4-8)

A taciturn peddler who pushes his cart from village to village and builds stone men to keep him company saves a village from a Cossack pogrom. Simple but winning illustrations.

ZAKON, MIRIAM STARK. *Gemarakup Returns (Gemarakup: Super Sleuth (2) series).* Brooklyn, NY: Tamar/Mesorah, 1993. 96 p. (10-14)

Brief stories followed by a question that tests the reader's knowledge of the sources against "Gemarakup's." Solutions are found at the end of the book. Part of a series. Glossary.

ZALBEN, JANE BRESKIN. *Happy New Year, Beni.* illus. by Jane Breskin Zalben. New York: Holt, 1993. unp. (4-8)

Their elders show the little bear cousins how the ancient customs of Rosh Hashanah can help them to resolve their disputes. Glossary; recipe for a round challah. Beautiful detailed illustrations in a mini-size book.

ZWEBNER, JANET. *UH! OH! Hidden Objects You'll (Almost) Never Find: Jewish Holidays.* illus. by Janet Zwebner. Yellow Brick Rd., 1993. unp. (8-12)

A Jewish "Where's Waldo" about Jewish holidays has hundreds of tiny figures and activities on each page for children to examine in order to solve the puzzle.

צבי ארני
ZVI ERENYI

יבול הספרות העברית באמריקה תשנ"ג-תשנ"ד

American Hebrew Books 1993–1994

The following bibliography of American Hebrew imprints includes original works, new editions and reprints with revisions or additions, but not unchanged reprints. In is based almost entirely on the holdings of the Mendel Gottesman Library of Hebraica-Judaica of Yeshiva University. For these reasons it is not exhaustive. For the sake of simplicity, all places of publication within New York City were listed as New York (i.e., Brooklyn - New York). The compiler welcomes any comments and suggestions.

ספר אבן שתיה שלם: תולדותיהם של צדיקים לבית קאסוב ויזניץ / חיים
כהנא. ניו יורק: מכון להוצאת ספרים פרי עץ חיים, תשנ"ד (מהדורה חדשה).
ספר אבני חושן: ביאור ובירור מקיף על עניני וגדרי שומע כעונה . . . /
שמואל ניימאן. מאנסי: המחבר, תשנ"ג.
ספר אבני שוהם (מועדים): ביאורים והערות בעניני המועדים והזמנים . . . /
נחום אייזענשטיין. ניו יורק: המחבר, תשנ"ג.
ספר אגרא דכלה על חמשה חומשי תורה: ביאורים, דרושים ע"ד הפרד"ס . . .
/ צבי אלימלך, אב"ד מדינאב. ניו יורק: הוצאת אמת, תשנ"ג.
אגרות נפלאות כוללות תורה, חכמה, מוסר ודקדוק אשר נדפסו בתחלת ספר
פרי מגדים של שלחן ערוך אורח חיים . . . / יוסף תאומים. ניו יורק: ישעי'
אשר אנשיל וייס, 1991 (מהדורה חדשה).
אגרות קודש / שמואל שניאורסאהן. ניו יורק: קהת, תשנ"ג (מהדורה חדשה).
ספר אגרת הפורים: חידושים וביאורים על מצות מחיית עמלק, מגילת אסתר
ומסכת מגילה (מכורך עם פירוש הרמב"ם על מגילת אסתר) / משה יצחק
וייסמאן. ניו יורק: המחבר, תשנ"ד.
אגרת שנית של רב שרירא גאון (תוספת לאגרש"ג), בצירוף מבוא,
ביאורים והערות מאת נתן דוד רבינוביץ / שרירא בן חנינא, גאון. ניו יורק:

יהושע ליינער, תשנ"א.

ספר אוצר אמת על חג הסוכות ומאמרים לחנוכה, עם קונטרס אגרת הפורים
וענייני ראש חודש / שמואל טייך. ניו יורק: ישיבת שערי דעה, תשנ"ד?

אוצר פתגמי חב"ד: 620 אמרות . . . וסיפורים . . . מלוקטים מספרי חב"ד /
אלתר אליהו פרידמן (מלקט). ניו יורק: קהת, תשנ"ג.

ספר אוצרות נפתלי: כתבי קודש וחידושי תורה, רזין דאורייתא שהובאו
בשני ספריו . . . ונקבצו כאן ושולבו ביחד עם הערות ומראי מקומות . . . /
נפתלי הורוויץ. ניו יורק: סיני הלברשטאם, תשנ"ג.

ספר אור שמונה בעניני חנוכה: ביאורים, פלפולים וחידושים, משולב
בדרושים ובאגדה עם הברכות והזמירות / יוסף חיים מאסקאוויטש. ניו יורק:
המחבר, תשנ"ג.

ספר אלה מסעי: בו יתואר פרשת נסיעת אדמו"ר מהר"מ ט"ב להשתטח על
קברות הצדיקים אשר במדינות אוקריינא, פולין, אונגארן, ראמעניע בחודש
תמוז תשנ"ב, עם סיפורי צדיקים ושיחות קודש . . . קרית יואל: אבני צדק,
תשנ"ד.

ספר אליבא דהלכתא: הלכות פסח, ערב פסח שחל להיות בשבת: ביאורי
פרטי ההלכות הנהוגות מז' ניסן עד ט"ו ניסן . . . / משה דוב שטיין. ניו יורק:
המחבר, תשנ"ד.

ספר אמירה נעימה על התורה . . . .: מחידושים ערבים . . . ,, דרושים נחמדים
על מדרשות ואגדות . . . / חיים גבריאל בלוך. ניו יורק: משה יחזקאל שרגא
גאלדענבערג, תשנ"ד (מהדורה שניה).

ספר אמרי אש, ונחלק לשלשה חלקים: א. מאורי האש: ביאורים באגדות
חז"ל ,, ב. עמודי אש: חדושים וביאורים על סדר הטור חושן משפט, ג. א. אש
אברהם: חדושים ובאורים בסוגיות בבא קמא ובבא בתרא / אוריאל אליהו
אביגס. לייקווד: מעיין החכמה, תשנ"ג.

ספר אמרי בינה על מגילת שיר השירים / צבי אריה בן אליעזר. ניו יורק:
חברה מפיצי תורה ממשפחת קול אריה, תשנ"א (מהדורה חדשה).

ספר אמרי דעה על שו"ע יורה דעה הלכות בשר בחלב סימנים צ"ג-צ"ז:
ביאור רחב ופירוש מספיק . . . / ירחמיאל משה ביטמאן. ניו יורק: המחבר,
תשנ"ג.

ספר אפנה ואשנה וקובץ שיעורים בנושאים שונים מפי מרן הגרי"ד
סולובייצ'יק / אלתר אשר ישעיה בלאו. ניו יורק: ישיבה אוניברסיטה, 1993.

ספר בא ישועה ונחמה: חיבור נפלא על חמשה חומשי תורה בדרך דרוש
ופלפול / ישעיה סג"ל. ניו יורק: אחים גאלדענבערג, תשנ"ג (מהדורה חדשה).

ספר באר אברהם: ביאורי סוגיות, הערות והארות בדברי הראשונים
והאחרונים בעניני מקואות, נדה, מועד ועניינים שונים / אברהם ישעי' סאווויץ.
לייקווד: המחבר, תשנ"ד.

באר החיים: חלק א': שאלות ותשובות וביאורים בענינים שונים, חלק ב':
חידושים בהלכות נדה סי' קצ"ו ועוד עניני הל' נדה . . . / אברהם חיים
שטיינווארצעל. ניו יורק: כולל מטה אפרים, תשנ"ד.

ספר באר מים חיים: ביאורים על פירש"י על התורה . . . עם הערות ומראה
מקומות בשם שרגא המאיר, ע"י שרגא פייוויש שנעעבאלג / חיים בן בצלאל.
ניו יורק: פ. שנעעבאלג, תשנ"ג.

ספר באר משה: ליקוטים, חידושים וביאורים על מסכת עירובין / משה
שטערן. ניו יורק: המחבר, תשנ"ב.

ספר באר משה: ליקוטים, חדושים ובאורים על מסכתות יומא-ביצה / משה
שטערן. ניו יורק: המחבר, תשנ"ג.

ספר באר שלמה: ליקוטים והקדמות נפלאות ממפרשי התורה ראשונים
ואחרונים מסודרים ע"פ א"ב / שלמה צוקער. ניו יורק: ש.א. בלוישטיין,
תשנ"ג (מהדורה שלישית).

ביאורים לפירוש רש"י על התורה: מלוקטים משיחות . . . / מנחם מענדל
שניאורסאהן. ניו יורק: קהת, תשנ"ג (מהדורה חדשה ומתוקנת).

ספר בית רחל משנה הלכות: דרך ישרה שיבור לו האדם לראות חיים עם
האשה אשר אהב . . . / מנשה קליין. ניו יורק: מכון משנה הלכות גדולות,
תשנ"ב.

בך אתפאר: סוד הגאווה היהודית / עזריאל טאובר. מאנסי: שלהבת, 1993.

ספר בכורי ראובן: חדושים וביאורים על מסכת גיטין / ראובן שיפנסקי. ניו
יורק: המחבר, תשנ"ג.

בנאות דשא: ביקורי כבוד קדושת אדמו"ר מנחם מענדל שניאורסאהן
מליובאוויטש במחנות הקיץ . . . בשנים התשט"ז, התשי"ז, התש"כ. ניו יורק:
קהת, תשנ"ג.

ספר בנה ביתך על הלכות נדה וטבילה . . . וגם פתחתי בו שער הבית ובו
יצויין על כל דיבור ודיבור מקור מקום מוצא הפנינים האלו . . . / אשר
אנשיל שעהר. ניו יורק: המחבר, תשנ"ג.

ספר בנין שלום על שו"ע או"ח הלכות ברכת הפירות / שלום נח וייס. ניו
יורק: המחבר, תשנ"ג.

ספר בצל הכסף: והוא ליקוט נפלא, מאמרים וסיפורים ואגרות קודש המדברים
בעניני גודל מעלת ושבחו של המחזיק ומרחיב דעת הצדיקים . . . / אברהם
יצחק האלצלער (מלקט). שיכון סקווירא: המלקט, תשנ"ג.

ספר ברית אברהם הכהן על מגדל עז לרבינו יעב"ץ: הלכות ומנהגי ברית
מילה . . .; קונטרס הנפלאות משנות הזעם / אברהם קאהן. ניו יורק: המחבר,
1993.

ספר ברכת השבת: ביאורים, חידושים וסיכומי הלכה בשו"ע או"ח הלכות שבת
/ אליהו פישר. ניו יורק: המחבר, תשנ"ג (מהדורה שניה).

ספר בשבילי הבבלי והירושלמי: ביאורים על חילוקי דיעות ושיטות בין
הבבלי והירושלמי בשני פרקים הראשונים של מסכת שבת / אברהם אזדאבא.
ניו יורק: המחבר, תשנ"ב.

בשורת הגאולה: מלוקט מספרי השיחות תש"נ-תשנ"ב / מנחם מענדל
שניאורסאהן. ניו יורק: קהת, תשנ"ג.

ספר גבעת שאול, עם תולדותיו, ועתה יצא לאור מחדש בתוספת מרובה . . . /

שאול הלוי מורטירא. ניו יורק: חיים אלעזר רייך, תשנ״א (צילום תרס״ב עם הוספות).

ספר גדולת מרדכי: כולל תולדות אדם . . . ונלוה אליו מכתבים ואגרות קודש . . . חוברו לו יחדיו ויו״ל לראשונה ע״י נכדו אהרן אליעזר דייטש / מרדכי יהודה לעוו. ניו יורק: אהרן אליעזר דייטש, תשנ״ג.

ספר דברי אהרן: כולל חידושים וביאורים, הארות והערות, עיונים ודיונים על מסכתות הש״ס וגם מכתבים של חידושי תורה / אהרן סדובסקי. ניו יורק: י. סדובסקי, תשנ״ג.

ספר דברי האגרת: פי׳ על אגרת מוסר מהרמב״ן לבנו . . . מאת אברהם יהושע רעטעק, ועם פירוש אגרת פתוחה . . . אשר יזם הרה״ג המחבר ונגמר ע״י . . . חיים ארי׳ ערלאנגער / משה בן נחמן. ניו יורק: מנחם משה רעטעק, תשנ״ד.

ספר דברי הפורים: מיוסד על עניני מגילה וד׳ פרשיות . . . / יחזקאל ראטה. ניו יורק: ב.ד. ראטה, תשנ״ג.

ספר דברי חיים דוב, חלק רביעי: פירוש על סה״ק פרי עץ חיים, שער התפילין (מכורך עם ספר משיבת נפש) / חיים דוב וייסבערג. ניו יורק: המחבר, תשנ״ב.

ספר דברי ישראל, חלק ראשון: דרוש על דברי חז״ל במדרשים ובש״ס על ספר בראשית / ישראל אברהם אבא קריגער. ניו יורק: יוסף גאלדבערג, תשנ״ב.

ספר דברי שיר על התורה ועל המועדים ולקוטים שונים / שמואל ראטה. ניו יורק: ב. טעללער, תשנ״א (צילום תרפ״ד עם הוספות).

ספר דברי שירה: עירובין / אליהו לוין. לייקווד: אוריתא, תשנ״ד.

ספר דברי שירה: שבת . . . / אליהו לוין. לייקווד: המחבר, תשנ״ג.

ספר דברי שמואל . . . מעט מזער מחידושי׳ אשר כתב בימי חרפו . . . (מכורך עם ספר אור הנערב) / שמואל בן אברהם, הצרפתי. ניו יורק: אחים גאלדענבערג, תשנ״ג.

ספר דודאים של משה: הן מאמרי קודש על סדר הפרשיות, מועדים והזמנים . . . „ חלק ב׳: כמה אמרי קודש מהקוה״ט אברהם יעקב, אדמו״ר הזקן מסאדיגורא . . . „ חלק ג׳: שני מאמרים מאת . . . אברהם יעקב שפירא / דוד משה שפירא. ניו יורק: יצחק מרדכי שפירא, תשנ״ב.

דיני מאכלי נכרים: דיני בישולי נכרים, פת, חלב, גבינה של נכרים ודיני יין נסך: פסקים, חקירות ובירורי הלכות / מיכאל פרק. ניו יורק: המחבר, תשנ״ב.

ספר הדקדוק לרמח״ל: יוצא לאור הדפוס בפעם ראשונה מתוך כתבי יד, עם הגהות ומראה מקומות בשם אשי בני ישראל, ממני אלעזר שמואל בריעגער / משה חיים לוצאטו. ניו יורק: אלעזר בריעגער, תשנ״ד.

ספר דרוש וחידוש מהרא״ץ בריסק: חידושי סוגיות, שאלות ותשובות . . . נערך ונסדר ויו״ל בתוספת . . . בכורי אביב מנאי . . . אליעזר יצחק בריסק / אהרן צבי בריסק. מאנסי: מכון מהר״ם ומהרא״ץ בריסק, תשנ״ג.

דרוש לשבת הגדול, פרשת צו: נכבדות מדובר בו משיעבוד וגלות של מצרים וגאולתינו מה׳ מתחת יד פרעה / אברהם שמשוני. ניו יורק: אחים

גאלדעגבערג, תשנ"ד (מהדורה שניה).

ספר דרשות קול בן לוי (מכורך עם ספר ערוך השלחן) / יחיאל מיכל
עפשטיין. הובוקן: כתב, תשנ"א.

הגדה. הגדה של פסח אור המלכות: ילקוט אמרות טהורות . . . מרבינו הק' אור
ישראל מרוזין וצאצאיו . . . אספתי ולקטתי . . . שמחה בונם פישמן. ניו יורק:
המלקט, תשנ"ד (מהדורה חדשה).

הגדה. סדר הגדה של פסח דברי חיים השלם, מכבוד אדמו"ר . . . חיים
הלברשטאם . . . מלוקט מתוך ספרו הקדוש דברי חיים וגם מה שהובא
בשמו . . . ; קונטרס עקבי חיים: והוא אוסף של הליכות והלכות . . . לכל ימי
חודש ניסן מרבינו הקדוש . . . ניו יורק: מכון „סגולה", תשנ"ד (מהדורה
חדשה).

הגדה. סדר הגדה של פסח עם פירוש . . . ויחי יוסף, אשר השאיר אחריו
ברכה . . . מרן יוסף גרינוואלד . . . ניו יורק: בני המחבר, תשנ"ב.

הגדה. הגדה של פסח עם פירוש יפה נוף . . . אשר חיבר . . . חיים גבריאל
בלוך . . . (מכורך עם ספר אמירה נעימה). ניו יורק: משה יחזקאל שרגא
גאלדעגבערג, תשנ"ד (מהדורה חדשה).

הגדה. הגדה של פסח ע"פ ליקוטי כלי יקר . . . מתורתו של הגאון . . . רבינו
שלמה אפרים . . . מחבר פי' כלי יקר עה"ת . . . לייקווד: מכון אבני שהם,
תשנ"ג.

הגדה. פירוש רבינו אליהו מווילנא על סדר ההגדה של פסח, עם פירוש
לפירושו ליקוטי דודאים על ביאור הגר"א, ליקוטי הלכות הגר"א, נערך
ונסדר ע"י ראובן דוד גרשון. קליבלנד: העורך, תשנ"ד.

הדרנים על הש"ס: כרך א': זרעים, מועד, נשים / מנחם מענדל שניאורסאהן.
ניו יורק: קהת, תשנ"ד.

ספר הוד שבהוד על עניני ל"ג בעומר: קובץ על יד מאמרי חז"ל מש"ס,
מדרשים וזוה"ק . . . / ברוך אלי' לעווי (מלקט). מונרו: המלקט, תשנ"ג.

הנהגות ישרות וסדר היום / שלום שכנא, מפרוביסטש. ניו יורק, תשנ"א.

ספר הסברות מהר"ם בומסלא על מסכת ברכות ואו"ח מסימן קס"ז עד סימן
רט"ז, הערות וציונים ומראה מקומות ע"י יצחק הערשקאוויטש / מאיר
בומסלא. ניו יורק: מכון הררי קדם, תשנ"ג.

ספר הרים משה על התורה ומועדים וחידושים (מכורך עם ספר ידות אפרים)
/ יצחק משה פאנעט. ניו יורק: מנחם עזריאל ראטה, תשנ"ג.

ספר ואתה ברחמיך הרבים על הלכות תשובה להרמב"ם, על שערי תשובה
לרבינו יונה, דברי הלכה ודברי אגדה / אליעזר גינזבורג. ניו יורק: המחבר,
תשנ"ב.

ספר וזאת ליהודה (מכורך עם ספר ישמח לב) / יהודה הלוי, מנײשטאדט.
מאנטריאל: א.ע. בינעטה, תשנ"ב.

ספר ויגד מרדכי על הגדה של פסח: חידושים, ביאורים וסנסנים קצרים
שבליל התקדש חג נאמרים . . . / מרדכי ישראל חיים סאמעט. ניו יורק:
המחבר, תשנ"ב.

ספר וידבר דוד: מאמר תורה אור, מאמר זה כתב בימי נעוריו בעניני יציאת
מצרים, קרי"ס וקנין תורה / משה דוד שטיינוווארצל. ניו יורק, תשנ"ד.

וידבר משה: דברים נעימים נפלאים . . . דברי הלכה ושמעתתא הנוגע
להסדרה, נושא ונותן בדברי רבותינו הראשונים ואחרונים . . . / משה
פאללאק. מאנסי: א. ראזענבערג, תשנ"ג (מהדורה חדשה).

ספר ויקהל דוד על ראש השנה ויום הכפורים: דברים ערבים ונחמדים
בעניינים שונים, אוסף נפלא על עניני סליחות . . . / דוד דוב מייזליש. ניו
יורק: המחבר, תשנ"ג.

ספר וירא פנחס: והוא ילקוט מדרשים ודרושים על פרשת מרגלים ומגדף
ומקושש, עם פירוש . . . של חידושים וביאורים ותקוני נוסחאות . . . / פנחס
וועכטער-ראבינאוויטץ (מלקט). ניו יורק: המלקט, תשנ"ג.

ספר זכרון: הוצאה מיוחדת לזכרון הקדוש ולע"נ . . . ר' משה פיינשטיין . . . ניו
יורק: ישיבה סטעטן איילנד, תשנ"ב.

ספר זכרון דוד עה"ת ומועדים דברים נחמדים מדבש ונופת צופים . . .
ועליו . . . קונטרס בנים על אבות ובו הערות . . . על ספר זכרון דוד . . .
מבנו . . . שלום קרויז / שמואל דוד קרויז. ניו יורק: כולל בית ישעי'
ד'אודוואארי, תשנ"א (מהדורה שניה).

ספר זכרון מנחם . . .: על מסכת קינים: ביאור צח וקל על המסכת כולה, בנוי
ומיוסד על דברי הרע"ב, תוס' יו"ט והתפא"י / יעקב מנחם יואל איצקאוויטש.
ניו יורק: המחבר, תשנ"ד.

ספר זכרון מנחם: תולדות אא"ז שמחה בונם אייגער אבדק"ק
מאטערסדארף . . . / יודא ארי' ליב יונגרייז. ניו יורק: המחבר, תשנ"ג?

ספר זכרון צבי מאיר: פרק אלו נערות: כולל משא ומתן, ביאורים והערות
על הרבה סוגיות בפרק שלישי דכתובות / משה שמעון חיים זילברברג.
מאנסי: המחבר, תשנ"ב.

ספר זכרון שמואל על מועדים / שמואל יששכר דוב טויבענפעלד. מאנסי:
בני המחבר, תשנ"ד.

ספר זכרון תפארת משה יצחק לזכרון הרה"ח . . . משה יצחק העכט. ניו
הייווען: מוסדות חינוך ליובאוויטש, תשנ"ב.

זמירות דברי יואל לחג המצות: והוא סדר הזמירות . . . משובץ באמרות ה'
אמרות טהורות, חידושי תורות . . . מאת . . . מרן יואל טייטלבוים. קרית יואל:
הוצאת דמתה לתמר, תשנ"ג.

(זמירות). ספר זרע יצחק אשר לקטנו מעט מזעיר לקיים רצון קדשו . . .
של . . . רבינו יצחק (מאמשינאוו). ניו יורק, תשנ"ד.

זמירות חיים ושלום לשבתות ומועדים ועתותי קודש . . . ע"פ מנהג
ונוסח . . . רבי חיים אלעזר שפירא, אבדק"ק מונקאטש . . . ניו יורק: יום טוב
ליפא וייס ובניו, תשנ"ב (מהדורה חדשה).

זמירות לשבת קודש עם פירוש רנו שמים . . . מאת . . . אדמו"ר מקאשוי,
נכתב ונסדר . . . על ידי . . . יוסף משה פרידמאן. בעדפארד הילס: יוסף משה
פרידמאן, תשנ"ג.

זמירות קדושת לוי על חנוכה, דרושים וחידושים . . . המובאים בספרו
הקדוש קדושת לוי ובספרי בניו ותלמידיו הקדושים / לוי יצחק בן מאיר,
מבארדיטשוב. מאנסי: הוצאת ספרים דקהל קדושת לוי ד׳בארדיטשוב, תדש״ן.
ספר זמירות שבת שירי דוד. לוס אנג׳לס: ב. קאהן, 1992.
ספר זרע יעקב: תוכו רצוף אהבה דברים עתיקים . . . אור אמונה והתחזקות
מפיקים . . . / יעקב הורוויץ. ניו יורק: בן ציון הלברשטאם, תשנ״ד.
חודש בחדשו. גליון א׳: ניסן תשנ״ד. ניו יורק: איחוד חסידי מונקאטש, תשנ״ד־
חדושי הגר״מ והגרי״ד: והם דברי תורה שנאמרו בחבורה של מרן הר׳ משה
סאלאווייצ״יק עם בנו ותלמידו מרן ר׳ יוסף דוב סאלאווייצ״יק . . .: עניני
קדשים . . . / משה סאלאווייצ״יק. ניו יורק: מורשה, תשנ״ג.
חידושי מהר״ם שיף על תנ״ך ע״ד אגדה / מאיר בן יעקב שיף. ניו יורק:
יעקב שיף, תשנ״ב (מהדורה חדשה).
ספר חידושי מרן הגר״ב סורוצקין על סדר נשים, חלק ב׳: נדרים, נזיר,
גיטין / רפאל ברוך סורוצקין. וויקליף: משפחת המחבר, תשנ״ג.
ספר חיי שלום: כולל חידושים וביאורים עמוקים, רובם בדרך הקבלה על
חמשה חומשי תורה ושאלות ותשובות וספרי דינים בהלכה / יחיא בן שלום,
הכהן. מאנסי: ע. אדמוני, תשנ״ג.
ספר חיים של ברכה: דיני ברכת שהחיינו וברכת הטוב והמטיב: אוצר הלכות
ומנהגים מלוקטים מתוך ספרי הפוסקים . . . / חיים יוסף פרידמאן (מלקט). ניו
יורק: המלקט, 1992.
ספר חסדי אבות: והוא חיבור נחמד פירוש על פרקי אבות . . . / אהרן בן
יהודה, הלוי. ניו יורק: אחים גאלדענבערג, תשנ״ג (מהדורה חדשה).
ספר החסידות: תורת ושיטת חסידות חב״ד, מהותה וחידושה, ענינה
ותפקידה . . . / חנוך גליצנשטיין (מלקט). ניו יורק: קהת, 1993.
ספר חפץ חיים . . .: הוא חבור מיוסד על הלכות איסורי לשה״ר ורכילות ואבק
שלהן . . . נלוה פירוש . . . חלקת בנימין . . . על ידי בנימין כהן / ישראל
מאיר, הכהן. ניו יורק: בנימין כהן, תשנ״ג.
ספר יבנה המקדש: מאמרים בעניני בית המקדש / שלמה ברעוודה (מלקט).
ניו יורק: המלקט, תשנ״ג.
ספר יג״ל יעקב על התורה: חדושי אגדות על חמשה חומשי תורה וכתבי קודש
וליקוטים בדרך פרדס . . . / חיים מרדכי יעקב גאטטליעב. ניו יורק: נכדי
המחבר, תשנ״ג.
ספר יד יחזקאל: מאמרי מוסר לפי סדר הפרשיות והמגילות . . . אשר נשמעו
רובם בישיבת מיר העתיקה בשנות גלותה וטלטולה משנת תש״א עד תש״ח,
לוקט מפיהם ומפי כתבם של תלמידיו הרבים / יחזקאל לעווינשטיין.
לייקווד: מ. גינזבורג, תשנ״ג.
ספר ידות אפרים על טו״ב סוגיות הש״ס / יצחק אייזיק ראזענפעלד. ניו
יורק: מנחם עזריאל ראטה, תשנ״ג (מהדורה חדשה).
ספר היובל: איגוד הרבנים ד׳אמריקא לכבוד שנת החמישים, תש״ב-תשנ״ב. ניו
יורק: איגוד הרבנים, תשנ״ב.

ספר היובל קרנות צדי״ק: קובץ מיוחד לדברי תורה ועיונים בהלכה . . .
לכבודו ולזכותו של . . . רבי מנחם מענדל שניאורסאהן . . . ניו יורק: קהת,
תשנ״ב.

ספר יחוס משפחת רוזענבלאט: והוא תולדות של הרב הנגיד המפורסם
אברהם דוד בן יעקב . . . / נ. רוזענבלאט. ניו יורק: המחבר, תשנ״ב.

ספר ייטב לב על מסכת גיטין / יקותיאל יהודה טייטלבוים. ניו יורק: מ.מ.
טייטלבוים, תשנ״ג.

ספר ייטב לב על מסכת מכות / יקותיאל יהודה טייטלבוים. ניו יורק: חברה
קנין ספרים דקהל עצי חיים סיגוט, תשנ״ד.

ילקוט אמרות טהורות: והוא ליקוט פנינים ומאמרים, מלוקט מתוך תורתם
של אדמו״ר מרן ה״פחד יצחק״ מבאיאן וכ״ק אדמו״ר הרמ״ש מבאיאן על
חנוכה / יצחק פרידמאן. ניו יורק, תשנ״ד.

ילקוט אמרות טהורות: והוא ליקוט פנינים ומאמרים, רובן מכ״ק אדמו״ר וגם
מאביו מרן אדמו״ר ה״פחד יצחק״ מבאיאן ואדה״ג מס״ג על הד׳ פרשיות
ופורים . . . / מרדכי שלמה פרידמאן. ניו יורק, תשנ״ד (מהדורה שניה).

ספר ילקוט ביאורים בית משה אליהו על מסכת גיטין: פנינים מחידושי
וביאורי רבותינו גדולי האחרונים מבואר בלשון צח וקל . . . / אריה ליב
שפיצער (מלקט). ניו יורק: המלקט, תשנ״ג.

ילקוט משיח וגאולה על התורה. ניו יורק: קהת, תשנ״ד (תדפיס מספר זה על
פרשת בראשית).

ספר ימי שמונה: והוא סדר הדלקת נר חנוכה עפ״י נוסח רבוה״ק מדעעש, עם
ליקוט אמרות טהורות על ימי החנוכה. ניו יורק: מכון מראה יחזקאל להוצאת
ספרי אדמו״רי בית דעעש, תשנ״ג.

ספר יצב אברהם: דברים ערבים, רמזים וענינים . . . על עניני חנוכה /
אברהם צבי גינצלער. ניו יורק: נתן נפתלי הורוויץ, תשנ״ד.

ספר יקב אפרים: עניני מצות השנה השביעית / יעקב קאפיל שווארץ. ניו
יורק: המחבר, תשנ״ג-

ספר יקב אפרים: רשימות של הערות וביאורים בפירושי רמב״ן על התורה /
יעקב קאפיל שווארץ. ניו יורק: המחבר, תשנ״ג.

ספר ישמח לב על התורה, נו״כ / משה שמעון בן יהודה, הלוי. מאנטריאל:
א.ע. בינעטה, תשנ״ב.

ספר כונת הלב: חידושים על הש״ס (מכורך עם ספר רני עקרה) / הילל
ליכטענשטיין. ניו יורק: יוסף ליכטער, תשנ״ג.

ספר כונת הלב: ליקוטי תשובות (מכורך עם ספר רני עקרה) / הילל
ליכטענשטיין. ניו יורק: יוסף ליכטער, תשנ״ג.

ספר כמו השחר: הערות מאירות כשחר עולות בסוגיות הלכות ואגדות . . . /
נתן נטע לנדא. ניו יורק: משפחת אונטערטער, תשנ״ב (צילום תרמ״ד עם הוספות).

ספר כסא שן: דיני והנהגת הסעודה וברכת המזון . . . בצרוף הגהות והשמטות
הג׳ המחבר ובצירוף ציונים ומראי מקומות ע״י אברהם יוסף סעקולא / יעקב
עמדין. ניו יורק: אברהם יוסף סעקולא, תשנ״ג.

ספר כרם יהושע: ובו פרקים בענין דרך הלימוד הנכונה וסדר לשינון וחזרה,
ביררוים בענין לימוד התורה ובכללי הש״ס . . . / יהושע כהן. מאנסי:
המחבר, תשנ״ד.

ספר כתבי ר׳ אייזיק על מסכת בבא קמא / אייזיק שווי. ניו יורק: קהת,
תשנ״ג.

ספר כתבנו לחיים: אוצר בתוכו ההסכמות שנתן . . . רבי חיים
הלברשטאם . . . עם תולדות המחברים וצילומי שערי הספרים / חיים
הלברשטאם. ניו יורק: ברוך שמשון הלברשטאם, תשנ״ג.

ספר לב יהודה על עניני ש״ס / יהודה ליב נוייורט. ליקוד: המחבר, תשנ״ג.

ספר להבת אש: קבלת הבעל שם טוב ותלמידיו, נערך ונסדר מדבריהם
הקדושים עם הערות והארות ופתיחת שעריהם / שמואל טייך (עורך). ניו
יורק: כולל לב האר״י, תשנ״ג.

ספר ליל שמורים בעניני ליל פסח, עם פירוש על הגדה של פסח: הכל מיוסד
על דברי חז״ל ורבותינו הראשונים והאחרונים / שלמה ברעוודה (מלקט). ניו
יורק: המלקט, תשנ״ב.

ספר לימודי ניסן על מסכת ביצה / ניסן ליפא אלפערט. מאנסי: מ. אלפרט,
תשנ״ג.

ליקוט פסוקי תנ״ך, מאמרי חז״ל וקטעים מספרים הק׳ . . . במצות קידוש שם
שמים . . . (חלק ג׳ מקונטרס שמחת עולם) / מרדכי צבי סאסנע (מלקט). ניו
יורק: ועד להרמת קרן התורה מצדיקי הרבים, תשנ״ד.

לקוטי אמרים על עניני ברכת המזון. ניו יורק, תשנ״ג.

ספר ליקוטי ישרים: והוא שלשה ספרים נפתחים: עניני חנוכה, יסודות חינוך
הבנים ועניני ד׳ פרשיות . . . / יוסף מגיד. ניו יורק: המחבר, תשנ״ב (מהדורה
שניה).

לקוטי ספורים: זכרונות, ספורים ופתגמין קדישין מכ״ק רבותינו . . . מה
ששמעתי . . . בעת למדי בישיבת תומכי תמימים בליובאוויטש . . . / חיים
מרדכי פערלאוו. ניו יורק: המחבר, תשנ״ב.

לקוטי ערכים בש״ס וברמב״ם: ערכים קצרים מלוקטים משיחות / מנחם
מענדל שניאורסאהן. ניו יורק: קהת, תשנ״ב.

ספר לכבוד צדיק: לזכות צדי״ק יסוד עולם, אדמו״ר שליט״א
מליובאוויטש . . . : ביאורים ודיוקים בשו״ע או״ח ושו״ע הרב / אלימלך יוסף
סילבערבערג. ניו יורק: המחבר, 1992.

ספר מאיר עיני חכמים, מהדורא תליתאי . . . על התורה ועל המועדים
בדרך חסידות ומוסר . . . / מאיר יחיאל האלשטוק. ניו יורק: י. מאנדעלבוים,
תשנ״ג.

מאמר התקשרות והמשך . . . / אברהם משה רבינוביץ. ארה״ב: מכון
להוצאת ספרי רבוה״ק, תשנ״ג.

ספר מאמר מרדכי על פורים: מאורות מרדכי על חנוכה / מרדכי אליהו
סמיילאוויץ. ויקליף: ישיבת טלז, תשנ״ג.

מגילת אסתר עם דברות קודש מאת רבי אהרן אויש, אבדק״ק לופעני ומבנו

רבי יחיאל אויש, אבדק"ק וואלקאן . . . נלקט ונסדר ע"י משולם זושא יצחק
נפתלי אויש. ניו יורק: זושא אויש, תשנ"ד.

מגילת אסתר עם פירוש על דברי חז"ל המובאים במדרש אסתר רבתי
ובילקו"ש וכו' וכן ביאור בפשטות המקרא . . ., עם מ"מ ופיסוק מלא ע"י משה
פלאהר / אלישע גאליקו. לייקווד: מכון אבני שוהם, תשנ"ד.

מגלת רות, עם פירוש ויאמר לקוצרים: הערות ובאורים ורעיונות / אליעזר
גינזבורג. ניו יורק: מחבר הפירוש, תשנ"ד.

ספר מהר"ם סופר: חלק ראשון: על התורה, חלק שני: שו"ת וחידושי
סוגיות . . ", בתוספות . . . ליקוטי בתר ליקוטי וגם מכתי"ק המחבר / . . .
משה סופר. ניו יורק: יואל אייליאוויטש, תדש"ן (בחלקו צילום תרפ"ח).

מחברת שלום ושלווה: מאמר שבת שלום: סנסן מחיבורי על מועדי
השנה . . . פסוקים ומאמרי חז"ל בדרך פרד"ס מבוארה לכבוד שמחת חתן
וכלה . . . / שלום וייס. ניו יורק: המחבר, תשנ"ג?

מחזור שבועות, עם פירוש דברי יואל, מלוקט מספרי . . . מרן יואל
טייטלבוים, ונלוים אליו מנהגי קודש . . . קרית יואל: הוצאת דמתה לתמר,
תשנ"ב.

ספר מטיב נגן . . .: ביאור טוב ויפה על כל הזמירות של שבת . . . / אברהם
הכהן. ניו יורק, תשנ"ד? (בחלקו צילום תרל"ט).

ספר מילואים לספר מראי מקומות לספר משנה תורה, הוא היד החזקה לרבינו
משה ב"ר מיימון, רמב"ם. ניו יורק: קהת, תשנ"ג (מהדורה חדשה).

ספר מימיני מיכאל: ביאורים ובירורים בסוגיות הש"ס ושיטות הראשונים
וגדולי הפוסקים במסכת פסחים / מיכל קלאגסבאלד. מאנסי: המחבר, תשנ"ד.

ספר מנהג ישראל תורה: מטרתו להראות מקור טהור למנהגי ישראל,
ובמיוחד בעניינים הנוגעים להלכה . . . על פי סדר הסימנים בשולחן ערוך
אורח חיים . . . / יוסף לעווי. ניו יורק: המחבר, תשנ"ג.

ספר מנחת שמואל: בעיות הזמן בהלכה: ליקוטי ענינים אקטואליים מספרי
שו"ת והלכה . . . / שמואל כאשכראמ[ן] (מלקט). (אטלאנטא) יוניאן סיטי:
המלקט, תשנ"ג.

המסורה הגדולה לתורה מידי שמואל בן יעקב בכתב יד (בעריכת) מרדכי
ברויאר / שמואל בן יעקב. ניו יורק: קרן מנשה רפאל ושרה ליהמן, תשנ"ב.

מסכת אבות עם פירוש רבינו עובדיה מברטנורא, ועל צבאם חונים . . . זרעא
חיא והוא ילקוט אמרי קודש מספרי . . . רבינו יוסף מאיר בעל אמרי יוסף
ובנו . . . רבינו יצחק אייזיק בעל חקל יצחק / יוסף מאיר [וייס]. ניו יורק:
ח.י. פרידמאן, 1993.

ספר מעוז לתם (משלי י':כ"ט): שיחות מוסר שנאמרו בישיבת רבינו יעקב
יוסף-עדיסאן / יצחק ליב קירזנר. ניו יורק: ברוך גרין ואחרים, תשנ"ב.

מעין חי . . .: רעיונות ושיחות לילדים ולנוער, מעובד על-פי שיחותיו / . . .
מנחם מענדל שניאורסאהן. ניו יורק: קהת, תשנ"ג-

ספר מצווה ועושה: חיבור גדול . . . לברר דיני וטעמי המצוות שמתחייב
בהם כל אדם מישראל מיום הכנסו לעול המצוות . . . / שמואל דוד

פריעדמאן. ניו יורק: המחבר, 1994.

ספר מצות המלך על ספר המצות להרמב"ם: יסודו לבאר שיטת הראשונים
וביחוד שיטת הר"מ בכל מצוה ומצוה, עם מקורות והערות בשם עין המלך /
עזריאל צימענט. ניו יורק: המחבר, תשנ"ב.

ספר מקור חיים: והוא פירוש על ספר חסידים (מכורך עם ספר החיים) /
שבתי ליפשיץ. ניו יורק: ש.י. פרייזלער, תשנ"ב.

ספר מראה כהן . . .: כולל כמה עניני תורה ומוסר ותפלה ששיכים ליום
הכפורים / שמרי' שולמאן. ניו יורק: המחבר, תשנ"ג.

ספר מראה משה: תוכו רצוף שאלות ותשובות בפלפול והלכה וחידושים
וביאורים בסוגיות הש"ס . . . / משה פירסט. ניו יורק: נכדי המחבר, תשנ"ג
(מהדורה שניה).

ספר מרגניתא טבא . . . על התורה, חידושי גמרא ותוס' וחידושי מדרשים /
דוד בן אריה ליב. ניו יורק: אחים גאלדענבערג, תשנ"ג (מהדורה חדשה).

ספר משבצות זהב: מאמרי חסידות על פרשת השבוע ומועדי השנה / מרדכי
מנשה זילבער. ניו יורק: ביהמ"ד תולדות יהודה, תשנ"ב.

ספר משיבת נפש על התורה / חיים דוב וויסבערג. ניו יורק: המחבר,
תשנ"ב.

משנה. משניות מסכת בכורים, עם פירוש רבינו עובדיה מברטנורא, ועם פירוש
סייעתא דשמיא . . . על ידי שמעי' גרינבוים. ניו יורק: הוצאת פירוש המשנה,
תשנ"ד.

משנה. משניות מסכת יומא, עם פירוש רבינו עובדיה מברטנורא ועם פירוש
בסגנון קל . . . בשם סייעתא דשמיא יקרא, חובר על ידי שמעי' גרינבוים. ניו
יורק: הוצאת פירוש המשנה, תשנ"ד.

משנה בפרק האיש מקדש: דעת תורה ובירור הלכה . . . כיצד להתנהג
מתחילת השידוכין עד אחר החתונה . . . (מכורך עם ספר בית רחל משנה
הלכות) / מנשה קלין. ניו יורק: מכון משנה הלכות גדולות, תשנ"ב.

ספר משנה הלכות, מדור התשובות / מנשה קלין. ניו יורק: מכון משנה
הלכות גדולות, תשנ"ב (מהדורה תניינא).

ספר משנת הלוי על מסכת קידושין: כולל הערות והארות, חידושים וביאורים
ועיקרי דברי הראשונים והאחרונים . . . דף על דף / רפאל שארר. מאנסי:
המחבר, תשנ"ד.

ספר משנת רבית על הלכות רבית והיתר עיסקא, כולל כל ההלכות
והדינים . . . עם מקורי הדינים, הערות והארות ונוסחאות הית"ע בלה"ק
ואנגלית / אברהם משה לבנוני (מלקט). ניו יורק: המלקט, תשנ"א.

נבואת חבקוק עם פירוש רבינו אליהו מוילנא, נערך על ידי ראובן דוד גרשון
/ אליהו בן שלמה. ויקליף: העורך, תשנ"ב.

ספר נחלי בינה על יום הושענא רבה ועל סדר הושענות: ליקוטים יקרים . . .
/ חיים יהודה כ"ץ (עורך). ניו יורק: העורך, תשנ"ב.

ספר נחלי בינה על מצות נטילת ארבעה מינים . . . / חיים יהודה כ"ץ. ניו
יורק: המחבר, תשנ"א.

ספר נחלי בינה על שמיני עצרת, שמחת תורה, הקפות, אסרו חג, שבת
בראשית: ליקוטים יקרים ונעימים . . . / חיים יהודה כ"ץ (מלקט). ניו יורק:
המלקט, תשנ"א.

ספר נחלי דבש על מסכת יבמות / דוד וילמן. לייקווד: המחבר, תשנ"ב.

ספר נחלת יעקב לחדש אדר ולימי פורים: פנינים יקרים . . . / יעקב חיים
אמסעל. ניו יורק: המחבר, תשנ"ד.

ספר נחלת יצחק: חידושים על מסכת גיטין: פלפולא דאורייתא לבאר דעתם
של רבותינו הראשונים והאחרונים / אברהם יגיד. מאנסי: המחבר, תשנ"ג.

נחמו נחמו עמי: קונטרס הכולל אגרת תנחומין ל־יהונתן אייבשיץ, סדר
לימוד משניות ואמירת קדיש ומאמר תועלת החסד לנפש. ניו יורק: מפעל
גומלי חסד באיאן, תשנ"ג.

ספר נטעי גבריאל־אהל רייזל: הלכות אבילות: מכיל דיני ומנהגי יום
פקודתו של אדם עלי אדמות . . . / גבריאל ציננער. ניו יורק: המחבר, תשנ"ג.

ספר נטעי גבריאל: הלכות חנוכה: מכיל הלכות ומנהגי חנוכה, ההדלקה
וחיובה, המנורה השמן והפתילות . . . / גבריאל ציננער. ניו יורק: המחבר,
תשנ"ד (מהדורה חדשה).

ספר נטעי גבריאל: הלכות נשואין: מכיל הלכות ומנהגי חתן וכלה, החל
משבת קודם החתונה . . . / גבריאל ציננער. ניו יורק: המחבר, תשנ"ג (מהדורה
חדשה).

ספר נטעי גבריאל: הלכות ערב פסח שחל בשבת . . . / גבריאל ציננער. ניו
יורק: המחבר, תשנ"ד (מהדורה חדשה).

ספר ניב שמעון: לקט חידושי אגדה על התורה ומועדים (מכורך עם קונטרס
עדות ביהוסף) / שמעון קורניצר. ניו יורק: אליהו כהן, תשנ"ג.

נר יונה וידהודית: אוסף פירושים על ספר מצות גדול־סמ"ג, לרבינו משה ב"ר
יעקב מקוצי: על הלכות חנוכה, עם חידושי רבינו רבי אליהו מזרחי . . .
לייקווד: מכון משנת רבי אהרן, תשנ"ג.

ספר נר מערבי: חידושי תורה בעניני מועד. ניו יורק: כולל דוועסט סייד,
תשנ"ב.

ספר נר למשפט מסכת סנהדרין: שיעורי הלכה שנאמרו בישיבת בית יוסף
ביליסטוק נברידוק, ברוקלין / יעקב חיים יפהן. ניו יורק: המחבר, תשנ"א.

סדר הגט מאיר עיני חכמים: סדר גט ראשון — מיד הבעל ליד האשה, סדר
גט שני — מיד הבעל ליד השליח / יהושע העשיל וואלהענדלער. ניו יורק:
המחבר, תשנ"א.

סדר הדלקת נר חנוכה על פי מנהגי ספינקא, ונלוה אליו ספר אמרי
יוסף . . . מאת יוסף מאיר . . . בק"ק ספינקא, וגם ילקוט אמרות טהורות
מבנו . . . יצחק מאיר, בעל חקל יצחק. ניו יורק: הוצאת ספרי בית ספינקא,
תשנ"ג.

סדר הדלקת נר חנוכה, עם מנהגי קודש וליקוטי דברי יואל . . . עם חידושי
תורה . . . מאת . . . מרן יואל טייטלבוים. קרית יואל: הוצאת דמתה לתמר,
תשנ"ג.

סדר (נוסח) הושענות לסוכות ולהושענא רבה, עם כל סדר התפלה להושענא
רבה כאשר נהגו בבית מדרשם של רבותינו מסיגגעט וסאטמאר . . . „ עם פירוש
צלא דמהימנותא . . . קרית יואל: הוצאת פאר, תשנ״ג (מהדורה שניה).

סדר הושענות, עם פירוש נחלי בינה (מכורך עם ספר נחלי בינה) / חיים
יהודה כ״ץ (מפרש). ניו יורק: חיים יהודה כ״ץ, תשנ״ב.

סדר הכנסת ספר תורה עפ״י מנהג רבותה״ק מבעלזא: פנינים לפרשת
השבוע . . . ניו יורק: ביהמ״ד לומדי תורה דחסידי בעלזא, תשנ״ב.

סדר הקבלה: היא הפתיחה לפירושו למסכת אבות. יוצא לאור מחדש על פי
כת״י לנינגראד, עם מבוא, שינויי נוסחאות . . . מאת שלמה זלמן הבלין /
מנחם בן שלמה מאירי. קליבלנד: מכון אופק, תשנ״ב.

סדר הקפות המפורש לשמיני עצרת ושמחת תורה עפ״י נוסח בית סיגגעט
וסאטמאר, עם ילקוט אמרי קודש . . . ממרן בעל דברי יואל, ועם לקוטים
יקרים . . . עצי תומר. ניו יורק: הוצאת ספרים מכון קודש הילולים, תשנ״ב.

סדר הקפות (ונלוה אליו מנהגים מחג הסוכות), נוסח נדבורנא, מאת כבוד
אדמו״ר . . . מרדכי מנדבורנא . . . ניו יורק: מוסדות תפארת איתמר
דבישטינא, תשנ״א (מהדורה חדשה).

סדר הקפות לשמיני עצרת ושמחת תורה הנאמרים בבית מדרשו של אדמו״ר
מבאבוב . . . מיוסד עפ״י נוסח של . . . מרן חיים הלברשטאם. ניו יורק: חברה
קנין ספרים של מתיבתא עץ חיים, תשנ״ד.

סדר יום שלש עשרה מדות: תוכו רצוף סדר קריאת הקרבנות עם קונטרס
שיח שפתותינו לברר ולבאר ענין קריאת פרשיות הקרבנות . . . / חיים יעקב
מאיר רבין (עורך) / ניו יורק: מכון „סגולה", תשנ״ג.

סדר נוסח האושפיזין וזמירות לחג הסוכות וסדר נוסח ההקפות . . . כאשר
נהגו בבית מדרשם של רבותינו מסיגגעט וסאטמאר . . . עם פירוש צלא
דמהימנותא . . . קרית יואל: ישראל חיים שטעסיל – הוצאת פאר, תשנ״ג.

סידור יצחק יאיר השלם: כולל כל התפילות של כל השנה . . . ניו יורק:
ארטסקרול-מסורה, תשנ״ג.

סידור כתר מלכות החדש, נוסח ספרד: כולל התפלות לכל השנה . . . ניו
יורק: זונדל ברמן, תש״ן.

סדור מנחם אלעזר, נוסח ספרד: כולל תפלות לכל השנה על פי נוסח ומנהגי
אדמו״ר . . . חיים אלעזר שפירא, אבדק״ק מונקאטש . . . נערך ע״י ירוחם
שמחה פרידמאן. ניו יורק: ירוחם שמחה פרידמאן, תשנ״ב.

סידור מעדני אשר: הוגה וסודר מחדש . . . עפ״י נוסח הרוו״ה והגר״א וע״פ
פסקי המשנה ברורה . . . ניו יורק: וויינרעב, תשנ״ג.

ספריית ליובאוויטש: סקירת תולדותיה על פי מכתבים, תעודות וזכרונות /
שלום דב לעווין. ניו יורק: קהת, תשנ״ג.

ספר סתרי תורה: אמרות טהורות, מאמרים קדושים . . . וסדר מגילת יוחסין /
ישכר בערצי בן יצחק. ניו יורק: מ. ווייסבלום, תשנ״ב (מהדורה חדשה).

ספר עבודת הלוי: דרושים על התורה . . . / אכסיל ראד בן יוסף סג״ל. ניו
יורק: אחים גאלדענבערג, תשנ״ד (מהדורה שניה).

ספר עטרה למלך: כולל מאמרים והערות, השקפות והדרכות ... / אברהם
יעקב פאם. ניו יורק: תלמידי המחבר, תשנ״ג.

ספר עם מרדכי על מסכת ברכות, ונלוה אליו קונטרס על עלא על עניני
אבלות / מרדכי יצחק וויליג. ניו יורק: ישיבה אוניברסיטה, 1992.

ספר עמק הבכא: ספר הקורות והתלאות אשר עברו על בית ישראל / יוסף בן
יהושע, הכהן. טורונטו: אוצרנו, תשנ״ב (מהדורה חדשה).

ספר ענף עץ אבות וויזשניץ סקווירא לזכרון ... רבי ישראל בער ליש. ניו
יורק: עוזר דוב פעלדמאן, תשנ״ב.

ספר עצי חיים על מסכת גיטין (מכורך עם ספר ייטב לב על מסכת גיטין) /
חיים צבי טייטלבוים. ניו יורק: מ.מ. טייטלבוים, תשנ״ג.

עקבי אהרן ופשר דבר על סדר נשים, הכולל מסכתות יבמות, כתובות, נדרים,
נזיר, סוטה, גיטין וקידושין: שלש מאות ושבעים ושתים הארות והערות ... /
יעקב ווהל (מלקט). ניו יורק: המלקט, 1993.

ספר ערוך השלחן על יורה דעה הלכות נדרים ושבועות מסימן ר״ג עד סימן
רל״ט / יחיאל מיכל עפשטיין. הובוקן: כתב, תשנ״א.

ספר פועל צדק: והוא סדר תרי״ג מצות ... ודרוש יקר מהנ״ל על „כמה
מעלות טובות למקום עלינו" (הגדת ליל פסח) ... / שבתאי בן מאיר, הכהן.
ניו יורק: עולם הספרים, תשנ״ד (מהדורה מחודשת).
(פירוש על ספר איוב). Commentary on the Book of Job / Moses
Kimhi. Atlanta: Scholars Press, 1992.

ספר פרי חיים ... אשר דרש מדי שבת ומועד / חיים קלוגר. ניו יורק: קהל
דברי חיים, תשנ״ג (מהדורה חדשה).

פרנס לדורו: התכתבות אליעזר ליפמן פרינץ עם חכמי דורו / אליעזר ליפמן
פרינץ. הובוקן: כתב, תשנ״ב.

ספר פתגמין קדישין מתורתו של ... מו״ה יעקב יצחק הלוי מלאנצוט ...
הנקרא בפי כל החוזה מלובלין: על התורה, מלוקט מספריו ... / יעקב יצחק
הורוויץ. מאנסי: יוסף יצחק ראזענפעלד, תשנ״ד.

ספר פתחי הלכה: כולל לקוטי דינים בהלכות ברכות, דיני עיקר וטפל, היסח
הדעת, שינוי מקום, קדימה בברכות וכללי כל ברכה ראשונה / בנימין
עובדיה פארסט (מלקט). ניו יורק: המלקט, תשנ״ב.

ספר צורת הבית: צורת בית המקדש העתיד הנראה ליחזקאל ... עם ציונים
וביאורים ... ע״י דוד שפוטץ: מגילת איבה ... להגיד הנס הגדול שניצל
ממות לחיים ... / יום טוב ליפמן בן נתן. ניו יורק: דוד שפוטץ, תשנ״ב
(מהדורה חדשה).

ספר צמח צדק: ספר השיחות / מנחם מענדל שניאורסאהן (1789-1866). ניו
יורק: קהת, תשנ״ג.

ספר קדושת הארץ: כולל חידושים וביאורים ופלפולים על ענינים מסדר
זרעים / אברהם שמשון בראדט. ניו יורק: המחבר, תשנ״ד.

ספר קדשי יחזקאל, מהדורא תנינא ... על התורה ועל המועדים (מכורך עם
ספר מאיר עיני חכמים) / יחזקאל הלשטוק. ניו יורק: י. מאנדעלבוים, תשנ״ג.

קובץ דמשק אליעזר. קונטרס א': כסליו תשנ"ג. ניו יורק: כולל דמשק
אליעזר, תשנ"ג.

קובץ י"א בניסן שנת הצדי"ק אל"ף. ניו יורק: קהת, תשנ"ב.

קובץ י"א בניסן שנת הצדי"ק בי"ת. ניו יורק: קהת, תשנ"ג.

קובץ משכנות יעקב. א': כסליו תשנ"ד. שיכון סקווירא: מכון משכנות יעקב,
תשנ"ד.

קובץ נר שלום: קובץ חידו"ת מגאוני וצדיקי קשישאי . . . „מרבנים ות"ח חברי
הכולל נר שלום דחסידי דאבוב במאנסי. מאנסי: כולל נר שלום, תשנ"ד.

קובץ סיפורים עם ביאורים והוראות בעבודת ה' – מלוקט משיחות . . . /
מנחם מענדל שניאורסאהן. ניו יורק: קהת, תשנ"ב.

קונטרס אגרת הפורים: הערות וביאורים על מצות מחיית עמלק, מגילת
אסתר ומסכת מגילה / משה יצחק וויסמאן. ניו יורק, תשנ"ג.

קונטרס אמרות טהורות / יואל טייטלבוים. ניו יורק: קופי קורנר, תשנ"ג.

קונטרס אני מאמין בענין האמונה בביאת המשיח והצפיי' לבואו / שמואל
חיים בלומינג. ניו יורק: המחבר, תשנ"ב.

קונטרס אסופות: דפי שערים מספרים שונים יקרי המציאות שיצאו לאור
מחדש . . . על ידינו המוציאים לאור אחים כ"ץ בוכבינדריי. ניו יורק: אחים
כ"ץ, 1991.

קונטרס בא יבא ברנה: חידושים ורמזים בתוה"ק / שמואל משה גאלד. ניו
יורק: המחבר, תשנ"ד.

קונטרס בדין מצות ישיבת סוכה / יצחק רייטפארט. ניו יורק: המחבר,
תשנ"ג.

קונטרס „בחדש השביעי": דרושים, ביאורים ומאמרים שנאמרו בחדש תשרי
בבית מדרשינו, בית מדרש קהל אגודת אברכים. ניו יורק: קהל אגודת
אברכים, תשנ"ג.

קונטרס בענין בל תוסיף ובל תגרע / יצחק רייטפארט. ניו יורק: המחבר,
תשנ"ג.

קונטרס בענין כפרת שעיר המשתלח / יצחק רייטפארט. ניו יורק:
המחבר, תשנ"ג.

קונטרס גט מעושה בערכאות – משנה הלכות: בירור נגד החוק לכוף לגרש
ע"י ערכאות ואיסור הליכה לערכאות והמסתעף לזה (מכורך עם שנו חכמים
בלשון המשנה) / מנשה קלין. ניו יורק: מכון משנה הלכות, תדש"ן.

קונטרס דרשות יהונתן: דרושים מתוקים, חידושים נפלאים ופלפולים
עמוקים . . . (בעריכת שניאור זלמן ליימן) / יהונתן אייבשיץ. ניו יורק: אחים
גאלדענבערג, תשנ"ד (מהדורה חדשה).

קונטרס דרשות מהרי"א / ישראל אברהם שטיין. ניו יורק: מנחם מענדל
שטיין, תשנ"ד.

קונטרס הבית דין צדק ובית המשפט בכפיה לגרש / ירמיהו בן אשר. ניו
יורק, תשנ"ג (מהדורה ב').

קונטרס היכל משה על ערב פסח שחל בשבת / נחום משה פארהאנד. ניו

יורק: ביהמ״ד היכל משה, תשנ״ד (מהדורה שלישית).

קונטרס הלכות ומנהגים לערב פסח שחל בשבת ע״פ מנהגי סקווירא /
יצחק שמעון וואזנער (עורך). שיכון סקווירא: העורך, תשנ״ד.

קונטרס המועדים / משה אהרן בלייך. ניו יורק: המחבר, 1993.

קונטרס הנה זה זה בא: ליקוט קטעים משיחות . . . (כ״ח ניסן תנש״א-ש״פ נח
תשנ״ב) ע״ד תקופתנו זו / מנחם מענדל שניאורסאהן. ניו יורק: קהת, תשנ״ב.

קונטרס הערות מסודרים ע״פ ערבי פסחי / אהרן שלמה צינמון. ניו יורק:
המחבר, תשנ״ב.

קונטרס הרבנית דבורה לאה: על דבר סיפור מסירת נפשה של הרבנית . . .
דבורה לאה, בת רבינו הזקן להצלת אילנא דחיי . . . מלוקט משיחות רבותינו
נשיאינו . . . ניו יורק: קהת, תשנ״ג.

קונטרס וטבל במים בענין שאלה חדשה העומדת על הפרק בדבר ההמצאה
שמכניסים מים שאובים-מים טמאים לתוך המקוה . . . / דוד ראזענבערג
(מלקט). מונרו: המלקט, תשנ״ב.

קונטרס וידבר דוד על עניני חודש ניסן ופסח / משה דוד שטיינוואראצל. ניו
יורק: אברהם חיים שטיינוואראצעל, תשנ״ד.

קונטרס וירא ישראל על הגדה של פסח: חידושים וביאורים וסנסנים
קצרים . . . / מרדכי ישראל סאמעט. ניו יורק: המחבר, תשנ״ד.

קונטרס זכרון ישעי׳: חלק א׳ (1) הערות בענין ברכת חתנים . . . „ 2) הערות
וברורים בענין ברכת הזימון . . . „ חלק ב׳: תשובות גדולי זמנינו והערותיהם
על הקונטרס הנוכחי . . . / אהרן יוסף בערגער. מאנסי: המחבר, תשנ״ג.

קונטרס זכרון תפארת חיים זלמן: כולל חידושים וביאורים על סוגיות הש״ס /
יהודה אריה מינץ. לייקוד: המחבר, תשנ״ב.

קונטרס זר זהב: ליקוטים ומרגליות, נופת צופים מאת רבותינו . . . בעניני ד׳
פרשיות . . . / יעקב קאפל שטראהלי (מלקט). ניו יורק: תפארת בחורים
ד׳באבוב, תשנ״ב.

קונטרס חידושי סוגיות / יואל טייטלבוים. ניו יורק: צבי הירש מייזליש,
תשנ״ג (מהדורה חמישית).

קונטרס ילקוט חילוקי תיבות: אוצר חילוקי תיבות וביאורי שמות
הנרדפים . . . / ברוך יהודה פריעדמאן (מלקט). ניו יורק: המלקט, תשנ״ד.

קונטרס לא תטע לך אשרה: להסביר חומר העון של הקמת „פאבליק סקול"
והחילול ה׳ שנעשה בקרית יואל בהקמתו . . . / משה דוב בעק. מאנסי:
המחבר, תשנ״ד.

קונטרס להודות ולהלל בעניני חנוכה, עם פירוש על תפלת על הנסים . . . /
שלמה ברעוודא (מלקט). ניו יורק: המלקט, תשנ״ג (מהדורה חדשה).

קונטרס להודות ולהלל: הלכות ברכת הגומל ליולדת, ביאורים והערות
בהלכה ואגדה בעניני הודאה וברכת הגומל . . . / שלמה זלמן פריעדמאן.
לייקוד: המחבר, תשנ״ג.

קונטרס ליל שמורים: ליקוט מדברי גדולי הפוסקים, הארות והערות ומראי
מקומות בעניני ליל הסדר לפי הסדר השלחן ערוך בסימן תע״ב-תע״ג / אברהם

שארר (מלקט) ניו יורק, תשנ״ב.

קונטרס ליקוטי שיעורים בעניני פסח / משה דוד שטיינוואראצל. ניו יורק:
חברה קנין ספרים דקהל שערי ציון ד׳באבוב, תשנ״ד.

קונטרס מגן וצנה החושף את האמת על כת הכופרים הנקראים „דרדעים"
ומגלה את פרצופו האמיתי של העומד בראשה. ניו יורק, תשנ״ד? (ברובו ד״צ).

קונטרס מועדים לשמחה על חג הסוכות: והוא ליקוט נפלא כולל בתוכו
פנינים, מנהגים וסיפורים בלה״ק ובאידיש . . . / יוחנן בירנהאק (מלקט).
מאנסי: המלקט, תשנ״ד.

קונטרס מילי דאבות על עניני נשואין / ישעי׳ ראזענבערג. ניו יורק: המחבר,
תשנ״ב.

קונטרס מילי דאבות: פירושים נאים ודרושים נפלאים על מסכת אבות / . . .
אהרן טייטלבוים. קרית יואל: תלמידי המחבר, תשנ״ג.

קונטרס מלחמת מצוה בענין חוק החדש הנקרא "Get Law": בו יבואר
בקצרה השתלשלות העניינים העומדים על הפרק . . . / דוד ראזענבערג
(מלקט). מונרו: המלקט, תשנ״ג.

קונטרס מצבת אבן: תורות הרה״ק מוהר״ר מרדכי . . . שפירא, אבד״ק
בערטש, מלוקט מכתבי בנו אלעזר שפירא על ידי נכדו זלמן ליב
אייכענשטיין / מרדכי שפירא. ניו יורק, תשנ״ד.

קונטרס מקור הברכה: קובץ הלכות על ערב פסח שחל בשבת והלכות פסח
הנוגעים לחברי ההצלה, הלכה למעשה ע״פ גדולי הפוסקים / אהרן ברוך
גאלדירינג. ניו יורק: המחבר, תשנ״ד.

קונטרס מקור טהרה על הלכות נדה: דינים, הלכות ומנהגים מספרי ראשונים
ואחרונים ומגדולי המורים . . . / אשר חיים שטרנבוך. ניו יורק: מכון יד
פנחס, תשנ״ג (מהדורה שניה).

קונטרס משאת שבת על הלכות רפואה בשבת, או״ח סימן שכ״ח: ביאורי
ובירורי מקורות ההלכה מן הגמרא, ראשונים ואחרונים / משה שמעון בינעטה
(עורך). מאנסי: כולל אברכים דחסידי בעלזא, תשנ״ב.

קונטרס משלוח מנות: בירורים בדין משלוח מנות ושושביניין לחופה, ונוסף
לזה מנהגי נישואין עפ״י מנהגי סטאלין קארלין / יהודה זבולון קליטניק. ניו
יורק: המחבר, תשנ״ד.

קונטרס נעשה ונשמע: ליקט על עניני תרי״ג מצות / אהרן צבי יוסף קליין
(מלקט). ניו יורק, תשנ״ב.

קונטרס ספר החיים על יום הדין של ראש השנה / גרשון ריבנר. לייקווד:
המחבר, תשנ״ג.

קונטרס עדות ביהוסף: חידושי אגדה על סדר במדבר, דרשות, חידושי
סוגיות ומכתבי תורה / יוסף נחמיה קורניצר. ניו יורק: אליהו כהן, תשנ״ג.

קונטרס עיונים בפרשה: ליקוט ביאורים וחידושים על עניני הלכה בפרשת
השבוע / אברהם שארר (עורך). ניו יורק: העורך, תשנ״ד־

קונטרס עקבי אהרן ופשר דבר על מסכת יבמות: ששים ותשעה הארות
והערות על נקודות וסוגיות מפורסמות הנלקטים מגדולי הראשונים והאחרונים

ומעט מזעיר הוספתי נופך משלי / יעקב ווהל. ניו יורק: המחבר, תשנ״ד.

קונטרס עקבי אהרן ופשר דבר על מסכת קידושין: ששים ושמונה הארות . . . / יעקב ווהל. ניו יורק: המחבר, תשנ״ד.

קונטרס ערב פסח שחל בשבת; דיני פרוזבול ושמיטה / יחזקאל ראטה. ניו יורק: שערי ציון קארלסבורג, תשנ״ד.

קונטרס פותח פתח: ביאורים והערות והארות על קונטרס פתח טוב-ליקוטי הלכות בנוגע לדיני מקוואות . . . (מאת) יוסף גרינוואלד (מכורך עם ספר שו״ת משפטים ליעקב) / יעקב יצחק נייאמאנן. ניו יורק: המחבר, תשנ״ב.

קונטרס צדי״ק למלך. ניו יורק, תשנ״ב-

קונטרס קול אריה על עניני חנוכה: קובץ חידושי תורה בהלכה ובאגדה מלוקט מספרן של גאוני וגדולי משפחת קול אריה . . . / יואל זיסמאן עהרענרייך (מלקט). ניו יורק: חברה מפיצי תורה ממשפחת קול אריה, תשנ״ד (מהדורה שניה).

קונטרס קיצור דיני ערב פסח שחל בשבת על-פי פסקי ומנהגי רבותינו הקדושים. ניו יורק: קהל מנחת אלעזר מונקאטש, תשנ״ד.

קונטרס תפארת אדם בענין הקפת הראש והזקן . . . בהוספת קונטרס על מכונת גלוח / ישראל מאיר, הכהן. ניו יורק: ועד תפארת אדם, תשנ״ב (בחלקו ד״צ).

קונטרס תקנת השבים / משה גרינוואלד. ניו יורק: משה יחזקאל שרגא גרינוואלד, תשנ״ד (מהדורה חדשה).

קונטרסי ישמח יהודה: כולל משא ומתן וביאורים על הדף בפרקים ממסכתות עירובין, חולין, נדה . . . / יצחק יהודה יאקובוביץ. לייקוּוד: המחבר, תשנ״ג.

ספר רונו ליעקב שמחה: הערות וביאורים על התורה, מועדים ומסכתות / יעקב שמחה אורליק. ניו יורק: המחבר, תשנ״ג.

רוקדים ובוכים: האמת על תנועת חב״ד / יורי ינובר. ניו יורק: משי, 1994.

ספר רני עקרה: מבאר הלכה ברורה . . . תקנת העגונות אחר כלות מלחמת העולם השני׳, תרצ״ח-תש״ה / הילל ליכטענשטיין. ניו יורק: יוסף ליכטער, תשנ״ג.

ספר רצון משה על אגדות ודרשות: דברים יקרים, אמרים נעימים . . . / משה שטיין. ניו יורק: מוסדות ראצפערט תפארת שמואל דוד, 1994.

ספר שאלות ותשובות אבני צדק / יקותיאל יהודה טייטלבוים. ניו יורק: ירושלים, תשנ״ג (צילום תרמ״ה עם הוספות).

שאלות ותשובות בענין הגאולה העתידה וביאת המשיח / שמואל חיים בלומינג. ניו יורק: המחבר, תשנ״ב.

ספר שאלות ותשובות דברי אור . . .: לברר ענינים שונים בד׳ חלקי השו״ע / יצחק הערשקאוויטש. ניו יורק: המחבר, תשנ״ג.

שו״ת מקדש ישראל על חג השבועות: כולל בירורים על שאלות המצויים בימי החג / ישראל דוד הארפענעס. ניו יורק: המחבר, תשנ״ג.

ספר שאלות ותשובות מקדשי השם . . . עם הגהות דברי צבי . . . / צבי

הירש מייזליש. ניו יורק: אלעזר מייזליש, תשנ״ג (מהדורה חדשה).

שאלות ותשובות משיב כהלכה על ארבעה חלקי שולחן ערוך (עם)
שאלות ותשובות משיב כהלכה החדשות / אברהם זאב וואלף פרענקל. ניו
יורק: נכדי המחבר, תשנ״ב (בחלקו צילום תרמ״ה).

ספר שאלות ותשובות משפטיך ליעקב . . . ונלוה אליו קונטרס על
הלכות טריפות . . . , ובתוכם הערות . . . בשם ויען יוסף מבן המחבר . . . /
יעקב יחזקאל גרינוואלד. ניו יורק: י.י. נimmann, תשנ״ב (מהדורה חדשה).

שו״ת נשמ״ת שבת (והוא ח״ד משו״ת מקדש השבת): כולל בירורי הלכות
בהל׳ שבת המצויים (השייכים לשו״ע סי׳ שי״ח-שכ״ז) / ישראל דוד
הארפענעס. ניו יורק: המחבר, תשנ״ג (מהדורה חדשה).

ספר שאלות ותשובות רבי אברהם שטנג, ובו תשובה לההגאון רבי חיים אחי
מהר״ל מפראג. יוצא לאור לראשונה מכת״י . . . (מכורך עם ספר שו״ת דברי
אור) / אברהם שטנג. ניו יורק: יצחק הערשקאוויטש, תשנ״ג.

ספר שארית ישראל: והמה ליקוטי אמרות טהורות . . . / ישראל דוב בער,
מוילדניק. ניו יורק, תשנ״ד.

שבח המועדים: והוא קיצור הלכות ומנהגי המועדים עפ״י מנהגי חב״ד /
שמואל הורוויץ (עורך). ניו יורק: העורך, תשנ״ג.

ספר שדה ברכה: מיוסד על מסכת ברכות לבאר דבר דבור על אופניו בגמרא,
רש״י ותוספות דף על דף . . . / שמואל דוד פריעדמאן. ניו יורק: המחבר,
תשנ״ג.

ספר השיחות, ה'ת״ש-ה'תש״ה / יוסף יצחק שניאורסאהן. ניו יורק: קהת,
תשנ״ב.

שיעורי רבי דוד ליפשיץ על מסכת חולין / דוד ליפשיץ. ניו יורק: תלמידי
המחבר, תשנ״ג.

ספר שירת דוד: ביאורים ופירושים על חמש מגילות / אהרן דוד גולדברג.
ויקליף: ישיבת טלז, תשנ״ד.

ספר שלום בחילך: חידושים וביאורים בסוגיות שונות / אלימלך אהרן פדר.
ניו יורק: המחבר, תשנ״ב.

שנו חכמים בלשון המשנה — משנה הלכות: בענין לימוד התורה בקדושה
ושלא להעתיק התורה מלשון הקודש ללשון העמים / מנשה קלין. ניו יורק:
מכון משנה הלכות, תדש״ין.

שערי חכמה העליונה: על החובה והזכות לעסוק בתורת החסידות, פנימיות
התורה בדורות האחרונים דוקא: משיחותיהם ומכתביהם של רבותינו נשיאי
חב״ד לדורותיהם / אברהם חנוך גליצנשטיין (עורך). ניו יורק: קהת, תשנ״ג.

ספר שערי רבית: פתיחת שער לעניני רבית ועיסקא / משה מנדל ברוס. ניו
יורק: המחבר, תשנ״ג.

ספר שעשועי תורה על סוגיות הש״ס ממס׳ יבמות, סנהדרין (פרק בן סו״מ)
ושבת ח״א . . . / יוסף שווארצמן. לייקוד: מכון יד ישראל, תשנ״ג.

שפע חיים: המדרש והמעשה: דברי תורה בהלכה ואגדה ושיעורים אשר דבר
בקדשו במשך זמן ביקורו בארה״ב בשנת תשל״א . . . / יקותיאל יהודה

הלברשטאם. ניו יורק: איגוד חסידי צאנז בארה"ב, תשנ"ג.

שפע חיים יהי אור: דברי תורה בהלכה ואגדה ליומין דחנוכה . . . אשר דבר
בקדשו בימי אורה ושמחה תשמ"ב / יקותיאל יהודה הלברשטאם. ניו יורק:
איגוד חסידי צאנז בארה"ב, תשנ"ב.

ספר שפתי מהר"ש (השלם) על התורה ומועדי השנה / שמואל ענגיל. ניו
יורק: ראובן ש. שארף, תשנ"ג (מהדורה רביעית).

ספר תורת אמך: והוא ביאור דיני באיסור דלימוד תורה לנשים, מקורו, מהותו,
גדריו ופרטי דיניו . . . ניו יורק: מכון מסורה והלכה, תשנ"ג.

ספר תורת אמת: בו יובא וידובר אודות תורתינו הקדושה . . . להגיע אליה
לאמיתה ולתכליתה . . . / אהרן ראזענבערג. מאנסי: המחבר, תשנ"ב.

ספר תורת המקדש: כולל חידושים וביאורים ופלפולים על ענינים מסדר
קדשים / אברהם שמשון בראדט. ניו יורק: המחבר, תשנ"ב.

תורת חיים על ספר בראשית / דובער שניאורסאהן. ניו יורק: קהת, תשנ"ג
(מהדורה ששית).

תורת מנחם: התוועדויות, שנת השי"ת . . . / מנחם מענדל שניאורסאהן. ניו
יורק: קהת, תשנ"ג.

תורת שלום: ספר השיחות, שיחות הקודש של . . . / שלום דובער
שניאורסאהן. ניו יורק: קהת, תשנ"ג (מהדורה רביעית).

ספר תיבת משה: הכולל הערות והארות, ביאורים ובירורים בעניני ט"ל
מלאכות שבת ועוד עניני שבת / משה בצלאל בראון. ניו יורק: המחבר,
תשנ"ג.

ספר תלת שמעתתא בעניני פורים ומסכת מגילה, עם מילי דאגדה ודברי
חיזוק / ישעיהו טוביה דירעקטאר. ניו יורק: המחבר, תשנ"ב (מהדורה ב').

ספר התמימים מיום ט"ו אלול תרנ"ז עד התחלת תש"י / יצחק גנזבורג
(מלקט). ניו יורק: קהת, תשנ"א (מהדורה חדשה).

ספר תנובת שדה על זמנים: הוא ביאור שיטות הפוסקים בזמן בין השמשות,
שיעור הנשף, י"ב שעות היום, גם הערות בדיני מקום גבוה / שמואל דוד
סיגל. בלטימור: המחבר, תשנ"א (מהדורה שניה).

ספר תפארת יהושע: מילי דאבות והנהגות קדושות, מלוקט מן ספר „זכרון
יהושע" ומספר „תולדות אנשי מופת" / יהושע העשיל פריעד. ניו יורק: דוד
שפוטץ, תשנ"ד.

ספר תפארת יואל . . .: עובדין טבין, אמרות טהורות והדרכות יקרות אשר
שמענו מפי . . . רבינו יואל טייטלבוים / אלימלך עוזר בודק. ניו יורק:
המחבר, תשנ"ג.

תקון קוראים המפואר: חמשה חומשי תורה, הפטרות, מגילות, מסלת הנקוד,
קצור הלכות ספר תורה. ניו יורק: יושר, 1994.

The compiler gratefully acknowledges the kind assistance of Leah Adler,
Zalman Alpert, Pearl Berger, Rebecca Malamud, and Rabbi Berish
Mandelbaum, all of the Yeshiva University Libraries, and Moshe and
Shlomo Biegeleisen, of the J. Biegeleisen Co.

משה זכריה בעקער
ZACHARY M. BAKER

דאָס ייִדישע בוך 1993־1994*

Yiddish Books 1993-1994

בעלעטריסטיק, אַנטאָלאָגיעס
FICTION, ANTHOLOGIES

בערגער, לילי. עכאָס פֿון אַ װײַטן נעכטן; דערצײילונגען, חומש־מעשׂהלעך,
עסייען און סקיצן. תל־אביב, ישׂראל־בוך, תשנ״ג — 1993. 228 זז׳.
די מחברין װױנט אין פּאַריז.

גאָרשמאַן, שׂירה. חנה׳ס שאָף און רינדער; ראָמאַן. תל־אביב, ישׂראל־בוך,
תשנ״ג — 1993. 199 זז׳, אילוס׳: מנדל גורשמן.
די מחברין איז געקומען קיין ישׂראל פֿון סאָװעטן־פֿאַרבאַנד אין די
1970ער יאָרן.

וואָרזאָגער, שלמה. אַ גט; נאָװעלע און צװײי דערצײילונגען. תל־אביב, ה.
לייװיק, תשנ״ג — 1993. 166 זז׳.
אינהאַלט: אַ גט. — אַ שנירעלע פּערל. — שכנים. דאָס 14טע בוך פֿון
מחבר.

יעלין, מאיר. בײַ די גלױענדיקע קױלן; דערצײילונגען אױף טעמעס פֿון דער
נאַצי־תקופֿה; דאָס געזאָגטע װאָרט: װעגן ייִדישן אומקום און
װידערשטאַנד. תל־אביב, ה. לייװיק, תשנ״ד — 1994. 302 זז׳.
דער מחבר, אַ געבוירענער אין סרעדניק, ליטע (1910), איז געקומען קיין
ישׂראל פֿון סאָװעטן־פֿאַרבאַנד אין די 1970ער יאָרן.

מאַש, יענטע. משנה מקום . . . דערצײילונגען. תל־אביב, י.ל. פּרץ, תשנ״ד —
1993. 262 זז׳.
זאַמלונג דערצײילונגען װעגן דער מחברינס באַסאַראַבער לאַנדסלײַט.

עסטרײַך, גענאַדי. מאַסקװער פּורים־שפּילן; דערצײילונגען. ראָװן ד׳וױילז,
פֿאַרלאַג „דרײַ שװעסטער", תשנ״ג — 1993. 151 זז׳.
נעמט אַרײַן 12 דערצײילונגען פֿון סאָװעטיש־געבױרענעם ייִדישן

---

* ביכער װאָס דער צונױפֿשטעלער האָט ניט געזען זײַנען באַצײכנט מיט אַ שטערנדל.
* Items not seen by the compiler have been asterisked.

שריבער.

קאַרפינאָװיטש, אַבֿרהם. װילנע. װילנע, מײַן װילנע; דערצײַלונגען. תל־אבֿיבֿ, י.ל.
פּרץ, 1993. 165 זז׳.

דאָס 10טע בוך פֿון מחבר.

רעכטער, ישעיהו. אין דער האַנט פֿון גורל; דערצײַלונגען. תל־אבֿיבֿ,
ישׂראל־בוך, תשנ״ג — 1992. 96 זז׳.

נעמט אַרײַן 7 דערצײַלונגען פֿון ישׂראלדיקן יידישן שריבער.

שלו־גאָרדאָן, חבֿיבֿה. צוריק צום שטאַם. תל־אבֿיבֿ, ישׂראל־בוך, תשנ״ג —
1993. 143 זז׳, פּאָרטרעט.

שפּריכװערטער, סקיצן, דערצײַלונגען און זכרונות. די מחברין איז
געבױרן געװאָרן אין ראשון־לציון, און אױפֿגעװאָקסן אין אַ יידיש־
רעדנדיקער הײם.

SHALEV-GORDON, HAVIVA. *Turning to the Roots.* Tel Aviv, Israel-Book,
1993. 143 p., port.

Proverbs, sketches, short stories and memoirs. The author was born
in Rishon Lezion, in a Yiddish-speaking home.

פּאָעזיע

POETRY

בנימין, ה. [הרשבֿ־הרושאָװסקי] טאַקע אױף טשיקאַװעס; געקליבענע לידער.
ראָװען ד׳װײלז, פֿאָרלאַג „דרײַ שװעסטער", תשנ״ד — 1994. 170 זז׳, אילוס׳:
מ. קופֿפֿערמאַן.

לידער, געשריבענע אין משך פֿון זעקס יאָרצענדליקער. דער מחבר, אַ
געבױרענער אין װילנע, האָט עולה געװאָרן קיין ישׂראל נאָך דער 2טער
װעלט־מלחמה. איצט איז ער פּראָפֿעסאָר פֿון ליטעראַטור בײַם יעיל־
אוניװערסיטעט.

BINYOMIN, H. [Harshav-Hrushovski] *For the Sake of Curiosity; Selected
Poems.* Rowen, Wales, Three Sisters Press, 1994. 170 p., illus.: M.
Kupferman.

Poems written during six decades. The author, a native of Vilna,
settled in Israel after World War II and is now professor of Comparative
Literature at Yale University.

בערנשטײן, משה. אױסגעלאָשענע ליכט; לידער און דערצײַלונגען. תל־
אבֿיבֿ, ה. ה. לייװיק, 1993. 30 זז׳, אילוס׳.

אַלבאָם־פֿאָרמאַט.

בר־חײַם, אסתּר. ערשטער בוך: פֿאַרװאָס לאָכט די כּלה? צװײטער בוך:
יורשלימער טיפֿן. ירושלים, נס, 1993. 211, [5] זז׳, אילוס׳, מוזיק.

דאָס ערשטער בוך אױף יידיש פֿון אַ מחברין װאָס װױנט אין ירושלים.

דזשאבלאָוסקי, אסתּר חרלף. דער הייליגער אוצר פֿון מײַן קוואַל.
JABLOWSKY, ESTHER CHARLOFF. *The Holy Treasure of My Source; a Collection of Poetry.* Compiled by Albert Jablowsky; English translation by Pearl Krupit. [New York], 1992. 87 p., ports.

Poems originally written in Yiddish, with English translations on facing pages. Most were first published in American Yiddish newspapers between 1940 and 1975.

האַלצבערג, אסתּר. אין זומערדיקײַט פֿון אויסגעמעקטער וועלט. [ישראל],
תשנ״ג – 1993. 189 זז׳, אילוס׳: ד״ר גרשון האַלצבערג.

לידער פֿון אַ דיכטערין וואָס איז געבוירן געוואָרן אין דער ליטע און איז
געקומען קיין ישראל פֿון סאָוועטן־פֿאַרבאַנד אין יאָר 1971.

ווערגעליס, אַרן. מײַן קלײנע אַנטאָלאָגיע: פֿון דער רוסישער דיכטונג און
צוואַנציקסטן יאָרהונדערט. העפֿט נומער 1. מאָסקווע, פֿאַרלאַג „די יידישע
גאַס״, 1993. 157 זז׳. (בײַלאַגע צום זשורנאַל „די יידישע גאַס״, נום. 3-4).

אײַנזאַמלונג פֿון קרוב 50 רוסישע דיכטער, איבערגעזעצט אויף יידיש.
VERGELIS, ARN. *My Small Anthology: Russian Poetry in the Twentieth Century.* Vol. 1. Moscow, Di Yidishe Gas, 1993. 157 p. (supplement to the journal "Di Yidishe Gas," no. 3-4)

Collection of poems by close to 50 Russian authors, in Yiddish translation.

זשיכלינסקי, רייזל. נײַע לידער. תּל־אביב, ישראל־בוך, תשנ״ג – 1993. 40
זז׳.

די 7טע לידער־זאַמלונג פֿון אַ דיכטערין וואָס האָט דעביוטירט אין
וואַרשע, 1936.

חרץ, מאיר, אנפֿאַס, אין פּראָפֿיל און הינטער די פּלייצעס. תּל־אביב, י.ל. פּרץ,
תשנ״ד – 1993. 176 זז׳, פּאָרטרעט.

לידער־זאַמלונג, ארויסג. אײן יאָר נאָך דער פּטירה פֿון מחבר.

טאוב, איטע. אין קלעם פֿון בענקשאַפֿט; לידער. ירושלים, פֿאַרלאַג „נס״,
תשנ״ג – 1993. 112 זז׳, אילוס׳: יאָסל בערגנער.

נעמט אַרײַן 3 לידער־ציקלען: בענקשאַפֿט; אין לײַכטן געמיט; יאָרן. די
מחברין וווינט אין ניו־יאָרק.

לודען, יוסף. געזאַמלטע לידער. 2טער באַנד. תּל־אביב, פּראָבלעמען, 1994,
133 זז׳, פּאָרטרעט.

דער 1טער באַנד איז ארויס אין יאָר 1990.

מאַגילנער, באָריס. ליקע־כאַמען; לידער. מאָסקווע, פֿאַרלאַג „די יידישע
גאַס״, 1993. 141 זז׳. (בײַלאַגע צום זשורנאַל „די יידישע גאַס״, נום. 1-2).

קאַטליאַר, יוסף. מײַן וועלט: לידער, משלים, מעשׂהלעך פֿאַר קינדער.
צונויפֿגעשטעלט און צוגעגרייט צום דרוק: ישראל רודניצקי; הקדמה: הירש
אָשעראָוויטש. תּל־אביב, י.ל. פּרץ, תשנ״ג – 1993. 265 זז׳, אילוס׳, פּאָרטרעט:
רפֿאל כּוואַלעס.

אײַנזאַמלונג פֿון די שאַפֿונגען פֿון פֿאַרשטאַרבענעם סאָװעטיש־ייִדישן
דיכטער (1908־1962).

קאַפּשטײן, ברכה. פֿון אַ גרױס גערעטעניש; לידער איבערגעזעצט פֿון
עברית אױף ייִדיש. תל־אביב, שלום, תשנ״ג — 1993. 79 זז׳.

לידער־אַפּקלײַב פֿון ישראלדיקע דיכטערס, איבערגעזעצט אױף ייִדיש.

קאַץ, מעינקע. דרײַ שװעסטער. 2טע אױפֿל. ראָװן ד׳װײַלז, פֿאַרלאַג „דרײַ
שװעסטער", תשנ״ג — 1993. 70 זז׳. אילוס׳: רימאַנטאַס דיכאַװיטשיוס
(װילנע).

די 1טע אױפֿל. איז ארױס אין מילװאָקי, 1932.

קאַץ, מעינקע. מעינקע סאָנעטן. ניו־יאָרק, דער שמיד, תשנ״ג — 1993. 57 זז׳.
אַרױסג. נאָך דער פּטירה פֿון דיכטער (1906־1991).

קערלער, יוסף. אַבֿי געזונט; לידער פֿון הײַנט און פֿון נעכטן. קלעזמאָרים־
טאַנץ און פּאָרטרעט פֿון מחבר: משה בערנשטײן. ירושלים, אײגנס, תשנ״ג —
1993. 106 זז׳.

GLATSTEIN, JACOB. *I Keep Recalling; the Holocaust Poems of Jacob Glatstein.* Tr. from the Yiddish by Barnet Zumoff; with an introduction by Emanuel S. Goldsmith; illustrations by Yonia Fain. [Hoboken, NJ] Ktav Publishing House, 1993. xxvi, 289 p., illus. port.

Text of poems in Yiddish and English (on facing pages). Includes 5 cycles of poems: Good Night, World; Shir — A Song; Divine Time; God's Thorn-Bush; Reb Leyvi Yitzkhok's Voice.

מוזיק, הומאָר

MUSIC HUMOR

באַגדאַנסקי׳ מאיר. לידער אַנטאָלאָגיע. [1993] Leibson's, London
94 זז׳, מוזיק.

געזאַנגען אױף ייִדיש (אין ייִדישן אלף־בית און לאַטײנישער
טראַנסקריפּציע).

בלאַך־לעדערער, לאה, רעד. די שענסטע געקליבענע ייִדישע לידער צום
זינגען. רמת־גן, 1992. 1 באַנד, מוזיק, פּאָרטרעטן.

נעמט אַרײַן אַן ערך 120 ייִדישע געזאַנגען (אין ייִדישן אלף־בית און
לאַטײנישער טראַנסקריפּציע).

סלוצקי־קאַהן, גרוניא. זינגט, קינדער! [מוזיק: שרה חזן.] מאָנטרעאַל, 1993.
109 זז׳, מוזיק, פּאָרטרעט.

נעמט אַרײַן לידער און געזאַנגען (טײל מיט נאָטן).

LEVITAN, RUTH. *Shlemiels—Shlimazls.* Written, tr. and adapted by Ruth Levitan. Brooklyn, 1993. 216 p., illus.: Jan Vidra.

Collection of Yiddish anecdotes, in transliteration.

OCHODLO, ANDRÉ HÜBNER. *Yiddish Songs.* Sopot, [Poland], The Art 2000
Foundation, 1993. 1 vol., illus., music + 1 tape cassette.

From a performance held on April 17, 1993, in the "Gdansk
Miniatura" Theater. Text of songs in transliterated Yiddish, Polish,
German and English.

ליטעראַטור־קריטיק, עסייען
LITERARY CRITICISM, ESSAYS

איזענבוד, משה, רעד. 50 יאָר יידישער „פֿאָלקס־צענטער" אין סידנעי.
סידנעי, אַרויסג. דורכן יידישן „פֿאָלקס־צענטער" אין סידנעי, 1993. 64, 19
זז'. אילוס'. פּאָרטרעטן.
זאַמבלאָך, אויף יידיש און טיילווײַז אויף ענגליש, געווידמעט אַ יידישן
צענטער וואָס איז געגרינדעט געוואָרן פֿון י.נ. שטיינבערג אין יאָר 1941. מיט
ביאָגראַפֿישע סקיצעס וועגן די בוירערס און טורערס וואָס זײַנען געווען
פֿאַרבונדן מיט צענטער.

AISENBUD, MOSHE, ed. *Jewish Folk Centre in Sydney: First Fifty Years 1941-
1991.* English text by Nate Zusman. Woollahra, Australia, Jewish Folk
Centre Library, 1993. 19, 64 p., illus., ports.

Collection, in Yiddish and partially in English, about a Jewish
community center in Sydney, founded by the Territorialist leader I. N.
Steinberg. Includes biographical sketches of personalities associated
with the center.

אליצקי, מ. עסיי און ליד. תל־אביב, ישראל־בוך, תשנ"ג — 1993. 117 זז'.
מיט אַ ספּעציעלער אָפּטייל, „אין מײַן ברודערס אָנדענק". נעמט אויך
אַרײַן „ברוך אליצקי: עסיי", פֿון יעקבֿ־צבֿי שאַרגעל.

*[בורג, יוסף.] אונטער אײן דאַך: יוסף בורג יובל־בוך. צונויפֿגעזאַמלט:
לעאָניד פֿינקעל. טשערנאָוויץ, א. שטיינבאַרג יידישע קולטור־געזעלשאַפֿט,
1992. 173 זז'.

וואַסערשטרום, יאַקוב. טײַערע נעמען. וואַרשע, דאָס יידישע וואָרט, 1993.
74 זז', פּאָרטרעטן.
קורצע עסייען וועגן 11 פֿון די גרעסטע יידישע שרײַבער.

טורניאנסקי, חוה, רעד. די יידישע ליטעראַטור אין נײַנצעטן יאָר־
הונדערטט; זאַמלונג פֿון יידישער ליטעראַטור־פֿאָרשנוג און קריטיק אין
ראַטן־פֿאַרבאַנד. אפּקלײַב און פֿאָרוואָרט: חנה שמערוק. ירושלים,
העברעיִשער אוניווערסיטעט אין ירושלים, ייִדיש־אָפּטייל; הוצאת ספרים
ע"ש י"ל מאגנס, תשנ"ג — 1993. 595 זז'.
נעמט אַרײַן 21 עסייען פֿון סאָוועטיש־ייִדישע קריטיקערס.

TURNIANSKY, CHAVA, ed. *Yiddish Literature in the 19th Century; an Anthology of Yiddish Literary Research and Criticism in the Soviet Union.* Selection and foreword by Chone Shmeruk. Jerusalem, The Hebrew University of Jerusalem, Department of Yiddish; Magnes Press, 1993. 595 p.

Includes 21 essays by Soviet Yiddish literary critics.

די ייִדישע גאַס; ליטעראַריש־קינסטלערישער כוידעש־זשורנאַל. נום. 1‏- הױפּט־
רעדאַקטאָר: אַ. װערגעליס. מאָסקװע, יאַנואַר 1993‏-

יורש פֿונעם זשורנאַל „סאָװעטיש הײמלאַנד", װאָס האָט אױפֿגעהערט
אַרױסצוגײן סוף 1991. נעמט אַרײַן דערצײילונגען, לידער און עסײען אױף
ייִדיש און רוסיש.

DI YIDISHE GAS; *Literary-Artistic Monthly.* No. 1- Editor-in-chief: A. Vergelis. Moscow, January 1993-

Successor to the journal "Sovetish Heymland," which ceased publication at the end of 1991. Includes stories, poems and essays in Yiddish and Russian.

סוצקעװער, אַבֿרהם. בײַם לײענען פּנימער; דערצײילונגען, דערמאָנונגען,
עסײען. אַפּגעקליבן און צוגעגרײט צום דרוק: אַבֿרהם נאָװערשטערן. תּל־
אָבֿיב, העברעיִשער אוניװוערסיטעט אין ירושלים, ייִדיש־אַפּטײל, תּשנ"ג —
1993. 301 זז, פּאָרטרעט: חײם אוריסאָן.

אַרױסג. צום 80סטן געבוירנטאָג פֿון גרױסן ייִדישן דיכטער.

SUTZKEVER, ABRAHAM. *Face Reading; Stories, Recollections, Essays.* [Selected by Abraham Nowersztern.] Jerusalem, The Hebrew University of Jerusalem, The Yiddish Department, 1993. 301 p., port.: Hayim Urison.

Published on the great Yiddish poet's 80th birthday.

ראָזשאַנסקי, שמואל. די טראַגיק און הערואָיִק פֿון 1492 און 1942 אין דער
ייִדישער ליטעראַטור. בוענאָס־איַרעס, ייִדישער װיסנשאַפֿטלעכער
אינסטיטוט — יִװואָ, תּשנ"ב — 1992. 30 זז.

סעפּאַראַט פֿון בוך „1492 . . . 500 יאָר נאָכדעם".

[שמערוק, חנא.] כמנהג אשכנז ופולין: ספר יובל לחנא שמרוק; קובץ
מחקרים בתרבות יהודית. עורכים: ישראל ברטל, חוה טורניאנסקי, עזרא
מנדלסון. [ירושלים], מרכז זלמן שזר לתולדות ישראל, תּשנ"ג — 1993. 428,
118 זז, פּאָרטרעט.

נעמט אַרײַן עסײִען װעגן ייִדיש און דער ייִדישער ליטעראַטור, ס'רובֿ פֿון
זײ אױף עברית און ענגליש, אַבֿער אױך טײילװיַיז אױף ייִדיש: געװידמעט
דעם אָנגעזעענעם ישראלדיקן ייִדישן ליטעראַטור־פֿאָרשטער.

[SHMERUK, CHONE.] *Studies in Jewish Culture in Honour of Chone Shmeruk.* Editors: Israel Bartal, Ezra Mendelsohn, Chava Turniansky. Jerusalem, The Zalman Shazar Center for Jewish History, 1993. 118, 428 p., port.

Essays about Yiddish and Yiddish literature, mostly in Hebrew or English, with some in Yiddish; dedicated to the distinguished Israeli Yiddish literary scholar.

זכרונות, ביאָגראַפֿיעס
MEMOIRS, BIOGRAPHY

בוכשטיין, דובה. פֿון רייזוויץ ביז ירושלים; זכרונות = מרייביץ עד ירושלים.
ירושלים, תשנ″ג — 1993. 181, 111 זז׳, פּאָרטרעטן.
אין ייִדיש און העברעיִש.

חײַמאָוויטש־הירש, מאַלי. מײַנע קינדער־יאָרן אין שאָטן פֿון חורבן. תל־
אביב, י.ל. פרץ, תשנ″ג. 1993. 73 זז׳.
זכרונות וועגן דער מחברינס קינדער־ און יוגנט־יאָרן אין ראַדעוויץ
(ראַדאַוץ), בוקאָווינע.

מינץ, מתתיהו. נײַע ציטן – נײַע לידער: בער באָראָכאָוו, 1914־1917. פֿון
עברית: בערל זרובבֿל. תל־אביב. י.ל. פרץ, תשנ″ד — 1993. 624 זז׳.
די העברעיִשע אויסגאַבע פֿון דער ביאָגראַפֿישער שטודיע וועגן דעם
באַוווּסטן פּועלי־ציוניסטישן טוער איז אַרויס אין 1988.

MINTZ, MATITYAHU. *New Times—New Tunes: Ber Borochov, 1914-1917.*
[From Hebrew: Berl Zerubavel.] Tel Aviv, I. L. Peretz, 1993. 624 p.

The Hebrew edition of this biographical study of the noted Poale Zion leader was published in 1988.

קאָפֿראָוו, אריזעל. מאָראַל, מוט און גלויבן. טאָראָנטאָ, אַרויסג. דורך אַ
קאָמיטעט, 1993. 10, 242 זז׳, אילוס׳, פּאָרטרעטן.
„די איבערלעבונגען פֿון אַ ייִדישער משפּחה" אין בעסאַראַביע. המשך פֿון
מחברס בוך „צווישן צוויי וועלט־מלחמות".

ייִדישע שפּראַך, פֿאָלקלאָר
YIDDISH LANGUAGE, FOLKLORE

גורי, י. סוף טוב, הכל טוב; קובץ פתגמים עברית, ייִדיש, רוסית, אנגלית =אַז
דער סוף איז גוט, איז אַלץ גוט; שפריכווערטער העברעיִש, ייִדיש, רוסיש,
ענגליש. ירושלים, תרבות: ירושלימער אוניווערסיטעט, אָפטיילונג פֿאַר
רוסישע לימודים, 1993. 63, 64 זז׳, אילוס׳: אירנה בת־צבי.
די פֿריִערדיקע אויסגאַבע (ירושלים, 1990) האָט אַרײַנגענומען
שפריכווערטער נאָר אויף עברית, ייִדיש און רוסיש.

GURI, Y. *All's Well that Ends Well; a Dictionary of Proverbs, English,
Russian, Yiddish, Hebrew = Vse Khorosho, Chto Khorosho*

Konchaetsia. Jerusalem, Tarbut, 1993. 64, 63 p., illus.: Irena Bat-Tsevi.

The previous edition (Jerusalem, 1990) included proverbs in Hebrew, Yiddish and Russian only.

צפֿתמן, שׂרה. רעד. ייִדישע פֿאָלקס־מעשׂיות פֿון מיזרח־אייראָפּע. ירושלים, ייִדיש־אָפּטייל, העברעיִשער אוניווערסיטעט, תשנ״ב — 1991. 196 זז׳, מאַפּעס.

‏„צונויפֿגעשטעלט . . . כּדי צו דינען ווי לייענ־מאַטעריאַלן פֿאַר. . . קורסן און סעמינאַרן וועגן דער ייִדישער פֿאָלקס־מעשׂה" (הקדמה).

ZFATMAN, SARA, ed. *Yiddish Folk Tales from Eastern Europe.* Jerusalem, Hebrew University of Jerusalem, Yiddish Department, 1991. 196 p., maps.

"Compiled... in order to serve as reading matter for... courses and seminars on the Yiddish folk tale" (Preface).

סודיט, שלום. גרויסער ווערטערבוך פֿון דער ייִדישער שפּראַך. נהריה, דפֿוס אופֿסט, 1992. 34 זז׳, פֿאַקסימ׳.

אָפּשאַצונגען וועגן דעם פּראָיעקט צונויפֿשטעלן אַן אויסשעפּיק ייִדיש־ ווערטערבוך.

קאַץ, הירשע־דוד. תּקני תּקנות; פֿראַגן פֿון ייִדישער סטיליסטיק. אָקספֿאָרד, פֿאָרלאַג „אָקספֿאָרדער ייִדיש", בשותּפֿות מיטן אָקספֿאָרדער צענטער פֿאַר העכערע העברעאישע סטודיעס, תשנ״ג — 1993. 349 זז׳, פֿאָרטרעטן, פֿאַקסימי׳.

‏„געבויט אויף פּרינציפּן וואָס זענען אויפֿגעשטעלט געוואָרן דורך דעם מחבּרס פֿאָטער, דעם ייִדישן פּאָעט מעינקע קאַץ ז״ל".

KATZ, DOVID. *Amended Amendments; Issues in Yiddish Stylistics.* Oxford, Oksforder Yidish Press, in cooperation with Oxford Centre for Postgraduate Hebrew Studies, 1993. 349., ports., facsims.

"Based upon principles established by the author's father, the Yiddish poet Menke Katz (1906-1991)."

קרישטאַלקע, שפֿרה שטערן. ייִדיש: אַ לעבעדיקע שפּראַך; אַ לערן־ פּראָגראַם פֿאַר לערער, טייל א. מאָנטרעאַל, [ייִדישע פֿאָלקסשולן און פּרץ־ שולן], 1992. 426 זז׳, אילוס׳.

נעמט אַריַין לידער, גראַמאַטישע איבונגען, שמועסן, מעשׂיות א״אַנד מאַטעריאַלן צו לערנען ייִדיש.

KRISHTALKA, SHIFRA SHTERN. *Yiddish: a Living Language; a Teaching Program for Teachers, Part A.* Montreal, Jewish People's and Peretz Schools, 1992. 426., illus.

Includes poems, grammatical exercises, conversations, stories and other materials for the teaching of Yiddish.

ריַיך, רבֿקה. לאָמיר לערנען ייִדיש; לערנבוך פֿאַר אָנהייבער. רמת־גן, אַרויסג. דורך דער ייִדיש־קאַטעדרע א.נ. פֿון רינה קאָסטא ביַים בר־אילן

אוניווערסיטעט: פֿאַרלאַג „ישראל־בוך", תשנ"ג — 1993. 104 זז׳.
הילפֿבוך פֿאַר ישראלדיקע תלמידים וואָס לערנען זיך יידיש.

REICH, RIVKA. *Yiddish Learn Book for Beginners*. Ramat Gan, Rina Kosta
Yiddish Chair at Bar-Ilan University; Israel-Book, 1993. 104 p.

Workbook for Israeli students of Yiddish.

שעכטער, מרדכי. יידיש צוויי; לערנבוך פֿאַר מיטנדיקע און וויטהאַלטערס.
ניו־יאָרק, ייִדיש־שפּראַכיקער רעסורסן־צענטער, ייִדיש־ליגע, 1993. 561, 23
זז׳, אילוס׳, מוזיק, מאַפּע.

די ערשטע אויפֿלאַגע פֿונעם לערנבוך איז אַרויס אין פֿילאַדעלפֿיע, 1986.

SCHAECHTER, MORDKHE. *Yiddish II; an Intermediate and Advanced
Textbook*. New York, Yiddish Language Resource Center, League for
Yiddish, 1993 xxiii, 561 p., illus. music, map.

The first edition of the textbook was published in Philadelphia.
1986.

UEDA, KAZUO. *Yiddisshugo kiso 6000 go [6000 Yiddish Words for Daily
Life]*. Tokyo, Daigakushorin Publishing House, 1993. xix, 407 p.

Words listed in alphabetical order: Yiddish (with Latin-alphabet
transcriptions) and Japanese equivalents.

חורבן

HOLOCAUST

גראַס, אַבֿרהם יקותיאל יודאַ הכּהן, צונויפֿשט. ספֿר חורבן אייראָפּע; אין
דער יידישער שפּראַך. [ברוקלין], באַר יהודה, 1993[1], 488, [14] זז׳, אילוס׳,
מאַפּעס.

אין 3 טיילן: מאורעות תרצ"ח-תש"ה; אין ליכט פֿון דער תורה; חרות על
הלוחות.

פֿײַטעלסאָן, אַלעקס (אַלטער). אין שטורעם און געראַנגל. ווילנע,
[ליטואַנוס], תשנ"ד — 1993. 420 זז׳, פּאָרטרעט.

זכרונות וועג חורבן־קאָוונע.

פֿײַנגאָלד, יהודה לייב. איך בין געבליבן לעבן; שילדערונגען פֿון אַ איד
וואָס האָט דורכגעלעבט די שרעקליכע יאָהרן פֿון תרצ"ט-תש"ה... לאָדזש
— וואַרשע — טרעבלינקע — אוישוויץ — בעלזן בערגן [!]. רעדאַקטירט און
בעאַרבעט דורך י. מאַנדל. ירושלים, י. מאַנדל, ה/תשנ"ג. 328 זז׳, אילוס׳,
פּאָרטרעטן.

זכרונות און פֿאַרצייכענונגען וועגן דער חורבן־תקופֿה.

[ריבאַטשוק, אַדאַ; מעלניטשענקאָ, וולאַדימיר.] דער רעקוויעם־בוך,
דער בוך פֿון אָנדענק. איבערזעצונג אַף ייִדיש: ה. פֿאַליאַנקער. קיעוו, 1991.
79 זז׳, אילוס׳.

קינסטלערישער אָנדענק-אַלבאָם, געווידמעט די אומגעקומענע ייִדן אין
באַבי-יאָר; אַרויסג. 50 יאָר נאָך דער גרויסער שחיטה. טעקסט אויף ייִדיש,
אוקראַיִניש, רוסיש און ענגליש.

[RYBACHUK, ADA; MELNICHENKO, VLADIMIR.] *Book —Requiem —Book —
Monument: In Memory of the Tragedy in the Babi Yar.* Kiev, 1991. 79
p., illus.

Album dedicated to the Jewish victims of the Babi Yar massacre,
published on its 50th anniversary. Text in Yiddish, Ukrainian, Russian
and English.

•שיין, בערל. מאָרגן וועט זײַן בעסער. Hallandale, FL, 1988 ,B. Shain
207 זז׳, פּאָרטרעטן.

וועגן מחברס איבערלעבונגען אין װײַסרוסלאַנד בעת דער 2טער וועלט-
מלחמה.

יזכּור-ביכער

MEMORIAL BOOKS

ספֿר יזכּור לקהילת לוקץ׳ (פּולין) = געדענק בוך פֿאַר די שטעטל לאָקאַטש. אסף:
אליעזר װערבה; ערך: שמעון מטלובסקי. ירושלים, שמעון מטלובסקי, תשנ״ג
1993. 98 [34] זז׳, אילוס׳, פּאָרטרעטן, מאַפּע. —

יזכּור-בוך, אויף עברית און ייִדיש, וועגן אַ וואָלינער שטעטל. נעמט אַרײַן
אַ הקדמה אויף ענגליש און אַ רשימה פֿון די קדושים.

LOKATCH (POLAND) MEMORIAL BOOK. Compiled by Eliezer Verba;
edited by Shimon Matlofsky. Jerusalem, Shimon Matlofsky, 1993.
[34], 98 p., illus., ports., map.

Memorial book, in Hebrew and Yiddish (with an English
introduction), about a Volhynian shtetl. Includes a list of Holocaust
victims.

מענדעלעוויטש, לעאָן/לייבל. פּנקס וואַשילקאָװער יזכּור בוך; אַ
ספּעציעלע אויסגאַבע װעגן לעבן, מאָרד און טויט פֿון אַ ייִדישן ישוב ...
איבערזעצט פֿון ייִדיש צו ענגליש: מאַרק לאַנגזאַם, בעני גאָטהײַנער.
מעלבורן, 1990. 339, 152 זז׳, אילוס׳, פּאָרטרעטן, מאַפּעס, פֿאַקסים׳.

צוויישפּראַכיקער באַנד (ייִדיש, ענגליש) וועגן אַ פּויליש שטעטל לעבן
ביאַליסטאָק. מיט רשימות פֿון די קדושים, אויף ייִדיש און ענגליש.

MENDELEWICZ, LEON. *The Wasilkower Memorial Book; Memories of Our
Town Wasilkow Which Has Been Annihilated by the Nazis.* Tr. from
Yiddish: Mark Langsam, Bene Gothajner. Melbourne, 1990. 152, 339
p., illus., ports., maps, facims.

Bilingual volume (Yiddish, English) about a town near Bialystok,

Poland. Includes lists of Holocaust victims, in Yiddish and English.

יקליין, הערי צבֿי. טשענסטאָכאָװ – אונדזער ירושה. מאָנטרעאַל, [הערי צבֿי קליין], 1993. 480 זז׳.

צוויישפּראַכיק (ייִדיש, ענגליש) בוך וועגן אַ פּויליש־ייִדישן ייִשובֿ. נעמט אַריַין זכרונות פֿון די ניצול־געװאָרענע ייִדישע קינדער פֿון טשענסטאָכאָװ.

שלנגר, יהודה [א"אַנד]. דברי ימי קהילות קושיצה. בני ברק, 1993. 92, [18], 340, 6 זז׳, אילוס׳, פּאָרטרעטן.

יזכור־בוך, אױף עברית, ייִדיש, ענגליש און אונגעריש, וועגן דער סלאָװאַקיש־ייִדישער קהילה קאַשוי (קאָשיצע). די ייִדיש־אָפּטיילונג איז געשריבן פֿון שרגאי פּרי: „500 יאָר אין קאַשוי – קושיצה; קורצע היסטאָרישע פֿאַקטן".

SCHLANGER, YEHUDA. *The Story of the Jewish Community of Kos&ice.* Tr. from the Hebrew: Gabriela Williams. Bene Berak, 1993. vi, 340, [18], 92 p., illus., ports.

Memorial book, in Hebrew, Yiddish, English and Hungarian, about a Slovakian Jewish community. Hungarian section by Görög Artur: "A Kassai Zsidoság története és gallériája"; Yiddish section by Shragai Peri: "500 Years in Kashoy —Kos&ice; Brief Historical Facts".

דערציִונג, קינדער־ליטעראַטור

EDUCATION, CHILDREN'S LITERATURE

*אידישע היסטאָריע; 1טער טייל: די ערשטע צוויי הונדערט פופֿציג יאָר פֿון די ניַיע ציַיט, פֿון גרוש ספֿרד ביז תקופֿת החסידות, ח׳רנ״ב – ח׳ת״ק. ירושלים, הוצאת מרגליות, מכון להוצאת ספרי חינוך ולימוד שע״י בית ברכה, מרכז מפעלי חינוך לבנות, תשנ״ב – 1992.

קיפֿניס, לעװין. אונטערן באָקסערבוים: פֿון ראַש־חשנה ביז פּסח; דערציילונגען פֿאַר קינדער, געשריבענע אין יודיש. תל־אביב, ישראל־בוך, 1993. 165 זז׳, פּאָרטרעט, אילוס׳: חײם רון.

KIPNIS, LEVIN. *Under the Carob Tree: [From Rosh Hashanah to Passover; Stories for Children, Written in Yiddish].* Tel Aviv, Israel Book, 1993. 165 p., port., illus.: Hayim Ron.

קיפֿניס, לעװין. אונטערן פֿיַיגנבוים: פֿון פּסח ביז ראָש־חשנה; דערציילונגען פֿאַר קינדער, געשריבענע אין יודיש. תל־אביב, ישראל־בוך, 1993. 167 זז׳, פּאָרטרעט, אילוס׳: חײם רון.

צוויי קינדערביכער פֿון אַ באַקאַנטן העברעיִשן שריַיבער װאָס האָט פֿריִער געשאַפֿן אין ייִדיש.

KIPNIS, LEVIN. *Under the Fig Tree: [From Passover to Rosh Hashanah; Stories for Children, Written in Yiddish].* Tel Aviv, Israel Book, 1993.

167 p., port., illus.: Hayim Ron.

Two children's books by a prominent Hebrew writer who earlier wrote in Yiddish.

רעליגיע

RELIGION

דער וועג צו שלימות; הערליכע ארטיקלען, טייערע מוסר רייד, געקליבענע
געדאנקען, לאגישע ווערטלעך, אמת'ע מעשיות, שיינע משלים,
ארויסגענומען פון מדרשי חז״ל און ספרי מוסר וחסידות. ברוקלין,
צוזאמענגעקליבען און ארויסגעגעבן דורך הוצאת זרע אהרן, תשנ״ד —
[19]93. 408 זז׳, אילוס׳.

אויסגעסדרט לויט פארשידענע טעמעס: אמת, אכילה, כיבוד אם ואם,
קנאה א״אנד.

[יעקב בן יצחק אשכנזי, פון יאנאװו]. ספר צאינה וראינה המקורית; א
פירוש אויף די פרשיות התורה... איבערגעארבעט און ארויסגעגעבן דורך
ר' יעקב משולם גרינפעלד. [ברוקלין], הוצאת עטרת, תשנ״ג — [19]93. 3 בענד
(576, 576, 576 זז׳).

אויך צוגעגעבן: „מוסר און מדות" און „קיצור תרי״ג מצות".

ניסנזאהן, ש. דאס מלכות'דיגע חסידות; א באשרײַבונג פון דעם הייליגען
ריזשינער רבין׳ן רבי ישראל זצוקלל״ה מיט זײַנע הייליגע קינדער זי״ע.
איבערגעארבעט און ארויסגעגעבן דורך ר' ראובן ש. שארף. ברוקלין,
תשנ״ד. 346 זז׳.

אנגעשריבן און צום ערשטן מאל ארויס אין ווארשע, תרצ״ז [1936/37].

פערקאוויטש, כואן; פראנקא, סוסאנא; פאלאטא, סעסאר. די פינף
מאגיקער פון נאטרע'דאם; הונדערט יאר פאר פינף אויגנבליק אן צײַט.
איבערזעצונג: איידל מייקלער. [בוענאס-אירעס], גאלדענע אויסגאבעס פון
דער בוענאס אירעסער יאגא-שול, 1993. 101 זז׳.

מיסטישער ווערק, איבערגעזעצט פון שפאניש.

TECHINAS; a Voice from the Heart, "As Only a Woman Can Pray". [Ed. by] Rivka Zakutinsky. Brooklyn, Aura Press, 1992. 430 p.

In Yiddish and English.

Anglo-Jewish Books
1993-1994

BIBLE STUDIES

BOSETTI, ELENA. *Yahweh: Shepherd of the People–Pastoral Symbolism in the Old Testament*. Tr. from the Italian by G. La Spina. Slough: St Pauls, 1993. 174 p.

BROWN, RAYMOND. *Message of Deuteronomy*. Leicester: Inter-Varsity, 1993. 288 p. (Bible Speaks Today Series).

CAVE, DAVE. *Ezra/Nehemiah: Free to Lead*. Nottingham: Crossway Books, 1993. 192 p. (Crossway Bible Guides, 4).

COLLINS, JOHN J. *Daniel*. London: SCM Press, 1994. 528 p.

CRYER, FREDERICK H. *Divination In Ancient Israel and its Near Eastern Environment: A Socio-Historical Investigation*. Sheffield: Sheffield Academic Press, 1994. 330 p. (JSOT Supplement Series, 142).

DENNIS, TREVOR. *And Sarah Laughed: Women in Old Testament Storytelling*. London: SPCK, 1993. 176 p.

DICOU, BERT. *Edom, Israel's Brother and Antagonist. Obadiah and the Other Oracles Against Edom, and the Jacob-Esau Stories in Genesis*. Sheffield: Sheffield Academic Press, 1994. 250 p. (JSOT Supplement Series, 169).

FRITZ, VOLKMAR. *An Introduction to Biblical Archeology*. Sheffield: Sheffield Academic Press, 1994. 240 p. (JSOT Supplement Series, 172).

GRAEME, AULD A. *Kings Without Privilege: David and Moses in the Story of the Bible's Kings*. Edinburgh: T & T Clark, 1994. 224 p.

KAMESAR, ADAM. *Jerome, Greek Scholarship, and the Hebrew Bible: A Study of the Quaestiones Hebraicae in Genesim*. Oxford: Clarendon Press, 1993. 240 p.

LIMBURG, JAMES. *Jonah*. London: SCM Press, 1993. 128 p. (Old Testament Library).

MASON, REX. *Zephaniah, Habakkuk, Joel*. Sheffield, JSOT Press, 1994. 128 p. (Old Testament Guides).

PARKER, T.H.L. *Calvin's Old Testament Commentaries*. Edinburgh: T & T Clark, 1994. 256 p.

PRICE, CHARLES W. *Joshua: Free to Follow*. Nottingham: Crossway

Books, 1993. 192 p. (Crossway Bible Guides).

RAD, GERHARD VON. *The Message of the Prophets.* London: SCM Press, 1993. 188 p.

ROBINSON, GNANA. *Let Us be Like the Nations: 1 and 2 Samuel.* Musselburgh: Handesel Press, 1993. 304 p. (International Theological Commentary on the Old Testament).

SAWYER, JOHN F.A. *Prophecy and the Biblical Prophets.* 2nd rev. ed. Oxford: Oxford Univ. Press, 1993. 184 p. (Oxford Bible Series).

STRACK, H.L. and G. STEMBERGER. *Introduction to the Talmud and Midrash.* Tr. by Markus Bockmueh. Edinburgh: T & T Clark, 1994. 412 p.

HISTORY AND BIOGRAPHY

AMISHAI-MAISELS, ZIVA. *Depiction and Interpretation: The Influence of the Holocaust on the Visual Arts.* Oxford: Pergamon Press, 1993. 567 p.

Antisemitism World Report 1993. London: Institute of Jewish Affairs, 1993. 182 p.

BOSWORTH, R.J.B. *Explaining Auschwitz and Hiroshima: History Writing and the Second World War, 1945-1990.* London: Routledge, 1993. 272 p. (New International History Series).

BURLEIGH, MICHAEL, ed. *Confronting the Nazi Past.* London: Collins & Brown, 1993. 160 p.

BURRIN, PHILIPPE. *Hitler and the Jews: Genesis of the Holocaust.* London: E. Arnold, 1994. 192 p.

BUTNARU, L. C. *Waiting for Jerusalem: Surviving the Holocaust in Romania.* London: Greenwood Press, 1993. 280 p. (Contributions in the Study of World History, 37).

CESARANI, DAVID, ed. *The Final Solution: Origins and Implementation.* London: Routledge, 1994. 328 p.

CHERNOW, RON. *The Warburgs: A Family Saga.* London: Chatto & Windus, 1993. 820 p.

CHEYETTE, BRYAN. *The Construction of the Jew in English Literature and Society: Racial Representations, 1875-1945.* Cambridge: Cambridge Univ. Press, 1993. 240 p.

COHN-SHERBOK, DAN. *Not a Job for a Nice Jewish Boy.* London: Bellview, 1993. 224 p.

ECKHARDT, ALICE L., ed. *Burning Memory: Times of Testing and Reckoning.* Oxford: Pergamon Press, 1933. 350 p.

ESKANAZI, TAMARA C. and KENT H. RICHARDS, eds. *Second Temple Studies. 2.: Temple and Community in the Persian Period.* Sheffield: Sheffield Academic Press, 1994. 250 p.

FEIN, HELEN. *Genocide: A Sociological Perspective.* New ed. London:

Sage Publications, 1993. 120 p.

FEUCHTWANGER, E. J. *From Weimar to Hitler: Germany 1918-1933.* London: Macmillan Press, 1993. 376 p.

FRANK, DANIEL. *Judah Halevi.* London: P. Halban, 1994. 176 p. (Jewish Thinkers).

FRIEDLANDER, ALBERT. *Riders Towards the Dawn: From Ultimate Suffering to Tempered Hope.* London: Constable, 1993. 328 p.

GALIPEAU, CLAUDE J. *Isaiah Berlin's Liberalism.* Oxford: Clarendon Press, 1993. 208 p.

GEARY, DICK. *Hitler and Nazism.* London: Routledge, 1993. 64 p.

GERSTENFELD-MALTIEL, JACOB. *My Private War: One Man's Struggle to Survive the Soviets and the Nazis.* London: Vallentine Mitchell, 1993. 336 p.

GILBERT, MARTIN. *Dent Atlas of the Holocaust.* London: Dent, 1993. 256 p.

GLEARY, RICHARD. *Hitler and Nazism.* London: Routledge, 1993. 96 p.

GOODMAN, ARNOLD. *Tell Them I'm On My Way.* London: Chapman, 1993. 464 p.

GOODMAN, MARTIN. *The Ruling Class of Judea The Origins of the Jewish Revolt Against Rome.* Cambridge: Cambridge Univ. Press, 1993. 251 p.

HANSEN, PHILLIP. *Hannah Arendt: Politics, History and Citizenship.* Oxford: Polity Press, 1993. 266 p.

HARMAN, GEOFFREY, ed. *Holocaust Remembrance: The Shapes of Memory.* Oxford: Blackwell, 1993. 306 p.

LANGBEIN, HERMANN. *Against all Hope: Resistance in the Nazi Concentration Camps 1938-45.* London: Constable, 1994. 480 p.

Leo Baeck Institute Year Book 1993. Vol. 38. London: Secker & Warburg for the Institute, 1993. 558 p.

LEVIN, BERNARD. *Utopia.* London: J. Cape, 1993. 304 p.

LEVY, ALAN. *The Wiesenthal File.* London: Constable, 1993. 463 p.

MARKS JANE. *The Hidden Children. The Secret Survivors of the Holocaust.* London: Piatkus Books, 1993. 308 p.

PELICAN, FRED. *From Dachau to Dunkirk.* London: Vallentine Mitchell, 1993. 224 p.

PERES, SHIMON. *Witness: An Autobiography.* London: Weidenfeld & Nicolson, 1994. 288 p.

REUTH, RALF GEORG. *Goebbels: The Life and Times of Joseph Goebbels, the Mephistophelean Genius of Nazi Propaganda.* Tr. from the German by K. Winston. London: Constable, 1993. 600 p.

RIDLEY, JANE and STEPHEN THOMAS. *Young Disraeli, 1804-1842.* London: Sinclair-Stevenson, 1993. 384 p.

ROSEN, SARA. *My Lost World: A Survivor's Tale.* London: Vallentine Mitchell, 1993. 320 p.

SCHARF, RAFAEL F., comp. *In the Warsaw Ghetto: Summer 1941.*

Photographs by Willy Georg. With passages from Warsaw Ghetto Diaries. Tr. from Yiddish. London: R. Hale, 1993. 112 p.

SHAHAK, ISRAEL. *Jewish History, Jewish Religion. The Weight of Three Thousand Years*. London: Pluto Press, 1993. 128 p.

SHAPIRO, DAVID H. *From Philanthropy to Activism: The Political Transformation of American Zionism in the Holocaust Years 1933-45*. Oxford: Pergamon Press, 1993. 250 p. (Holocaust Series.)

SLATER, ROBERT. *Rabin of Israel: A Biography*. 2nd rev. ed. London: Robson Books, 1993. 486 p.

SLOWE, PETER. *Manny Shinwell: An Authorised Biography*. London: Pluto Press, 1993. 352 p.

SMELSER, RONALD and RAINER ZITELMANN, eds. *The Nazi Elite*. Tr. by Mary Fischer. London: Macmillan, 1993. 259 p.

WEINTRAUB, STANLEY. *Disraeli: A Biography*. London: H. Hamilton, 1993. 731 p.

WERMUTH, HENRY. *Breathe Deeply My Son*. London: Vallentine Mitchell, 1993. 232 p.

WILSON, DEREK. *The Rothschilds*. 2nd rev. ed. London: Deutsch, 1994. 528 p.

ISRAEL, ZIONISM AND THE MIDDLE EAST

ABADI, JACOB. *Israel's Leadership: From Utopia to Crisis*. London: Greenwood Press, 1994. 208 p.

AL MADFAI, MADIHA RASHID. *Jordan, the United States and the Middle East Peace Process, 1974-91*. Cambridge: Cambridge Univ. Press, 1993. 279 p. (Cambridge Middle East Library, 28).

ASSALHA, OMAR. *Towards the Long-Promised Peace: a History of the Israeli-Palestinian Conflict*. London: Saqi Books, 1994. 330 p.

BAR-ON, MORDECAI. *Gates of Gaza: Israel's Road to Suez and Back, 1955-57*. London: Macmillan, 1994. 400 p.

BEGIN, ZE'EV B. *A Zionist Stand*. London: F. Cass, 1993. 160 p.

BROMLEY, SIMON. *Rethinking Middle East Politics: State Formation and Development*. Oxford: Polity Press, 1993. 200 p.

CORBIN, JANE. *Gaza First: The Secret Norway Channel to Peace Between Israel and the PLO*. London: Bloomsbury, 1994. 213 p.

ELLIS, MARC H. *Renewal of Palestine in the Jewish Imagination*. London: Alhani International Books, 1993. 176 p.

GILBERT, MARTIN. *Dent Atlas of the Arab-Israeli Conflict*. 6th ed. London: Dent., 1993. 152 p.

GILBERT, MARTIN. *Jerusalem Illustrated History Atlas*. 3rd rev. ed. London: Vallentine Mitchell, 1994. 114p.

GOMI, YOSEF. *The State of Israel in Jewish Public Thought: The Quest* for Collective Identity. London: Macmillan, 1994. 432 p.

GRADUS, YEHUDA, ERAN RAZIN and SHAUL KRAKOVER. The Industrial Geography of Israel. London: Routledge, 1993. 255 p.

GUTMANN, EMANUEL, ed. Ben Gurion to Rabin: The Development of the Israeli Prime Ministership. London: Hurst, 1993. 240 p.

HAIDER, AZIZ. The Arab Population in the Israeli Economy, 1949-1990. London: Hurst, 1993. 174 p.

HOURANI, ALBERT, PHILIP KHOURY, and MARY WILSON, eds. The Modern Middle East: A Reader. London: I.B. Tauris, 1993. 600 p.

ISRAELI, RAPHAEL. Muslim Fundamentalism in Israel. London: Brassey's, 1993. 203 p.

KLIOT, NURIT. Water Resources and Conflict in the Middle East. London: Routledge, 1993. 368 p.

KYLE, KEITH and JOEL PETERS, eds. Whither Israel? The Domestic Challenges. London: Royal Institute of International Affairs in association with I. B. Tauris, 1993. 292 p.

LEVENBERG, HAIM. Military Preparations of the Arab Community in Palestine, 1945-1948. London: Vallentine Mitchell, 1993. 288 p.

LEVETT, GORDON. Flying Under Two Flags: An Ex-RAF Pilot in Israel's War of Independence. London: F. Cass, 1993. 296 p.

LOWI, MIRIAM R. Water and Power: The Politics of a Scarce Resource in the Jordan River Basin. Cambridge: Cambridge Univ. Press, 1993. 300 p.

MASSALHA, OMAR. Towards the Long-Promised Peace. London: Saqi Books, 1994. 346 p.

MORRIS, BENNY. Israel's Border Wars, 1949-1956: Arab Infiltration, Israeli Retaliation, and the Countdown to the Suez War. Oxford: Clarendon Press, 1993. 451 p.

NETANYAHU, BENJAMIN. Place Among the Nations: Israel and the World. London: Bantam Press, 1993. 448 p.

NETTLER, RONALD L., ed. Studies in Muslim Jewish Relations. Vol. 1. London: Harwood Academic Publishers with the Oxford Centre for Postgraduate Hebrew Studies, 1993. 205 p.

O'NEILL, DAN and DON WAGNER. Peace or Armageddon? Unfolding Drama of the Middle East Accord. London: Marshall Pickering, 1994. 112 p.

PERES, SHIMON. Battling for Peace: Memoirs. London: Weidenfeld & Nicolson, 1994. 288 p.

PETERS, JOEL and KEITH KYLE, eds. Whither Israel? The Domestic Challenges. London: I.B. Tauris, 1993. 288 p.

RICE, MICHAEL. False Inheritance: Israel in Palestine and the Search for a Solution. London: Kegan Paul International, 1994. 237 p.

SANDLER, SHMUEL. State of Israel, the Land of Israel: The Statist and Ethnonational Dimensions of Foreign Policy. London: Greenwood Press, 1993. 320 p. (Contributions in Political Science, 32).

SMITH, BARBARA J. *The Roots of Separatism in Palestine: British Economic Policy, 1920-1929.* London: I. B. Tauris, 1993. 352 p.

TILL, JULIE. *Jerusalem: Its Political Signficance in the Palestinian-Israeli Peace Talks.* London: Gulf Centre for Strategic Studies, 1994. 41 p. (Contemporary Strategic Issues in the Middle East Series).

UNITED NATIONS. *Life of the Palestinians Under Israeli Occupation.* London: HMSO, 1993. 64 p.

RELIGION AND PHILOSOPHY

ALBERTZ, RAINER. *A History of Israelite Religion in the Old Testament Period.* Vol. 1.: *From the Beginnings to the End of the Monarchy.* Tr. from the German by John Bowden. London: SCM Press, 1994. 384 p.

COHN-SHERBOK, DAN. *The Jewish Faith.* London: SPCK, 1993. 272 p.

EVERETT, ROBERT ANDREW. *Christianity Without Antisemitism: James Parkes and the Jewish-Christian Encounter.* Oxford: Pergamon Press, 1993. 336 p. (Studies in Antisemitism).

GUINESS, MICHELE. *A Little Kosher Seasoning.* London: Hodder, 1994. 256 p.

JACOBS, JULIAN G. *Judaism Looks at Modern Issues.* London: Aviva Press, 1993. 216 p.

JACOBS, LOUIS. *Hasidic Prayer.* London: Littman Library of Jewish Civilization, 1993. 206 p.

LACHS, SAMUEL TOBIAS. *Humanism in Talmud and Midrash.* London: Associated Universities Presses, 1993. 150 p.

LEVINAS, EMMANUEL. *Outside the Subject.* London: Athlone Press, 1994. 224 p.

MARTIN, JAMES D. *Davidson's Introductory Hebrew Grammar.* 27th ed. Edinburgh: T & T Clark, 1994. 240 p.

NOY, DAVID. *Jewish Inscriptions of Westem Europe.* Vol. 1. Cambridge: Cambridge Univ. Press, 1993. 300 p.

REIF, STEFAN C. *Judaism and Hebrew Prayer: New Perspectives on Jewish Liturgical History.* Cambridge: Cambridge Univ. Press, 1993. 450 p.

ROSE, GILLIAN. *Judaism and Modernity: Philosophical Essays.* Oxford: Blackwell, 1993. 309 p.

RYCE-MENUHIN, JOEL, ed. *Jung and the Monotheisms: Judaism, Christianity and Islam.* London: Routledge, 1993. 288 p.

SANDERS, JACK T. *Schismatics, Sectarians, Dissidents, Deviants: The First One Hundred Years of Jewish-Christian Relations.* London: SCM Press, 1993. 448 p.

SCHWARZFUCHS, SIMON. *The History of the Rabbinate.* Oxford:

Blackwell, 1993. 224 p.

SOGGIN, J. ALBERTO. *An Introduction to the History of Israel and Judah.* London: SCM Press, 1993. 448 p.

WEEKS, STUART. *Early Israelite Wisdom.* Oxford: Clarendon Press, 1993. 224 p. (Oxford Theological Monographs).

SOCIAL STUDIES

ALDERMAN, GEOFFREY and COLIN, HOLMES, eds. *Outsiders and Outcasts: Essays in Honour of William J. Fishman.* London: Duckworth, 1993. 214 p.

CESARANI, DAVID *The Jewish Chronicle and Anglo-Jewry, 1841-1991.* Cambridge: Cambridge University Press, 1994. 350 p.

COHN-SHERBOK, DAN. *Atlas of Jewish History.* London: Routledge, 1994. 224 p.

ENGLANDER, DAVID, ed. *A Documentary History of the Jews in Britain, 1840-1920.* London: Pinter Press, 1993. 395 p.

FRIEDLANDER, ALBERT. *Riders Towards the Dawn: From Ultimate Suffering to Tempered Hope.* London: Constable, 1993. 256 p.

GILBERT, MARTIN. *Dent Atlas of Jewish History.* 5th ed. London: Dent, 1993. 136 p.

LINDSAY, PAUL. *The Synagogues of London.* London: Vallentine Mitchell, 1993. 144 p.

POLONSKY, ANTONY, ed. *The Jews in Old Poland, 1000-1795.* London: I.B. Tauris, 1993. 340 p.

POLONSKY, ANTONY, ed. *From Shtetl to Socialism Studies from Polin.* London: The Littman Library of Jewish Civilization for the Institute for Polish-Jewish Studies, Oxford, 1993. 581 p.

SEGAL, J. B. *A History of the Jews of Cochin.* London: Vallentine Mitchell, 1993. 134 p.

TAYLOR, SIMON. *A Land of Dreams: A Study of Jewish and Afro-Caribbean Migrant Communities in England.* London: Routledge, 1993. 224 p.

TURNER, BARRY. *The Long Horizon: 60 Years of the CBF World Jewish Relief.* London: CBF World Jewish Relief, 1993(?). 103 p.

WEBBER, JONATHAN, ed. *Jewish Identities in the New Europe.* London: Littman Library of Jewish Civilization for the Oxford Centre for Hebrew and Jewish Studies, 1994. 307 p. (Littman Library of Jewish Civilization).

ZIV, AVNER and ANAT ZAJDMAN, eds. *Semites and Stereotypes: Characteristics of Jewish Humour.* London: Greenwood Press, 1993. 224 p. (Contribution in Ethnic Studies Series, 31).

FICTION

ABERBACH, DAVID. *Realism, Caricature and Bias: The Fiction of Mendele Mocher Sefarim.* London: Littman Library of Jewish Civilization, 1993. 131 p. (Littman Library of Jewish civilization).

GALFORD, ELLEN. *The Dyke and the Dybbuk.* London: Virago, 1993. 224 p.

RAYNER, CLAIRE. *First Blood.* London: M. Joseph, 1993. 384 p. First in a new series of medical crime novels featuring a lady pathologist in an inner city hospital.

RAYNER, CLAIRE. *Cottage Hospital.* London: Severn House, 1993. 192 p. Another in her series of nursing romances.

ROTH, HENRY. *Mercy of a Rude Stream.* Vol. 1.: A *Star Shines Over Mt. Morris Park. A Novel.* London: Weidenfeld & Nicolson, 1994. 292 p.

SHMUELI, ALFRED. *Murder on the Kibbutz.* London: Independent Writers Publications, 1993. 308 p.

CHILDREN'S FICTION

DILLON, ELLIS. *Children of Bach.* London: Penguin, 1993. 160 p. A novel of suspense set in war-torn Europe at the end of the 1930s. The escape of three children from Hungary after the parents were taken by the Nazis.

MISCELLANEOUS

BURR, GILLIAN and MARION COHEN, eds. *Yesterday's Kitchen: Jewish Communities and Their Food Before 1939.* London: Vallentine Mitchell, 1993. 266 p.

CLINES, DAVID J. A., ed. *The Dictionary Of Classical Hebrew.* Vol. 1.: *Aleph.* Sheffield: Sheffield Academic Press, 1993. 475 p.

GOULD, ALLAN and DANNY SIEGEL. *The Unorthodox Book of Jewish Records and Lists.* London: Robson Books, 1993. 196 p.

MASSIL, STEPHEN W., ed. *The Jewish Yearbook 1994.* London: Vallentine Mitchell in association with the Jewish Chronicle, 1994. 362 p.

SÁENZ-BADILLOS, ANGEL. *A History of the Hebrew Language.* Tr. from the Spanish by John Elwolde. Cambridge: Cambridge Univ. Press, 1993. 400 p.

יוסף גלרון-גולדשלגר

JOSEPH GALRON-GOLDSCHLÄGER

מבחר ספרים עבריים ממדינת ישראל תשנ"ג-תשנ"ד

Selected Hebrew Books from Israel 1993–1994

‏1. ביבליוגרפיה, אנציקלופדיות, לקסיקונים

אלפסי, יצחק. שרי התורה: מאורות מעולם הרבנות / יצחק אלפסי. –
ירושלים: כרמל, תשנ"ג 1993. 370 עמ'. „דיוקנותיהם של 70 דמויות מעולם
התורה והרבנות – מרש"י ועד זמננו. כולל פרטים ביוגרפיים
וביבליוגרפיים".

אנציקלופדיה לבית ישראל: בעשרים כרכים / העורך – הרב רפאל
הלפרין. – כרך א-ג. – [בני-ברק]: הקדש רוח יעקב, תשנ"ג 1993. 3 כר'.
(כרך א. א-או. 240 עמ'. – כרך ב. אז-אל. 240 עמ'. – כרך ג. אמ-את. 240
עמ'). „. . . ריכוז תמציתי של מידע על כל מושגי התרבות האנושית בעולם
הרוח ובעולם החומר . . . מתוך נאמנות לדיוק מדעי ולמסורת היהדות".

בורשטין, מנחם. שמיטה – תדריך למודי: ביבליוגרפיה: כיצד ומהיכן ללמוד
וללמד עניני שמיטה: שמיטה הלכה למעשה: פסקי הלכות שביעית / מאת
מנחם בורשטין. – ירושלים: מדרשת התורה והארץ, תשנ"ד 1993. 292 עמ'.

הטל, אברהם. יהדות צפון-אפריקה – ביבליוגראפיה / אברהם הטל. – מהד'
ב מורחבת. – ירושלים: מכון בן-צבי לחקר קהילות ישראל במזרח, תשנ"ג
1993. יב, 672, CIII עמ'. נוספו שער, מבוא ומפתחות בצרפתית.

וונדר, מאיר. אלף מרגליות: ספר עזר לחקר יוחסין: תולדות חייהם ושלשלת
יחוסם של יותר מאלף אבות משפחתנו . . . מימי קדם עד אבינו . . . מוהר"ר
ישראל אריה מרגליות / . . . נערכו ונסדרו . . . על ידי הרב מאיר וונדר. –
ירושלים: המכון להנצחת יהדות גליציה, תשנ"ג. טו עמ', 776 עמודות, [46]

Special thanks to the Melton Center for Jewish Studies at The Ohio
State University which supported this bibliography.

עמ'. [46] העמ' כוללים: ספר מעלות היוחסין / אפרים זלמן מרגליות ושער נוסף באנגלית.

וינוגרד, ישעיהו. אוצר הספר העברי: רשימת הספרים שנדפסו באות עברית מראשית הדפוס העברי בשנת רכ"ט (1469) עד שנת תרכ"ג (1863) / מאת ישעיהו וינוגרד. — ירושלים: המכון לביבליוגרפיה ממוחשבת, תשנ"ד 1993. <כרך ב>. שער נוסף באנגלית. התוכן: חלק ב. רשימת הספרים ערוכה לפי מקומות הדפוס.

הטיפול במשפחה בישראל: ביבליוגרפיה נבחרת ותקצירים 1980-1993 / עורך מדעי – יונתן רבינוביץ', עורכת – נעמי מי-עמי. — ירושלים: מכון הנרייטה סאלד, תשנ"ג 1993. 303, [1] עמ'. — (פרסום / מכון הנריטה סולד: מס' 705) "החוברת יוצאת לאור בשיתוף עם השירות לרווחת הפרט והמשפחה משרד העבודה והרווחה". שער נוסף באנגלית.

יודלוב, יצחק. מפתח כללי לקטלוגים של "יודאיקה ירושלם": א, ניסן תשמ"ז . . . – טו, סתיו תשנ"ג . . . / [י. יודלוב]. — [ירושלים]: יודאיקה ירושלם, [תשנ"ג]. 181 עמ'.

לקסיקון התרבות היהודית בזמננו: מושגים, תנועות, אמונות / עורכים: ארתור א. כהן ופול מנדס-פלור; עורך המהדורה העברית: אברהם שפירא. — תל-אביב: עם עובד, תשנ"ג 1993. ז, 597 עמ'.

רוטנשטרייך, נתן. אפרים אלימלך אורבך – ביו-ביבליוגרפיה מחקרית / נתן רוטנשטרייך . . . ,, יעקב זוסמן . . . ,, בתיה בן-שמאי; העורך – דוד אסף. — ירושלים: האיגוד העולמי למדעי היהדות, תשנ"ג 1993. 133 עמ'. — (מוסף מדעי היהדות / במת האגוד העולמי למדעי היהדות; 1)

תבורי, יוסף. רשימת מאמרים בעניני תפילה ומועדים / מאת יוסף תבורי. — ירושלים: בית הספרים הלאומי והאוניברסיטאי, 1993. — ז, 792 עמ'. — (פרסומי בית הספרים, מס' 32) (קרית ספר. מוסף לכרך סד)

2. מקרא, מגילות מדבר-יהודה

אמינוף, עירית. אחד מקרא ושנים מדרש / עירית אמינוף; איורים ועטיפה: גיל מוזס. — קרית-ביאליק: אח, 1993. 176 עמ'.

אליצור, יהודה. אטלס דעת מקרא: אוצר ערכים גיאוגרפיים-היסטוריים / כתובים וערוכים בידי יהודה אליצור, יהודה קיל. — ירושלים: מוסד הרב קוק, תשנ"ג 1993. XVI, 343, [1] עמ'.

אפשטיין, קלונימוס קלמן. ספר מאור ושמש השלם: על התורה ומועדים / קלונימוס קלמן הלוי עפשטיין; ליקט ערך והביא לדפוס מנחם אברהם בראון. — ירושלים: מכון אור הספר, תדש"ן [ז"א תשנ"ד] 1993. 1 כרך. סודר מחדש עם ציוני מקורות, ביאורים, הערות והשוואות.

אררט, ניסן. אמת וחסד במקרא / ניסן אררט. — ירושלים: הרשות המשותפת לחינוך יהודי ציוני – המחלקה לחינוך ולתרבות תורניים בגולה, תשנ"ג, 364,

[1] עמ'. — (ספריית אלינר)

אשכנזי, שלמה. פנינים ואבני חפץ על התורה / שלמה אשכנזי; נערך ע"י
אליעזר ברנע (ברלין). — קרית־אונו: ספרי תבונה, תשנ"ג-תשנ"ד. 2 כר'.
התוכן: [א]. בראשית. [ב]. שמות.

ויסבליט, שלמה. הוראת המקרא בעזרת המילון / שלמה ויסבליט, מנחם צבי
קדרי. — [תל־אביב]: אור־עם, תשנ"ג 1993. 111 עמ'.

זהרי, מנחם. נתיבות בשירה המקראית / מאת מנחם זהרי. — ירושלים: כרמל,
תשנ"ג 1993. 135 עמ'.

חמישה חומשי תורה: עם פירוש רש"י ועם ביאור רבינו לוי בן גרשום
(רלב"ג) / בעריכת ברוך ברנר, אלי פריימן. — מהד' מדויקת על פי כתבי יד
עם שינויי נוסחאות, ציוני מקורות וביאורים. — מעלה אדומים: מעליות,
תשנ"ג 1993. 1 כרך.

כהנא, מאיר דוד. פירוש המכבי על ספר שמות / הרב מאיר דוד כהנא. —
ירושלים: המכון להוצאת כתבי הרב מאיר כהנא, תשנ"ד. תנט, [3] עמ'. כולל
פרוש רק על פרקים א-ג מספר שמות בתוספת קטעי פרושים לספרים
אחרים. נוספו שער ומבוא באנגלית.

מאק, חננאל. הפרשנות הקדומה למקרא / חננאל מאק. — תל־אביב: משרד
הבטחון־ההוצאה לאור, מטכ"ל — קצין חינוך ראשי — גלי צה"ל, תשנ"ג 1993.
123 עמ'. — (ספריית אוניברסיטה משדרת)

סיון, דניאל. דקדוק לשון אוגרית / מאת דניאל סיון. — ירושלים: מוסד
ביאליק, תשנ"ג 1993. 213 עמ'. — (ספריית האנציקלופדיה המקראית; ט)

ספר במדבר בארמית חדשה בניבם של יהודי זאכו: ונוספו עליו
טקסטים בניבים אחרים של ארמית חדשה ומילון / מאת יונה צבר. —
ירושלים: האוניברסיטה העברית, המכון למדעי היהדות, מפעל מסורות
הלשון של עדות ישראל, תשנ"ג. לד, 147, [5] עמ'. — (עדה ולשון; טז)

עמרוסי, שמואל. 3500 שו"ת בקיאות ו-250 מדרשים מתורה ומנביאים
ראשונים: ללימוד בקיאות בעיון לחידוני תנ"ך והעמקת ידע / [חיבר, כתב
וערך שמואל עמרוסי]. — [צפת: ש' עמרוסי, תשנ"ג]. [9], 264, [2], 23, כד, [2]
עמ'. כולל גם: תולדות חידוני התנ"ך / מאת יוסף שער.

פיש, הראל. שירת מקרא: עדות ופואטיקה / א' הראל פיש; [מאנגלית סמדר
מילוא]. — רמת־גן: אוניברסיטת בר־אילן, תשנ"ג 1993. 208 עמ'.

פנקובר, יצחק שרגא.א. נוסח התורה בכתר ארם־צובה: עדות חדשה / מאת
יצחק ש' פנקובר. — רמת־גן: אוניברסיטת בר־אילן, תשנ"ג 1992. 144 עמ'. —
(מקורות ומחקרים; ו)

קמרון, אלישע. ארמית מקראית / מאת אלישע קימרון. — ירושלים: מוסד
ביאליק, תשנ"ג 1993. י, 147 עמ'. — (ספריית האנציקלופדיה המקראית; י)

שיפמן, יהודה. הלכה, הליכה ומשיחיות בכת מדבר יהודה / יהודה שיפמן;
תרגום ועריכה — טל אילן; [המערכת המדעית אברהם גרוסמן . . . ואחרים;
מרכז המערכת יצחק כהן] ירושלים: מרכז זלמן שזר לתולדות ישראל, 1993.
391 עמ'

שנאן, אביגדור. מקרא אחד ותרגומים הרבה: סיפורי התורה בראי תרגומיהם
הארמיים / אביגדור שנאן. — תל־אביב: הקיבוץ המאוחד, 1993. 191 עמ'. —
(ספריית „הילל בן חיים")

התנ״ך: מבחר פרקי פרוזה / עורך: דרור גרין; [איורים: גוסטב דורה]. —
ירושלים: ספרים, 1993. 2 כר'.

3. משנה, תלמוד, מדרשים, הלכה ומשפט עברי

אדרת, שלמה בן אברהם אבן (רשב״א). חידושי הרשב״א — מסכת
שבועות / לרבינו שלמה ב״ר אברהם אדרת: יו״ל על־פי כתבי־יד ודפוסים
ראשונים, בצירוף מבוא, ציוני מקורות, מקבילות, הערות וביאורים / מאת
הרב יעקב דוד אילן. — ירושלים: מוסד הרב קוק, תשנ״ג 1993. [10] עמ', רסו
עמודות, [1] עמ'.

אובדן ושכול בחברה הישראלית / עורכים — רות מלקינסון, שמשון
רוביז, אליעזר ויצטום. — ירושלים: כנה, תשנ״ג. 1993, 268, XXVI עמ'.
כולל הערות ביבליוגרפיות.

אליהו בן שלמה זלמן (הגר״א). קבלת הגר״א / . . . [ערוך] על ידי יוסף
אביב״י: [הסדרה] בעריכת ישעיהו וינוגרד. — ירושלים: מכון כרם אליהו,
[הקד' תשנ״ג]. קנב עמ'. — (סדרת ספרים על הגר״א: ספר א). התוכן: [א].
גילוי אליהו: מבוא לקבלת הגר״א, ערוך על פי החיבורים הנדפסים מכבר.
— [ב]. עשרה כללים מאת הגר״א מווילנא, יוצאים לאור על פי כתב יד
שנתגלה עתה.

אפרתי, יעקב אליהו. מסכת יום טוב — פרק שלישי: בצירוף צילום דפוס
שונצינו משנת ה' רמ״ד . . . עם מבוא, הערות, בירורים וביאורים: ועליהם
נספח שינויי הנוסחאות עפ״י עשרים כת״י מן המשנה והתלמיד[!] / יעקב
אליהו אפרתי, אפרים יצחקי. — פתח־תקוה: אגודת בני אשר, תשנ״ג. כח, 290
עמ'.

גליק, שמואל. אור וניחומים: להתפתחותם של מנהגי „ניחום אבלים" במסורת
ישראל / שמואל גליק. — אפרת: קרן אורי, תשנ״ג 1993. 210 עמ'.

דנציג, נחמן. מבוא לספר הלכות פסוקות: עם תשלום הלכות פסוקות / מאת
נחמן דנציג. — ניו־יורק וירושלים: בית המדרש לרבנים באמריקה, תשנ״ג
1993. [15], 708, [2] עמ'. שער נוסף באנגלית.

הגר־לאו, יהושע. העוז והענוה: בירור נושאי בטחון, צבא ומלחמה בהשקפת
הרמב״ם מתוך ספריו: משנה תורה — יד החזקה, ספר המצוות, מורה נבוכים,
פירוש המשנה, אגרות ותשובות / מאת יהושע הגר־לאו. — בית־יתיר:
המכינה הקדם־צבאית ישיבתית, תשנ״ג 1993. [9], י, 363 עמ'.

הלבני, דוד. מקורות ומסורות: ביאורים בתלמוד. כרך ה: מסכת בבא קמא /
דוד הלבני. — תל־אביב: דביר, תשנ״ג, 1993. 1 כר'.

וינפלד, יוסף שלום. ספר מבוא לש״ס וילנא: כולל שלשה מדורים / ערכתי

סדרתי יוסף שלום הלוי וינפלד. — ירושלים: אשכול, תשנ״ד 1994. תקעו עמ׳.
התוכן: מדור א. אוסף שערים — מדור ב. נושאי כליו של הש״ס: האישים
שדברי תורתם נדפסו בתוך הש״ס. . . — מדור ג. המפרשים לפי סדר
המסכתות.

ולר, שולמית. נשים ונשיות בסיפורי התלמוד / שולמית ולר. — [תל־אביב]:
הקיבוץ המאוחד, 1993. 143 עמ׳. — (ספריית ״הילל בן־חיים״)

זהרי, חיים. מקורות רש״י: מדרשי הלכה ואגדה בפירושיו / חיים זהרי; ערך
מנחם זהרי. — ירושלים: כנה, תשנ״ג 1993. 16 כר׳.

יום־טוב בן אברהם מאשבילי. חידושי הריטב״א: מסכת שבועות / יום טוב
[בן] אברהם אלאשבילי: יו״ל על־פי כתבי־יד ודפוסים ראשונים בצירוף
מבוא, ציוני מקורות, מקבילות, הערות ובאורים מאת אליהו ליכטנשטיין. —
ירושלים: מוסד הרב קוק, תשנ״ג 1993. תקכב עמ׳. — (חדושי הריטב״א על
הש״ס)

כהן, ישראל מאיר בן אריה זאב. ספר משנה ברורה . . . והוא פירוש . . . על
שו״ע אורח חיים . . . עם חידושי דינים שהשמיט . . . מו״ה משה איסרליש,
עם . . . באר הגולה . . . באר היטב . . . שערי תשובה . . . ביאור הלכה . . .
/ חברתי . . . ישראל מאיר בר׳ אריה זאב הכהן . . .; בתוספת הארות והגהות
ותרגום מילים . . . בתוספת טבלאות וציורים, שיעורים וזמנים . . . עם הגהות
והערות איש מצליח לספרדים ועדות המזרח. — חלק א. — ירושלים: א׳
בלום, [הסכ׳ תשנ״ד]. 1 כר׳. כולל בסופו קטעים מחזון איש, שינון הלכה.

הכינוס הבינלאומי לרפואה, אתיקה והלכה: תמוז תשנ״ג – יולי 1993:
אסופת מאמרים בנושאי הכינוס . . . / העורך, מרדכי הלפרין. — ירושלים:
המכון ע״ש ד״ר פלק שלזינגר ז״ל לחקר הרפואה על־פי התורה, [תשנ״ג
1993]. 400, 92 עמ׳. עברית ואנגלית.

לוי, יהודה. מול אתגרי התקופה: שיחות על היהדות / יהודה לוי. — ירושלים:
עולם הספר התורני, תשנ״ג 1993. שטו עמ׳.

מאיר, עפרה. סוגיות בפואטיקה של סיפורי חז״ל / עפרה מאיר. — [תל־אביב]:
ספרית פועלים, תשנ״ג 1993. 184 עמ׳. — (פואטיקה וביקורת)

מסכת שביעית — חקר ועיון: כולל: א. המשנה עם שנויי נוסחאות ב. פירוש
רבי יצחק בן מלכי צדק . . . ג. פירוש רבי שמשון משנץ בצירוף הערות /
סודרו ונערכו . . . על פי כתב יד ודפוסים ראשונים על ידי קלמן בן
לאאמו״ר בנימין זאב כהנא. — מהד׳ מתוקנת וערוכה מחדש. — ירושלים: בית
מדרש גבוה להלכה בהתישבות חקלאית, תשנ״ג. 14, [2], קצה עמ׳.

מסכת שביעית מן תלמוד ירושלמי: עם הגהות הגר״א וביאורי הגר״א על־
פי כתבי־היד וכפי שנדפסו ב״שירי ירושלמי״, בצירוף הגהות הגר״א כפי
שנדפסו בחיבורים אחרים ועם לקט ביאורים . . . / נערכו וסודרו . . . על ידי
קלמן בן ללאמו״ר בנימין זאב . . . כהנא. — מהד׳ מתוקנת וערוכה מחדש. —
ירושלים: בית מדרש גבוה להלכה בהתישבות חקלאית, תשנ״ג. 12, [2], קצז
עמ׳. בסוף הספר: ״לחקר ביאורי הגר״א לירושלמי ולתוספתא סדר זרעים״.

משה בן נחמן. חדושי הרמב״ן השלם: מסכתות בבא מציעא, בבא בתרא, מכות,

קונטרס דינא דגרמי. — ירושלים: מכון מערבא, תשנ״ג 1993. 1 כר׳. „מוגה ע״פ כתבי־יד ודפוסים ראשונים וספרי תלמידיו, וע״י צוות תלמידי חכמים, בציון מראי המקומות למובאות בדבריהם".

נסים בן ראובן גירונדי. חידושי הר״ן: מסכת שבת / נסים [בן] ראובן גירונדי; יו״ל על־פי כת״י בצירוף מבוא, ציוני מקורות, מקבילות, הערות ובאורים מאת ישראל סקלר. — ירושלים: מוסד הרב קוק, תשנ״ד 1993. 16 עמ׳, תרל עמודות. — (חדושי הר״ן) כולל גם: חידושי הר״ן: מסכת מועד קטן. ירושלים: מוסד הרב קוק, תשנ״ד.

נתן בן יחיאל. הערוך על התלמוד הירושלמי / נתן בן יחיאל. מוסף הערוך / בנימין מוספיא: מסודר לפי סדר דפי התלמוד עם הערות והסברים מאת מאיר מיזליש. — בני ברק: נתיבה, תשנ״ד 1993. 2 כר׳.

עמרם גאון, המאה ה־7. סדר רב עמרם גאון: ששיגר רב עמרם בר ששנא . . . לרבינו יצחק בר׳ שמעון . . . בתור תשובה לשאלתו בדבר נוסח התפלה ומנהגי בית הכנסת. — בני ברק: [חמו״ל], תשנ״ד 1993. רנג עמ׳. מהדורת „גרש ירחים" ערוכה בידי גרשום הרפנס.

פסקי דין מבית הדין לבירור יהדות של הרבנות הראשית לירושלים / ערוכים ע״י הרב אברהם דב לוין . . . — מהד׳ א. — כרך א־ ב. — ירושלים: המועצה הדתית, תשנ״ג-תשנ״ד. 2 כר׳. כרך ב יצא בתוך: פסקי דין מבית הדין לדיני ממונות ולבירור יהדות, עמ׳ [רנז]-רצה.

פסקי דין מבית הדין לדיני ממונות של הרבנות הראשית לירושלים / ערוכים ע״י הרב אברהם דב לוין . . . — מהד׳ א. — כרך א־ ב. — ירושלים: המועצה הדתית, תשנ״ג-תשנ״ד. 2 כר׳. כרך ב: פסקי דין מבית הדין לדיני ממונות ולבירור יהדות של הרבנות הראשית לירושלים.

קוק, אברהם יצחק. שבת הארץ: [הלכות שביעית]: עץ הדר: [היתרון אשר לאתרוגים הכשרים המשומרים של אחינו בני המושבות באה״ק ופסולן של המורכבים] / מאת אברהם יצחק הכהן קוק. — מהד׳ ג. — ירושלים: מוסד הרב קוק, תשנ״ג 1993. קלב, קו עמ׳.

קוק, אברהם יצחק. שבת הארץ: הלכות שביעית / מאת אברהם יצחק הכהן קוק. — כפר דרום, חוף עזה: מכון התורה והארץ, תשנ״ג 1993. 2 כר׳. „עם תוספת שבת", „עם הוספות מכתי״ק תוספת שבת, מקורות, ציונים והערות נכתבו ונערכו . . . ע״י צוות מכון התורה והארץ".

רקובר, נחום. איכות הסביבה: היבטים רעיוניים ומשפטיים במקורות היהודיים / נחום רקובר. — ירושלים: מורשת המשפט בישראל, תשנ״ד 1993. 160 עמ׳. — (ספרית המשפט העברי)

שבתאי בן מאיר הכהן. ספר פועל צדק: על תרי״ג מצות . . . / לבעל הש״ך. — [ירושלים]: מכון „לב אריה", תשנ״ג 1993. כה, [22] עמ׳. מחולק לפי ימי השבוע וימי החודש. „עם קיצור הוספות מטעמי המצות מספר החינוך להרא״ה"

שינובר, צבי. איכות החיים והסביבה במקורות היהדות / צבי שינובר, יצחק גולדברג. — נחלים: מופת, תשנ״ד 1993. 264 עמ׳.

שנאן, אביגדור. תרגום ואגדה בו: האגדה בתרגום התורה הארמי המיוחס
ליונתן בן עוזיאל / אביגדור שנאן. – ירושלים: הוצאת ספרים ע"ש י"ל
מאגנס, תשנ"ג. 234, [6] עמ'. – (סדרת ספרים לחקר המקרא מיסודו של ס"ש
פרי)

4. זרמים רוחניים ביהדות. פילוסופיה יהודית

אברבנאל, יצחק בן יהודה. ראש אמנה / יצחק אברבנאל: ההדיר בצירוף
מבוא, הערות ונספחים מנחם קלנר. – רמת־גן: אוניברסיטת בר־אילן, תשנ"ג
1993. 198 עמ'.

אידל, משה. קבלה – היבטים חדשים / משה אידל: [תירגם אבריאל בר־לבב:
בעריכת המחבר]. – ירושלים: שוקן, תשנ"ג 1993. 434 עמ'.

אלפסי, יצחק. מאורות מעולם הקבלה והחסידות / יצחק אלפסי. – [תל־אביב]:
דעת יוסף, [תשנ"ד]. 574 עמ'.

דריפוס, תאודור. דו־שיח בין חכמים / תיאודור דרייפוס. – רמת־גן:
אוניברסיטת בר־אילן, תשנ"ג 1993. 188 עמ'.

דריקרמן, יעקב. תמימי דרך. תמימי דרך / יעקב דריקרמן: הוצאה ביקורתית עם מבוא,
הערות ומפתחות מאת גדליה נגאל. – ירושלים: כרמל, תשנ"ד 1993. 140 עמ'.

הלל, משה. בעלי שם: סיפורם המופלא של רבי אליהו בעל־שם מוורמייזא,
רבי יואל בעל־שם מזאמאשטש, רבי אדם בעל־שם מרופשיץ / . . . ליקט
וערך – הרב משה הלל. – ירושלים: מכון בני יששכר, תשנ"ג. [3], VI, 384
עמ'. "מנהיגי חבורת ה'צדיקים הנסתרים' אשר בעזרתה הפיצו את תורת
הקבלה באירופה ובכך הכשירו את הקרקע לצמיחת תנועת החסידות ע"י רבי
ישראל בעל־שם טוב".

כהנא, קלמן. תרומת כהן: קובץ שיחות ומאמרים / של . . . הרב קלמן
כהנא . . . קווים לדמותו. – חפץ חיים, תשנ"ג. 192 עמ'. נערך על ידי שרגא
שטיפל, שמואל עמנואל.

מאימראן, ישראל. חופש הבחירה בהגותו של רבי אברהם אזולאי / מאת
ישראל מאימראן. – ירושלים: מכון בני יששכר, הספריה הספרדית, תשנ"ג
1993. 195 עמ'.

מיזליש, שאול. מן ההר אל העם: חייו ופועלו של הראשון לציון . . . הרב
יצחק נסים . . . / אסף והכין שאול מייזליש; ערך . . . מאיר בניהו. – תל־
אביב: ידיעות אחרונות, 1993. 283 עמ'.

מנחה לשרה: מחקרים בפילוסופיה יהודית ובקבלה: מוגשים לפרופסור שרה
א' הלר וילנסקי / בעריכת משה אידל, דבורה דימנט, שלום רוזנברג. –
ירושלים: הוצאת ספרים ע"ש י"ל מאגנס, האוניברסיטה העברית, 1994. ח,
403 עמ'.

משואות: מחקרים בספרות הקבלה ובמחשבת ישראל מוקדשים לזכרו של
פרופ' אפרים גוטליב ז"ל / עורכים מיכל אורון, עמוס גולדרייך. –

ירושלים: מוסד ביאליק , תשנ"ד 1994. יז, 510 עמ'.

קוק, אברהם יצחק. דרשות הראי"ה לימים נוראים / מאת הרב אברהם יצחק הכהן קוק. – ירושלים: המכון ע"ש הרצי"ה, תשנ"ב. [8], קז עמ'.

קוק, אברהם יצחק. הקריאה הגדולה לארץ ישראל: קשר החיים בין הארץ לעם השב אליה . . . / הרב אברהם יצחק הכהן קוק; [עריכה, ביאורים ומקורות – בנימין אלון; שיכתוב ־אמונה אלון]. – ירושלים: אמונים, [תשנ"ג]. 58 עמ'. לקט קטעים מכתביו. המקורות מנוקדים.

רז, שמחה. מלאכים כבני אדם: הרב אברהם יצחק הכהן קוק / שמחה רז. – ירושלים: קול מבשר, תשנ"ד 1993. יד, 497 עמ'.

שטינפלד, צבי אריה. רש"י – עיונים ביצירתו / בעריכת צבי אריה שטינפלד. – רמת־גן: אוניברסיטת בר־אילן, תשנ"ג 1993. 220, VLX עמ'.

שרשבסקי, עזרא. החכם מלייפציג: הרב שמעון הלוי הורוויץ . . . חייו וכתביו / מאת עזרא שרשבסקי. – ירושלים: ר' מס, תשנ"ג 1993. – 174, 76, [1] עמ'.

שתיל, יונתן. פסיכולוג בישיבת ברסלב: מיסטיקה יהודית – הלכה למעשה / יונתן שתיל. – תל־אביב: פפירוס, 1993. 216, [3] עמ'.

5. תפלה, מחזור השנה ומנהגיו, גמטריה

אליצור, שולמית. מחזורי שבעתות לסדרים ולפרשות / שולמית אליצור. – ירושלים: האיגוד העולמי למדעי היהדות, תשנ"ג. 317, [2] עמ'. – (מקורות לחקר תרבות ישראל: 1)

אלעזר בן יהודה, מגרמיזא. שירת הרוקח: פיוטי רבי אלעזר מוורמייזא / יוצאים לאור על פי כתבי יד ודפוסים עתיקים, בצירוף חילופי נוסח ביאורים ומפתחות בידי יצחק מיזליש. – ירושלים: [חמו"ל], תשנ"ג. 322, [3] עמ'. נוספו שער, תוכן ענינים ומבוא קצר באנגלית.

בואי כלה: זמירות לשבת / שאול מייזליש. – ירושלים: ש.זק, 1993. 128 עמ'.

גורן, שלמה. ספר מועדי ישראל: בו: מחקרים וחשיפת תכנים חדשים בנושא: מועדי ישראל ורגליו / מאת שלמה גורן. – [תל־אביב]: ידיעות אחרונות: ספרי חמד, 1993. שסד עמ'.

מחזור פסח: לפי מנהג בני אשכנז . . . כולל מנהג אשכנז (המערבי) מנהג פולין ומנהג צרפת לשעבר / מוגה ומעובד בידי יונה פרנקל. – ירושלים: קורן, תשנ"ג 1993. ס, 672 עמ'. „על־פי שיטתו של דר' דניאל גולדשמיט"

6. ספרות וחקר הספרות

ספרות כללית ועברית:

30 שנה, 30 סיפורים: מבחר הסיפור העברי הקצר משנות הששים עד שנות

התשעים / בחר וערך: זיסי סתוי: מסה: דן מירון. – תל־אביב: ספרי ידיעות אחרונות, 1993. 429 עמ'.

חביבי, אמיל. סראיא, בת השד הרע: חוראפייה / אמיל חביבי: מערבית: אנטון שמאס. – תל־אביב: הקיבוץ המאוחד, תשנ"ג 1993. 169 עמ'. – (ספרי סימן קריאה) (הספריה החדשה: 1993)

פסטיבל משוררים בינלאומי, ירושלים 93 – השירים / [עורכים איל מגד, וויאן אדן]. – משכנות שאננים, ירושלים: כתר, 1993. 172 עמ'.

פרייל, גבריאל. אספן סתווים: שירים, 1972־1992 / גבריאל פרייל: [ערך והוסיף מסה על שירת פרייל דן מירון]. – ירושלים: מוסד ביאליק, תשנ"ג 1993. 380 עמ'. כולל מסה של דן מירון „בין הנר לכוכבים".

שירה אחרת: לקט מן השירה הגרמנית הפוסט־נאצית / ליקט, תירגם והוסיף אחרית־דבר ידידיה פלס. – [תל־אביב]: הקיבוץ המאוחד, 1993. 143 עמ'.

חקר הספרות:

אבישי, מרדכי. שערים ברוח: סופרים עבריים ויהודים בספרות העולם / מרדכי אבישי. – ת"א [ז"א תל־אביב]: גולן, 1993. 203 עמ'.

בר, עמוס. המשוררת מכנרת: סיפורה של רחל / עמוס בר. – ירושלים: יד יצחק בן־צבי, תשנ"ג 1993. 186 עמ'. – (סדרת ראשונים בארץ)

ברויאר, זאב זכריה. שירת הקודש של ר' שלמה אבן גבירול: תוכן וצורה / זאב ז. ברויאר. – ירושלים: י"ל מאגנס, תשנ"ג. 402, [6] עמ'.

הולצמן, אבנר. הכרת פנים: מסות על מיכה יוסף ברדיצ'בסקי / אבנר הולצמן. – תל־אביב: רשפים, תשנ"ד 1993. 256 עמ'.

זמיר, ישראל. אבי, יצחק בשביס־זינגר / מאת ישראל זמיר. – תל־אביב: ספרית פועלים: ידיעות אחרונות: ספרי חמד, 1994 / c. 291 עמ'.

יצחקי, ידידיה. הפסוקים הסמויים מן העין: על יצירת א"ב יהושע / ידידיה יצחקי. – רמת גן: אוניברסיטת בר־אילן, תשנ"ג 1992. 336 עמ'. כולל שלושה סיפורים גנוזים מאת א"ב יהושע.

לונדון, ירון. קישון: דו־שיח ביוגרפי / ירון לונדון. – תל־אביב: ספרית מעריב, תשנ"ג 1993. 247 עמ'.

לי, רנה. עגנון והצמחונות: עיונים ביצירותיו של ש"י עגנון מן ההיבט הצמחוני / רנה לי. – תל־אביב: רשפים, תשנ"ד 1993. 283 עמ'.

לשם־עזרא, דנה. חנוך לוין: חפץ / מאת דנה לשם־עזרא. – [תל־אביב]: אור־עם, תשנ"ג 1993. 112 עמ'. – (סדרה לביקורת ספרותית)

מלצר, אלון. אמנון שמוש: מישל עזרא ספרא ובניו / מאת אלון מלצר. – [תל־אביב]: אור־עם, תשנ"ג 1993. 151 עמ'. – (סדרה לעיון וללימוד)

מלצר, אלון. יהושע סובול: ליל העשרים / מאת אלון מלצר. – [תל־אביב]: אור־עם, תשנ"ג 1993. 159 עמ'. – (סדרה לעיון וללימוד)

מלצר, אלון. יצחק בשביס־זינגר: העבד / מאת אלון מלצר. – [תל־אביב]: אור־עם, תשנ"ג 1993. 157 עמ'. – (סדרה לעיון וללימוד)

מלצר, אלון. שולמית לפיד: גיא אוני / מאת אלון מלצר. – [תל־אביב]: אור־

עם, תשנ"ג 1993. 134 עמ'. — (סדרה לעיון וללימוד)

נוה, חנה. בשבי האבל: האבל בראי הספרות העברית החדשה / חנה נוה. — [רמת-גן]: הקיבוץ המאוחד, 1993. 249 עמ'. דיון בעיקר בהיבטים הפסיכולוגיים.

נקודות מפנה בספרות העברית וזיקתן למגעים עם ספרויות אחרות: [ספר הכנס הבין-אוניברסיטאי הששי לחקר הספרות העברית] / ערכו זיוה שמיר ואבנר הולצמן. — תל-אביב: אוניברסיטת תל-אביב — מכון כ"ץ לחקר הספרות העברית, תשנ"ג 1993. 290 עמ'.

נתן, אסתר. הדרך ל"מתי מדבר": על פואמה של ביאליק והשירה הרוסית / אסתר נתן; [ערך: ידידיה פלס]. — [תל-אביב]: הקיבוץ המאוחד, 1993. 223 עמ'. מבוסס על דיסרטציה. האוניברסיטה העברית בירושלים, תשמ"ז 1986.

סדן: מחקרים בספרות עברית. כרך ראשון / עורך, דן לאור. — [תל-אביב]: אוניברסיטת תל-אביב, מפעלים אוניברסיטאיים, תשנ"ד 1994. 296 עמ'. "שנתון הנושא את שמו של דב סדן". כולל מחקרים בספרות עברית והשלמה לביבליוגרפיה של כתבי דב סדן.

"עד עצם היום הזה" . . .: על אמנות ההיגוד של המספר העממי: אסופת מאמרים / בעריכת תמר אלכסנדר. — מהד' ב. — תל-אביב: אופיר, 1993. 230 עמ'. בתחתית השער: פסטיבל גבעתיים למספרי סיפורים תשנ"ג.

עוז, עמוס. שתיקת השמים: עגנון משתומם על אלוהים / עמוס עוז. — ירושלים: כתר, 1993. 219 עמ'.

על "והיה העקוב למישור": מסות על נובלה לש"י עגנון / מבוא ועריכה יהודה פרידלנדר. — [רמת-גן]: אוניברסיטת בר-אילן, תשנ"ג 1993. 224 עמ'. — (סדרת אופקי מחקר)

פגיס, דן. השיר דבור על אופניו: מחקרים ומסות בשירה העברית של ימי הביניים / דן פגיס; ערך והתקין לדפוס עזרא פליישר. — ירושלים: הוצאת ספרים ע"ש י"ל מאגנס, תשנ"ג 1993. 386 עמ'.

קצנלסון, גדעון. גולף הכלים של הכסף: מסות על שירת אורי צבי גרינברג / גדעון קצנלסון; [מבוא ועריכה אבידב ליפסקר]. — תל-אביב: י' גולן, 1993. 234 עמ'.

שביט, עזי. חרוז ומשמעות: עיונים בפואטיקה היסטורית של השירה העברית / עוזי שביט. — ירושלים: מוסד ביאליק, תשנ"ג 1993. 187 עמ'. דן גם בחרוז ומשמעות בשירת אלתרמן.

שוורצבוים, חיים. שורשים וענפים: מבחר כתבים בחקר הפולקלור / חיים שוורצבוים: ליקט מן העזבון וערך עלי יסיף. — באר שבע: הוצאת הספרים של אוניברסיטת בן-גוריון בנגב, תשנ"ד 1993. 220 עמ'.

שמיר, זיוה. להתחיל מאלף: שירת רטוש: מקורויות ומקורותיה / זיוה שמיר: [ערכה: לאה שניר]. — [תל-אביב]: הקיבוץ המאוחד, 1993. 238 עמ'.

שקד, גרשון. ספרות אז, כאן ועכשיו / גרשון שקד. — תל-אביב: זמורה-ביתן, תשנ"ג 1993. 330 עמ'. — (עמודים לספרות עברית: עיון)

7. לשון

אלמוג, עוז. תת-תרבות גלי צה"ל: תרבות בני הנוער בקיבוץ בראי שפתם / עוז אלמוג. — רמת אפעל: יד טבנקין, מרכז מחקרי, רעיוני ותיעודי של התק"ם, 1993. 98, IX עמ'. — (מחקר "הקיבוץ במפנה המאה-משבר, שינוי, המשכיות" חוברת ו') נוספו שער ותמצית באנגלית.

הרמתי, שלמה. בני עלייה: מנחילי-לשון בכירים בדורות האחרונים תרומותיהם ללשון העברית ולהנחלתה / מאת שלמה הרמתי. — תל-אביב: י. גולן, 1993. 272 עמ'.

הרמתי, שלמה. סוד שיח: דיבור עברי במאות ט"ז-י"ט / שלמה הרמתי. — תל-אביב: י' גולן, 1992. 290 עמ'.

וינברך, ליאורה. רב-מילון: מילון דידקטי תלת לשוני: עברי-רוסי-אנגלי / ליאורה וינברך, עדנה לאודן; הרחבת המילון ועריכתו נעשו בשיתוף עם צפורה רמון; רוסית: ב. פודולסקי . . . [ואחרים]; אנגלית: מרים שני. — תל-אביב: עד, 1993. 849, 109 עמ'. שער נוסף ברוסית.

חקק, הרצל. טעות, חזור!: לקסיקון חקק לשיפור הלשון / הרצל ובלפור חקק; עריכה לשונית: רבקה שביט. — ירושלים: שלהבת ירושלים, תשנ"ג 1993. 363 עמ'.

חקרי עבר וערב: מוגשים ליהושע בלאו: על ידי חבריו ותלמידיו במלאת לו שבעים / עורך: ח' בן-שמאי. — [תל-אביב]: אוניברסיטת תל-אביב, הפקולטה למדעי הרוח, בית הספר למדעי היהדות ע"ש חיים רוזנברג. האוניברסיטה העברית בירושלים, המכון ללימודי אסיה ואפריקה, קרן מקס שלסינגר, תשנ"ג 1993. ח, 606 עמ'. נוספו שער ותוכן ענינים באנגלית.

מסכת שביעית במסורות הקריאה של שלוש עדות / מאת קציעה כ"ץ. — ירושלים: האוניברסיטה העברית, המכון למדעי היהדות, מפעל מסורות הלשון של עדות ישראל, תשנ"ד. 121, [2] עמ'. — (עדה ולשון; יז)

סיון, ראובן. בהתחדש לשון: חליפות ותמורות בעברית של ימינו / ראובן סיון. — [תל-אביב]: משרד הבטחון — ההוצאה לאור, תשנ"ג 1993. 167 עמ'.

קומי, אריה. מלון עברי-ספרדי — [ספרדי-עברי]: מחדש ומעדכן / אריה קומי, דב ירדן. — מהד' ג. — תל-אביב: אחיאסף, תשנ"ג 1993. 695, 453 עמ'.

8. תולדות עם-ישראל (מחוץ לגבולות ארץ-ישראל), היסטוריוגרפיה, ציונות, שואה

50 שנה למרד הגיטאות 1943-1993. — תל-אביב: בית עדות ע"ש מרדכי אנילביץ, 1993. 237 עמ'. — (ילקוט מורשת; 54)

אביטבול, מיכאל. מכרמיה לפטן: אנטישמיות באלג'יריה הקולוניאלית 1870-1940 / מיכאל אביטבול. — ירושלים: מרכז זלמן שזר לתולדות ישראל, תשנ"ד 1993. 209, [5] עמ'. — (הסדרה לתולדות האנטישמיות)

אבני, שמעיה. יוסף עבר־כהן ובני דורו: פרקים בתולדות הציונות ברומניה
1923־1957 / ש׳ אבני. — תל־אביב: רשפים, תשנ״ג 1993. 190 עמ׳.

אופנהיים, ישראל. תנועת החלוץ בפולין, 1929־1939 / ישראל אופנהיים. —
קריית שדה־בוקר: המרכז למורשת בן־גוריון, תשנ״ג 1993. ד, 673 עמ׳. נוספו
שער ותכן באנגלית.

האטלס ההיסטורי: תולדות עם ישראל מימי האבות עד ימינו / עורך ראשי
— אלי בר־נביא; עורך המהדורה העברית — מולי מלצר; מפות — מישל
אופטובסקי. — [תל־אביב]: ידיעות אחרונות; ספרי חמד, 1993. 299 עמ׳.
המקור בצרפתית. תורגם גם לאנגלית.

אלבוים־דרור, רחל. המחר של האתמול / רחל אלבוים־דרור. — ירושלים: יד
יצחק בן צבי, תשנ״ג 1993. 2 כר׳. שער נוסף באנגלית. התוכן: כרך א.
האוטופיה הציונית — כר׳ ב. מבחר האוטופיה הציונית.

בין זיכרון להכחשה: גזירות ת״ח ות״ט ברשימות בני הזמן ובראי הכתיבה
ההיסטורית / יואל רבא. — תל־אביב: המרכז לחקר תולדות היהודים בפולין
ומורשתם — המכון לחקר התפוצות — אוניברסיטת תל־אביב, תשנ״ד 1994.
VII ,381 עמ׳. — (פרסומי המכון לחקר התפוצות: 98)

בן־סימון, אניס. חסן השני והיהודים: סיפור העלייה החשאית ממרוקו / אניס
בן־סימון; [עברית — מיכאל אביב]. — תל־אביב: ידיעות אחרונות; ספרי חמד,
1993. 199, [1] עמ׳. כולל הערות ביבליוגרפיות.

גוטמן, ישראל. מרד הנצורים: מרדכי אנילביץ׳ ולחימת גיטו וארשה /
ישראל גוטמן. — מהד׳ 3 מתוקנת. — תל־אביב: מורשת, 1993. 423 עמ׳.

גורני, יוסף. אוטופיה במדיניות: פתרונות פדרליים במחשבה המדינית הציונית
/ יוסף גורני. — תל־אביב: המרכז לפיתוח על־שם פנחס ספיר ליד
אוניברסיטת תל־אביב, 1992. 149 עמ׳. — (סדרת נירות דיון / המרכז לפתוח
על־שם פנחס ספיר; מס׳ 92־6)

גירוש ושיבה: יהודי אנגליה בחילופי הזמנים / עורכים — דוד כ״ץ, יוסף
קפלן. — ירושלים: מרכז זלמן שזר לתולדות ישראל, תשנ״ד 1993. 163 עמ׳.

גרוס, אברהם. ר׳ יוסף בן אברהם חיון: מנהיג קהילת ליסבון ויצירתו. — רמת־
גן: אוניברסיטת בר־אילן, תשנ״ג 1993. 293 עמ׳.

דברי הימים של פאס: גזירות ומאורעות יהודי מארוקו כפי שרשמום בני
משפחת אבן דנאן לדורותיהם, ונלוה אליהם תלאות ומצוקות יהודי פאס
מחיבורו של רבי שאול סירירו / איזן, חקר ותיקן מאיר בניהו. — [תל־אביב]:
מכון למחקר התפוצות — אוניברסיטת תל־אביב, תשנ״ג. [2], 200, [2] עמ׳. —
(פרסומי המכון לחקר התפוצות: ספר 94)

הילברונר, עודד. עליית המפלגה הנאצית לשלטון: אזור היער השחור כדגם
מחקרי / עודד היילברונר. — ירושלים: הוצאת ספרים ע״ש י״ל מאגנס,
האוניברסיטה העברית, תשנ״ג 1993. 327 עמ׳. בראש השער: האוניברסיטה
העברית בירושלים, המרכז להיסטוריה גרמנית על שם ר׳ קבנר.

הרצשטרק, זושא. דם ודמע בגיטו לודז׳ / מאת זושא הארצשטארק. —
ירושלים: מוסד הרב קוק, תשנ״ד 1993. 288 עמ׳.

וימן, דוד ס. הפקרת היהודים: אמריקה והשואה, 1941־1945 / דיוויד ס' ויימן;
תרגמה סמדר מילוא. – ירושלים: יד ושם, תשנ"ג 1993. כ, 475 עמ'.

זוהר, צבי. מסורת ותמורה: התמודדות חכמי ישראל במצרים ובסוריה עם
אתגרי המודרניזציה, 1880־1920 / צבי זוהר. – ירושלים: מכון בן־צבי,
תשנ"ג 1993. 319, XVI עמ'. נוספו שער ותקציר באנגלית.

זנד־לנדאו, ריטה. מי הנהר אדמו – / ריטה זנד־לנדאו. – תל־אביב: רשפים,
תשנ"ג 1992. 414 עמ'. סיפור חייה של נערה יהודיה מבוקובינה, לפני
המלחמה ובימי השואה, במחנה הריכוז, טרנסניסטריה.

חמישים שנה למרד גיטו וארשה, 19 באפריל 1943 — 19 באפריל
1993 / עריכה, צביקה דרור. – תל־אביב: בית לוחמי הגיטאות: הקיבוץ
המאוחד, 1993. 223 עמ'. – (עדות: ט)

יוסף בן יהושע הכהן. עמק הבכא / ליוסף הכהן מאויניון: [ערך וההדיר
משה הלל]. ספר הזכירה / לאפרים בן יעקב מבונא: [ערך וההדיר משה
הלל]. – ירושלים: הספריה הספרדית, תשנ"ג 1993. 231, 38 עמ'. "שני ספרים
נפתחים: קורות ותלאות עם ישראל בארצות צרפת, אשכנז, פורטוגל, ספרד
ואיטליה".

כמנהג אשכנז ופולין: ספר יובל לחנא שמרוק: קובץ מחקרים בתרבות
יהודית / עורכים ־ישראל ברטל, חוה – ורניאנסקי, עזרא מנדלסון. –
ירושלים: מרכז זלמן שזר לתולדות ישראל, תשנ"ג 1993. 428, 118 עמ'.
עברית, יידיש ואנגלית, עם שער נוסף באנגלית: Studies in Jewish
Culture.

כץ, שמואל. ז'בו: ביוגרפיה של זאב ז'בוטינסקי / שמואל כץ. – תל־אביב:
דביר, 1993. 2 כר' (1219 עמ'.) כולל ביבליוגרפיה.

לאופר, יוסף. כחיית השדה: לשרוד בשדות אוקראינה / סיפורו של יוסף
לאופר: נכתב בידי חיים טל. – תל־אביב: משרד הבטחון – ההוצאה לאור,
תשנ"ג 1993. 128 עמ'. – (לחיות! עדויות הישרדות מהשואה)

ליפשיץ, משה. ציונות: עם ישראל בדורות האחרונים / משה ליפשיץ. – מהד'
א. – [תל־אביב]: אור־עם, תשנ"ג 1993. 2 כר' (483 עמ'.) התוכן: א. 1882־1939
– ב. 1939־1949.

מאי, חנה. קבקבי־עץ: [קורותיה של ילדה יהודיה בשואה] / חנה מאי, מלכה
מאי. – תל־אביב: י. גולן, תשנ"ב 1993. 80 עמ'. – (ילדים יהודים אלמונים)

מחתרת הצלה: בני־עקיבא בהונגריה בתקופת השואה / מבוא והערות מאת
נעמי בלנק, חיים גניזי. רמת־גן: אוניברסיטת בר־אילן, תשנ"ג 1933. 197,[3]
עמ'. – (עיונים במחתרת ובמרי: 8) כולל הערות ביבליוגרפיות.

מיכאל, ראובן. הכתיבה ההיסטורית היהודית: מהרנסנס עד העת החדשה /
ראובן מיכאל. – ירושלים: מוסד ביאליק, תשנ"ג 1993. 554 עמ'.

מעין, שמואל. יוסף קפלן: קורותיו של צעיר יהודי בשירות תנועתו – תנועת
"השומר הצעיר" בפולין. חלק ב. בגיטו וארשה ובפולין הכבושה מארס 1940־
ספטמבר 1942 / שמואל מעין. – מעינית: ש. מעין, תשנ"ג 1993. 355 עמ'.

נאור, מרדכי. גשר חי / מרדכי נאור. – [תל־אביב]: משרד הבטחון – ההוצאה

לאור, תשנ"ד 1993. 389 עמ'. על חיילי הבריגדה שסייעו לפליטי השואה
באירופה.

עיונים בתקומת ישראל: מאסף לבעיות הציונות, היישוב ומדינת ישראל.
כרך ג. – קריית שדה בוקר: המרכז למורשת בן־גוריון: [באר שבע]:
אוניברסיטת בן־גוריון בנגב, תשנ"ג 1993. 590, xix עמ'.

הפזורה היהודית הספרדית אחרי הגירוש / מיכאל אביטבול . . .
[ואחרים]. – [ירושלים]: מרכז זלמן שזר לתולדות ישראל, תשנ"ג 1992. 144
עמ'.

פטרן, גילה. האם מאבק על הישרדות: הנהגת יהודי סלובקיה בשואה 1938-
1944 / גילה פטרן; ערך לוי דרור. – תל־אביב: מורשת – בית עדות ע"ש
מרדכי אנילביץ, 1992. 333 עמ'.

פינקוס, בנימין. תחייה ותקומה לאומית: הציונות והתנועה הציונית בברית
המועצות, 1947-1987 / בנימין פינקוס. – באר־שבע: המרכז למורשת בן־
גוריון, תשנ"ג 1993. 737 עמ'. נוספו שער ותוכן באנגלית.

פלד, יעל. קרקוב היהודית, 1939־1943: עמידה, מחתרת, מאבק / יעל פלד
(מרגולין). – [תל־אביב]: בית לוחמי הגיטאות והקבוץ המאוחד בשיתוף
"משואה", תשנ"ג 1993, 360, [8] עמ'.

פריסטר, רומן. דיוקן עצמי עם צלקת / רומן פריסטר. – תל־אביב: דביר,
תשנ"ד 1993. 382 עמ'. "חשבון נפש של סופר ועיתונאי שעבר את המלחמה
כנער במחנות ריכוז, היה עיתונאי בפולין ועלה ב־1957 לישראל".

צפורי־דיר, אירנה. דפים שניצלו מאש / אירנה ציפורי־דייר: תרגם
מפולנית: עמי שפיר. – תל־אביב: בית לוחמי הגיטאות, תשנ"ג 1993. 96 עמ'.
– (פנקסי עדות)

צפתמן־בילר, שרה. בין אשכנז לספרד: לתולדות הסיפור היהודי בימי־
הביניים / שרה צפתמן. – ירושלים: הוצאת ספרים ע"ש י"ל מאגנס,
האוניברסיטה העברית, תשנ"ג 1993. 244 עמ'.

קהן, מאיר. חומת השתיקה נפרצה: כחו של עתון / מאיר <מרק> קהאן; [ערכו
יצחק אלפסי, יוסף קיסטר]. – תל־אביב: מכון ז'בוטינסקי, תשנ"ד 1993. 174
עמ'. אודות העתונים היידיים: היינט ודער מאמענט.

קובנר, אבא. מגילות העדות / אבא קובנר; עורך ומביא לאור – שלום לוריא.
– ירושלים: מוסד ביאליק, תשנ"ג 1993. טו, 277 עמ'.

קוטיק, מאיר. נאשמים ללא אשם: משפטים בצל האנטישמיות / מאיר קוטיק. –
תל־אביב: מלא, תשנ"ג 1993. 322 עמ'. נוספו שער באנגלית.

קצבורג, נתנאל. אנטישמיות בהונגריה, 1867־1944 / נתנאל קצבורג. –
ירושלים: מרכז זלמן שזר לתולדות ישראל; החברה ההיסטורית הישראלית;
המרכז הבינלאומי לחקר האנטישמיות ע"ש וידאל ששון, האוניברסיטה
העברית, תשנ"ג 1993. 203 עמ'. (הסדרה לתולדות האנטישמיות)

קרן, נילי. רסיסי ילדות: חינוך הילדים והנוער בגיטו טרזיאנשטאט ובאושוויץ־
בירקנאו. – [תל־אביב]: בית לוחמי הגיטאות והוצאת הקיבוץ המאוחד, תשנ"ג
1993. 160 עמ'.

רוזן, משה. והסכנה איננו אוכל: זכרונות מתקופות המאבק להצלת יהודי רומניה / מאת דוד משה רוזן. – ירושלים: שם, תשנ"ג 1993. 390 עמ'.

רינגלבלום, עמנואל. כתבים מימי המלחמה / עמנואל רינגלבלום: מבואות, עריכה, הערות -ישראל גוטמן, יוסף קרמיש, ישראל שחם. [כרך א']. – ירושלים: יד ושם – רשות הזיכרון לשואה ולגבורה, תשנ"ג 1. כר'. התוכן: כרך א. יומן ורשימות מתקופת המלחמה – גיטו וארשה: ספטמבר 1939- דצמבר 1942.

רמון, אורי. ז'בוטינסקי: מונולוג (עבר והווה) / אורי רמון. – תל-אביב: אופיר, תשנ"ג 1993. 164 עמ'.

רפסודיה לתכלת לבן: קורות תנועת הנוער תכלת לבן-אל על בצ'כוסלובקיה – השומר הצעיר נוער צופי חלוצי (נצ"ח) / עריכה והבאה לדפוס, דב קוסטלר. – עין-גב: העמותה לתולדות „תכלת לבן-אל על" בצ'כוסלובקיה, 1993. 373, [2] עמ'.

שניר, מילק. קריעות קטנות / מילק (ירחמיאל) שניר: [הביא לדפוס מרדכי יעקובוביץ']. – נוה-איתן, תשנ"ג 1993 . [5], 307 עמ'. „בהוצאת המשפחה וקיבוץ נוה-איתן". „סיפורו האישי של מילק על רקע מלחמת העולם השניה".

9. ארץ-ישראל

טבע הארץ:

בן-דרור, מיכאל. אל פינות החמד: מדריך למטייל בארץ פלגי מים / מיכאל בן-דרור. – ירושלים: הוצאת ספרים אריאל, 1993. 208 עמ'. – (אריאל; 89-90)

הלר, יוסף. שבלולי ארץ ישראל: אורחות חיים ומגדיר / יוסף הלר: איורים – טוביה קורץ. – [תל-אביב]: משרד הביטחון, תשנ"ג 1993. 271 עמ'.

הראובני, עמנואל. פסגות: טיולים לפסגות הרים ואל נקודות תצפית / עמנואל הראובני: [צילומים – עמנואל הראובני]. – [תל-אביב]: כנרת, 1993. 213, [11] עמ'.

הראובני, עמנואל. קום התהלך בארץ: מדריך שמורות טבע בישראל / עמנואל הראובני. – מהד' חדשה, מתוקנת ומורחבת. – תל-אביב: זמורה, ביתן, תשנ"ג 1993. [14], 404 עמ'.

שלמון, בני. מדריך היונקים בישראל: וסימני השדה לנוכחותם / כתב וערך בני שלמון: ציורי היונקים – טטיאנה קופיאן, איורים – עזרא חדד. – ירושלים: כתר, 1993. 216 עמ'. – (מדריכי שדה). כולל ביבליוגרפיה.

גאוגרפיה, מקומות:

אילת – אדם, ים ומדבר / ערכו מאיר כהן ואלי שילר, בהשתתפות חנה צוקרמן-מזרח. – ירושלים: אריאל, תשנ"ג 1993. 368 עמ'. – (אריאל: כתב עת לידיעת ארץ-ישראל; שנה טו 93-94)

אפרת, אלישע. ישראל – גיאוגרפיה בת־זמננו: עם היבטים לקראת המאה ה־
21 / אלישע אפרת. – תל־אביב: אחיאסף, 1993. 224 עמ'.

ארץ הגולן והחרמון / עורכים אבי דגני, משה ענבר. – תל־אביב: משרד
הבטחון – ההוצאה לאור, תשנ"ד 1993. 2 כר' – (ארץ)

בחזרה לסיני: מדריך לטיולים ולחופים בדרום סיני – 1993/1994 / עורך –
אברהם שקד; [כתבו רויטל בר־יוסף . . . ועוד]. – מהד' א. – תל־אביב: מסע
אחד – מגאזין חובק עולם, 1993. 170 עמ'. – (ספריית מסע אחר)

בר־גל, יורם. מולדת וגיאוגרפיה במאה שנות חינוך ציוני / יורם בר־גל;
[עריכה: אילנה שמיר]. – תל־אביב: עם עובד, תשנ"ג 1993. 233 עמ'.

דרור, צביקה. שותפות במעשה הבריאה: הסיפור של בית־הערבה / צביקה
דרור. – תל־אביב: הקיבוץ המאוחד, 1994. 199 עמ'.

וילן, יעקב. בדרך אל נגבה: פרקי חיים / יעקב (קובה) וילן. – תל־אביב:
אופיר, תשנ"ב 1993. 376 עמ'.

יהב, דן. קיבוצים במושבות בשנות השלושים והארבעים: רמת השרון: "אביב",
"הרצליה", "בנתיב" ו"נחשונים": 70 למושבה, 1923־1993 / דן יהב. – תל־
אביב: מאה – הפקה והוצאה לאור, תשנ"ג 1993. 104 עמ'.

לוין, גדעון. עד קצה הגבול: חמש השנים הראשונות להתישבות של קבוץ
להבות הבשן [1950־1945] / גדעון לוין. – להבות הבשן, תשנ"ג 1993. 112
עמ'.

לוינגר, פרץ. יקנעם הכפר החריג: 1935־1985 / פרץ לוינגר. – [יקנעם: פ'
לוינגר]: ועד מקומי יקנעם: מועצה מקומית יקנעם עלית: מועצה מקומית
מגידו, 1993. 278 עמ'.

לטייל בגליל התחתון / ערכו – יוסי בוכמן, עזריה אלון. – [תל־אביב]:
משרד הבטחון – ההוצאה לאור, החברה להגנת הטבע, תשנ"ג 1993. 246 עמ'.

מגי, ג'ויבנה. מצדה וים המלח: יריחו, חירבת קומראן, עין גדי / ג'ויבנה מגי.
– בני־ברק: סטימצקי, 1993. 63 עמ'.

ניר, דב. עיונים בגיאוגרפיה פיסית של ארץ־ישראל ודרום סיני: אסופת
מאמרים / דב ניר. – ירושלים: אריאל, 1993. 159 עמ'.

נשרי, יצחק. התחלות קשות: קיבוץ ארז, ישוב־משלט סוג א' 1949־1959 /
יצחק נשרי: קריקטורות: אליעזר שרף. – קבוצת ארז: י. נשרי, תשנ"ג 1993.
149 עמ'.

ארכיאולוגיה:

אמנות הפסיפס בבתי כנסת עתיקים בארץ־ישראל מהמאה
הרביעית עד המאה השביעית / [אוצר התערוכה – אשר עובדיה;
אנגלית – עריכה לשונית, דפנה רז]. – תל־אביב: אוניברסיטת תל־אביב –
הגלריה האוניברסיטאית לאמנות ע"ש גניה שרייבר, 1993. 85, [3] עמ'. עברית
ואנגלית.

היימן, מרדכי. מפת הר חמרן דרום־מזרח (199) / מרדכי היימן. – ירושלים:
רשות העתיקות ־האגודה לסקר ארכיאולוגי של ישראל, תשנ"ג 1993. 131, 76

עמ'. – (סקר ארכיאולוגי של ישראל).

זרטל, אדם. סקר הר מנשה / אדם זרטל. – [תל־אביב]: משרד הבטחון –
ההוצאה לאור, תשנ"ב 1992. 1 כר'. – (פרסומי סקר הר מנשה). התכן: א. קער
שכם.

סקר ארכיאולוגי בארץ בנימין / עורכים יצחק מגן, ישראל פינקלשטיין.
– ירושלים: המינהל האזרחי ביהודה ובשומרון, קצין מטה ארכיאולוגיה:
רשות העתיקות, תשנ"ג 1993. 466, 70 עמ'.

קמפינסקי, אהרן. מגידו – עיר־מדינה כנענית ומרכז ממלכתי ישראלי /
אהרון קמפינסקי; תרגמה: דבי הרשמן. – תל־אביב: הקיבוץ המאוחד:
החברה לחקירת ארץ ישראל ועתיקותיה, 1993. 208 עמ'.

היסטוריה:

בן־שלום, ישראל. בית שמאי ומאבק הקנאים נגד רומי / ישראל בן־שלום. –
ירושלים: יד יצחק בן־צבי, תשנ"ד 1993. יד, 366 עמ'.

דרורי, יוסף. אבן אל־ערבי מסביליה: מסע בארץ ישראל (1095-1092) / יוסף
דרורי. – רמת־גן: אוניברסיטת בר־אילן, תשנ"ג 1993. 201 עמ'.

הראובני, דוד. סיפור דוד הראובני: על פי כתב־יד אוקספורד בצרוף כתבים
ועדויות מבני הדור, עם מבוא והערות / ערוך בידי א"ז אשכולי; מבואות –
משה אידל ואליהו ליפינר. – מהד' ב מורחבת. – ירושלים: מוסד ביאליק,
תשנ"ג 1993. LXVI, רמ, 254 עמ'.

יוסף בן מתתיהו פלויוס. מלחמת היהודים / יוסף בן מתתיהו־יוספוס
פלביוס; תרגום חדש על־ידי שמואל חגי. – מהד' ה מתוקנת בצירוף מפתח
השמות והענינים, מפות ואיורים. – ירושלים: ר' מס, תשנ"ג (1993). 349, [3]
עמ'.

מדינת החשמונאים: לתולדותיה על רקע התקופה ההלניסטית: קובץ
מאמרים / ליקטו וערכו אוריאל רפפורט וישראל רונן. – ירושלים: יד יצחק
בן־צבי, תשנ"ד 1993. 525 עמ'. בתחתית השער: האוניברסיטה הפתוחה.

מנהיג והנהגה: קובץ מאמרים / עורכים עירד מלכין, זאב צחור. –
[ירושלים]: מרכז זלמן שזר לתולדות ישראל, החברה ההיסטורית הישראלית,
תשנ"ב 1992. 349 עמ'.

ריבלין, אברהם בנימין. זה קרה בארץ־ישראל: אירועים ופרשיות / מאת
אברהם ב. ריבלין. – ירושלים: ר' מס, תשנ"ג 1993. 127 עמ'.

שפרבר, דניאל. תרבות חומרית בארץ־ישראל בימי התלמוד / דניאל שפרבר.
– ירושלים: יד יצחק בן־צבי, תשנ"ד 1993. 198 עמ'.

תולדות ירושלים:

ביר, אהרן. מוסדות תורה וחסד יהודיים ברובע המוסלמי בירושלים העתיקה /
מאת אהרן ביר. היישוב היהודי המתחדש ברובע המוסלמי, תשל"ב־תשנ"ג /
מאת ברכה סליי. – ירושלים: [חמו"ל], תשנ"ג 1993. עט עמ' + מפה מקפלת.

בן־גור, אליצור. יומן ירושלים, תש"ח: ברובע הנצור ובשבי הלגיון / אליצור

בן־גור. – ירושלים: אריאל, 1993.

גונן, רבקה. לגור בירושלים / רבקה גונן, דוד קרויאנקר; [עיצוב אורה יפה].
– ירושלים: מוזיאון ישראל, תשנ״ג 1993. 193 עמ׳. – (קטלוג / מוזיאון
ישראל, ירושלים; 349)

וילנאי, זאב. אנציקלופדיית וילנאי לירושלים / זאב וילנאי; עדכן: נתנאל
ליפשיץ. – ירושלים: אחיעבר, תשנ״ג 1993. 2 כר׳.

חלום בהקיץ: ירושלים הלא־בנויה / אוצר התערוכה: דוד קרויאנקר; [עיצוב
הקטלוג: סטודיו קו־גרף]. – [ירושלים]: מגדל דוד, המוזיאון לתולדות
ירושלים, [1993]. 225 עמ׳. הטכסט בעברית, אנגלית וערבית.

טופורובסקי, יהודית. מאה שערים שלי: קורות משפחת שלום ומלכה אזולאי
בשכונת מאה שערים כאספקלריה לחיי הישוב הישן בין השנים 1919־1924 /
יהודית טופורובסקי. – ירושלים: ר׳ מס, תשנ״ד 1993. 106 עמ׳.

כהן, אמנון. יהודים בבית המשפט המוסלמי: חברה, כלכלה וארגון קהילתי
בירושלים העות׳מאנית, המאה השש־ עשרה / אמנון כהן, אלישבע סימון־
פיקאלי ובהשתתפות עובדיה סלאמה. – ירושלים: יד יצחק בן־צבי, תשנ״ג
1993. 418 עמ׳.

מנחה לירושלים: במלאות כ״ה שנים לאיחודה / ערך אלי שילר; ייעץ
ישראל קמחי. – ירושלים: אריאל, 1993. 223 עמ׳. – (אריאל: כתב עת
לידיעת ארץ־ישראל; שנה יד 91־92)

קמחי, ישראל. כ״ה שנים לאיחוד ירושלים: היבט סטטיסטי / ישראל קמחי. –
ירושלים: מכון ירושלים לחקר ישראל, 1993. [4], 35 עמ׳. – (היבט מס׳ 3)

קרויאנקר, דוד. אדריכלות בירושלים: הבנייה בעיר העתיקה / דוד
קרויאנקר. – ירושלים: כתר; מכון ירושלים לחקר ישראל; עיריית ירושלים;
הקרן לירושלים, 1993. 500 עמ׳. כולל ביבליוגרפיה.

קרויאנקר, דוד. סיפור קריית העירייה, ירושלים / דוד קרויאנקר. –
ירושלים: אריאל, תשנ״ג 1993. 467 עמ׳.

קרניאל, שלמה. אטלס מטרופוליטני ירושלים / שלמה קרניאל, חוה גורדון.
– תל־אביב: מדריך ישראל – אטלס, 1993. 176 עמ׳.

תולדות הישוב החדש והמאבק לעצמאות:

בוגנר, נחום. ספינות המרי: ההעפלה 1945־1948 / נחום בוגנר. – [תל־אביב]:
משרד הבטחון – ההוצאה לאור, תשנ״ג 1993. 371 עמ׳.

בן־גוריון, דוד. לקראת קץ המנדט: (זכרונות מן העיזבון: 29 ביוני 1946־מרס
1947) / דוד בן־גוריון; ערך וליווה במבואות ובהארות מאיר אביזוהר. –
תל־אביב: עם עובד, תשנ״ג 1993. יב, 448 עמ׳.

בן־עזר, אהוד. ג׳דע: סיפורו של אברהם שפירא שומר המושבה / אהוד בן
עזר. – ירושלים: יד יצחק בן־צבי, תשנ״ג 1993. 231 עמ׳. – (סדרת ראשונים
בארץ)

ברמן, יצחק. בימי סער / יצחק ברמן. – [תל־אביב]: משרד הבטחון – ההוצאה
לאור, תשנ״ג 1993. 156 עמ׳. „חלק מקטעי זכרונות".

גוזס־סבוראי, איה. ספרי לי ספרי לי: חברות פלמ״ח מספרות / איה גוזס־
סבוראי. – תל־אביב: המרכז לתולדות כח המגן – "ההגנה" ע״ש ישראל
גלילי: הקיבוץ המאוחד, 1993. 199 עמ׳.

גורני, יוסף. מדיניות ודמיון: תכניות פדרליות במחשבה המדינית הציונית,
1917־1948 / יוסף גורני. – ירושלים: יד יצחק בן־צבי, תשנ״ג 1993. י, 244
עמ׳.

דוד, אברהם. עלייה והתיישבות בארץ־ישראל במאה הט״ז / מאת אברהם דוד.
– ירושלים: ר׳ מס, תשנ״ג 1993. [5], 260, [1] עמ׳.

הרשלג, פועה. שליחות של אהבה: סיפורו של אנצו סרני / פועה הרשלג. –
ירושלים: יד יצחק בן־צבי, תשנ״ג 1993. 218 עמ׳. – (סדרת ראשונים בארץ)

זית, דוד. חלוצים במבוך הפוליטי: התנועה הקיבוצית 1927־1948 / דוד זית. –
ירושלים: יד יצחק בן־צבי, תשנ״ג 1993. 281 עמ׳. נוספו שער ותוכן באנגלית

חסון, יצחק. הזקן ואני: סיפורו האישי של ראש המודיעין של הלח״י (מחלקה ו)
/ יצחק חסון. – תל־אביב: בריירות, תשנ״ג 1993. 223 עמ׳.

כהן, גדעון. צללים: זכרונות בין שתי מלחמות 1918־1939 / גדעון כהן;
[מאנגלית – עדנה תדמור]. – ירושלים: ר׳ ח׳ הכהן, תשנ״ג. 128 עמ׳.

כתבים לתולדות חיבת ציון וישוב ארץ ישראל / ליקט וערך לראשונה
אלתר דרויאנוב , ההדירה וערכה מחדש שולמית לסקוב. כרך שביעי, 1889־
1890. – [תל־אביב]: אוניברסיטת תל־אביב: הקיבוץ המאוחד, תשנ״ג 1993.
592 עמ׳. – (סדרת מחקרים ומקורות / תל־אביב. אוניברסיטה. המכון לחקר
הציונות ע״ש חיים ויצמן)

לאו־לביא, נפתלי. עם כלביא / נפתלי לאו־לביא. – תל־אביב: ספרית
מעריב, תשנ״ג 1993. 448 עמ׳.

מאירי, שלמה. בנתיבי מחתרת ובארץ גזרה: מפתח־תקוה לקניה וחזרה /
שלמה מאירי ("בנימין"). – תל־אביב: מלוא, תשנ״ג 1993. 472 עמ׳.

סגל, ירושלים. ירושלים בתל־אביב: זכרונות / ירושלים סגל; [עריכה, עיצוב
הספר והעטיפה: יעקב גרוס]. – תל־אביב: מולדת, תשנ״ג 1993. 415 עמ׳.

ספר עולי הסרטיפיקאטים: זיכרונות, תעודות, איגרות / בעריכת סיני
לייכטר וחיים מילקוב. – ירושלים: הוצאת ספרים ע״ש י.ל. מאגנס,
האוניברסיטה העברית, תשנ״ג 1993. VII ,337, עמ׳. – (פרסומי הר הצופים)

עקביה, אברהם. אורד וינגייט – חייו ופועלו / אברהם עקביה; [עורך: צבי
עופר]. – תל־אביב: מערכות, 1993. 282 עמ׳.

ראובני, יעקב. ממשל המנדט בא״י, 1920־1948: ניתוח היסטורי־מדיני / יעקב
ראובני. – רמת־גן: אוניברסיטת בר־אילן, תשנ״ג 1993. 245 עמ׳. – (סדרת
עיונים במשק ובחברה)

רובינשטין, שמעון. ברקיע הציפיות: המדיניות הקרקעית של "ועד הצירים"
ב־1918 / שמעון רובינשטיין: בצרוף הקדמה מאת גדעון ביגר. – תל־אביב:
י. גולן, 1993. 315, [4] עמ׳.

רובינשטין, שמעון. מברלד עד מעברת ראש־פינה: על מאבק הקיום
וההסתגלות של משפחת עולים מרומניה בגליל (1950־1956): שיח בין נתן

ואַרנה רובינשטיין, הבן שמעון והנכד אפרים / שמעון רובינשטיין; מבוא
ירחמיאל אסא וצבי שילוני; איורים וציור העטיפה גרטי רובינשטיין. – תל־
אביב: י. גולן. 1993. 654, II עמ'.

שביט, יעקב. חרושת הטקסטיל בארץ ישראל 1854־1956: מתעשייה חלוצית
לתעשייה מובילה / יעקב שביט. – תל־אביב: האגודה הישראלית לטקסטיל,
1992. 304, [6], [1] עמ'.

שנות המחנות העולים: עשור שלישי, תש"ו (1945)־תשט"ז (1956) / ערך
יחזקאל אבנרי. – [תל־אביב]: הקיבוץ המאוחד, תשנ"ד, 1993.

שפר, אליעזר. סיפורי הזמן והמקום / אליעזר שפר. – ירושלים: מוסד
ביאליק, תשנ"ג 1993. 130 עמ'.

תולדות היישוב היהודי בארץ־ישראל מאז העלייה הראשונה.
[כרך ב.] חלק א. תקופת המנדט הבריטי / עורך – משה ליסק. – ירושלים:
האקדמיה הלאומית הישראלית למדעים, תשנ"ד 1993. כח, 542, [7] עמ'. כולל
ביבליוגרפיה.

10. מדינת־ישראל

ערביי ישראל:

אוסצקי־לזר, שרה. אקרית ובירעם – הסיפור המלא / שרה אוסצקי־לזר. –
גבעת־חביבה: המכון ללימודים ערביים, 1993. 40 עמ'. – (סקירות על
הערבים בישראל; מס' 10)

ביילי, יצחק. קסם נאקות: שירה בדווית מסיני והנגב / יצחק ביילי: תרגום
השירים – פרץ־דרור בנאי. – [צופית]: המרכז לחקר החברה הערבית
בישראל, תשנ"ג 1993. 130 עמ'. – (כחול ירוק: עיונים במציאות יהודית־
ערבית). כולל גם טקסט בערבית.

בן־דוד, יוסף. יישוב הבדווים בנגב: מדיניות ומציאות, 1967־1992 / יוסף בן־
דוד. – ירושלים: משרד הבינוי והשיכון: מכון ירושלים לחקר ישראל, 1993.
129 עמ'. – (מחקרי מכון ירושלים לחקר ישראל; 49).

גאנם, אסעד. הערבים בישראל לקראת המאה ה־21: סקר תשתית בסיסית /
אסעד גאנם. – גבעת חביבה: המכון לחקר השלום, 1993. 98, [1] עמ'.

הורוביץ, דני. כמו גשר תקוע: שיחות עם השחקנים מוחמד בכרי, סלווה
נקארה־חדאד, מכרם כורי, ח'אולה חאג' וסלים דאו / דני הורוביץ. –
[צופית]: המרכז לחקר החברה הערבית בישראל, בית ברל, תשנ"ג 1993. 139
עמ'. – (כחול ירוק)

לנדאו, יעקב מ. המיעוט הערבי בישראל: 1967־1991: היבטים פוליטיים /
יעקב מ. לנדאו. – תל־אביב: עם עובד, תשנ"ג 1993. VI, 215 עמ'. – (ספרית
אשכולות)

רכס, אלי. המיעוט הערבי בישראל: בין קומוניזם ללאומיות ערבית, 1965־1991
/ אלי רכס. – תל־אביב: מרכז משה דיין, אוניברסיטת תל־אביב, תשנ"ג
1993. 271 עמ'. – (קו אדום)

העולם הערבי, הסכסוך הישראלי־ערבי. האינתיפדה:

האסלאם הפונדמנטליסטי: אתגר ליציבות אזורית / עורך – דוד מנשרי. – תל־אביב: מרכז משה דיין ללימודי המזרח ואפריקה, 1993. 83, [2] עמ'. – (סקירות / אוניברסיטת תל־אביב. מרכז משה דין ללמודי המזרח התיכון ואפריקה: 114)

זיסר, איל. אסד של סוריה – המנהיג ותדמיתו / איל זיסר. תל־אביב: אוניברסיטת תל־אביב – מרכז משה דיין ללימודי המזרח התיכון ואפריקה – מכון שילוח, 1993. [2], 27 עמ'. – (נתונים וניתוח)

זמיר, איל. „אדמות היהודים״ ביהודה, שומרון, חבל עזה ומזרח ירושלים / איל זמיר, איל בנבנשתי. – ירושלים: מכון ירושלים לחקר ישראל, 1993. 320 עמ'. – (מחקרי מכון ירושלים לחקר ישראל: 52)

זמיר, מאיר. כינונה של לבנון המודרנית / מאיר זמיר; [תרגום מאנגלית – יורם שדה]. – תל־אביב: מערכות, 1993. 320 עמ'.

טרור איסלאמי וישראל: חיזבאללה, ג'יהאד איסלאמי פלסטיני, חמאס / [עורכים]: ענת קורץ, משכית בורגין, דוד טל. – תל־אביב: פפירוס, 1993. 209 עמ'. בתחתית השער: מל״א, המרכז למחקרים אסטרטגיים ע״ש יפה, אוניברסיטת תל־אביב.

ישראל בראי הקריקטורה הערבית 1987־1992: מבחר קריקטורות מעתוני מצרים, ירדן, סוריה, לבנון, סעודיה, סודן, מרוקו, אלג'יריה, לוב, עירק, מדינות המפרץ, ערביי פלשתין. – תל־אביב: י' גולן, 1993. 189 עמ'.

לפידות, רות. אוטונומיה / רות לפידות. – [ירושלים: מכון ירושלים לחקר ישראל, [1993]. 79 עמ'. – (דפי דיון / מכון ירושלים לחקר ישראל)

מדיניות חוץ ובטחון. צה״ל:

אלדר, מייק. שייטת 13: סיפורו של הקומנדו הימי / מייק אלדר. – תל־אביב: ספרית מעריב, 1993. 712 עמ'.

אהרנסון, שלמה. הפוליטיקה והאיסטרטגיה של נשק גרעיני במזרח התיכון: ערפול, תיאוריה ומציאות, 1948־1993 / מאת שלמה אהרונסון בסיועו של עודד ברוש: [מאנגלית צילה אלעזר]. – ירושלים: אקדמון, תשנ״ד 1994. 1 כר'. התוכן: א. בן־גוריון והאופציה הגרעינית, 1948־1963.

בונה, עודד. להיות תותחן / עודד בונה. – תל־אביב: מערכות, 1993. 279, [1] עמ'.

גולד, דורי. האסטרטגיה הצבאית האמריקנית במזרח התיכון: ההשלכות של המערך הפיקודי של ארצות־הברית באזור (CENTCOM) על ישראל / דורי גולד: [מאנגלית רמי טל וברוך קורות]. – תל־אביב: משרד הבטחון – ההוצאה לאור, המרכז למחקרים אסטרטגיים ע״ש יפה – אוניברסיטת תל־אביב, תשנ״ג 1993. 226 עמ'.

גלבע, איתן. ארצות־הברית – ישראל: תשתית היחסים המיוחדים / איתן גלבוע; מאנגלית: יוסף ארגמן. – תל־אביב: משרד הבטחון – ההוצאה לאור, תשנ״ד 1993. 353 עמ'.

זעירא, אלי. מלחמת יום־הכיפורים: מיתוס מול מציאות / אלי זעירא; (עורך
רמי טל). – תל־אביב: ידיעות אחרונות, 1993. 288 עמ'.

יחסים נורמליים: יחסי ישראל־גרמניה / בעריכת משה צימרמן ועודד
היילברונר; [תרגם מגרמנית: ארנון מגן]. – ירושלים: הוצאת ספרים ע"ש י"ל
מאגנס, האוניברסיטה העברית, תשנ"ג 1993. XV, 167 עמ'. נוספו שער, תוכן
ומבוא באנגלית. שער נוסף בגרמנית. בראש השער: האוניברסיטה העברית
בירושלים, המרכז להיסטוריה גרמנית על שם ר' קבנר.

מודריק, עודד. שפיטה צבאית / עודד מודריק. – [תל־אביב]: משרד הבטחון
– ההוצאה לאור, תשנ"ג 1993. 248 עמ'.

מילשטיין, אורי. סיירת שקד: המנע ובטחון שוטף בתולדות צה"ל / אורי
מילשטיין, דב דורון. – תל־אביב: ידיעות אחרונות, 1994. 383 עמ'. "תיאור
מבצעיה של סיירת שקד בתוספת ניתוח החשיבה הצבאית בישראל".

מימון, דוד. טרור שנוצח: דיכוי הטרור ברצועת עזה 1972־1971 / דוד מימון;
[עריכה – מיכל גיל]. – [תל־אביב]: סטימצקי, תשנ"ב 1993. 222 עמ'.

עלי, כמאל חסן. לוחמים ועושי־שלום / כמאל חסן עלי; [תרגם מערבית
אברהם רובינזון]. – תל־אביב: מערכות, 1993. 390 עמ'.

פלד, יוסי. איש צבא / יוסי פלד; [כתבה רונית ורדי]. – תל־אביב: ספרית
מעריב, תשנ"ג 1993. 376 עמ'. אוטוביוגרפיה.

פרס, שמעון. המזרח התיכון החדש: מסגרת ותהליכים לעידן השלום / שמעון
פרס; [עם אריה נאור]. – בני־ברק: סטימצקי, 1993. 171 עמ'.

שושן, יצחק. הקרב האחרון של המשחתת אילת / יצחק שושן. – תל־אביב:
ספרית מעריב, תשנ"ד 1993. 271 עמ'. "מפקד המשחתת שטובעה כותב את
גירסתו".

שלו, אריה. שלום ובטחון בגולן / אריה שלו. – תל־אביב: מל"א – המרכז
למחקרים אסטרטגיים ע"ש יפה, אוניברסיטת תל־אביב, 1993. 269 עמ'. שער
נוסף באנגלית.

שפירא, דני. לבד בשחקים / דני שפירא עם דני שלום. – תל־אביב: ספרית
מעריב, תשנ"ד 1994. 398 עמ'. "סיפורו של מי שנחשב אחד הטייסים המהוטבים
בעולם".

נשים בישראל:

אדר, גילה. נשים פעילות ונשים לא פעילות בתפקידים ציבוריים־פוליטיים
בקיבוץ / מאת גילה אדר. – חיפה: אוניברסיטת חיפה, המכון לחקר
הקיבוץ, 1993. 89 עמ'. – [פרסום; מס' 129)

רפפורט, גיזי. על הפמיניזם ומתנגדיו / גיזי רפפורט. – תל־אביב: דביר, 1993.
170 עמ'. – (מה? דע!)

חברה וכלכלה:

אביב, אביבה. החברה הישראלית: מתחים ומאבקים / אביבה אביב. – תל־
אביב: משרד הבטחון – ההוצאה לאור, מטכ"ל – קצין חינוך ראשי – גלי

צה״ל, תשנ״ג 1993. 102 עמ'. (ספריית אוניברסיטה משודרת)

אברהם, אלי. התקשורת בישראל — מרכז ופריפריה: סיקורן של עיירות הפיתוח / אלי אברהם. תל־אביב: בריחות, תשנ״ג 1993. 164 עמ'.

אגסי, יוסף. בין דת ולאום: לקראת זהות לאומית ישראלית / יוסף אגסי. — מהד' 2, מורחבת ומתוקנת. — תל־אביב: פפירוס, 1993. 320 עמ'. נוסף שער באנגלית.

אורון, יאיר. זהות יהודית ישראלית: מחקר על יחסם של פרחי־הוראה מכל זרמי החינוך ליהדות בת־זמננו ולציונות / יאיר אורון. — תל־אביב: ספרית פועלים: מכללה לחינוך־סמינר הקיבוצים, תשנ״ג 1993. 204 עמ'. — (ספרי דעת זמננו: הסדרה: יהדות)

איזנשטדט, שמואל נח. עדות בישראל ומיקומן החברתי / ש״נ אייזנשטדט, משה ליסק, יעקב נהון. — ירושלים: מכון ירושלים לחקר ישראל, 1993. [4], 171 עמ'. — (מחקרי מכון ירושלים לחקר ישראל; מס' 46)

איכילוב, אורית. חינוך לאזרחות בחברה מתהווה: פלשתינה א״י — מדינת ישראל / אורית איכילוב. — תל־אביב: ספרית פועלים, תשנ״ג 1993. 148 עמ'. — (סדרת עיון)

איכילוב, אורית. חינוך לאזרחות בדמוקרטיה / אורית איכילוב. — [תל־אביב]: אוניברסיטת תל־אביב, בית הספר לחינוך, היחידה לסוציולוגיה של החינוך והקהילה, 1993. 99 עמ'. — (סדרת חינוך וחברה)

אליצור, יואל. מיסוד השיגעון: משפחות, טיפול וחברה / יואל אליצור, סלוודור מנוחין ופרק מאת מרדכי קאפמן: [מאנגלית — יהודית כפרי־מאירי]. — ירושלים ותל־אביב: שוקן, תשנ״ב 1992. 288 עמ'.

בן־רפאל, אליעזר. תפיסות של שינוי בקיבוץ / אליעזר בן־רפאל, עידית גייסט. — רמת אפעל: יד טבנקין — מרכז מחקר רעיוני ותיעודי של התק״ם, 1993. VI, 74 עמ'. — (מחקר הקבוץ במפנה המאה — משבר, שנוי, המשכיות; חוב' ח) נוספו שער ותקציר באנגלית.

גרינברג, לב. ההסתדרות מעל הכל / לב לואיס גרינברג. — ירושלים: נבו, 1993. 254 עמ'.

הורוביץ, דן. תכלת ואבק: דור תש״ח — דיוקן עצמי / דן הורוביץ; עורך אבי כצמן. — ירושלים: כתר, 1993. 150 עמ'. — (תעודת זהות)

הראל, יהודה. הקיבוץ החדש / יהודה הראל; עורך: אבי כצמן; איורים: מושיק לין. — [ירושלים]: כתר, 1993. 248 עמ'.

החברה הישראלית — היבטים ביקורתיים / [ערך] אורי רם. — תל־אביב: בריחות, תשנ״ד 1993. 363 עמ'.

לוינגר, אסתר. אנדרטות לנופלים בישראל / אסתר לוינגר. — תל־אביב: הקבוץ המאוחד, 1994. 192 עמ'. "מעבר לדיון במסרים הסמליים של האנדרטות דן הספר בשאלות יסוד של ההיסטוריה של האידיאולוגיה הישראלית ושל המיתולוגיה הציונית".

לניר, יוסף. המשבר הדמוגרפי בקיבוץ. א. גורמים כמותיים כמשתני שינוי והתפתחות במבנה הדמוגרפי של הקיבוץ / יוסף לניר. — רמת אפעל: יד

333

טבנקין, 1993. 130, [3] עמ'. — (סדרת מחברות מחקר; חוברת ל')

מדיניות תשתיות טכנולוגיות לחידוש הצמיחה / עורכים – משה יוסטמן, אהוד זוסקוביץ ומוריס תובל. — ירושלים: מכון ירושלים לחקר ישראל, 1993. [8], 316 עמ'. — (סדרת מחקרים / מכון ירושלים לחקר ישראל; 48)

פישר, רונאל. סלומון אבו – גנגסטר יהודי / רונאל פישר, דני דור. — תל־אביב: ספרית מעריב, תשנ"ד 1993. 376 עמ'. סיפורו של שודד ורוצח ישראלי.

פסי, רוזליה. הבולגרים של יפו / רוזליה פסי. — תל־אביב: משרד הבטחון – ההוצאה לאור, תשנ"ג 1993. 152 עמ'.

פרידמן, יצחק. יחסי־גומלין בין מורים לתלמידים: נקודת המבט של התלמיד: מבחר היגדים / מאת יצחק פרידמן, נועה קרונגולד. — ירושלים: מכון הנרייטה סאלד, המכון הארצי למחקר במדעי ההתנהגות, תשנ"ג 1993. 109 עמ'. — (דו"ח מחקר; 248) (פרסום מס' 704)

פרידמן, יצחק. לחץ ושחיקה בהוראה: גורמים ודרכי מניעה / יצחק פרידמן, אילה לוטן. — ירושלים: מכון הנרייטה סאלד – המכון הארצי למחקר במדעי ההתנהגות, תשנ"ג 1993. 175 עמ'. בראש השער: עמותת המורים לקידום ההוראה והחינוך מיסודה של הסתדרות המורים, משרד החינוך והתרבות – המינהל לכח אדם בהוראה, הכשרה והשתלמות.

פרס, יוחנן. קהילתיות בחינוך: הצלחה או כישלון?: מחשבות, נתונים, המלצות / יוחנן פרס, רחל פסטרנק. — תל־אביב: איתאב, תשנ"ד 1993. 108 עמ'.

צוקרמן, משה. שואה בחדר האטום: ה"שואה" בעתונות הישראלית בתקופת מלחמת המפרץ / משה צוקרמן. — [תל־אביב]: הוצאת המחבר, 1993. XII, 368 עמ'.

צלח, שמחה. בגוף ראשון רבים: קידום שכונות כתהליך של התעוררות פנימית / שמחה צלח. — תל־אביב: ברירות, 1993. 140 עמ'.

קונדור, יעקב. משק במחתרת בישראל ובעולם / יעקב קונדור; [עריכה: עפרה פרי]. — תל־אביב: צ'ריקובר, 1993. 150 עמ'. — (גומא ספרי מדע ומחקר)

קרע בין הכיפות: חשבון נפש על דור הכיפות הסרוגות / [משתתפים: אורי אליצור . . . ואחרים; מנחה ישראל הראל; עורך זאב גלילי]. — ירושלים: מרכז ספיר, תשנ"ג 1993. 207 עמ'.

קשתי, יצחק. בתי־ספר פנימיתיים בצמתים של שינוי / יצחק קשתי. — תל־אביב – רמות – אוניברסיטת תל־אביב, תשנ"ג 1993. 120 עמ'.

משפט:

ברזילי, גד. בית המשפט העליון בעין החברה הישראלית / גד ברזילי, אפרים יער־יוכטמן, זאב סגל. — תל־אביב: פפירוס, תשנ"ד 1994. 231, X עמ'.

כהן, חיים הרמן. צדק במשפט / חיים ה' כהן. — תל־אביב: משרד הבטחון – ההוצאה לאור, מטכ"ל – קצין חינוך ראשי – גלי צה"ל, תשנ"ג 1992. 114, [5] עמ'. — (ספריית אוניברסיטה משודרת)

מאוטנר, מנחם. ירידת הפורמליזם ועליית הערכים במשפט הישראלי / מנחם
מאוטנר. – תל־אביב: מעגלי דעת, תשנ״ג 1993. 167 עמ׳.

סגל, זאב. זכות העמידה בבית־המשפט הגבוה לצדק / זאב סגל. – מהד׳ ב
מעודכנת. – תל־אביב: פפירוס, תשנ״ד 1993. 307, X עמ׳.

שפטל, יורם. פרשת דמיאניוק: עלייתו ונפילתו של משפט ראווה / יורם
שפטל. – תל־אביב: אדם, 1993. 411 עמ׳.

שרון, יוסף. בניין בית המשפט העליון, ירושלים / [כתב וערך – יוסף שרון;
צילומים – ריצ׳ארד בריאנט]. – ירושלים: יד הנדיב, קרן רוטשילד, 1993.
180 עמ׳.

שרשבסקי, בנציון. דיני משפחה / מאת בנציון שרשבסקי. – מהד׳ ד
מורחבת. – ירושלים: ר׳ מס, תשנ״ג 1993. I, 471 עמ׳. – (פרסומי הפקולטה
למשפטים של האוניברסיטה העברית; 5)

אמנות ותרבות:

מנור, דליה. מיכאל ארגוב / דליה מנור; [עיצוב רוני רכב]. – [תל־אביב]:
ספרית פועלים, תשנ״ג 1993, 120 עמ׳. – (אמנות). עברית ואנגלית.

צבע מהטבע: על צבעים טבעיים בעת העתיקה / בעריכת חגית שורק ואיתן
איילון; [עריכה והבאה לדפוס: גניה דורון; תרגום לאנגלית: ג׳אי יעקובסון].
– תל־אביב: מוזיאון ארץ־ישראל, תשנ״ג 1993. 102, 37 עמ׳. עברית ואנגלית.
התערוכה נערכה בביתן הבולאות במוזיאון ארץ־ישראל, חורף תשנ״ג.

שגל, מרק. שאגאל – חלומות ומחזות: עבודות מוקדמות וציורי הקיר לתיאטרון
היידי ברוסיה / בעריכת רות אפטר־גבריאל; [עיצוב הספר נירית צור:
עיצוב התערוכה דוד גל]. – ירושלים: מוזיאון ישראל, 1993. 60, 43 עמ׳. –
(קטלוג / מוזיאון ישראל, ירושלים: 352). עברית ואנגלית.

שלטון ומינהל, מפלגות:

אורברך, אורי. ישראל צחקה מרבין: בדיחות פוליטיות אקטואליות / ערך אורי
אורברך; אייר ניסים. – ירושלים: אביטל, תשנ״ג 1993. 60, [1] עמ׳.

בגין, זאב בנימין. קווי עימות / זאב בנימין בגין. – [תל־אביב]: נהר, 1993.
384 עמ׳.

בילין, יוסי. ישראל – 40 פלוס: פרופיל פוליטי של החברה הישראלית בשנות
התשעים / יוסי בילין. – תל־אביב: ידיעות אחרונות, תשנ״ג 1993. 211 עמ׳.

גלעדי, דן. לוי אשכול: קברניט ההתיישבות ההמונית 1952-1948: (כולל תקציר
עברי ואנגלי) / דן גלעדי. – תל־אביב: מכון גולדה מאיר לחקרי עבודה
וחברה, 1993. [2], 58 עמ׳. – (נייר דיון; מס׳ 71). כולל ביבליוגרפיה.

דיסקין, אברהם. הבחירות לכנסת השלוש־עשרה / אברהם דיסקין. –
ירושלים: מכון ירושלים לחקר ישראל, 1993. 102 עמ׳. – (סדרת מחקרי מכון
ירושלים לחקר ישראל; 50)

חוק המפלגות בישראל: בין מסגרת חוקית לסדר דמוקרטי / [ערך] דן
אבנון. – תל־אביב: הקיבוץ המאוחד, המכון הישראלי לדמוקרטיה, תשנ״ג

1993. 128 עמ'. – (הספריה הדמוקרטית)

חזן, יעקב. ילדות ונעורים: פרקים אוטוביוגרפיים / יעקב חזן; עורך שלמה שאלתיאל; עורך לשוני דני פלג: עיצוב יעקב גוטרמן. – [תל-אביב]: ספרית פועלים, תשנ"ג 1993. 68 עמ'.

יעקבי, גד. העתיד מתחיל עכשיו / גד יעקבי. – תל-אביב: זמורה-ביתן, תשנ"ג 1993. 252 עמ'.

ממשל חדש לישראל: חלופה אינטלקטולית-פוליטית / אורי מילשטין . . . [ואחרים]. – מהד' א. – קראון: שרידות, 1993. 157, 173 עמ'. בעברית ובאנגלית.

נאור, אריה. בגין בשלטון – עדות אישית / אריה נאור. – תל-אביב: ידיעות אחרונות, 1993. 348 עמ'.

ספוקויני, יעקב. תפיסותיו המדיניות של מנחם בגין והשפעתן על תוצאות ועידת קמפ-דיוויד / יעקב ספוקויני. – רמת-גן: אוניברסיטת בר-אילן, תשנ"ג 1993. [4], 157, [5] עמ'.

פרס, שמעון. המזרח התיכון החדש: מסגרת ותהליכים לעידן השלום / שמעון פרס; [עם אריה נאור]. – בני-ברק: סטימצקי, 1993. 171 עמ'. "חזון השלום ופרטים על השגתו".

שמיר, יצחק. סיכומו של דבר / יצחק שמיר. – תל-אביב: עידנים, תשנ"ד 1994. 319 עמ'. "זכרונותיו של לוחם מחתרת, איש 'מוסד', חבר כנסת, שר החוץ וראש ממשלת ישראל לשעבר".

עליה וקליטה:

בבא, שרה. הבריחה: נסיעתי לארץ-ישראל / שרה באבא. – תל-אביב: י. גולן, 1993. 190 עמ'. – (סידרת ברקאי לפרוזה מקורית איכותית)

יגנס-יערי, חוה. ושבו בנים לגבולם / חוה יגנס-יערי. – תל-אביב: טרקלין, תשנ"ג 1993. 239 עמ'.

צמרת, צבי. ימי כור ההיתוך: ועדת חקירה על חינוך ילדי העולים (1950) / צבי צמרת. – קריית שדה-בוקר: המרכז למורשת בן-גוריון, תשנ"ג 1993. 263 עמ'. כולל גם את הדו"ח המלא של הועדה.

11. שונות

אוחנה, דוד. מסדר הניהיליסטים: לידתה של תרבות פוליטית באירופה 1870-1930 / דוד אוחנה. – ירושלים: מוסד ביאליק, 1993. כב, 574 עמ'. "התשתית התרבותית של המשטרים הפוליטיים הבלתי דמוקרטיים של תקופתנו, משמאל ומימין. מישור הדיון הוא מטה-פוליטי".

אונא, יששכר. פיסיקת הקוונטים / יששכר אונא. – תל-אביב: משרד הבטחון – ההוצאה לאור, מטכ"ל – קצין חינוך ראשי – גלי צה"ל, תשנ"ג 1993. 100, [2] עמ'. – (ספריית אוניברסיטה משודרת)

אליאב־פלדון, מירי. חמש־מאות שנה לגילוי אמריקה / מירי אליאב־פלדון;
(עורכת צילה דרורי). — תל־אביב: משרד הבטחון — ההוצאה לאור, מטכ"ל
— קצין חינוך ראשי — גלי צה"ל, תשנ"ג 1992. 112 עמ'. — (ספריית
אוניברסיטה משודרת)

ארן, לידיה. בודהיזם / לידיה ארן. — תל־אביב: דביר, תשנ"ג 1993. 207 עמ'.
— (מה? דע!)

בלפר־כהן, אנה. תולדות האדם הקדמון / אנה בלפר־כהן. — תל־אביב: משרד
הבטחון — ההוצאה לאור, מטכ"ל — קצין חינוך ראשי — גלי צה"ל, תשנ"ג
1992. 139, [5] עמ'. — (ספריית אוניברסיטה משודרת)

גרודזינסקי, יוסף. פסיכולוגיה ושפה / יוסף גרודזינסקי; [עורכת מפיקה:
שרה סורני]. — ירושלים: מכון ון ליר, תשנ"ג 1993. 92 עמ'. — (הקשרים)

הורן, שפרה. חוויה יפנית / שפרה הורן. — תל־אביב: ספרית מעריב, תשנ"ג
1992. 336 עמ'.

חזן, חיים. השיח האנתרופולוגי / חיים חזן. — תל־אביב: משרד הבטחון —
ההוצאה לאור, מטכ"ל — קצין חינוך ראשי — גלי צה"ל, תשנ"ג 1992. יא, [9]־
108, [5] עמ'. — (ספריית אוניברסיטה משודרת)

פרויד ודורה / זיגמונד פרויד . . . [ואחרים]; עריכה: עמנואל ברמן. — תל־
אביב: עם עובד, תשנ"ד 1993. 208 עמ'. — (סדרת פסיכואנליזה)

פרלשטין, יוסף. רוסיה של אתמול: על פי מקורות סוביייטים ומערביים / יוסף
פרלשטין. — [תל־אביב]: ספרי ליאור, 1993. 192 עמ'. בראש העמודים: הכר
את רוסיה.

קרפין, מיכאל. רשימות מכיכר פושקין / מיכאל קרפין. — תל־אביב: ידיעות
אחרונות, 1993. 294 עמ'.

רכילות / אהרון בן־זאב, אבינועם בן זאב (עורכים); בהשתתפות שולמית
אלמוג. — תל־אביב: הקיבוץ המאוחד, 1993. 191 עמ'. — (סדרת אורנים)

שיזף, צור. דרך המשי / צור שיזף. — תל־אביב: ידיעות אחרונות, 1993. 425
עמ'. — (ספריית מסעות)

שפיגל, נתן. אמנות השכנוע — הנואם וקהלו / נתן שפיגל. — ירושלים: הוצאת
ספרים ע"ש י.ל. מאגנס, האוניברסיטה העברית, תשנ"ג 1993. 240 עמ'. —
(פרסומי הר הצופים)

CAROLYN STARMAN HESSEL

Jewish Book Council
1993-1994

1993-94 was a pivotal period in the fifty-year history of the Jewish Book Council (JBC). On January 1, 1994, the Jewish Community Centers Association (formerly JWB) ceased their funding of JBC as they reevaluated their own focus. The Board of Directors of the Jewish Book Council voted to continue as a separate not-for-profit corporation after attempts to merge with another organization did not materialize. And so the Jewish Book Council, Inc. came into being.

The JBC remains committed to its original mission and mandate. It is the only organization in the North American Jewish community created to serve as a national clearinghouse for Jewish literary activity and responsible for ensuring the reading, writing, publishing and publicizing of the Jewish content book.

The goals are furthered through JBC programs which must now become self supporting.

JEWISH BOOK MONTH

Jewish Book Month runs annually during the thirty days before Hanukkah, and is designed to encourage the purchasing and reading of Jewish books. The 1994 dates are October 27th – November 27th. JBC has issued a colorful poster, prepared by Leonard Everett Fisher, which is exhibited in schools, libraries, synagogues, community centers and organizations throughout the country. Together with the Jewish Book Month kits it serves as the national reminder to read Jewish books.

The Jewish Book Month kit, prepared annually by the

JBC, sells over 1,000 sets. It includes two copies of the *Adventure With Jewish Books* poster, 50 adult and 50 children's bookmarks with reading lists, and the new bibliographies, *Something Special for Hanukkah* and *A Taste of Jerusalem: A Bibliography for All Ages for Jerusalem 3,000.* The latter title is only available with the kit. It will be expanded in 1995-96 when the JBC joins the worldwide Jewish community in celebrations of 3,000 years since the founding of Jerusalem.

The poster also serves as the logo for Jewish book fairs held nationwide. JBC serves as an advisor to communities in the preparation of their fairs. This includes preparation and distribution of an all new and extensive listing of "Selected Books for A Jewish Book Fair," advice about author availability for on-site visits, and listings of Judaic and general publishers who should be contacted.

JEWISH BOOK ANNUAL

Jewish Book Annual, volume 52, which appears under the editorship of Dr. Jacob Kabakoff, remains the leading record of the Jewish literary output in English, Yiddish and Hebrew of the preceding year. The publication finds its way into Jewish, general and academic libraries throughout the world, including Cairo, New Dehli, and Latvia. It often is one of only a few Jewish content reference books in general libraries. The JBA Editorial Advisory Board welcomed four new members to its roster: Pearl Berger, Dean of Libraries at Yeshiva University, Dr. Barry Holtz, Senior Education Officer of the Council for Initiatives in Jewish Education (CIJE); Dr. Abraham J. Karp, Professor Emeritus of Jewish Studies, the University of Rochester; and Dr. Monty Noam Penkower, Professor of History, Touro College.

JEWISH BOOK WORLD

Jewish Book World published Vol. 11:2 and Vol. 12:1 and 12:2 up through the Fall of 1994. Beginning with Vol. 12:2 it welcomed a new editor, Esther Nussbaum, Director, Ramaz

Upper School library. Mrs. Nussbaum is maintaining the regular format of presenting over 150 new titles with informative annotations and longer reviews by noted authorities. In addition, there will be a special focus on media, cybernetics and art literature to reflect new emphases in the 1990s. The journal, to be issued three times a year, is now by subscription at $20.00 annually. To encourage advertisers' participation it will be issued to coincide with the selling season for Rosh Hashanah, Hanukkah and Pesah.

JEWISH BOOK FAIR

Judaic Book and Crafts MARKETPLACE, sponsored by the JBC in cooperation with the Association of Jewish Libraries (N.Y. Metro Area), is the model for Jewish book fairs around the country. Taking place at the New York Hilton Hotel during Jewish Book Month the array of Judaica is the most extensive in the metropolis with the greatest Jewish population outside of Israel.

NATIONAL JEWISH BOOK AWARDS

National Jewish Book Awards is the Council's premier program. Under the professional direction of Dr. Marcia Posner, the awards are presented in 14 categories of Jewish interest. Included this year is a new category, Jewish Education. A distinct award reflects the current emphasis in the American Jewish community.

The 1993 awards, covering books published through December 31, 1992, were presented at the 92nd Street Y in Manhattan in June, 1993. The 1993-94 award cycle was changed in order to present the honors during National Jewish Book Month in November at a gala reception in mid-Manhattan. During this transition period the presentation covers a longer publication period. It will revert back to the annual cycle in 1995.

PUBLICATIONS

Publications is an ongoing program of the JBC. This
includes focused bibliographies on current topics of interest,
suggestions to authors on book publishing, materials for
publishers on distribution of Jewish books, materials for
synagogue librarians and more. The 1994 *List of Publications*
includes seventeen new publications among its offering of
twenty-eight separate titles. A renewed interest in intergener-
ational literature is reflected in *Grandparents in Jewish
Children's Literature: A Historical Overview* by Dr. Marcia W.
Posner. The Jewish continuity campaign, with its stress on
Jewish family life, which has been adopted by many American
Jewish communities, is credited for the all new *Jewish
Holidays: A Family Resource Guide.*

ADMINISTRATION

The Board of Directors accepted the resignation of its
long-time Director, Paula Gribetz Gottlieb, who will be
pursuing other career goals. During her eight-year tenure new
and successful programs were initiated. On November 1, 1993,
the JBC welcomed a new Executive Director, Carolyn
Starman Hessel, a long time Jewish educator, former Director
of the National Education Resource Center at the Jewish
Education Service of North America (JESNA) and active on
behalf of the Coalition for the Advancement of Jewish
Education (CAJE).

Contributors and Editors

Dr. Marc D. Angel, Rabbi of Congregation Shearith Israel, New York, and author of works on Sephardic Jewry.

Zachary M. Baker, head librarian, YIVO Institute for Jewish Research.

Jennifer Breger, author of studies on Hebrew printing and on women's literature.

Dr. Michael Chernick, professor of Jewish Jurisprudence and Social Justice, New York school of HCU-JIR.

Zvi Erenyi, Collection Development Librarian, Mendel Gottesman Library, Yeshiva University.

Dr. Morris M. Faierstein, Jewish Chaplain, now stationed overseas in Germany.

Joseph Galron-Goldschlager, Hebraica and Jewish Studies bibliographer, the Ohio State University Libraries.

Dr. Lewis Glinert, Reader in Hebrew at the School of Oriental and African Studies of the University of London and author of works on the Hebrew language.

Dr. Leonard S. Gold, chief, Jewish Division, New York Public Library.

Dr. Emanuel S. Goldsmith, professor of Yiddish, Queens College of CUNY.

Carolyn Starman Hessel, director, Jewish Book Council.

Dr. Avner Holtzman, lecturer in Hebrew literature at the Tel-Aviv University.

Dr. Jacob Kabakoff, professor emeritus of Hebrew and Jewish Studies, Lehman College.

Dr. Reuven Kimelman, professor of Near Eastern and Judaic Studies, Brandeis University.

Dr. Sol Liptzin, who lives in Jerusalem, is professor emeritus, City College of CUNY and author of many works.

Dr. Joseph Lowin, director of cultural services at the National Foundation for Jewish Culture.

Dr. Marcia W. Posner, library consultant, Jewish Book Council and Federation of Jewish Philanthropies, New York.

DR. MENAHEM SCHMELZER, professor in Medieval Jewish Literature and Jewish Bibliography, Jewish Theological Seminary.

PATRICIA A. SCHOTTEN, librarian, Institute of Jewish Affairs, London, England.

LEVI SHALIT, who lives in Israel, is an author and former editor of the *Idisher Tseitung*, Johannesburg.

ROBERT SINGERMAN, bibliographer and head, Price Library of Judaica, University of Florida at Gainesville.

DR. EZRA SPICEHANDLER, professor of Hebrew literature, HUC-JIR, Cinncinati.

SUZANNE M. STAUFFER, Judaica cataloger, library of the New York school of HUC-JIR.

RABBI THEODORE WIENER, Judaica cataloger, Subject Cataloging Division, Library of Congress.

ייִדישער
בוך
אַלמאַנאַך

תשנ"ה

כרך נ"ב

ייִדישער ביכער-ראַט פֿון אַמעריקע

שנתון
הספר
היהודי

תשנ"ה

כרד נ"ב

המועצה למען הספר היהודי באמריקה